POET OF EXILE

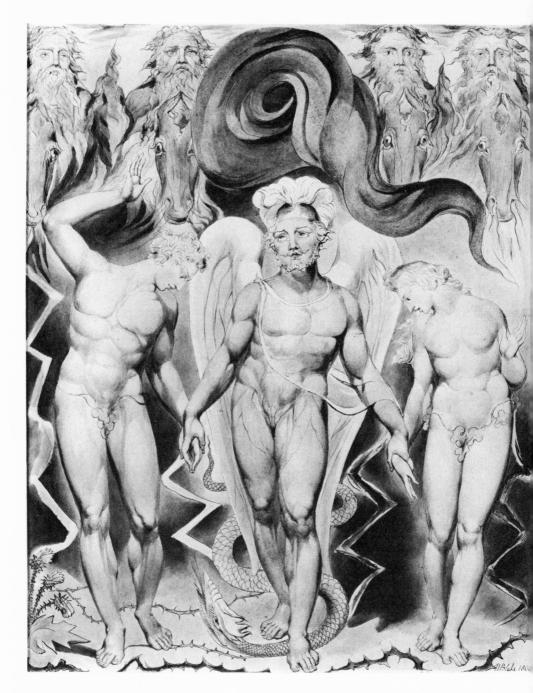

William Blake, "Expulsion from Paradise," Museum of Fine Arts, Boston.

Louis L. Martz

Poet of Exile

A Study of Milton's Poetry

New Haven and London
Yale University Press
1980

Published with assistance from
the Mary Cady Tew Memorial Fund.

Designed by Sally Harris
and set in VIP Baskerville type.
Printed in the United States of America by
Murray Printing Company, Westford, Mass.

Published in Great Britain, Europe, Africa, and
Asia (except Japan) by Yale University Press,
Ltd., London. Distributed in Australia and
New Zealand by Book & Film Services, Artarmon,
N.S.W., Australia; and in Japan by Harper & Row,
Publishers, Tokyo Office.

Library of Congress Cataloging in Publication Data

Martz, Louis Lohr.
    Poet of exile.

    Includes bibliographical references and index.
    1. Milton, John, 1608-1674—Criticism and
interpretation—Addresses, essays, lectures.
I. Title.
PR3588.M376   821'.4   79-64079
ISBN 0-300-02393-6

For Edwine

Contents

Preface

An account of the origins of this book may help to explain some of its characteristics. It has been now more than fifteen years since I first laid careful plans for a book that would deal with the whole body of Milton's poetry in a consistent, coherent way. But other obligations intervened, both administrative and scholarly, and I could keep my design alive only by accepting invitations to give lectures at various institutions or to engage in some scholarly symposium. Whenever possible, on such occasions, I suggested a talk on some aspect of Milton's poetry. The result was nine published essays; but they were composed for particular occasions, in no particular order, and they appeared in publications that ranged, if not exactly from China to Peru, certainly from Portugal to California.

At last, in 1977–78, through the generosity of the National Endowment for the Humanities and my own university, a year appeared in which to contemplate these various essays, along with the preliminary essay on *Paradise Lost* in *The Paradise Within* (1964) and the older essay on *Paradise Regain'd,* first published in 1960. I found that I had some three hundred published pages on Milton's poetry—but not a book. I thought of simply putting them together as "collected essays" on Milton—but, to echo William Carlos Williams, I wanted to write a book. As a result I set about revising most of the essays drastically, while folding them within more than a hundred pages of new writing, here first published. I have tried to make it all cohere. Each chapter can be read separately, but I hope that each chapter will mean more when read within the context of the whole. The original essays sometimes resisted revision tenaciously; words in print take on a life of their own, and they seem to dislike change. But by a combination of force and persuasion, great changes have been made. I have listed

in my notes the original places of publication for various portions
of the book.

I am greatly indebted to the National Endowment for the
Humanities for granting the fellowship that enabled me to com-
plete this work; and I wish to thank the following for permission
to include here materials previously published: Yale University
Press, Columbia University Press, University of California Press,
The Johns Hopkins University Press (*ELH*), University of
Pittsburgh Press (*Milton Studies*), *English Literary Renaissance,
Ocidente, Yale French Studies*, and *Ventures*. I am deeply grateful to
Maynard Mack, Bernard Schilling, Douglas Bush, Ellen Graham,
and the late Isabel MacCaffrey for their warm encouragement of
this study, and also to Gordon Williams for advice concerning
pastoral poetry and Ovid's poetry. I wish also to thank Sally
Serafim for her scrupulous styling of the manuscript, and Sally
Harris for her deep interest in the book's physical design. I wish to
express my appreciation to the anonymous reader of this manuscript for the Yale University Press, whose wise and tactful suggestions have greatly improved several parts of this book. Finally, I
am very grateful to Andrea Snell for assistance in research and for
many creative suggestions made over the past two years, and to
Alice Kaplan for assistance in research and for the adept typing
and retyping of this manuscript.

L. L. M.

Saybrook College
Yale University

PART I

The Shepherd's Trade:
Poems of Mr. John Milton, Both English and Latin
London, 1645

What leaf-fring'd legend haunts about thy shape
Of deities or mortals, or of both,
In Tempe or the dales of Arcady?

Keats

BELL'S EDITION.
The POETS of GREAT BRITAIN
COMPLETE, FROM
CHAUCER to CHURCHILL,

MILTON VOLUME IV,
My Muse with Angels did divide to Sing;
Par. r.

CHAPTER 1

The Pastoral Music:
A Maske Presented at Ludlow Castle

At the close of the seventh idyll of Theocritus, the poet Simichidas and his companions arrive at the scene of the harvest festival of Demeter, after Lycidas has gone another way, giving his stick to Simichidas "to pledge our friendship in the Muse." Their friendly exchange of songs in the earlier part of the idyll has prepared the way for the harmonious scene at the end where nature and man and the Muses mingle in a happy concord:

> Tall elms and poplars murmured in profusion overhead;
> near by, the sacred water from the Nymphs' own cave
> bubbled up and sparkled; among the shady branches,
> inky crickets chattered busily; far away,
> the tree-frog's croak was muffled in deep thistledown.
> Larks and linnets made their song, the dove his moan,
> bees hummed and hovered round the springs.
> The harvest's richest smells were everywhere;
> the air was filled with fruit-time's fragrance.
> Pears lay round our feet, apples by our side,

3

> rolling in abundance; wild plums in bunches
> weighed the boughs right down to the ground.
> We broke the wine-jars' four-year seals.

But there is more than wine to drink here. Amid the rich vitality, the murmuring, chattering, humming, and singing of nature in its harmonious fulfillment, the nymphs have graciously served from their spring a drink to mix with the wine, a drink that for Milton and the Renaissance could only mean poetical inspiration—the gift that has created the pastoral music of this entire Theocritean idyll. Gratitude to Demeter for her gift of food combines with gratitude to the Muses for their gift of song: both are mingled here as nature and man join in grateful appreciation of the gods' bounty:

> Nymphs of Castalia, high on Parnassus' slopes,
> was it quite such a vintage as this
> old Chiron poured for Heracles in Pholus' rocky cave?
> Was it quite such nectar had Polyphemus dancing
> around his folds by the Anapus? Polyphemus the shepherd,
> the mighty man who heaved mountains at ships?

In this context the allusion to Chiron reminds one of his skill in music, healing, and other arts, while the allusion to Polyphemus suggests his pastoral role as singer and piper;[1] the two allusions thus lead into the closing account of the "drink" served by the nymphs to Simichidas and his companions:

> Say, Nymphs, was either quite such a drink
> as you served for us from your spring that day
> by the shrine of Demeter of the Threshing-Floor?

Then the idyll ends with a prayer for the continuation of all these gifts, addressed to the mother-goddess who presides over the fruits of the earth:

> I pray that I may one day plant again
> the great winnowing fork in her heap of corn
> as the goddess smiles her blessing on us,
> with wheatsheaves and poppies in either hand.
>   [7.135–end; trans. Holden][2]

Such is the pastoral music that, in Milton's *Maske,* will answer the parody of nature's bounty that Comus pours forth in such cloying abundance:

> Wherefore did Nature powre her bounties forth
> With such a full and unwithdrawing hand,
> Covering the earth with odours, fruits and flocks,
> Thronging the Seas with spawn innumerable,
> But all to please, and sate the curious taste?   [710–14]

In Theocritus this bounty is full and unwithdrawn, but it never overwhelms, for eating is accompanied with prayer, drinking is accompanied with song. The "all-giver" is thanked by man's profound appreciation, not only by the act of consumption.

Milton had already provided a glimpse of his answer to Comus's temptation when, a year or so before his *Maske*, he wrote the pastoral entertainment *Arcades* to honor the mother-in-law of the Earl of Bridgewater for whom the *Maske* was presented at Ludlow Castle. *Arcades* is "Part of an entertainment presented to the Countess Dowager of *Darby* at *Harefield*, by som Noble persons of her Family, who appear on the Scene in pastoral habit, moving toward the seat of State with this Song"—"Look Nymphs, and Shepherds look." After this opening song has presented its tribute to the Countess as reigning deity, "the genius of the Wood appears" in a role almost certainly enacted by Henry Lawes—foreshadowing his appearance as the Attendant Spirit in the *Maske*. But here the Genius represents a fostering and healing power within nature, not above it, a power related to the healing and the fostering power of words and music:

> For know by lot from *Jove* I am the powr
> Of this fair Wood, and live in Oak'n bowr,
> To nurse the Saplings tall, and curl the grove
> With Ringlets quaint, and wanton windings wove.
> And all my Plants I save from nightly ill,
> Of noisom winds, and blasting vapours chill.
>
> . . . .
> And early ere the odorous breath of morn
> Awakes the slumbring leaves, or tasseld horn
> Shakes the high thicket, haste I all about,
> Number my ranks, and visit every sprout
> With puissant words, and murmurs made to bless . . .
>   [44–49,56–60]

Then from these fostering words and murmurs on earth the Genius moves on to describe how at night he listens

> To the celestial *Sirens* harmony,
> That sit upon the nine enfolded Sphears,
> And sing to those that hold the vital shears,
> And turn the Adamantine spindle round,
> On which the fate of gods and men is wound.
> Such sweet compulsion doth in musick ly,
> To lull the daughters of *Necessity*,
> And keep unsteddy nature to her law,
> And the low world in measur'd motion draw
> After the heavenly tune, which none can hear
> Of human mould with grosse unpurged ear . . .   [63–73]

One cannot miss the implications of the Orphic theory of music so widely held throughout the Renaissance: a theory traced to Orpheus, whose disciples, tradition said, passed this knowledge on to Pythagoras, from whom it passed to Plato and his followers.[3] Thus the neoplatonic "Daemon," the name given to the Attendant Spirit in the manuscripts of Milton's *Maske,* is associated with the Orphic theory of music as the principle that fosters harmony throughout the universe.

Arcades then closes with two songs, apparently sung by the Genius, demonstrating the power of music by voice and string.[4] The final song ties the whole entertainment together: it echoes the opening address of the first song ("Nymphs and Shepherds") and repeats the last two lines of the second song; and it brings together a cluster of Arcadian myths, evoked by the opening and closing allusions to the musical myth of Syrinx:

> Nymphs and Shepherds dance no more
>   By sandy *Ladons* Lillied banks.
> On old *Lycaeus* or *Cyllene* hoar,
>   Trip no more in twilight ranks,
> Though *Erymanth* your loss deplore,
>   A better soyl shall give ye thanks.
> From the stony *Maenalus,*
> Bring your Flocks, and live with us,
> Here ye shall have greater grace,
> To serve the Lady of this place.
>   Though *Syrinx* your *Pans* Mistres were,

> Yet *Syrinx* well might wait on her.
> Such a rural Queen
> All *Arcadia* hath not seen. [96–109]

The Arcadian place-names tie the song to the opening lines of the speech of the Genius:

> Of famous *Arcady* ye are, and sprung
> Of that renowned flood, so often sung,
> Divine *Alpheus,* who by secret sluse,
> Stole under Seas to meet his *Arethuse* . . . [28–31]

for three of the place-names in the song, Cyllene, Erymanth, and Maenalus, occur together in Arethusa's account of her flight from Alpheus: "Right on past Orchomenus and Psophis, past Cyllene and the ridges of Maenalus, past chill Erymanthus and Elis, I kept on running" (*Metamorphoses,* 5.607–09, trans. Innes).[5] The mountain Maenalus, one may recall, was the scene of the Arcadian myth in which the nymph Callisto is seduced by Jove (*Met.* 2.405–65). The other place-names are directly associated with the myth of Syrinx: in Ovid's tale, this wood nymph was living in "the chill mountains of Arcadia" when one day Pan saw her "as she was returning from Mount Lycaeus"; she refused his proposals and fled "through the pathless forest till she came to the still waters of sandy Ladon"—"donec harenosi placidum Ladonis ad amnem / venerit" (*Met.* 1.689,699,702–03, trans. Innes). There occurred her transformation into marsh reeds in the arms of Pan: "and while he sighed in disappointment, the soft air stirring in the reeds gave forth a low and complaining sound. Touched by this wonder and charmed by the sweet tones, the god exclaimed: 'This union, at least, shall I have with thee.'" Then he created the reed-pipe that bears her name. (*Met.* 1.690–712, trans. Miller).[6]

So too in Milton's masque at Ludlow Ovid's myths of transformation mingle with the Orphic music as the Attendant Spirit (or Daemon) becomes a presiding musical presence, healing or causing to be healed, by his pastoral harmonies, all nature's harms, and especially those caused by the wiles of Comus. But we do not realize for quite some time that the masque being presented is a pastoral, since the first half of the work is almost entirely given over to anti-pastoral or un-pastoral elements.

First comes the long prologue, like the prologue of a god in
Euripides, foretelling trouble in the world of men, and at the very
close revealing the promise of the pastoral music to come:

> But first I must put off
> These my skie robes spun out of *Iris* Wooff,
> And take the Weeds and likenes of a Swain,
> That to the service of this house belongs,
> Who with his soft Pipe, and smooth-dittied Song,
> Well knows to still the wilde winds when they roar,
> And hush the waving Woods . . .   [82–88]

The wit of the passage depends upon the sort of recognitions
peculiar to the masque-genre, for the audience knows that the
Spirit is describing the musician enacting the role, thus paying a
compliment to his own musical abilities and also a compliment to
the poet who wrote the ditties, that is, the words, for his song—the
poet who indeed wrote this compliment itself! But I do not think
the Spirit changes his garb here: he leaves the scene to change his
gorgeous heavenly costume for that of a shepherd, and he is at
once replaced by Comus and his crew, "their Apparel glistring,"
with Comus himself clad in some sort of "quaint habits," strange
and exquisite clothing, which he fears will astonish the Lady (157)
and cause her to flee. So he throws the "Magick dust" in her eyes
which causes him to appear as "som harmless Villager / Whom
thrift keeps up about his Country gear" (165–67).

In actual performance[7] a brilliant effect is created if Comus
does not change his garb here—and indeed the lines require no
change. As he hurls his "dazling Spells" into the air, "Of power to
cheat the eye with blear illusion," (154–55) the Lady sees Comus
as a shepherd, while the audience continues to see him in his
original "quaint" attire. Her illusion is then stressed by the way in
which she repeatedly addresses this figure in glistering garb with
the words "gentle Shepherd," "Gentle villager," "good Shepherd,"
"Shepherd I take thy word, / And trust thy honest offer'd
courtesie,"—and finally, "Shepherd lead on." Meanwhile Comus
in his own words supports the "blear illusion" by addressing her as
a goddess with Orphic powers of pastoral song:

> Hail forren wonder
> Whom certain these rough shades did never breed
> Unlesse the Goddes that in rurall shrine
> Dwell'st here with *Pan,* or *Silvan,* by blest Song
> Forbidding every bleak unkindly Fog
> To touch the prosperous growth of this tall Wood.   [265–70]

And he creates for himself a pastoral persona by his vital imagery of natural growth:

> I saw them under a green mantling vine
> That crawls along the side of yon small hill,
> Plucking ripe clusters from the tender shoots . . .
> I know each lane, and every alley green
> Dingle, or bushy dell of this wilde Wood,
> And every bosky bourn from side to side . . . [294–96,311–13]

Yet the stichomythic dialogue at the outset of their interview (277–90) creates a touch of "ill-beseeming" artifice that stresses the illusory quality of the scene; such dialogue belongs to a genre widely differing from pastoral.

Moreover, at her entrance the Lady has spoken anti-pastoral words, describing the harvest festivals of the local swains as a turbulent wassail quite unlike the harvest festival of Theocritus and even more significantly unlike the pious, harmonious festivals offered by these same swains in honor of Sabrina, as we are to hear near the close of the masque:

> For which the Shepherds at their festivals
> Carrol her goodnes lowd in rustick layes,
> And throw sweet garland wreaths into her stream
> Of pancies, pinks, and gaudy Daffadils.   [848–51]

But here the Lady fears a different scene, evoked by the "riotous and unruly noise" of Comus and his crew:

> This way the noise was, if mine ear be true,
> My best guide now, me thought it was the sound
> Of Riot, and ill manag'd Merriment,
> Such as the jocond Flute, or gamesom Pipe
> Stirs up among the loose unleter'd Hinds,
> When for their teeming Flocks, and granges full
> In wanton dance they praise the bounteous *Pan,*
> And thank the gods amiss. I should be loath

> To meet the rudenesse, and swill'd insolence
> Of such late Wassailers . . .   [170–79]

The contrast between these two versions of pastoral measures the distance that the Lady and the masque must travel to reach the meaning and the motive of true pastoral music.

As the Lady leaves with her false shepherd, the Elder Brother breaks even the slight illusion of pastoral as he unbuckles his schoolboy rhetoric:[8]

> Unmuffle ye faint stars, and thou fair Moon
> That wontst to love the travailers benizon,
> Stoop thy pale·visage through an amber cloud,
> And disinherit *Chaos*, that raigns here
> In double night of darknes, and of shades;
> Or if your influence be quite damm'd up
> With black usurping mists, som gentle taper
> Though a rush Candle from the wicker hole
> Of som clay habitation visit us
> With thy long levell'd rule of streaming light,
> And thou shalt be our star of *Arcady*,
> Or *Tyrian* Cynosure.   [331–42]

The Younger Brother, in his own more forthright way, also stresses their distance from pastoral as, in his simpler language, he longs for simple things:

> Or if our eyes
> Be barr'd that happines, might we but hear
> The folded flocks pen'd in their watled cotes,
> Or sound of pastoral reed with oaten stops,
> Or whistle from the Lodge, or village cock
> Count the night watches to his feathery Dames,
> 'Twould be som solace yet, som little chearing
> In this close dungeon of innumerous bowes.   [342–49]

Then Elder Brother, in his long-winded way, retails the lessons he has learned from "vertues book," recalling legends that show the power of chastity, and summoning up evidence from "the old schools of Greece." Well-schooled he surely is—but we see his lack of experience when he declares:

> So dear to Heav'n is Saintly chastity,
> That when a soul is found sincerely so,

> A thousand liveried Angels lacky her,
> Driving far off each thing of sin and guilt . . .   [453–56]

He knows his Plato well and overawes the younger brother—but we have just seen their sister leaving the stage with Comus.

Amid all this deception, naiveté, schoolboy learning, and ambitious rhetoric, we have nevertheless had one moment of the true pastoral music, in the Lady's song to Echo, where she creates a natural setting for the nymph, a *locus amoenus* such as Ovid so often provides for his metamorphoses, while she sings of the stories of Echo, Narcissus, and Philomela; and then, like the Genius in *Arcades,* she closes by associating earthly music with the music of the heavens:

> Sweet Echo, sweetest Nymph that liv'st unseen
>   Within thy airy shell
>   By slow *Meander's* margent green,
> And in the violet-imbroider'd vale
>   Where the love-lorn Nightingale
> Nightly to thee her sad Song mourneth well.
> Canst thou not tell me of a gentle Pair
>   That likest thy *Narcissus* are?
>   O if thou have
>   Hid them in som flowry Cave,
>   Tell me but where
> Sweet Queen of Parly, Daughter of the Sphear,
> So maist thou be translated to the skies,
> And give resounding grace to all Heav'ns Harmonies.
>   [230–43]

But the last line in the song that Lawes has set to music reads differently and in some ways more effectively in the musical manuscripts: "And hold a Counterpoint to All Heavn's Harmonies."[9] Milton's revision has the advantage of adding the overtones of heavenly "grace," but it lacks the power of the word "Counterpoint," which indeed represents the central principle of the masque: the attempt to create, by earthly sounds and words, a melody that will work in counterpoint with heaven's harmonies—the music of the spheres and the music of the higher Heaven.

Such is the music that the Attendant Spirit recalls in the first of the three great pastoral arias (as we might call them) by which he brings the imagery of music to bear upon the riot and disorder of

Comus. At line 489 the Spirit at last appears "habited like a Shepherd," and his musical function is at once indicated by the name bestowed upon him by the Elder Brother—*Thyrsis,* the name of the skillful singer of the elegy to Daphnis in the first Idyll of Theocritus, a performance that gives the name Thyrsis an archetypal significance in the Orphic tradition, as the Elder Brother makes clear in his compliment of greeting:

> *Thyrsis?* Whose artful strains have oft delaid
> The huddling brook to hear his madrigal,
> And sweetn'd every muskrose of the dale . . .   [494–96]

Then both he and Thyrsis combine to build a strong pastoral setting as they converse, creating thus a verbal antidote to the actual scene in this dark "dungeon of innumerous bowes":

> How cam'st thou here good swain? hath any ram
> Slip't from the fold, or young Kid lost his dam,
> Or straggling weather the pen't flock forsook?   [497–99]

And the Spirit answers:

> I came not here on such a trivial toy
> As a stray'd Ewe, or to pursue the stealth
> Of pilfering Woolf, not all the fleecy wealth
> That doth enrich these Downs, is worth a thought
> To this my errand, and the care it brought.   [502–06]

Then he tells the brothers the story of Comus, developing a contrast between an harmonious pastoral setting and the riot of Comus and his crew:

> this I have learn't
> Tending my flocks hard by i'th hilly crofts,
> That brow this Bottom glade, whence night by night
> He and his monstrous rout are heard to howl
> Like stabl'd wolves, or tigers at their prey . . .   [530–34]

Against this story he now proceeds to build a much stronger abode for the pastoral music, as he describes the vitality of nature amid which, like the shepherd of Vergil's *Eclogues,* he "meditates" his song:[10]

> This evening late by then the chewing flocks
> Had ta'n their supper on the savoury Herb

Of Knot-grass dew-besprent, and were in fold,
I sate me down to watch upon a bank
With Ivy canopied, and interwove
With flaunting Hony-suckle, and began
Wrapt in a pleasing fit of melancholy
To meditate my rural minstrelsie . . .   [540–47]

The echo of the "bank where the wild thyme blows . . . Quite over-canopied with luscious woodbine" (*Midsummer Night's Dream,* II.i.249–51), has often been noted, but not so often hints of another "bank" in Shakespeare, famous for its musical atmosphere: the scene with Jessica and Lorenzo in the *Merchant of Venice* (V.i):[11]

How sweet the moonlight sleeps upon this bank!
Here will we sit, and let the sounds of music
Creep in our ears. Soft stillness and the night
Become the touches of sweet harmony.   [V.i.54–57]

Any similarities between this scene and the words of Thyrsis are no doubt mainly due to the power of the general Orphic tradition, and yet the additional Shakespearean echoes that accompany the Spirit's account of hearing the Lady's song enforce the echo of Lorenzo's scene; for in these lines we hear echoes of *Romeo and Juliet, Macbeth,* and *Antony and Cleopatra,*[12] and also perhaps an echo of Nerissa's answer to Portia's remark that the music of Lorenzo's scene "sounds much sweeter than by day": "Silence bestows that virtue on it, madam" (V.i.100–01).

"But ere a close," the Spirit continues, before he could finish even one cadence of his meditated song,

The wonted roar was up amidst the Woods,
And fill'd the Air with barbarous dissonance,
At which I ceas't, and listen'd them a while,
Till an unusuall stop of sudden silence
Gave respit to the drowsie frighted steeds
That draw the litter of close-curtain'd sleep.
At last a soft and solemn breathing sound
Rose like a steam of rich distill'd Perfumes,
And stole upon the Air, that even Silence
Was took e're she was ware, and wish't she might
Deny her nature, and be never more
Still to be so displac't. I was all eare,

> And took in strains that might create a soul
> Under the ribs of Death . . .   [548–62]

A distant suggestion of the strains of Orpheus in Pluto's realm
may evoke the passage in Lorenzo's scene where he explains to
Jessica the power of music over wild beasts:

> For do but note a wild and wanton herd,
> Or race of youthful and unhandled colts,
> Fetching mad bounds, bellowing and neighing loud,
> Which is the hot condition of their blood;
> If they but hear perchance a trumpet sound,
> Or any air of music touch their ears,
> You shall perceive them make a mutual stand,
> Their savage eyes turn'd to a modest gaze
> By the sweet power of music: therefore the poet
> Did feign that Orpheus drew trees, stones, and floods;
> Since nought so stockish, hard, and full of rage,
> But music for the time doth change his nature.   [V.i.71–82]

"But O ere long," the Spirit says,

> Too well I did perceive it was the voice
> Of my most honour'd Lady, your dear sister.
> Amaz'd I stood, harrow'd with grief and fear,
> And O poor hapless Nightingale thought I,
> How sweet thou sing'st, how neer the deadly snare!
> [562–67]

Thus he picks up the imagery of Philomela in the Lady's song and
reminds us of the temporary quietening effect that her pastoral
music has had upon the "rout" of Comus:

> Then down the Lawns I ran with headlong hast
> Through paths, and turnings oft'n trod by day,
> Till guided by mine ear I found the place
> Where that damn'd wisard hid in sly disguise
> (For so by certain signes I knew) had met
> Already, ere my best speed could praevent,
> The aidless innocent Lady his wish't prey . . .   [568–74]

One need not take this to indicate that Comus has actually donned
a disguise here, for the Spirit, as usual, is telling the story in
keeping with his own disguise. What we should notice here is the
emphasis upon the "air" and the "eare",[13] for, in conjunction with

all the other reminiscences of renaissance musical theory, these words summon up a well-known passage where Ficino is explaining why the sense of hearing affects the human spirit more than any other of the senses. It is, he says, because sound is motion transmitted through the air:

> Although visual impressions are in a way pure, yet they lack the effectiveness of motion, and are usually perceived only as an image, without reality; normally therefore, they move the soul only slightly. Smell, taste and touch are entirely material, and rather titillate the sense-organs than penetrate the depths of the soul. But musical sound by the movement of the air moves the body: by purified air it excites the aerial spirit which is the bond of body and soul: by emotion it affects the senses and at the same time the soul: by meaning it works on the mind [Ficino is clearly thinking here of the words that live within a song]: finally, by the very movement of the subtle air it penetrates strongly: by its contemperation it flows smoothly: by the conformity of its quality it floods us with a wonderful pleasure: by its nature, both spiritual and material, it at once seizes, and claims as its own, man in his entirety.[14]

"I was all eare"—"Guided by mine ear"—thus music begins to play its role in the rescue.

But other pastoral properties are needed to complete the mission, and these Thyrsis explains in his second pastoral aria, where he tells of the rare herb *Haemony* that he received from a "certain Shepherd Lad." (619) The recent definitive article by Charlotte Otten[15] makes it plain that Milton is here describing a real plant belonging to the genus called in Milton's day *Hypericum,* a genus which "includes a number of species with an array of vernacular and scientific names such as St. John's Wort, Fuga Daemonum, Perforata (Porosa), and Androsaemon." All the plants of this genus bear a yellow flower, but it is from the last, Otten argues, that Milton has taken his name: *Andros-haemon,* a name derived from the Greek genitive for *man,* plus the Greek *haima, blood*—the latter part of the name indicating "the blood-red juice (a characteristic of the entire genus *hypericum*)." The leaf of this plant is "deep green," with "prickles" in the sense of perforations (not thorns); and it is a plant that, according to Lyte's popular *Herball,* "groweth not in this country, except in gardens where as it is sowen and planted." It was a plant for which "no pharmaceutical

uses" had been established, and therefore, as Lyte's *Herball* reports, it is "unknowen to the Apothecaries." But it was everywhere
known for its powers of putting evil demons to flight (as one of its
names indicates), and thus it was regarded as a cure for all kinds
of "harms" caused by malicious spirits. In short, nearly every detail of Milton's description of *Haemony* finds a parallel in the her-
bals of Milton's day:

> Amongst the rest a small unsightly root,
> But of divine effect, he cull'd me out;
> The leaf was darkish, and had prickles on it,
> But in another Countrey, as he said,
> Bore a bright golden flowre, but not in this soyl:
> Unknown, and like esteem'd, and the dull swayn
> Treads on it daily with his clouted shoon,
> And yet more med'cinal is it then that *Moly*
> That *Hermes* once to wise *Ulysses* gave;
> He call'd it *Haemony,* and gave it me,
> And bad me keep it as of sov'ran use
> 'Gainst all inchantments, mildew blast, or damp
> Or gastly furies apparition . . .   [629–41]

Otten suggests that Milton's description of the "bright golden
flowre" (which, it seems, does not appear in English soil) may
allude to the variety described by a German herbalist as bearing
"Goldfarben blümen," not simply yellow. But other varieties of
the genus, especially St. John's Wort, grow throughout the English landscape.

Milton, then, is describing the qualities of an actual plant popu-
larly regarded as an antidote to enchantments caused by evil
powers—an aspect of the plant well known to Henry Lawes, according to an amusing anecdote told by Aubrey and quoted by
Otten in her article. According to Aubrey, Lawes had a musical
friend whose house was haunted by some spirit by which "the
Curtains would be rashed at Night, and awake the Gentleman that
lay there" (*rashed* means "torn or drawn violently").[16] "*Henry Laws*
to be satisfied did lie with him; and the curtains were rashed so
then: The Gentleman grew lean and pale with the frights, One
Dr. —— Cured the House of this disturbance, and Mr. *Laws*
said, that the principal Ingredient was *Hypericon* put under his
Pillow."[17] It seems quite possible that Lawes may have told this

story to Milton, and that the description of *Haemony* is yet another of those witty personal recognitions characteristic of the masque-genre.

At the same time, through the allegorical nature of the masque-genre, the plant is bound to take on "mysterious" qualities. Its blood-red juice and its ambiguous "prickles" may accord with the interpretation of those who find in the plant's "divine effect" some indications of the redemption accomplished by the blood of Christ.[18] Meanwhile those may also be right who feel in the name *Haemony* an allusion to Thessaly, frequently called Haemonia by Ovid, and so called by Milton in his second elegy, when he refers to the rejuvenation of Jason's father by Medea, using a concoction of herbs and roots gathered in a valley of Haemonia:

> O dignus tamen Haemonio juvenescere succo,
> Dignus in Aesonios vivere posse dies . . .   [7–8]

Certainly the magical implications of Thessaly are appropriate, but much more significant, in this context, are the other implications of Haemonia as a region dedicated to poetry. It was in Haemonia that Apollo fell in love with Daphne, daughter of the river-god Peneus; it was here that Apollo wooed her with words describing his powers of prophecy, poetry, and medicine: especially his power of curing through the use of herbs:

> per me, quod eritque fuitque
> estque, patet; per me concordant carmina nervis . . .
> inventum medicina meum est, opiferque per orbem
> dicor, et herbarum subiecta potentia nobis.
> ei mihi, quod nullis amor est sanabilis herbis
> nec prosunt domino, quae prosunt omnibus, artes!

> By me what shall be, has been, and what is are all revealed; by me the lyre responds in harmony to song. . . . The art of medicine is my discovery. I am called Help–Bringer throughout the world, and all the potency of herbs is given unto me. Alas, that love is curable by no herbs, and the arts which heal all others cannot heal their lord!
>
> [*Met.* 1.517–18,521–24, trans. Miller]

And it is here, on the banks of the river Peneus, that Daphne calls upon her father for help, and she is changed into the laurel tree,

sacred to Apollo (*Met.* 1.545–67). Immediately after this comes
Ovid's description of the vale of Tempe in Haemonia:

> Est nemus Haemoniae, praerupta quod undique claudit
> silva: vocant Tempe; per quae Peneus ab imo
> effusus Pindo spumosis volvitur undis
>
> . . . .
>
> haec domus, haec sedes, haec sunt penetralia magni
> amnis, in his residens facto de cautibus antro,
> undis iura dabat nymphisque colentibus undas.

> There is a grove in Haemonia, shut in on every side by steep
> wooded slopes. Men call it Tempe. Through this grove flow the
> foaming waters of Peneus, gushing out from the bottom of Pindus'
> range. . . . This was the home, the dwelling, the most secret haunt
> of the great river. Sitting here, in a cave hewn out of the cliffs, he
> was dispensing justice to the waves and to the nymphs who inhab-
> ited his stream.   [1.568–70,574–76, trans. Innes]

This is a passage that Milton seems to have remembered when he
created his compliment to Manso, weaving together various
motifs concerned with the region of Haemonia:

> Men will say that, of his own free will, Apollo dwelt in your house,
> and that the Muses came like servants to your doors. Yet that same
> Apollo, when he was a fugitive from heaven, came unwillingly to
> King Admetus' farm, although Admetus had been host to mighty
> Hercules. When he wanted to get away from the bawling
> ploughmen Apollo could, at any rate, retreat to gentle Chiron's
> famous cave, among the moist woodland pastures and leafy shades
> beside the river Peneus. There often, beneath a dark oak tree, he
> would yield to his friend's flattering persuasion and, singing to the
> music of his lute, would sooth the hardships of exile. Then neither
> the river banks, nor the boulders lodged in the quarry's depths
> stayed in their places: the Trachinian cliff nodded to the tune, and
> no longer felt its huge and familiar burden of forest trees; the
> mountain ashes were moved and came hurrying down their slopes,
> and spotted lynxes grew tame as they listened to the strange
> music.   [*Mansus* 54–69, trans. Carey][19]

After the renaissance fashion, one is expected to admire the wit of
this very free commingling of Thessalian and Thracian themes.
The Orphean incident where the trees of Thrace gathered round
the singer (*Met.* 10.86–105) is here transferred to Haemonia,
scene of Apollo's exile from heaven while he served as herdsman

to Admetus, while the allusion to Hercules recalls the story of the
Alcestis (where of course Hercules came to the house of Admetus
after, not before Apollo) and especially the great chorus of
Euripides:

> Apollo of the beautiful lyre
> Deigned to dwell in you
> And to live a shepherd in your lands!
> On the slope of the hillsides
> He played melodies of mating
> On the Pipes of Pan to his herds.
>
> And the dappled lynxes fed with them
> In joy at your singing;
> From the wooded vale of Orthrys
> Came a yellow troop of lions;
> To the sound of your lyre, O Phoebus,
> Danced the dappled fawn
> Moving on light feet
> Beyond the high-crested pines
> Charmed by your sweet singing.   [570–87, trans. Aldington][20]

Having thus mingled the singing of Orpheus and Apollo, Milton merges the cave of Chiron with the cave of Peneus: for Chiron's cave was on mount Pelion, not beside the river Peneus.[21] The stories easily blend, for after the death of that Haemonian girl Coronis, Apollo had taken the child Aesculapius to the cave of Chiron for upbringing (*Met.* 2.630), and therefore might often have visited that cave.

All these associations, then, show how the name *Haemony* would recall *Haemonia,* how that region would in turn suggest the powers of music, and how that in turn would suggest a recognition of the shepherd lad who gave his virtuous plants to Thyrsis and would often beg him to sing:

> a certain Shepherd Lad
> Of small regard to see to, yet well skill'd
> In every vertuous plant and healing herb
> That spreds her verdant leaf to th'morning ray,
> He lov'd me well, and oft would beg me sing,
> Which when I did, he on the tender grass
> Would sit, and hearken even to extasie,
> And in requitall ope his leather'n scrip,
> And shew me simples of a thousand names

> Telling their strange and vigorous faculties;
> Amongst the rest a small unsightly root,
> But of divine effect, he cull'd me out;
> The leaf was darkish, and had prickles on it . . .   [619–31]

And indeed the leaf of the genus *Hypericum,* in color and in shape, bears a strong resemblance to the laurel leaf (as we may see in part from the illustration of St. John's Wort in Otten's article). Can one avoid the implication that Haemony has something to do with poetry, that it represents the power of poetry and song (as united in the word *carmen*), and that here is a pastoral account of the close relation between Milton and the music and voice of Henry Lawes? Is the "divine effect" of Haemony a tribute to the doctrine of the Orphic powers of music? Such a meaning may emerge if we look more closely at the presence of music throughout the masque.[22]

II

In this exploration I shall use the word "music" in all the senses held by the word *carmen:* "tune, song; poem, verse; an oracular response, a prophecy; a form of incantation", or in a broader sense also implied in the Latin, "every kind of poetical production."[23] I shall move from the musical scores that actually exist to hints of further music that may have existed, and from there to the fabric of musical allusions and analogies that bring the entire work into harmony.

The five songs for which the music exists include (as the second, third, and fourth in the musical manuscripts) three of the verses noted as "Song" in the work itself: the Lady's Song, beginning, "Sweet Echo," the Spirit's invocation, "Sabrina Fair," and the double song of the Spirit, "Back Shepherds, back," followed by the address, "Noble Lord, and Lady Bright." The fifth song consists of the last twelve lines of the Spirit's epilogue, beginning, "Now my task is smoothly don."[24]

The last four of these appear in the acting version, that is, in the Bridgewater manuscript,[25] at the points where they occur in the other texts. But the first song in the musical manuscripts has a special interest, for the Bridgewater version shows that it was designed to be sung at the very beginning of the performance.

For this purpose Lawes has set to music fourteen lines that, in all other versions of the masque, occur with some variations at the opening of the Spirit's epilogue. Lawes clearly wished to open the production with song rather than with the spoken prologue in blank verse which immediately follows in the acting version. To accomplish this, the opening line of Milton's epilogue, "To the Ocean now I fly," has been changed to read: "From the Heavn's now I fly," while the rest of the song follows closely the lines of the Spirit's epilogue:

> From the Heavn's now I fly,
> And those happy Climes that lie
> Where day never shuts his eye,
> Up in the broad Fields of the Sky,
> There I suck the liquid Air
> All amidst the Garden fair
> Of Hesperus and his daughters three
> That Sing about the golden Tree:
> Iris there with humid Bow
> Waters the od'rous Banks that blow
> Flowers of more mingled Hew
> Than her purfled scarfe can shew,
> Beds of Hyacinths and Roses
> Where many a Cherub soft reposes.[26]

In Milton's published epilogue the equivalent of the last line reads, "Where young *Adonis* oft reposes," and the poem then continues with the allusions to Venus, Cupid, and Psyche. There is an important advantage in opening the poem with a song, particularly with a song that includes a reference to the singing of the daughters of Hesperus, for in this way Lawes can prepare us to grasp the significance of musical imagery and theme throughout the masque. From the outset the Spirit is thus identified as a *musical* presence: a neoplatonic "daemon" who helps to create a universal harmony.[27] It is an effect that should always be retained in any actual performance of the work.

In addition to these five songs, the manuscripts and the printed version[28] of the poem contain a great deal of evidence that further music of some kind was at least planned. Sabrina's answer, "By the rushy-fringed bank," is preceded by the direction, "Sabrina rises, attended by water-Nymphes, and sings."[29] At the same time, the last words of Sabrina's song, "I am here," form a rhyme with the Spirit's answer, "Goddess dear" (901–02). As Haun says, "To carry over the rhyme without carrying over the music would have been an error in taste which Milton with his sensitivity and Lawes with his knowledge of masque-technique would not have been likely to have committed."[30] Then thirty-five lines after this, immediately following the line, "With Groves of myrrhe and cinnamon," we find in the manuscripts the significant direction: "Songe ends," a direction that may be taken to imply that the intervening thirty-five lines have all been designed for music.

In a similar way, immediately after the Spirit's song of invocation, "Sabrina fair," the succeeding lines are introduced in the Bridgewater manuscript with the direction: "The verse to singe or not,"[31] and then the following twenty-three lines of the poem are divided in this manuscript among three speakers: the elder brother, the younger brother, and the "Daemon":

> listen and appeare to vs
> in name of greate Oceanus,
> by th'earth-shakinge Neptunes mace,
> and Tethis grave maiestick pace,
> *El bro:* by hoarie Nereus wrincled looke,
> and the Carpathian wizards hooke,
> *2 bro:* by scalie Tritons windinge shell,
> and ould sooth-sayinge Glaucus spell,
> *El br:* by Lewcotheas lovely hands,
> and her sonne that rules the strands,
> *2 bro:* by Thetis tinsel-slipperd feete,
> and the songs of sirens sweete,
> *El br:* by dead Parthenopes deare tombe,
> and fayer Ligeas golden Combe,
> wherewith she sitts on diamond rocks,
> sleekinge her soft alluringe locks,
> *De:* By all the Nimphes of nightly daunce,
> vpon thy streames with wilie glaunce,
> rise, rise, and heave thy rosie head,
> from thy Corall paven bed,
> and bridle in thy headlonge wave,
> till thou our summons answered have,
>   Listen & save.   [Bridgewater MS. 788–810]

It seems then that this section was designed to be sung, provided that the boys could do the singing. This division of parts is highly

effective in performance, and should be retained, for thus we
hear the brothers' voices enclosed by and inspired by the voice of
the guardian spirit. We have powerful evidence, then, that the
concluding portion of the masque, from the invocation of Sabrina
to the end (128 lines in the acting version), was dominated by
music and perhaps very largely set to music, with the result that
Haun describes when he says, "If this does not make *Comus* an
opera, at least it makes it operatic."[32]

Meanwhile there are clear indications of instrumental music at
three points: the dances at the very close; the scene of Comus's
temptation of the Lady, where the stage direction of the published
version requires "soft Musick" at the outset; and the dance of
Comus and his monsters near the beginning of the work, where
some kind of wild "noise"—perhaps with the pipe and flute
suggested by the Lady—would seem to be required, for after the
entering speech of Comus, the manuscripts have the stage direction: "The measure in a wild, rude, & wanton Antick."[33] (The
published version spoils the effect by giving simply "The Measure.") In connection with the last point, one should note that the
entering words of Comus are written mainly in the same swift
tetrameter that is elsewhere set to or associated with music; and
indeed the opening speech of Comus suggests poetry very close to
the lyric form of the Anacreontic:

> Mean while welcom Joy, and Feast,
> Midnight shout, and revelry,
> Tipsie dance, and Jollity.
> Braid your Locks with rosie Twine
> Dropping odours, dropping Wine.
> Rigor now is gon to bed,
> And Advice with scrupulous head,
> Strict Age, and sowre Severity
> With their grave Saws in slumber ly.   [102–10]

But shortly after this, in keeping with the loss of rigor and
scrupulosity here urged, the tetrameter begins to expand into
pentameter, with significant variations that ebb and flow throughout the remainder of Comus's speech, as the imagery serves to
suggest:

> The Sounds, and Seas with all their finny drove
> Now to the Moon in wavering Morrice move,

> And on the Tawny Sands and Shelves,
> Trip the pert Fairies and the dapper Elves.   [115–18]

It is a wavering morris dance, indeed; these irregularities form a
striking contrast with the strict tetrameter form that dominates
the end of the masque, a regularity symbolizing the return of
order to the scene, as indicated also by the dancers at the conclusion.[34] In the original performance, this contrast would have been
reinforced by opening the masque with Lawes's song in strict
tetrameter form, binding together beginning and end.

In addition to actual music, a great many allusions to and descriptions of music help to develop this theme of disorder versus
harmony, as we have seen. The theme is stressed at the end of the
"Antick" dance by Comus and his crew when Comus breaks off
the "measure" with a metrical pun: "Break off, break off, I feel
the different pace / Of som chast footing neer about this ground"
(145–46). As Comus thus shifts his "footing" from tetrameter
couplets to blank verse, he alerts us to the way in which music and
dance merge into the music of poetry.

The Lady then enters and at once reinforces the theme by the
harmonies of her song to Echo. Some readers have felt, perhaps
rightly, that her isolation is stressed by the fact that no echo here
responds,[35] yet the Lady's words to Comus may indicate some
kind of echo:

> Not any boast of skill, but extreme shift
> How to regain my sever'd company
> Compell'd me to awake the courteous Echo
> To give me answer from her mossie Couch.   [273–76]

Would she refer to "courteous Echo" if Echo had not already in
some way answered her? It is hard to believe that Lawes would
have passed up a chance to perform this song with echoes, which
the pauses in the musical phrasing would allow. Perhaps he himself sang the echoes.

In any case, there is counterpoint, as Comus receives the song
within himself and responds, adding another melody:

> Can any mortal mixture of Earths mould
> Breath such Divine inchanting ravishment?
> Sure somthing holy lodges in that brest,

And with these raptures moves the vocal air
To testifie his hidd'n residence . . .   [244–48]

Comus here is forced to recognize the truth of the pythagorean-
platonic view of music as the emanation of the soul. Then, echoing Juliet's passionate wish for Romeo's presence,[36] he moves toward another kind of music, with his characteristic mutation into
sensuous imagery, as of someone's hair being stroked:

How sweetly did they float upon the wings
Of silence, through the empty-vaulted night
At every fall smoothing the Raven doune
Of darkness till it smil'd . . .   [249–52]

And from here we move quickly into the world of Ovidian
metamorphosis, where Circe and her crew put on an operatic
performance all their own:

I have oft heard
My mother *Circe* with the Sirens three,
Amid'st the flowry-kirtl'd *Naiades*
Culling their Potent hearbs, and balefull drugs,
Who as they sung, would take the prison'd soul,
And lap it in *Elysium, Scylla* wept,
And chid her barking waves into attention,
And fell *Charybdis* murmur'd soft applause:
Yet they in pleasing slumber lull'd the sense,
And in sweet madnes rob'd it of it self,
But such a sacred, and home-felt delight,
Such sober certainty of waking bliss
I never heard till now. Ile speak to her
And she shall be my Queen.   [252–65]

Thus Comus is impelled to pay powerful tribute to the harmoniz-
ing effect of song that is holy, sacred, or blessed, in contrast to the
"balefull" kind of song that Comus remembers.

Soon the two brothers enter, aged nine and eleven at the original performance; and they proceed to hold their schoolboy conversation about their sister and the power of chastity. Here is a
good example of Milton's way of creating an operatic effect
through poetry. When we watch an early opera by Monteverdi,
such as his *Orfeo,* we are aware that the interest cannot reside in
what we ordinarily call dramatic tension. The interest often re-

sides in watching two performers work their skillful ways through
contrasting parts, each part a set piece, a show piece, designed to
draw forth the utmost power of the performer's vocal skill, while
evoking the essence of the character or the dilemma represented.
So here, each brother is characterized by his poetry. The nine-
year-old is closer to earth and natural fears; the eleven-year-old is
full of superior knowledge, all out of books, able to quote Ovid
and Plato to excess in order to quell his brother's fears. Thus the
younger brother cries out:

> But O that haples virgin our lost sister
> Where may she wander now, whether betake her
> From the chill dew, amongst rude burrs and thistles?
> Perhaps som cold bank is her boulster now
> Or 'gainst the rugged bark of som broad Elm
> Leans her unpillow'd head fraught with sad fears.
> What if in wild amazement, and affright,
> Or while we speak within the direfull grasp
> Of Savage hunger, or of Savage heat?   [350–58]

And the elder brother replies with a highly condescending tone:

> Peace brother, be not over-exquisite
> To cast the fashion of uncertain evils;
> For grant they be so, while they rest unknown,
> What need a man forestall his date of grief,
> And run to meet what he would most avoid?   [359–63]

But when the younger brother has the temerity to continue with
his fear that some "ill greeting touch" may harm his sister, the
elder brother answers with an even more supercilious tone in the
following interchange:

> My sister is not so defenceless left
> As you imagine, she has a hidden strength
> Which you remember not.
> 2 Bro. What hidden strength,
> Unless the strength of Heav'n, if you mean that?
> Eld. Bro. I mean that too, but yet a hidden strength
> Which if Heav'n gave it, may be term'd her own:
> 'Tis chastity, my brother, chastity.   [414–20]

I do not see how any audience, particularly the original audience,
could do anything but smile at this encounter: the whole scene

could, and should, I think, be acted or imagined in such a way as
to create something of the effect of a school play on Parents' Day.

Then, when the brothers fail to rescue the Lady, through their
inexperience, the Attendant Spirit himself moves to the rescue
through poetical (musical) means described in his third pastoral
aria:

> Som other means I have which may be us'd,
> Which once of *Melibaeus* old I learnt
> The soothest Shepherd that ere pip't on plains.

(The heavy alliteration serves to identify the shepherd as Edmund
Spenser.)

> There is a gentle Nymph not farr from hence,
> That with moist curb sways the smooth Severn stream,
> *Sabrina* is her name, a Virgin pure . . .
> . . . .
> And, as the old Swain said, she can unlock
> The clasping charm, and thaw the numming spell,
> If she be right invok't in warbled Song,
> For maid'nhood she loves, and will be swift
> To aid a Virgin, such as was her self
> In hard besetting need, this will I try
> And adde the power of som adjuring verse.   [821–26,852–58]

Then follows the operatic conclusion to the poem in which song,
dance, and orchestral music serve to create a harmony in which
the oppositions of life are reconciled, and nature and spirit are
brought into a rich union represented by Sabrina's song:

> By the rushy-fringed bank,
> Where grows the Willow and the Osier dank,
>   My sliding Chariot stayes,
> Thick set with Agat, and the azurn sheen
> Of Turkis blew, and Emerauld green
>   That in the channell strayes,
> Whilst from off the waters fleet
> Thus I set my printless feet
> O're the Cowslips Velvet head,
>   That bends not as I tread,
> Gentle swain at thy request
>   I am here.   [890–91]

Indeed, the more we ponder the work, the sounder Gretchen

Finney's basic argument appears to be: that the masque, as Milton developed it, resembles the form that opera was beginning to take in the early part of the seventeenth century.[37] To see the work as thus related to opera may help to resolve some of our critical problems. The operatic analogy seems to be the best way of answering the usual criticism of the work, as put by Samuel Johnson, who complained that the speeches "have not the spriteliness of a dialogue animated by reciprocal contention, but seem rather declamations deliberately composed and formally repeated on a moral question. The auditor therefore listens as to a lecture, without passion, without anxiety." From this point of view, Johnson contends: "The dispute between the Lady and Comus is the most animated and affecting scene of the drama, and wants nothing but a brisker reciprocation of objections and replies, to invite attention and detain it."[38]

But if we listen operatically, we will not seek a brisker reciprocation, which would prevent the greatest delight of opera: the listening, with passion, to an aria deliberately composed and formally repeated by a skillfull performer. From this standpoint Comus's great aria of temptation is a showpiece designed to outdo all previous exhortations of the *carpe diem* kind, including Thomas Randolph's recent Cavalier piece:[39] while the Lady's answer, strengthened by Milton's addition in the published version (778–805), provides her with a worthy response, as she utters her own operatic climax:

> Thou art not fit to hear thy self convinc't;
> Yet should I try, the uncontrouled worth
> Of this pure cause would kindle my rap't spirits
> To such a flame of sacred vehemence,
> That dumb things would be mov'd to sympathize,
> And the brute Earth would lend her nerves, and shake,
> Till all thy magick structures rear'd so high,
> Were shatter'd into heaps o're thy false head.   [792–99]

Thus the Lady proves to have a power of eloquence that defeats the sensual music of Comus.[40] "She fables not," Comus admits to himself; "I feel that I do fear / Her words set off by som superior power" (800–01).

For us today Milton's masque must have its value, I believe, in

its demonstration of Milton's vital belief in the civilizing power of
poetry and music. I do not mean to say that we should ignore the
many studies that have shown the importance of Milton's moral
and religious themes in the masque. But we should not lose sight
of the fact that Milton's simple plot, like his whole volume of 1645,
is designed to show a progress toward maturity.[41] Perhaps that is
why he has allowed his young lady of fifteen to utter that famous
substitution of chastity for charity:

> O welcome pure-ey'd Faith, white-handed Hope,
> Thou hovering Angel girt with golden wings,
> And thou unblemish't form of Chastity . . .   [213–15]

The full power of chastity is represented, not in the Lady, but in
Sabrina, who combines the spirit of music with the spirit of charity
and evokes throughout the countryside, not the riotous noise that
the Lady has feared to meet in her earlier speech, but rather the
music of a Theocritean festival:

> still she retains
> Her maid'n gentlenes, and oft at Eeve
> Visits the herds along the twilight meadows,
> Helping all urchin blasts, and ill luck signes
> That the shrewd medling Elfe delights to make,
> Which she with pretious viold liquors heals.
> For which the Shepherds at their festivals
> Carrol her goodnes lowd in rustick layes,
> And throw sweet garland wreaths into her stream
> Of pancies, pinks, and gaudy Daffadils.   [842–51]

The spirit of music which the Lady has revealed in her opening
song shows that she has within herself a richer nature than her
philosophic speeches to Comus can reveal. Like Sabrina, she will
live to fulfill that promise, until her own shepherds, at their festivals, will "Carrol her goodnes lowd in rustick layes."

Milton's masque, then, is a recital, "musical as is Apollo's lute,"
performed with all the arts that Milton has now mastered from
various models.[42] It is a poem that displays a mastery of the blank
verse of Shakespeare and the Jacobean drama. It displays a mastery of the art of madrigal and air. It displays to perfection the
Jonsonian mode of couplet-rhetoric, especially in the form of the

tetrameter. It echoes the whole range of Elizabethan and Jacobean dramatic productions, from the *Old Wives' Tale* to the latest
masques by Thomas Carew and Aurelian Townshend.[43] It displays the prologue of the supernatural agent derived from
Euripides, along with the stichomythic dialogue of the Greek
drama. It can draw upon the whole range of pastoral poetry from
Theocritus to Spenser, along with the myths of Ovid. It is indeed
a mannerist display of poetical mastery, with the young Milton, at
the age of twenty-five, showing himself now almost ready to embark upon the great baroque work for which he has been so carefully preparing his powers.[44]

CHAPTER 2

The
Rising
Poet

It is hard to maintain a clear view of Milton's volume of 1645, since the editions that we are most likely to be using have broken up Milton's groupings and have rearranged the poems in chronological order, interspersed with other poems that Milton did not choose to publish here. I do not mean to quarrel with these rearrangements, which have the advantage of allowing one to trace the development of Milton's early poetical career. And indeed Milton himself has taken the lead in making such a view of his career possible, since his volume of 1645 takes care to date many of the poems and arranges them in rough chronological order, within various groups.[1] At the same time Milton's original arrangement creates the growing awareness of a guiding, central purpose that in turn gives the volume an impressive and peculiar sense of wholeness. In order to regain the significant integrity of the volume one must, now and then, go back to the original.

Perhaps the best way into the volume is to follow Milton's own description of it, in the Latin ode that he sent in January, 1646–47, to John Rouse, Bodley's librarian, with a copy of the book. This is a mock-heroic poem of remarkably high spirits, written in an unprecedented form that MacKellar calls a "metrical experi-

ment or jest."[2] The manner is one of learned wit that makes translation almost impossible; I give here a composite version of the
first strophe, with intermittent comments:[3]

> Gemelle cultu simplici gaudens liber,
> Fronde licet geminâ,
> Munditiéque nitens non operosâ,
> Quam manus attulit
> Juvenilis olim,
> Sedula tamen haud nimii Poetae;
> Dum vagus Ausonias nunc per umbras
> Nunc Britannica per vireta lusit
> Insons populi, barbitóque devius
> Indulsit patrio, mox itidem pectine Daunio
> Longinquum intonuit melos
> Vicinis, & humum vix tetigit pede . . .

"Book in twin parts, rejoicing in a single cover, yet with a double
leaf" [these are "Poems of Mr. John Milton, both English and
Latin," with a separate title page for the Latin poems and separate
pagination for the English and the Latin parts; the "double leaf,"
however, may allude not only to the two title pages, or the two
parts, but at the same time may suggest the double wreath of
laurel that the poet has won for his performance in two
languages], "and shining with unlabored elegance which a hand
once young imparted—a careful hand, but hardly that of one who
was too much a poet—" [that is, not yet a master-poet] "while he
played, wandering, now in the forest-shades of Ausonia and now
on the lawns of England" [*Ausonias umbras:* the phrase may be
taken to include a reference to his own Italian journey, to the
poems in the Italian language, to the Latin poems, and to the
pervasive atmosphere of Greek and Roman pastoral that plays
throughout the volume: Ausonia includes Magna Graecia]; "aloof
from the people, and forsaking the common paths, he indulged
his native lute, and presently in like fashion with Daunian quill
called forth for his neighbors a melody from far away, his foot
scarcely touching the ground" [*pectine Daunio:* the song and instrument of ancient Italy].

Here is the picture of a youthful poet, free from adult cares,
sometimes wandering alone, amusing himself, sometimes making
music for his friends or acquaintances, sometimes writing in his

native vein, sometimes evoking a strain from idealized antiquity—but with a light and dancing posture that we do not
usually associate with John Milton: *et humum vix tetigit pede*. It is
clear, from many indications, that Milton has designed his book
with great care to create this impression.

The entire volume strives to create a tribute to a youthful era
now past—not only the poet's own youth, but a state of mind, a
point of view, ways of writing, ways of living, an old culture and
outlook now shattered by the pressures of maturity and by the
actions of political man. Even the frontispiece, by William Marshall, attempts to set this theme. The aim of the engraving is
clearly to present the youthful poet surrounded by the Muses,
with a curtain in the background lifted to reveal a pastoral landscape of meadow and trees, where a shepherd is piping in the
shade, while a shepherd and a shepherdess are dancing on the
lawn. The legend around the portrait identifies it as a picture of
the poet in his twenty-first year—but in fact the portrait presents
the harsh and crabbed image of a man who might be forty or fifty!
Marshall could do better than this, as his engraving of the youthful Donne testifies; one almost suspects deliberate sabotage here.[4]
If so, Milton performed slyly an appropriate revenge. For under
the portrait, neatly engraved in Greek—engraved no doubt by
Marshall himself—we have the following comment by Milton:

> That an unskilful hand had carved this print
> You'd say at once, seeing the living face;
> But, finding here no jot of me, my friends,
> Laugh at the botching artist's mis-attempt.

With this learned practical joke, the volume begins in high spirits;
how can we doubt, after this, that Milton had a considerable sense
of humor?

Meanwhile, the facing title page prepares us for a volume that
will contain songs of unlabored elegance, in the recent courtly
style: "The Songs were set in Musick by Mr. Henry Lawes Gentleman of the Kings Chappel, and one of His Maiesties Private
Musick"—a notice quite in line with Moseley's preface, which associates Milton's volume with the poems of Waller that Moseley
had published a year before. Waller, as everyone knew, had been

exiled for his plot against the Parliament on the King's behalf; nevertheless Moseley insists on saying: "that incouragement I have already received from the most ingenious men in their clear and courteous entertainment of Mr. *Wallers* late choice Peeces, hath once more made me adventure into the World, presenting it with these ever-green, and not to be blasted Laurels." This bland ignoring, or bold confronting, of the political situation, with its emphasis upon the transcendent values of art, is maintained by reprinting here, from the 1637 edition, Henry Lawes's eloquent dedication of Milton's *Maske* to a young nobleman with strong royalist associations; by the Latin poems in memory of the bishops of Winchester and Ely; by the complimentary writings prefixed to the Latin poems, showing the high regard that Milton had won in Catholic Italy; and by the sonnet beginning: "Captain or Colonel, or Knight in Arms, / Whose chance on these defenceless dores may sease."

> Lift not thy spear against the Muses Bowre,
>   The great *Emathian* Conqueror bid spare
>   The house of *Pindarus,* when Temple and Towre
> Went to the ground: And the repeated air
>   Of sad *Electra's* Poet had the power
>   To save th' *Athenian* Walls from ruine bare.

But will the King's Captain do the same for one who is not yet "too much a poet"? There is room for doubt, and hence the plea, with its undertone of self-irony;[5] but there is no doubt at all about the power of poetry and this poet's hopes to achieve the immortality of Fame. He has told us this through the motto on the title page, there identified as coming from Vergil's seventh eclogue:

> —————Baccare frontem
> Cingite, ne vati noceat mala lingua futuro.

The whole context is essential: the lines are spoken by Thyrsis as he opens his answer in the singing match with Corydon, *Arcades ambo:*

> Pastores, hedera crescentem[6] ornate poetam,
> Arcades, invidia rumpantur ut ilia Codro;
> aut, si ultra placitum laudarit, baccare frontem
> cingite, ne vati noceat mala lingua futuro.

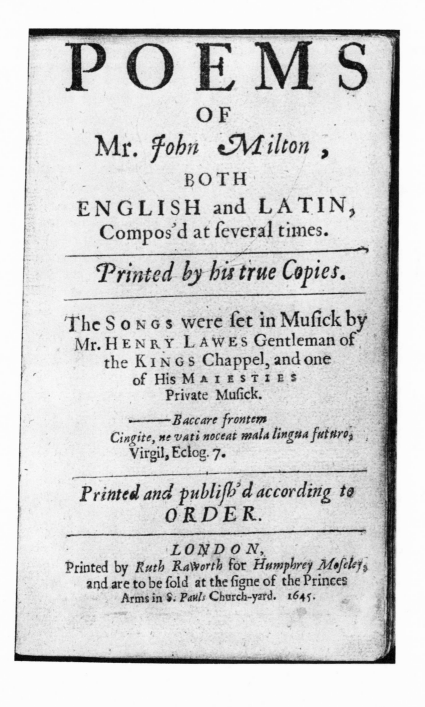

POEMS

OF
Mr. *John Milton*,

BOTH
ENGLISH and LATIN,
Compos'd at several times.

Printed by his true Copies.

The Songs were set in Musick by
Mr. Henry Lawes Gentleman of
the Kings Chappel, and one
of His Maiesties
Private Musick.

——*Baccare frontem*
Cingite, ne vati noceat mala lingua futuro,
Virgil, Eclog. 7.

Printed and publish'd according to
ORDER.

LONDON,
Printed by *Ruth Raworth* for *Humphrey Moseley*,
and are to be sold at the signe of the Princes
Arms in *S. Pauls* Church-yard. 1645.

Bring ivy-leaves to decorate your rising poet, shepherds of Arcady,
and so make Codrus burst his sides with envy. Or, if he tries to
harm me with excessive praise, twine foxglove round my brows, to
stop his evil tongue from hurting your predestined bard.
                                                      [7.25–29, trans. Rieu][7]

Thyrsis loses the match, but other contests no doubt lie ahead; he
ends by sending his love to his friend Lycidas.

That epigraph, summoning up the world of Vergil's *Eclogues*,
prepares the way for the many Vergilian characters and scenes to
be encountered in the English poems here: Corydon and Thyrsis,
Phillis and Thestylis, in *L'Allegro;* Thyrsis and Meliboeus in the
Maske; Lycidas, with Amaryllis, and Damoetas, and the setting of
Vergil's seventh eclogue, "where the Mincius embroiders his
banks with a green fringe of bending rushes";[8] and the shepherds
of *Arcades*—the entertainment at Harefield. The epigraph prepares us too for the echoes of Vergil's Messianic eclogue that
occur in the volume's opening poem, the Nativity Ode; and, above
all, it prepares us to watch, as we read the Latin poems, the poet's
growth away from the light elegy toward the Vergilian mode in
which Milton wrote the most mature and the finest of all the Latin
verses in this volume: *Ad Patrem, Mansus,* and *Epitaphium Damonis,*
all three of which confirm the "rising poet's" place as a "predestined bard."

The *Epitaphium Damonis,* spoken by Thyrsis, becomes appropriately the final poem of the entire volume, for with all its echoes
of Greek pastoral it is the most deliberately Vergilian poem in the
book. Here, clustered together, are those pastoral names that
Vergil drew together in his *Eclogues:* Thyrsis and Damon,
Daphnis, Tityrus, Alphesiboeus, Aegon, Amyntas, Mopsus,
Aegle, and Menalcas; the use of the refrain recalls Vergil's eighth
eclogue, the singing match between Damon and Alphesiboeus,
while the words of Milton's refrain are modeled upon a line from
the seventh eclogue (7.44) and also upon the final line of the last
eclogue; the account of the two cups which Manso gave the poet is
bound to recall the pairs of cups carved by Alcimedon, as described in Vergil's third eclogue; and verbal echoes of Vergil are
so frequent that the poem seems to grow within a Vergilian ma-
trix.[9]

The unity of Milton's volume, from title page to final poem, is
further suggested by the fact that the *Epitaphium Damonis* laments
the death of the very friend to whom the first Latin poem in the
book had been written—*Elegia prima,* that playful and thoroughly
Ovidian elegy composed by the arrogantly clever and quite unrepentant sophomore during his rustication. At the same time, the
reader is bound to recall that *Elegia sexta* and the fourth sonnet
have also been explicitly addressed to this same friend, Charles
Diodati. The final poem, then, in paying tribute to a friend of
youth, becomes a farewell to the pleasures and attitudes of youth,
including the pleasures of pastoral poetry and the imitative pleasures of writing such Latin verse—a farewell that Milton appropriately gives with unmistakable echoes of Vergil's *Eclogues:*

> Ipse etiam, nam nescio quid mihi grande sonabat
> Fistula, ab undecimâ jam lux est altera nocte,
> Et tum forte novis admôram labra cicutis,
> Dissiluere tamen rupta compage, nec ultra
> Ferre graves potuere sonos, dubito quoque ne sim
> Turgidulus, tamen & referam, vos cedite silvae.

And I—for I know not what my pipe was grandly sounding—it is
now eleven nights and a day—and then perhaps I had put my lips
to new pipes, but they burst asunder, broken at the fastening,
and could no more bear the deep tones—I hesitate too lest I seem
puffed up, yet I will tell the tale—give place then, O forests.

[155–60, trans. MacKellar]

Milton's *vos cedite silvae* is a clear echo of the *concedite silvae* with
which Gallus bids farewell to Arcadian pleasures in Vergil's last
eclogue (10.63); while Milton's following farewell to Latin poetry
and Latin themes is based explicitly on the wording of Vergil's
seventh eclogue:

> aut, si non possumus omnes,
> hic arguta sacra pendebit fistula pinu.   [7.23–24]

Thus, after the famous passage in which Milton tells of his resolve
to write an epic on British themes, he cries:

> O mihi tum si vita supersit,
> Tu procul annosa pendebis fistula pinu
> Multum oblita mihi, aut patriis mutata camoenis

Brittonicum strides, quid enim? omnia non licet uni
Non sperâsse uni licet omnia . . .

Ah! then if life remain, you, my pipe, shall hang on some aged pine
far off and forgotten, unless forsaking your native songs you shrilly
sound a British theme. Why not a British theme? One man cannot
do all things, cannot hope to do all things.

[168–72, trans. MacKellar]

MacKellar's version of these lines helps to bring out the complexity of the state of mind here expressed. The poet is resolved to
leave behind the *fistula,* the reed pipe of his pastoral muse, and he
will turn instead to write of those deeper themes which have already on one occasion proved to be stronger than that youthful
pipe could bear. At the same time the *fistula* may represent Latin
poetry, and the words *patriis camoenis* may thus suggest the Latin
language itself.[10] That is to say, the poet is contemplating deeper
themes, British themes, and themes composed in English. The
power of poetry represented by these early compositions on the
fistula will not be developed unless the poet can commit himself to
English. Perhaps he has already tried those deeper themes in
Latin, but without success: the rising poet knows, as Vergil says in
the eighth eclogue, *non omnia possumus omnes* (63); and he foresees
that his future fame must be entrusted to his native tongue.

His maturing prowess in that tongue has already been demonstrated in the other pastoral monody that, with beautiful symmetry, closes the series of his shorter English poems in the first
part of his double book. *Lycidas,* like the *Epitaphium Damonis,* represents the climax of its part; each monody is the culmination of
the many strands of experimentation that have been growing
throughout each part. The Ludlow *Maske* is printed after *Lycidas,*
as a work distinctly separate from the preceding groups; it is
provided with elaborate introductory matter and a separate half-
title—almost a full title-page, for it bears the imprint "Anno Dom.
1645." The pagination, however, is continuous throughout the
English part. The whole book, then, displays particular care for
balance and harmony in all its proportions, while the poems
themselves have been arranged to convey a sense of the predestined bard's rising powers.

II

The theme of poetical development is particularly clear in the Latin poems, most of which, as the Latin title page points out, were written *intra Annum aetatis Vigesimum:* that is, before his twentieth year had ended. In keeping with this emphasis, Milton has taken unusual care in dating his Latin poems, so as to make clear their youthfulness and the rising poet's precociousness. This atmosphere is borne out, in the elegies, by their heading *Liber primus*—a first book, a primer, for which no second book follows; and also by the retractation which ends the sequence of the seven numbered elegies. There is no need to suspect a misprint in the dating of the seventh, which comes out of chronological order,[11] for the placing of this elegy seems to be dictated by the presence of the retractation, evidently written for the seventh elegy alone, and not for this whole set of elegies; yet placed here as it is, the retractation covers any similar materials in the preceding poems and puts last the latest piece of composition, the retractation itself. This palinode creates the impression of having been composed for some special occasion (such as, perhaps, a recitation of the seventh elegy before one of those "privat Academies in *Italy*," where Milton tells us that he presented "some trifles . . . compos'd at under twenty or thereabout"),[12] when it was appropriate for the poet to speak of this youthful love poem with a tone of humorous exaggeration and a touch of mock-heroic banter:

> Haec ego mente olim laevâ, studioque supino
> 	Nequitiae posui vana trophaea meae.
> Scilicet abreptum sic me malus impulit error,
> 	Indocilisque aetas prava magistra fuit.
> Donec Socraticos umbrosa Academia rivos
> 	Praebuit, admissum dedocuitque jugum.
> Protinus extinctis ex illo tempore flammis,
> 	Cincta rigent multo pectora nostra gelu.
> Unde suis frigus metuit puer ipse Sagittis,
> 	Et Diomedéam vim timet ipse Venus.

These are the monuments to my wantonness that with a perverse spirit and a trifling purpose I once erected. Obviously, mischievous error led me astray and my undisciplined youth was a vicious teacher until the shady Academy offered its Socratic streams and

taught me how to escape from the yoke to which I had submitted.
From that hour those flames were extinct and thenceforward my
breast has been rigid under a thick case of ice, of which the boy
himself fears the frost for his arrows, and Venus herself is afraid of
my Diomedean strength.   [trans. Hughes]

After this coda to the formal elegies Milton adds his epigrams
written in the same verse form: first, a group of five pieces related
to the Gunpowder Plot, which we assume must be early, because
of their relation to *In quintum Novembris, Anno aetatis 17;* and lastly,
three epigrams that we know to be late, since they deal with the
singer Leonora Baroni, whom Milton heard during his visits to
Rome in 1638–39.[13] By this method of grouping Milton has man-
aged to end his section devoted to elegiac verse with poems that
give exalted praise to the Orphic powers of voice and verse, married in song:

> Altera Torquatum cepit Leonora Poëtam,
>   Cujus ab insano cessit amore furens.
> Ah miser ille tuo quantò feliciùs aevo
>   Perditus, & propter te Leonora foret!
> Et te Pieriâ sensisset voce canentem
>   Aurea maternae fila movere lyrae,
> Quamvis Dircaeo torsisset lumina Pentheo
>   Saevior, aut totus desipuisset iners,
> Tu tamen errantes caecâ vertigine sensus
>   Voce eadem poteras composuisse tuâ;
> Et poteras aegro spirans sub corde quietem
>   Flexamino cantu restituisse sibi.

> Another Leonora captivated the poet Torquato, who for fren-
> zied love of her went mad. Ah, poor unfortunate! How much more
> happily had he been lost in your times and for love of you, Leonora!
> He would have heard you singing with Pierian voice as the golden
> strings of your mother's lyre moved in harmony. Though he had
> rolled his eyes more fiercely than Dircean Pentheus, or all insensible
> had raved, yet you by your voice could have composed his senses
> wandering in their blind whirl; and, inspiring his distempered
> heart with peace, you could have restored him to himself with your
> soul-moving song.   [trans. MacKellar]

The same Orphic theme dominates the conclusion to the second, much longer grouping here, the *Sylvarum Liber,* poems in
various meters, where the growth toward maturity of poetic
power is marked by the poet's growing appreciation of the

philosophic and religious meaning of music's power in the universe. The first poem in this section is headed *Anno aetatis 16. In obitum Procancellarii medici,* with the date given special prominence by thus forming part of the title; and the same is true of the two following poems dated *Anno aetatis 17.* Thereafter the poems are not dated, but the first three headings have served to suggest a chronological movement while implicitly apologizing for the immaturity (and by the way implying perhaps the precocity?) of these opening pieces. After the two academic exercises that follow, the remaining poems are drawn together by interlocking themes, above all by the theme of poetical dedication set forth in *Ad Patrem*—still, as he says, one of his youthful works (*iuvenilia carmina*)—but nevertheless a poem that by its fervor and wit and firm command of hexameter marks the beginning of this poet's mature strength:

> Nec tu vatis opus divinum despice carmen,
> Quo nihil aethereos ortus, & semina caeli,
> Nil magis humanam commendat origine mentem,
> Sancta Promethéae retinens vestigia flammae.
> Carmen amant superi, tremebundaque Tartara carmen
> Ima ciere valet, divosque ligare profundos,
> Et triplici duros Manes adamante coercet.

> Scorn not the poet's song, a work divine, which more than aught else reveals our ethereal origin and heavenly race. Nothing so much as its origin does grace to the human mind, possessing yet some sacred traces of Promethean fire. The gods love song, song that has power to move the trembling depths of Tartarus, to bind the nether gods, and restrain the cruel shades with triple adamant.
>   [17–23, trans. MacKellar]

The implicit allusion to Orpheus is made explicit a few lines later, after Milton has imagined "the bard, seated at the festal board," singing of "the feats of heroes" and of "chaos and the broadly-laid foundations of the world."

> Denique quid vocis modulamen inane juvabit,
> Verborum sensusque vacans, numerique loquacis?
> Silvestres decet iste choros, non Orphea cantus,
> Qui tenuit fluvios & quercubus addidit aures
> Carmine, non citharâ, simulachraque functa canendo
> Compulit in lacrymas; habet has à carmine laudes.

And finally, what will the empty modulation of the voice avail, void
of words and sense, and of eloquent numbers? That song will do for
the sylvan choirs, but not for Orpheus, who with song and not with
lute held back the rivers, and gave ears to the oaks, and moved the
shades of the dead to tears; these praises he has from song.

[50–55, trans. MacKellar]

This passage prepares the way for the Orphic allusion at the close
of the poem written to the Roman poet Salzilli, where Milton
hopes that this poet's illness may be cured so that he may resume
his writing, with the result that "Swollen Tiber himself, charmed
by the song, will favor the annual hope of the husbandmen" (36–
37, trans. MacKellar).

But what shall we make of the two poems in Greek that lie
between *Ad Patrem* and *Ad Salsillum*? The first of these, the Greek
version of Psalm 114, can be securely dated in November 1634, as
we know from Milton's letter to Alexander Gill, in which he describes how he was inspired to adapt this work of the "truly divine
poet . . . to the rules of Greek Heroic song."[14] The poem thus
follows chronologically after *Ad Patrem,* if we believe, as I do, that
Ad Patrem dates from 1631–32, or, as Parker has argued, from the
earlier part of 1634.[15] But more important, the Greek version of
the psalm follows naturally after the gratitude that the poet has
just expressed to his father for encouraging him to learn, not only
Latin, but also Greek, French, Italian, and Hebrew. By his skill
in adapting and expanding the Hebrew original into Greek
hexameters we may see how far this poet has travelled intellectually since that time when, "at fifteen yeers old,"[16] he had made an
English paraphrase of the same psalm in the style of Sylvester's
Dubartas, using the current English versions as his guides. The
brief Greek epigram that follows is easily brought in here
(whenever it was written) as further evidence of linguistic command.

Then the whole volume closes with the two latest and most
complex of his Latin poems, *Mansus* and the *Epitaphium Damonis,*
bound together by Milton's elaborate description in the *Epitaphium* (181–97) of the two "cups" (*pocula*) that Manso gave to
Milton—gifts that Milton had hoped to show to Diodati—books,
perhaps, that they might have discussed together, as in their

younger days.[17] But above all, these two closing poems are linked
by their revelation of this poet's hopes to write a British epic:

> O mihi și mea sors talem concedat amicum
> Phoebaëos decorâsse viros qui tam bene norit,
> Si quando indigenas revocabo in carmina reges,
> Arturumque etiam sub terris bella moventem;
> Aut dicam invictae sociali foedere mensae,
> Magnanimos Heroas, & (O modo spiritus ad sit)
> Frangam Saxonicas Britonum sub Marte phalanges.

O, if my lot might but bestow such a friend upon me, a friend who
understands how to honor the devotees of Phoebus—if ever I shall
summon back our native kings into our songs, and Arthur, waging
his wars beneath the earth, or if ever I shall proclaim the mag-
nanimous heroes of the table which their mutual fidelity made in-
vincible, and (if only the spirit be with me) shall shatter the Saxon
phalanxes under the British Mars!

[*Mansus*, 78–84, trans. Hughes]

> Ipse ego Dardanias Rutupina per aequora puppes
> Dicam, & Pandrasidos regnum vetus Inogeniae,
> Brennúmque Arviragúmque duces, priscúmque Belinum,
> Et tandem Armoricos Britonum sub lege colonos;
> Tum gravidam Arturo fatali fraude Jögernen
> Mendaces vultus, assumptáque Gorlöis arma,
> Merlini dolus.

I would tell of Dardanian ships along the Rutupian Sea, and of the
ancient realm of Imogen, Pandrasus' daughter, of the leaders
Brennus and Arviragus, and old Belinus, and of colonists in Ar-
morica under British laws; then I would tell of Igraine pregnant
with Arthur by a fatal fraud, of the seeming face and counterfeit
arms of Gorlois, Merlin's artifice.

[*Epitaphium*, 162–68, trans. MacKellar]

"Quid enim?" Milton asks—"Why not a British theme?"

III

The dating of the English poems is less explicit in most cases,
but the mode of arrangement is clear. As with the Latin poems,
the over-arching structure runs from poems of early youth to
poems that enact a movement toward the broader visions of
maturity. Within this larger movement the poems are then sorted

into subordinate groupings: devotional poems, secular poems in
the Jonsonian mode, sonnets, and pastoral poems; and within
each of these a rough chronological arrangement can be discerned.[18]

The group headed "Sonnets," for example, opens with the English love sonnet that echoes Italian addresses to the Nightingale,
but basically follows the medieval and pseudo–Chaucerian tradition of the Cuckoo and the Nightingale. Then follow the five
sonnets in Italian, with their *Canzone,* paying tribute to the Petrar-
chans by using, as Milton says, "the language of which Love makes
his boast" ("Questa e lingua di cui si vanta Amore").[19] These are all
poems written in the atmosphere of the "young, unassuming and
artless lover" suggested by the opening line of Sonnet 6 ("Giovane
piano, e semplicetto amante"), and dramatized in the *Canzone,*
where the poet shows himself surrounded by "Amorous young
men and maidens . . . jesting."[20] After these playful exercises in a
fading, once-popular mode, the stern lines of Sonnet 7, on the
flight of his three-and-twentieth year, come with the shock of a
sudden recognition, setting a severe Calvinist view of life against
these early trifles:

> All is, if I have grace to use it so,
> As ever in my great task Masters eye.

The meaning of these lines, I think, is clarified if we take the word
"grace" in a strict Calvinist sense: the speaker's future lies completely in the hands of God.[21] Though Time has stolen away his
youth, all his hopes remain as valid as they ever were; nothing has
really changed, for the use of his life depends upon the timeless
will and eye and grace of God. Nothing could form a sharper
contrast with the preceding sonnets; and yet the sternness of the
doctrine itself may suggest a veering from one youthful extreme
to another—especially since the movement of the sonnet still
maintains a conventional, end-stopped, balanced manner. The
succeeding sonnet on the military threat to London shows (as the
earlier discussion has implied) a greater maturity, reflected in its
ironic posture and in the graceful sentence that winds its sinewy
length over the last five lines.

Then the group closes with two more sonnets addressed to

women, both sonnets forming a tacit contrast with the Petrarchan mode, in theme and in technique. Recalling the "Donna" of Milton's Italian sonnets, we are alert to appreciate the growth and change represented in the suspended opening of Sonnet 9:

> Lady that in the prime of earliest youth,
>   Wisely hast shun'd the broad way and the green,
>   And with those few art eminently seen,
>   That labour up the Hill of heav'nly Truth,
> The better part with *Mary,* and [with] *Ruth,*
>   Chosen thou hast . . .

Lastly, Sonnet 10, with an even greater suspension and involution,[22] addresses a married lady who in herself maintains the virtues that once ruled in England, before the turmoil of the present age began:

> Daughter to that good Earl, once President
>   Of *Englands* Counsel, and her Treasury,
>   Who liv'd in both, unstain'd with gold or fee,
>   And left them both, more in himself content,
> Till the sad breaking of that Parlament
>   Broke him, as that dishonest victory
>   At *Chaeronèa,* fatal to liberty
>   Kil'd with report that Old man eloquent,
> Though later born, then to have known the dayes
>   Wherin your Father flourisht, yet by you
>   Madam, me thinks I see him living yet;
> So well your words his noble vertues praise,
>   That all both judge you to relate them true,
>   And to possess them, Honour'd *Margaret.*

Thus the syntax involves the troubled, more inclusive vision of maturity, while the *disio amoroso* of the Italian sonnets lies far in the past.

Similarly, it is helpful to read *L'Allegro* and *Il Penseroso* in the context of Milton's chosen arrangement; for these two poems come at the end of a group that might best be described as Jonsonian: poems in the mode of the "terse" couplet characteristic of Jonson and his Sons. First, the "witty" *Epitaph on the Marchioness of Winchester;* next, that perfect distillation of the Elizabethan madrigal, the *Song On May morning;* then the rather labored epigram on Shakespeare, dated 1630, and marked as early by the archaic

"Star-ypointing"; and then the two jocular epitaphs for the University Carrier. Out of these experiments arise the two great companion poems, or twin poems, or the double poem, as we have come to call them. Reading these two poems in their original context may guide us toward a slight modification or qualification of these descriptive phrases. They are companion poems, certainly, but they are not of equal strength and stature.[23] Their relation is rather that of Younger Brother to Elder Brother. The parallels between them, so familiar to everyone, should not lead us to read the poems in parallel, as though they were two sides of a coin, or two sides of an academic debate. For the poems develop a linear, sequential effect, moving from youthful hedonism toward the philosophic, contemplative mind.[24]

It has often been noted that *L'Allegro* is looser in its handling of versification and syntax than *Il Penseroso*. According to Sprott, for example, the basic iambic tetrameter is varied with trochaic lines thirty-two percent of the time in *L'Allegro,* but only sixteen percent of the time in *Il Penseroso*.[25] Hence the subtle effect of "uncertainty" that Weismiller finds in reading the rhythms is much greater in *L'Allegro* than in *Il Penseroso*.[26] As for syntax, its occasional looseness in *L'Allegro* may be indicated by the sharp debate[27] that has arisen over these lines:

> To hear the Lark begin his flight,
> And singing startle the dull night,
> From his watch-towre in the skies,
> Till the dappled dawn doth rise;
> Then to com in spight of sorrow,
> And at my window bid good morrow,
> Through the Sweet-Briar, or the Vine,
> Or the twisted Eglantine.   [41–48]

Is it the lark or is it L'Allegro who comes to the window to greet the speaker in his bed? At first "to com" may seem to be in parallel with "to hear". Yet consideration of the context indicates that this cannot be so, for the lines immediately following, and all the rest of the poem, present L'Allegro as the receiver of impressions from without—"list'ning," "walking," measuring the landscape with his eye, hearing tales about the "lubbar Fend," and so on. No, "to com" is rather in rough parallel with "begin." It is the lark who greets L'Allegro with his song, just as in the next lines "the Cock with lively din, / Scatters the rear of darknes thin."

A greater freedom of syntax occurs in the speaker's memory of the tales about the goblin:

> She was pincht, and pull'd she sed,
> And he by Friars Lanthorn led
> Tells how the drudging *Goblin* swet,
> To ern his Cream-bowle duly set . . .   [103–06]

In the edition of 1673 the second line is altered to read "And by the Friars Lanthorn led"—but this change does not affect the colloquial looseness of the phrasing.

Such syntactical looseness is hardly a defect in the poem, any more than the striking variations in meter: these are all part of a poem designed with "wanton heed, and giddy cunning," the poem of "fancies child," warbling "his native Wood-notes wilde," a poem that moves with "light fantastick toe" to celebrate "The Mountain Nymph, sweet Liberty." Freedom of movement, without concentration of mind, is implicit in those floating participles: "list'ning" (53) and "walking" (57), which relate to the wish of the "I" and "me" (34–35) some twenty lines before. Indeed the pronouns "I" and "me" occur only four times in *L'Allegro,* as compared with eleven times in *Il Penseroso.* Instead it is "mine eye"— an "it"—that measures the lawn and sees the towers; and when the "upland Hamlets . . . invite," they invite no particular person, but everyman; and later on "Towred Cities please *us.*" In every possible way a generalized receiver of shifting impressions is created, so that at the close even Orpheus becomes, not a singer, but a listener! For the speaker wishes

> That *Orpheus* self may heave his head
> From golden slumber on a bed
> Of heapt *Elysian* flowres, and hear
> Such streins as would have won the ear
> Of *Pluto,* to have quite set free
> His half-regain'd *Eurydice.*   [145–50]

All this presents a sharp contrast with the poem of "the fixed mind" whose presiding goddess, "Sober, stedfast, and demure," is urged to keep her "wonted state, / With eev'n step, and musing gate." The "Cherub Contemplation" here works within a personal

presence whose mind not only receives impressions from without, but also actively addresses and "woos" their action:

> Sweet Bird that shunn'st the noise of folly,
> Most musicall, most melancholy!
> Thee Chauntress oft the Woods among,
> I woo to hear thy eevn-Song . . .   [61–64]

This speaker does not float with loose participles; his stance is
precise, active, personal: "I walk," "I hear". He hopes to set his
lamp in the lonely tower in order to spend the night in deep study
of Hermes, Plato, and the great tragedians, while his mind longs
to behold Orpheus in vital action:

> But, O sad Virgin, that thy power
> Might raise *Musaeus* from his bower,
> Or bid the soul of *Orpheus* sing
> Such notes as warbled to the string,
> Drew Iron tears down *Pluto's* cheek,
> And made Hell grant what Love did seek.   [103–08]

And after his dreams, set in an harmonious Theocritean landscape, he hopes to hear the music represented in *Arcades* and the
Ludlow *Maske:*

> And as I wake, sweet musick breath
> Above, about, or underneath,
> Sent by som spirit to mortals good,
> Or th'unseen Genius of the Wood.   [151–54]

But even such listening is too passive for this speaker: he soon
directs himself "To walk the studious Cloysters pale," and to
"love" the beauties of Gothic architecture, while "the pealing Or-
gan" and "the full voic'd Quire" will, he hopes, inspire the contemplative mind to its highest reaches, and

> through mine ear
> Dissolve me into extasies,
> And bring all Heav'n before mine eyes.   [164–66]

Looking back now, we can see that the first poem has summed
up a youthful world of Elizabethan poetry now past; the tone has
been set in the opening archaism, "In Heav'n ycleap'd *Eu-
phrosyne.*" It is full of all the maying and the pastoral joys cele-

brated in hundreds of Elizabethan airs and madrigals, including the famous "Come live with me," strongly echoed near the beginning (39) and at the very end; and it remembers too those popular legends about Mab and the drudging goblin, celebrated by Shakespeare and Drayton. Then there are the allusions to the "high triumphs" of archaic chivalry, to the courtly "Ladies, whose bright eies / Rain influence" in Petrarchan fashion, to "mask, and antique Pageantry," to Jonson's comedies, and to Shakespeare in his comic and pastoral vein.[28] It is a joyous celebration and recreation of an era, a state of mind, now past; but we note that it ends with hints that suggest this is not the highest mode of harmony. As every Platonist knew, Plato had condemned the "soft *Lydian* Aires," and Milton subtly recalls the condemnation, while seeming to ignore it:

> With wanton heed, and giddy cunning,
> The melting voice through mazes running . . .   [141–42]

But the words "wanton," "giddy," and "melting" recall the implications of the *Republic:*

> Again, drunkenness, effeminacy, and inactivity are most unsuitable in Guardians. Which are the modes expressing softness and the ones used at drinking-parties?
> There are the Ionian and certain Lydian modes which are called "slack."
> You will not use them in the training of your warriors?
> Certainly not.   [III.398c–400c, trans. Cornford][29]

The final picture of Orpheus heaving up his head "From golden slumber on a bed / Of heapt *Elysian* flowres" carries on, however beautifully, the "softness" of the Lydian mode, in contrast to the potent, active Orpheus of *Il Penseroso.* Furthermore, this second reference to Orpheus is subsumed within the middle of *Il Penseroso,* where he is only one of many great poets and thinkers. The spirit of Plato's "shady Academy"[30] (derived traditionally from Orpheus and Pythagoras) dominates *Il Penseroso,* from the opening salutation of the Goddess "sage and holy" to the grand musical close which extends this poem two dozen lines beyond the length of *L'Allegro.* All is, however, subtly qualified at the very end, as the poem presents a picture that is too obviously archaic and senti-

mental to be taken solemnly: its excess tells us that Melancholy too
needs tempering:

> And may at last my weary age
> Find out the peacefull hermitage,
> The Hairy Gown and Mossy Cell,
> Where I may sit and rightly spell,
> Of every Star that Heav'n doth shew,
> And every Herb that sips the dew;
> Till old experience do attain
> To somthing like Prophetic strain.
> These pleasures *Melancholy* give,
> And I with thee will choose to live.

That echo of "Come live with me" is phrased more positively than
the closing couplet of *L'Allegro:*

> These delights, if thou canst give,
> Mirth with thee, I mean to live.

Yet the echo reminds us that either choice involves a limitation.

Thus the two poems move from youth to age—the word
"youthfull" is invoked twice in *L'Allegro,* and not at all in *Il
Penseroso*—while in their movement these two unequal but compatible companions suggest the growth toward maturity that constitutes this volume's dominant theme.

IV

Turning now, finally, to the devotional group that begins Milton's book, we note that he has carefully stressed the youthfulness
of the four opening poems. First, out of strict chronological order,
we have the poem headed: *On the morning of Christs Nativity. Compos'd 1629.*—with the date thus given prominence as part of the
title.[31] Then come the two psalms, "don by the Author at fifteen
yeers old," as the headnote tells us. Then the unfinished poem on
the Passion, with the famous note at the end: "This Subject the
Author finding to be above the yeers he had, when he wrote it,
and nothing satisfi'd with what was begun, left it unfinisht." One may
wonder why Milton bothered to include this acknowledged failure
and fragment, when he did not include the more interesting and
at least completed English poems that he added in 1673: the poem

On the Death of a fair Infant, and the lines from the *Vacation Exercise.* But the inclusion of the fragment has a clear function: to stress the immaturity of these opening pieces, to suggest the ambitious young man outreaching his powers, and achieving poetical success only when he can subject his muse to some deliberate limitation. What he can accomplish is then demonstrated in the three short pieces that follow: *On Time, Upon the Circumcision,* and *At a solemn Musick;* these are undated, and thus, we assume, not quite so youthful. *Upon the Circumcision,* in particular, suggests a new beginning, in a less venturous mode, after the false start of *The Passion;* here the poet, by skillfully imitating the stanza-form of Petrarch's canzone to the Virgin, creates a carefully controlled meditation on the love of the suffering Infant.[32] The other two lyrics are experiments in the handling of the canzone, anticipating the flexible verse-form of *Lycidas. At a solemn Musick* bears a special significance as the final poem in this group, for its transcendent praise of the wedded powers of voice and verse links with the view of music's power to be found in *Arcades,* the Ludlow *Maske,* the epigrams to Leonora, *Ad Patrem,* and *Mansus.* It is thus a poem that helps to tie the entire volume together, as well as this small opening group, where the final lyric recalls the heavenly music heard by the shepherds in the long youthful poem on the Nativity that Milton has wisely chosen to open his book, as prologue to the rising poet's achievement.

The dating, "Compos'd 1629," accords with the Nativity poem's relation to an age and mode of English poetry now outgrown, both by the nation and by the poet. In understanding this poetical mode, one may gain important clues from Milton's description of the Nativity Ode in his sixth Latin elegy—especially when we read this elegy in Milton's chosen context, between the Ovidian celebration of Spring in *Elegia quinta* and the mildly Ovidian eroticism of *Elegia septima.* Read thus, *Elegia sexta* does not lend itself easily to the widely held view that the Ode "teaches us to read the contrast of the elegiac and the heroic vein as a repudiation of the former, to transliterate the description of the heroic poet into Christian terms as the account of a dedicated spirit divinely inspired."[33] This elegy begins with a broad joke about Diodati's feasting at the Christmas season:

> Mitto tibi sanam non pleno ventre salutem,
>   Quâ tu distento forte carere potes.

> With a stomach anything but full, I send you a prayer for sound
> health, of which, perhaps, you, with your stomach stretched to its
> uttermost, may be in sore need.   [trans. Knapp][34]

Then follows lively praise of festive poetry and the "light elegy,"
in a passage twice as long as the subsequent praise of epic: wine,
feasting, maidens, and dancing inspire, says Milton, an excellent
kind of poetry, blessed by many gods. Of course, he adds, if a poet
wants to write on grand epic themes, then he must live quite
differently; and Milton proceeds to write a hyperbolical account
of the ascetic life required for such a bard:

> Ille quidem parcè Samii pro more magistri
>   Vivat, & innocuos praebeat herba cibos;
> Stet prope fagineo pellucida lympha catillo,
>   Sobriaque è puro pocula fonte bibat.

> let him live sparingly, like the Samian teacher [Pythagoras] and let
> herbs furnish his innocent diet. Let the purest water stand beside
> him in a bowl of beech and let him drink sober draughts from the
> pure spring.   [59–62, trans. Hughes]

He goes on to express his belief in the exalted power of this kind
of bard, but he does not wholly lay aside the tone of "Ovidian
banter" that Rand has found in the earlier part.[35] Milton no doubt
hopes to reach that higher vein himself; but he does not appear to
be saying so here. When he turns to discuss himself at the end of
the poem, he makes a clean break with the previous discussion of
elegy and epic; both are excellent in their kinds, the poet implies,
but he is not writing in either vein at the moment:

> At tu siquid agam, scitabere (si modò saltem
>   Esse putas tanti noscere siquid agam)
> Paciferum canimus caelesti semine regem,
>   Faustaque sacratis saecula pacta libris,
> Vagitumque Dei, & stabulantem paupere tecto
>   Qui suprema suo cum patre regna colit.
> Stelliparumque polum, modulantesque aethere turmas,
>   Et subitò elisos ad sua fana Deos.
> Dona quidem dedimus Christi natalibus illa,
>   Illa sub auroram lux mihi prima tulit.   [79–88]

One must stress the *At tu siquid agam, scitabere:* "But if you will
know what I am doing (if only you think it of any importance to
know whether I am doing anything)"—note how he maintains the
familiar tone with which the poem has opened—"I am singing the
heaven-descended King, the bringer of peace, and the blessed
times promised in the sacred books—the infant cries of our God"
[which in fact are not mentioned in the Nativity poem as we have
it; but Milton is emphasizing the poem's allegiance to the naïve
tradition of the Christmas carol, as his next words further indi-
cate] "and his stabling under a mean roof who, with his Father,
governs the realms above. I am singing the starry sky and the
hosts that sang high in air, and the gods that were suddenly destroyed in their own shrines. These are my gifts for the birthday
of Christ—gifts which the first light of its dawn brought to me"
(trans. Hughes). In that last clause Milton seems to be saying only
that the writing of the poem began at dawn; there seems to be no
indication of a special experience of religious dedication.

In this elegy's final couplet the opening *Te quoque* has allowed
various interpretations:[36]

> Te quoque pressa manent patriis meditata cicutis,
>   Tu mihi, cui recitem, judicis instar eris.

In some versions it appears that Milton is referring to certain *other*
English poems that he has also written; but the *quoque* modifies *te;*
or, rather, it is pleonastic and is best omitted, as in the revised
translation of Hughes, which makes it plain that the passage is still
alluding to the Nativity poem: "For you these simple strains that
have been meditated on my native pipes are waiting; and you,
when I recite them to you, shall be my judge." *Patriis meditata
cicutis:* meditated on the native hemlock pipes of the humble
shepherd. Milton has suggested here the Nativity poem's basic
decorum.

It is, first of all, a poem that declares, in many ways, this poet's
indebtedness to his predecessors in the line of English poetry. The
four prefatory stanzas, written in a variation of rhyme royal,
suggest the use of this ancient stanza-form by Chaucer and the
Chaucerians, by Spenser, in *The Ruines of Time* and the *Fowre
Hymnes,* and by Shakespeare, in *Lucrece;* while the modification

into hexameter in the final line declares a further allegiance to
Spenser and the Spenserians. The stanza of the Hymn proper is
even more significant, for its first six lines suggest the movement
of a popular song or carol:

> It was the Winter wilde,
> While the Heav'n-born-childe,
>   All meanly wrapt in the rude manger lies;
> Nature in aw to him
> Had doff't her gawdy trim,
>   With her great Master so to sympathize.

The use of three-foot and five-foot lines, in various combinations,
is found in many Elizabethan songs: thus among Thomas Mor-
ley's canzonets we find this stanza running 335335335, though the
rhyme differs from Milton's:[37]

> I follow, lo, the footing
> Still of my lovely cruel,
> Proud of herself that she is beauty's jewel.
>   And fast away she flieth,
>   Love's sweet delight deriding,
> In woods and groves sweet Nature's treasure hiding.
>   Yet cease I not pursuing,
>   But since I thus have sought her,
> Will run me out of breath till I have caught her.

But the first six lines of Milton's stanza also suggest another pattern: the combination of two- and three-foot lines, with Milton's
rhyme scheme, found in some of the ancient Christmas carols:

> The God Almyght
> And Kyng of Lyght,
>   Whose powr is ouer all,
> Gyue vs of grace
> For to purchas
>   Hys realme celestyall.
>
> Wher hys aungels
> And archangels
>   Do syng incessantly,
> Hys princypates
> And potestates
>   Maketh gret armony.
>
> The cherubyns

> And seraphyns
>   With ther tvnykes mery,
> The trones al,
> Most musycall,
>   Syng the heuenly Kery.[38]

Then, by allowing his last line to swell out into a Spenserian alexandrine, Milton draws his poem out of the realm of the popular song into the larger area of this poet's predestined goals. In stanza after stanza we may feel this change from the simple language and steady beat of the ballad into the realms of a more ambitious art:

> But wisest Fate sayes no,
> This must not yet be so,
>   The Babe lies yet in smiling Infancy,
> That on the bitter cross
> Must redeem our loss;
>   So both himself and us to glorifie:
> Yet first to those ychain'd in sleep,
> The wakefull trump of doom must thunder through the deep.
>   [149–56]

With all the poem's lofty expansions in rhythm, in language, and in rich allusion, the poet's chosen method of control never falters: he clings to the central mode of the ancient naïve, the mode of the Nativity ballad, the mode that Milton points to in his prologue when he calls his poem a "humble ode" that he seeks to lay "lowly at his blessed feet." The touches of archaic, Spenserian language sprinkled throughout, very lightly, are all adjusted to maintain this effect, as in the "ychain'd" of the stanza just quoted, the "lusty Paramour" of the Hymn's opening stanza, the "silly thoughts" of the shepherds, or the "dusky eyn" of the doomed god Osiris. At the same time touches of old-fashioned heavy alliteration recall the style, not only of Spenser, but of all those lesser writers whom Sidney mocked for their "rimes, running in ratling rowes."

This decorum of an ancient and traditional simplicity pervades every aspect of the poem, versification, language, scene painting, imagery, and theme.[39] The scenes and images are given in broad and simplified terms, as in some old tapestry or pageant. The

original line (143) in which Truth and Justice wear "Th'enameld
Arras of the Rainbow" is more closely in accord with the poem
than Milton's more sophisticated revision: "Orb'd in a Rain-bow."
Thus Nature seeks to hide her "guilty front" with "The Saintly
Vail of Maiden white"; and "the meek-eyd Peace . . . crown'd
with Olive green, came softly sliding / Down through the turning
sphear" (39,42,46–48). "The Shepherds on the Lawn . . . Sate
simply chatting in a rustick row"; then

> At last surrounds their sight
> A Globe of circular light,
>   That with long beams the shame-fac't night array'd,
> The helmed Cherubim
> And sworded Seraphim,
>   Are seen in glittering ranks with wings displaid.
>   [85,87,109–14]

One should note, too, in these quotations, the curious mixture
of past and present tense, which Lowry Nelson has ably interpreted to indicate the poem's sense of a timeless world;[40] this is so,
yet Milton's manner of thus mixing past and present also adds to
the effect of the naïve, as though the poet were artlessly following
the instinct of a momentary mood or were using past and present
tense as the needs of rhythm and rhyme might, for a moment,
require.

Then, in the latter half of the poem, this effect is strongly
heightened by Milton's treatment of the various characters that
here are shown in action. The Dragon of Revelation is presented
in the guise of a dragon out of folklore:

> And wrath to see his Kingdom fail,
> Swindges the scaly Horrour of his foulded tail.   [171–72]

And his antagonist, the blessèd Babe, is likewise shown in the
manner of some ancient folk-hero, some infant Hercules:

> Our Babe to shew his Godhead true,
> Can in his swadling bands controul the damned crew. [227–29]

Meanwhile, in the superb rendition of the fall of the pagan deities,
it is helpful, while we recognize the foreshadowing of *Paradise
Lost,* to notice also how utterly lacking in sophistication this ac-

count is, when compared with Milton's later roll call of the fallen
angels. In *Paradise Lost* it is made plain that these are devils adored
as deities, and the horror of the deception is brought home by
showing in detail the effect of these devils upon mankind:

> First *Moloch,* horrid King besmear'd with blood
> Of human sacrifice, and parents tears,
> Though for the noyse of Drums and Timbrels loud
> Their childrens cries unheard, that past through fire
> To his grim Idol. Him the *Ammonite*
> Worshipt in *Rabba* and her watry Plain . . .   [1.392–97]

and so on for eight more lines of particular detail, showing the
ravages wrought by Moloch on the earth.

But here in the Nativity poem Moloch is simply mentioned as a
totally defeated character, while the scene of his idolatry is represented in elementary colors and sounds:

> And sullen *Moloch* fled,
> Hath left in shadows dred,
>   His burning Idol all of blackest hue,
> In vain with Cymbals ring,
> They call the grisly king,
>   In dismall dance about the furnace blue.   [205–10]

These vanquished gods are not devils in disguise; they are the
supernatural beings of antique folklore, who exist in their own
right as a part of nature, a part of man's primitive consciousness
of forces that lie beyond his control:

> The lonely mountains o're,
> And the resounding shore,
>   A voice of weeping heard, and loud lament;
> From haunted spring, and dale
> Edg'd with poplar pale,
>   The parting Genius is with sighing sent,
> With flowre-inwov'n tresses torn
> The Nimphs in twilight shade of tangled thickets mourn.
>   [181–88]

Finally, bringing to a brilliant close this basic effect of the simple
and naïve, Milton ends with two stanzas that sum up the basic
techniques and attitudes of the poem. First we have the poem's
most extravagantly naïve image—one that would have offended at

the outset—but, now, with our minds attuned to the poem's peculiar decorum, we can perhaps accept it as a youthful excess:

> So when the Sun in bed,
> Curtain'd with cloudy red,
>   Pillows his chin upon an Orient wave . . .   [229–31]

Then come the ghosts and fairies of folklore, treated with sympathy and even affection:

> The flocking shadows pale,
> Troop to th'infernall jail,
>   Each fetter'd Ghost slips to his severall grave,
> And the yellow-skirted *Fayes,*
> Fly after the Night-steeds, leaving their Moon-lov'd maze.
>   [232–36]

And lastly, we return to the traditional scene, ten thousand times
represented in ancient poetry and painting: the manger scene
upon which this technique of the naïve has been based:

> But see the Virgin blest,
> Hath laid her Babe to rest.
>   Time is our tedious Song should here have ending.

Here, still, is the simple, humble singer, who is well aware of his
defects, but nevertheless has been led by gratitude to sing this
song of praise:

> Heav'ns youngest teemed Star,
> Hath fixt her polisht Car,
>   Her sleeping Lord with Handmaid Lamp attending:

All Heaven, whether physical or spiritual, stands fixed in a service
of unlabored elegance:

> And all about the Courtly Stable,
> Bright-harnest Angels sit in order serviceable.

The last rhyme seems to call attention to the way in which
Milton has contrived, within his chosen mode, to make even the
poem's defects appear as virtues, contributing to the total effect of
the youthful singer writing as well as he can in an ancient, traditional manner of tribute. The poem is a total success because
Milton has chosen and maintained a mode of writing that does not
tempt him beyond the range of his precocious powers.

That is not to say that the poem is simple-minded in the range of its implications, but that the chosen mode of simplicity creates a world in which theological problems are pushed beyond the fringe of our vision; there is no sense of struggling with theological issues, no sense that we need to consult the church fathers, no sense of attempting to enforce anything but the most easily grasped and broadly acceptable truths. This, says the poet, is the happy morn when, as everyone knows,

> the Son of Heav'ns eternal King,
> Of wedded Maid, and Virgin Mother born,
> Our great redemption from above did bring.   [2–4]

Everyone shares the story, how the Son laid aside the majesty that was his due as part of Trinal Unity,

> and here with us to be,
> Forsook the Courts of everlasting Day,
> And chose with us a darksom House of mortal Clay.   [12–14]

How can we express our gratitude for this gift of the Almighty? By a song of praise for the peace and harmony that the divine child has brought to earth, not only on the day of his birth, and in the long-range future, but, in some measure, now: it "now begins," as this poet can best testify by writing a song that in itself represents a simple and unworried harmony.

But—"Compos'd 1629." More difficult and much more complex harmonies lie ahead for the rising poet, the predestined bard.

CHAPTER 3

Lycidas:
Building the
Lofty Rhyme

Nothing could pay a higher tribute to Milton's sense of significant balance and contrast than the placement of the Nativity Ode and *Lycidas* in his volume of 1645: at the beginning and the end of his shorter English poems. Both poems have a personal prologue and an objective conclusion in one stanza, while the body of each poem displays a movement that modulates into three sequences.[1] But there the similarity ends. The Nativity poem shows its origins in English poetry and popular song by the stanza that ends the opening sequence of the Hymn:

> The Shepherds on the Lawn,
> Or ere the point of dawn,
>   Sate simply chatting in a rustick row;
> Full little thought they than,
> That the mighty *Pan*
>   Was kindly com to live with them below;
> Perhaps their loves, or els their sheep,
> Was all that did their silly thoughts so busie keep.   [viii]

But *Lycidas,* moving far beyond such deliberate naiveté, recalls within its intricate measure the entire range of European pastoral, ancient and modern.[2]

A figure named Lycidas plays an important role in the seventh idyll of Theocritus and the ninth eclogue of Vergil. In Theocritus the character named Lycidas is a goatherd: "nor could one that saw him have mistaken him, for beyond all he looked the goatherd. On his shoulders he wore the tawny skin of a thick-haired, shaggy goat reeking of fresh curd, and round his breast an aged tunic was girt with a broad belt; in his right hand he grasped a crooked club of wild olive."[3] There is not much resemblance, it would seem, to the young Cambridge graduate whose death has provided the occasion for Milton's poem. But if we read on in this idyll some relationships will emerge. The idyll is told in the first person by the poet Simichidas, who seems to represent a persona of Theocritus; on the way to a harvest festival, this poet meets with Lycidas and greets him thus:

> Friend Lycidas, all tell me you are
> a piper without all peer among herdsmen or reapers.
> And happy I am to hear it—yet I've a lurking
> hope I may prove your equal . . . .
>   let's sing
> country-style: the pleasure may well be mutual.
> I too am a sounding reed of the Muses, and called by all
> an excellent poet—though Zeus knows, I'm no gull!
> I am not, in my own conceit, a match as yet
> for the noble Samian Sicelidas, nor Philetas.
> I should rival their song as a frog vies with cicadas!
>   [27–31,36–41, trans. Rist]

Lycidas, with a hearty laugh, offers to give Simichidas his olive stick because of the younger poet's lack of pretensions. "But let us begin the singing," he continues, "See here, friend, if you like / a trifling thing I laboured over lately on the hillside." Lycidas proceeds to sing a song in which he wishes fair voyage to Mitylene for his friend Ageanax, hoping he may "find all weather to his turn and reach his haven"—a fate quite the opposite of that which overtakes Milton's Lycidas. Now Simichidas answers:

> Lycidas, friend, I too
> have herding on the mountains learned from the nymphs
> many a noble theme—it may be fame
> has borne them even to the throne of Zeus! But this

I shall regale you with is by far the foremost.
Hear me, then, for dear you prove to the Muses.

[91–95, trans. Rist]

Then after Simichidas sings a rather comic love-song, the idyll quickly concludes as Lycidas takes another road, giving Simichidas his olive stick "as a token of our friendship from the Muses," while Simichidas and his friends turn "toward Phrasidamus' farm" to celebrate the harvest festival of Demeter described in my opening chapter.

This is, then, an idyll which represents man and nature in perfect harmony, fulfilling at the close the harmony promised by the two songs that we have just heard; and above all it is an idyll about poets and poetry. The figure of Lycidas here has been interpreted by Gilbert Lawall as a "goatherd-satyr" who "embodies the pastoral hillside world and is by nature a consummate musician or piper." "The hillside is a world of poetry, where Lycidas composed his song and where Simichidas learned his from the nymphs." Lycidas, in short, is a symbol of the "perfect poet," while the poem's frame of the harvest festival may be interpreted as "an allegory of poetic inspiration."[4] Whether or not one wholly agrees with this interpretation, the mere fact that such a view is possible and plausible suggests a powerful reason for Milton's choice of this name out of all the pastoral names available.

When the figure Lycidas[5] reappears in Vergil's Eclogue Nine, he is still a poet who appreciates other poets, and especially he appreciates the poems of one Menalcas, often regarded as a persona for Vergil himself. In Eclogue Nine we find that the life of the absent Menalcas has been endangered by disputes over the expropriation of property, as Lycidas exclaims:

To think, Menalcas, how near we came to losing you and, with you, all you did to cheer our lives! Who would have sung to us about the Nymphs? Who would have strewn wild flowers on the ground or given our springs green cover from the sun? Who else could have written the lines I overheard you sing the other day, quite unaware of me, as you were on your way to see our darling Amaryllis?

[17–22, trans. Rieu]

This seems to be the Amaryllis celebrated in Eclogue One, and mentioned in two other eclogues; a girl derived from that Amaryllis who is comically serenaded in the third idyll of Theocritus:

Charming Amaryllis, why no more dost thou peep out of this thy cave and call me in—me, thy sweetheart? Dost hate me? Am I, then, snub-nosed to thy eye on closer view, maiden? And does my beard stick out? Thou'lt make me hang myself. [6–9, trans. Gow]

In Vergil's ninth eclogue, however, a sad note of imminent destruction is eroding the pastoral harmony in which the Lycidas of Theocritus had flourished. Nevertheless, Vergil's Lycidas is optimistic and still trusts in the power of song, saying, "I too am a poet who has found some favour with the Muse. I too have written songs. I too have heard the shepherds call me bard." And then he adds an echo of a passage that I have quoted from Theocritus: "But I take it from them with a grain of salt: I have the feeling that I cannot yet compare with Varius or Cinna, but cackle like a goose among melodious swans" (32–36). His friend Moeris, however, is quite despondent, saying, "Time carries everything away, even our memories. How often as a boy I sang through the long summer day and put the sun to bed! So many songs forgotten! And now my very voice is failing me" (51–54). But Lycidas encourages him, finding still a harmony in nature and finding still a time for song: "Now is the moment—look around! Through all its length the lake lies calm and hushed for you; the blustering wind has fallen: not a murmur left . . . here, Moeris, let us sing. Rest your kids now, and we shall still reach town. Or, if it looks as though the night might turn to rain before we are in, why not go forward singing all the way?" (57–65; trans. Rieu).[6]

Among the followers of Vergil, singers named Lycidas play important roles in the third and sixth eclogues of Calpurnius Siculus (first century A.D.) and in the fourth eclogue of Nemesianus (third century A.D.); these poems were well known in the Renaissance (see below, chapter 13). But for Milton perhaps the most important of the later appearances of the singer Lycidas in Latin poetry occurs in the first "Piscatorial Eclogue" of Sannazaro, which seems to have exerted an influence upon the latter part of Milton's poem.[7] In Sannazaro Lycidas is again a poet, who, in a setting among the fishermen by the Bay of Naples, sings a lament for his beloved Phyllis, buried on the shore. "Sweet are the sounds of your singing, Lycidas," says the fisherman Mycon, as he urges Lycidas to repeat the song. But Lycidas, overcome by sorrow, declines, adding:

Yet these and many others besides shall I sing for you, and better perhaps, if the Muse will be with me as I sing. But these too I shall some day inscribe to be seen by the sailing ships, whether under the spreading cliff of Procida or Miseno, and shall trace in rust great letters which the passing sailor may scan from the open sea and say: "Lycidas, Lycidas made these songs."   [119–25; trans. Nash][8]

It is clear that the creative powers of Lycidas have been in no way weakened by his loss of Phyllis; his songs will dominate the scene, while man and sea and land survive in pastoral harmony.

But now in Milton's poem it appears that the destruction feared by Moeris in Vergil has in fact overtaken both Lycidas and his pastoral harmony: a loss that Milton's opening stanza evokes in every possible way, by imagery, by statement, by faltering verse and rhymes (for one line is short and two of the lines are un-rhymed). Milton's prologue suggests a sonnet, for it consists of fourteen lines containing echoes of the familiar Petrarchan rhyme-scheme;[9] but the form is eroded and disrupted by sorrow and fear:

> Yet once more, O ye Laurels, and once more
> Ye Myrtles brown, with Ivy never-sear,
> I com to pluck your Berries harsh and crude,
> And with forc'd fingers rude,
> Shatter your leaves before the mellowing year.
> Bitter constraint, and sad occasion dear,
> Compels me to disturb your season due . . .   [1–7]

Thus in faltering form the prologue speaks of the disruption of the order of seasonal growth, the disruption of that "mellowing year" celebrated by Theocritus in his imagery of the harvest festival.

Meanwhile the repetition of the words "once more" in Milton's opening unrhymed line evokes echoes of language that lies far beyond the realm of Theocritus and Vergil; for the line echoes a passage from the Epistle to the Hebrews (12:25–27):[10]

See that ye refuse not him that speaketh. For if they escaped not who refused him that spake on earth, much more shall not we escape, if we turn away from him that speaketh from heaven: Whose voice then shook the earth [at Mt. Sinai]: but now he hath promised, saying, Yet once more I shake not the earth only, but also heaven. And this word, Yet once more, signifieth the removing of those things that are shaken, as of things that are made, that those things which cannot be shaken may remain.

The modern translation of the Jerusalem Bible[11] makes the point for Milton's *Lycidas* as clear as possible: "The words *once more* show that since the things being shaken are created things [i.e., laurels, myrtle, ivy, poetry, men], they are going to be changed, so that the unshakeable things will be left."

Thus even within the sad and shaken opening of Milton's poem, there seems to lie a secret promise of redemption, for the passage from the Epistle to the Hebrews contains a promise that the things of earth will be shaken, in order that certain immortal things may be revealed. But we cannot see this promise now, so deep is the speaker's sorrow:

> For *Lycidas* is dead, dead ere his prime
> Young *Lycidas,* and hath not left his peer:
> Who would not sing for *Lycidas*? he knew
> Himself to sing, and build the lofty rhyme.
> He must not flote upon his watry bear
> Unwept, and welter to the parching wind,
> Without the meed of som melodious tear.   [8–14]

A heavy emphasis falls upon that word *welter,* occurring as it does in an unrhymed line, and linked by sound to "watry," "wept," and "wind." What does it mean—*welter*? "To rise and fall tumultuously, or roll, toss, or tumble, as if by the motion of waves; hence, figuratively, to be agitated or disturbed; to be in a turmoil; as, the people's passions *weltered* in revolution; a vessel *weltering* in the trough of the sea."[12]

The poem indeed begins and for a long time continues in what might be called a *weltering* motion, with the lines rocking and repeating, as if in some directionless agony:

> For *Lycidas* is dead, dead ere his prime
> Young *Lycidas,* and hath not left his peer:
> Who would not sing for *Lycidas*?

This sort of repetition, inherited from previous pastoral elegists,[13] becomes by Milton's accentuation a very theme of the poem, a sign of the poem's anguish:

Begin then, Sisters of the sacred well,
That from beneath the seat of *Jove* doth spring,
Begin, and somwhat loudly sweep the string.   [15–17]

Yet the repeated "Begin" contains the stabilizing power of tradition, as it echoes the refrains from the first idyll of Theocritus
and the *Lament for Bion:* "Begin, dear Muses, begin the pastoral
song"; "Begin, Sicilian Muses, begin the dirge" (trans. Gow). The
repetition thus prepares the way for the living poet's hope that at
his own death some fellow-singer will pay him tribute, even as he
is now paying tribute to his own poetical friend and to the whole
line of poets who sang under the name Lycidas:

Hence with denial vain, and coy excuse,
So may som gentle Muse
With lucky words favour my destin'd Urn,
And as he passes turn,
And bid fair peace be to my sable shrowd.   [18–22]

It is a pagan consolation, in which the succession of poets passes
by the funeral bier and preserves in poetry the memory of the
singer, as Bion's pupil had once done with a floral tribute:

Now orchards, sorrow with me; sigh, groves;
flowers, breathe grief from your tight clusters;
now roses, deepen your red in mourning; and yours,
anemones; now hyacinth, let your lettering speak,
your leaves chatter their grief.
The beautiful flute-player is dead.
. . . .
Thrice-beloved, who now will play your pipe?
Who will put your flute to his mouth?
What man would dare? For your lips and your breath
live on; the sound of your music still echoes
in those reeds.   [3–7,51–54; trans. Holden]

Nevertheless, toward the end of this dirge for Bion a belief in the
power of poetry provides a consolation in the sense of poetical
succession:

For I am no stranger
to pastoral song, but a pupil of yours,
an heir to your Dorian style,
honoured, when others inherited
your wealth, to be left your music.   [93–97]

The poem concludes with a memory of the visit of Orpheus to the realm of Hades, and a hope that Bion may be singing there:

> Let it be some song of Sicily,
> for Persephone, some sweet country song,
> for she too is Sicilian, she once played
> on Etna's shores; she knows Dorian music;
> your singing would not go unrewarded.
> As once she granted Orpheus, for the rhythms
> of his harp, the return of his Eurydice,
> so shall she return you, Bion, to the hills.
> Could my pipe ever match the magic of his harp,
> I would myself have sung for you to Hades.   [119–26]

In Milton's poem this pagan view of the succession of poets leads into a pagan vision of the succession of hours, days, and seasons in the cyclic year that grants an immortality to *kinds,* but not to individual beings. At first this long passage of traditional pastoral imagery takes us back to the hillside world of Theocritus, where the happy life of man is found to be in tune with nature. It is the landscape of the seventh idyll, which Lawall describes in words that will aptly apply to Milton:

> The world inhabited by Lycidas is not wholly equivalent to the actual geography of Cos; he lives in a mental landscape of his creator, Theocritus. Just as Lycidas is Theocritus' fictional poetic exemplar, so this world of the mind is an inner realm of poetic imagination. Peopled by nymphs and Muses in addition to wondrous goatherd-satyrs, it is a world into which the pastoral poet retires (by a process of psychological introspection, as it were) to shepherd his flock and compose his poetry.   [p. 85]

> For we were nurst upon the self-same hill,
> Fed the same flock, by fountain, shade, and rill.
>   Together both, ere the high Lawns appear'd
> Under the opening eye-lids of the morn,
> We drove a field, and both together heard
> What time the Gray-fly winds her sultry horn,
> Batt'ning our flocks with the fresh dews of night,
> Oft till the Star that rose, at Ev'ning, bright
> Toward Heav'ns descent had slop'd his westering wheel.
> Mean while the Rural ditties were not mute,
> Temper'd to th'Oaten Flute;
> Rough *Satyrs* danc'd, and *Fauns* with clov'n heel,

> From the glad sound would not be absent long,
> And old *Damaetas* lov'd to hear our song.   [23–36]

But now, as in the *Lament for Bion,* this happy landscape seems utterly shattered, in a passage that begins by weltering in heavy repetitions:

> But O the heavy change, now thou art gon,
> Now thou art gon, and never must return!
> Thee Shepherd, thee the Woods, and desert Caves,
> With wilde Thyme and the gadding Vine o'regrown,
> And all their echoes mourn.
> The Willows, and the Hazle Copses green,
> Shall now no more be seen,
> Fanning their joyous Leaves to thy soft layes.
> As killing as the Canker to the Rose,
> Or Taint-worm to the weanling Herds that graze,
> Or Frost to Flowers, that their gay wardrop wear,
> When first the White thorn blows;
> Such, *Lycidas,* thy loss to Shepherds ear.   [37–49]

It is the loss of the whole harmonious world of pastoral in which Lycidas, that ancient figure of the poet, once sang. No one could help to save the poet. Milton's Lycidas was as helpless as Bion—or Vergil's Menalcas before the soldiers of the State, as Moeris says to Vergil's Lycidas in Eclogue Nine, "But this poetry of ours, Lycidas, can do no more against a man in arms than the doves we have heard of at Dodona, when an eagle comes their way" (11–13; trans. Rieu).

Now Milton's poem becomes even more deeply troubled in its measure, as the poet addresses the Nymphs, but breaks off abruptly, shattering the rhythm of his lines with words that are harsh and crude:

> Where were ye Nymphs when the remorseless deep
> Clos'd o're the head of your lov'd *Lycidas?*
> For neither were ye playing on the steep,
> Where your old *Bards,* the famous *Druids* ly,
> Nor on the shaggy top of *Mona* high,
> Nor yet where *Deva* spreads her wisard stream:
> Ay me, I fondly dream!
> Had ye bin there—for what could that have don?   [50–57]

Yet even within this despairing cry, we can feel the singer reso-
lutely and skillfully maintaining his place in the poetic succession,
for this passage gives the most explicit imitation of Theocritus and
Vergil in the whole poem. In his first idyll, Theocritus has Thyrsis
begin his lament for Daphnis with the question:

> Where were you, nymphs, when Daphnis lay dying? Where
> were you, nymphs? In Peneus' precincts or about Pindus?
> You surely held not to the great River Anapus,
> nor the summit of Etna, and holy waters of Acis.
>   [66–69; trans. Rist]

Then Vergil begins the lament for Gallus in his tenth eclogue with
the imitative question:

> Where were you, gentle Naiads, in what high woods or in what
> glades, while Gallus lay dying of unrequited love? Nothing de-
> tained you on Parnassus; nothing on any ridge of Pindus; and
> nothing at Aonian Aganippe's spring.   [9–12; trans. Rieu]

Thus even as the living poet laments the death of Orpheus, with
anguished repetitions, we may feel that the ending on Sappho's
island carries more than a hint of poetic succession:

> What could the Muse her self that *Orpheus* bore,
> The Muse her self, for her inchanting son
> Whom Universal nature did lament,
> When by the rout that made the hideous roar,
> His goary visage down the stream was sent,
> Down the swift *Hebrus* to the *Lesbian* shore.
>   Alas! What boots it with uncessant care
> To tend the homely slighted Shepherds trade,
> And strictly meditate the thankles Muse . . .   [58–66]

Even in the depth of this despair, however, he is echoing the
words of Vergil's *Eclogues: musam meditaris* (1.2) and *meditabor . . .
musam* (6.8). Perhaps the shepherd's trade is not so slighted, after
all.

Now, from that cry "Alas!" the poem moves toward its first
great crest, the first of three great crests (or crescendos, as Arthur
Barker has called them)[14] in this weltering of poetical waves. Now
we have the great meditation on the possible futility of striving to

achieve great poetry—but again, with significant echoes of names immortalized by other poets:[15]

> Were it not better don as others use,
> To sport with *Amaryllis* in the shade,
> Or with the tangles of *Neaera's* hair?
> *Fame* is the spur that the clear spirit doth raise
> (That last infirmity of Noble mind)
> To scorn delights, and live laborious dayes;
> But the fair Guerdon when we hope to find,
> And think to burst out into sudden blaze,
> Comes the blind *Fury* with th'abhorred shears,
> And slits the thin spun life.   [67–76]

It seems that we have reached here a crest of anguish, but then the line is suddenly capped by an unexpectedly higher movement, as the poet hears the words of a power beyond this crest—words that begin with an echo of Vergil's Eclogue Six (3–5):

> But not the praise,
> *Phoebus* repli'd, and touch'd my trembling ears;
> *Fame* is no plant that grows on mortal soil,
> Nor in the glistering foil
> Set off to th'world, nor in broad rumour lies,
> But lives and spreds aloft by those pure-eyes,
> And perfet witnes of all judging *Jove;*
> As he pronounces lastly on each deed,
> Of so much fame in Heav'n expect thy meed.   [76–84]

There is then something that remains; there is a meed beyond the meed of a melodious tear, though the promise exists here only as assertion, not as a full poetic action.

The first wave of grief is thus expended, and the poem sinks back to the pastoral mode of Theocritus and Vergil, in which the poet rests for a time, pondering further issues and gaining strength for a new cresting of poetic and redemptive power:

> O Fountain *Arethuse,* and thou honour'd floud,
> Smooth-sliding *Mincius,* crown'd with vocall reeds,
> That strain I heard was of a higher mood:
> But now my Oate proceeds . . .   [85–88]

In this pastoral mode the poet now listens to a procession of mythological figures, inquiring into and lamenting the disaster—

a passage that clearly echoes similar processions in the first idyll of Theocritus and in Vergil's tenth eclogue. But Triton and Hippotades suggest no answer except an ugly superstition that explains nothing:

> It was that fatall and perfidious Bark
> Built in th'eclipse, and rigg'd with curses dark,
> That sunk so low that sacred head of thine.   [100–02]

Next comes the world of learning, but the reverend Camus has only a cry for an answer, "Ah; Who hath reft (quoth he) my dearest pledge?"—"Last came, and last did go / The Pilot of the *Galilean* lake . . ." (107–09). The Pilot, of course, is generally identified as St. Peter, but there are strong overtones of Christ in the passage.[16] Thus the line, "The Pilot of the *Galilean* lake," seems designed to evoke the vision and voice of Christ speaking through the figure of his earthly representative and denouncing the latest generation of money-changers in the temple. This whole anti-clerical polemic gathers power as it goes; the satirist's fierce indignation has a purifying, strengthening effect, with the result that the ending of the denunciation takes the stable form of a passage in *ottava rima:*

> What recks it them? What need they? They are sped;
> And when they list, their lean and flashy songs
> Grate on their scrannel Pipes of wretched straw,
> The hungry Sheep look up, and are not fed,
> But swoln with wind, and the rank mist they draw,
> Rot inwardly, and foul contagion spread:
> Besides what the grim Woolf with privy paw
> Daily devours apace, and nothing sed,
> But that two-handed engine at the door,
> Stands ready to smite once, and smite no more.
>   [122–31]

I take my stand with those who interpret the famous "engine" as an allusion to the "sharp two-edged sword" that comes forth from the mouth of God in the first chapter of the book of Revelation (verse 16), a sword that in the nineteenth chapter of Revelation (verse 15) is associated with the "Word of God" and is promised as an instrument that God will use to "smite the nations."[17] It is an image of Divine Justice, an image of the Day of Judgment. Thus the whole speech helps to confirm the promise of the poem's opening words, "Yet once more," for the Pilot's final words signify "the removing of those things that are shaken, as of things that are made, that those things which cannot be shaken may remain."

From that fearsome crest of prophetic vision (worthy of Amos or Ezekiel), the poem yet once more drops back to the mode of pastoral:

> Return *Alpheus,* the dread voice is past,
> That shrunk thy streams; Return *Sicilian* Muse,
> And call the Vales, and bid them hither cast
> Their Bels, and Flourets of a thousand hues.   [132–35]

The power of this long floral offering arises from its revelation of the poet's love of natural beauty. Despite the hints of sorrow and death, created nature is a place of comfort and rest,[18] when properly appreciated, but alas, it is one of the things that are made, and nature's consolation can be no more than temporary:

> Bid *Amaranthus* all his beauty shed,
> And Daffadillies fill their cups with tears,
> To strew the Laureat Herse where *Lycid* lies.
> For so to interpose a little ease,
> Let our frail thoughts dally with false surmise.
> Ay me!   [149–54]

With this echo of the earlier "Alas!" that began the meditation on poetic fame, the poem now begins its third great movement from depths to crest, as the poet faces clearly the destruction of the body that was made:

> Ay me! Whilst thee the shores, and sounding Seas
> Wash far away, where ere thy bones are hurld,
> Whether beyond the stormy *Hebrides,*
> Where thou perhaps under the whelming tide
> Visit'st the bottom of the monstrous world . . .   [154–58]

As in the earlier passage on fame, this depth of despair is answered by the voice of faith, although here the transition toward the redemptive moment is more gradual:

> Or whether thou to our moist vows deny'd,
> Sleep'st by the fable of *Bellerus* old,
> Where the great vision of the guarded Mount

> Looks toward *Namancos* and *Bayona's* hold;
> Look homeward Angel now, and melt with ruth.
> And, O ye *Dolphins*, waft the haples youth.   [159–64]

The poet's vision has shifted from depth to height, from a vision of the world of sea-monsters in the ocean depths to a vision of the Archangel Michael, guardian of England's southern shore. With that vision the "moist vows" are answered, as the poet appeals directly to the Angel and receives within his mind a consoling answer:[19]

> Weep no more, woful Shepherds weep no more,
> For *Lycidas* your sorrow is not dead,
> Sunk though he be beneath the watry floar . . .   [165–67]

It is an answer that forms a striking contrast with the ending of Bion's lament for Adonis, which concludes with an allusion to the annual feast of Adonis: "Cease thy laments today, Cytherea; stay thy dirges. Again must thou lament, again must thou weep another year" (trans. Gow). But now the cycles of the day and of the seasons and the fluctuations of the poet's grief are all transmuted into the imagery of Christian death and resurrection, in a movement toward a crest that fulfills the secret promise of the poem's opening line and reveals, through allusions to the Book of Revelation,[20] the faith that cannot be shaken:

> So sinks the day-star in the Ocean bed,
> And yet anon repairs his drooping head,
> And tricks his beams, and with new spangled Ore,
> Flames in the forehead of the morning sky:
> So *Lycidas* sunk low, but mounted high,
> Through the dear might of him that walk'd the waves
> Where other groves, and other streams along,
> With *Nectar* pure his oozy Lock's he laves,
> And hears the unexpressive nuptiall Song,
> In the blest Kingdoms meek of joy and love.
> There entertain him all the Saints above,
> In solemn troops, and sweet Societies
> That sing, and singing in their glory move,
> And wipe the tears for ever from his eyes.   [168–81]

Finally, with that third cresting of poetic power, Milton's poem can end securely within the pastoral setting. First the poem returns, in two serene couplets, to the poem's classical basis:

> Now *Lycidas* the Shepherds weep no more;
> Hence forth thou art the Genius of the shore,
> In thy large recompense, and shalt be good
> To all that wander in that perilous flood.   [182–85]

And then the poet can replace that eroded sonnet of prologue
with a perfect concluding stanza of *ottava rima,* a stanza that ac-
cepts the daily movements of time and reaches out with hope
toward another day. The modern shepherd-poet is seen once
more in harmony with nature, prepared to build the lofty rhyme:

> Thus sang the uncouth Swain to th'Okes and rills,
> While the still morn went out with Sandals gray,
> He touch'd the tender stops of various Quills,
> With eager thought warbling his *Dorick* lay:
> And now the Sun had stretch'd out all the hills,
> And now was dropt into the Western bay;
> At last he rose, and twitch'd his Mantle blew:
> To morrow to fresh Woods, and Pastures new.   [186–93]

There is a special decorum in this concluding metrical form;
whereas the sonnet is dedicated to intimate, personal utterance,
this traditional eight-line stanza is best known as a form used for
objective narration. Appropriately, as the stanza builds its perfect
rhyme, the mode of the poem shifts to the third person, and
Milton brings a new figure into his poem: a detached observer,
whose poise and serenity give a new vitality to the shepherd-
singer, as we see him move away into the sunset.[21] Or rather, it
might be better to say that Milton at the close reveals the presence
of the mature consciousness that has guided the words of his
"uncouth Swain" throughout the poem.

Who, then, is Lycidas? He is a composite figure to be seen
simultaneously in several aspects. He is the robust, smiling
goatherd-satyr of Theocritus, who sings in joyful harmony with
nature. He is the troubled singer of Vergil, whose friend makes
him aware of worldly power, time, and death, but who has not yet
lost his faith in the possibility of singing happy songs in an harmonious landscape. The name Lycidas therefore prepares us
from the outset for the poem's movement beyond the limitations
of the pastoral elegy into the broader reaches of the pastoral
eclogue, with its awareness of the world of history.[22] He is also the

sorrowful singer of Sannazaro's eclogue, whose songs transcend and dominate the seaside. He is the dead singer of Milton's poem, who at first seems to have no home except the whelming tide, but who is at last reborn within a supernatural landscape, through the faith and imaginative power of his fellow-poet. And finally, through the theme of poetical succession, the name Lycidas is related to the detached observer who sings that final stanza: the mature consciousness whose underlying presence in the poem has provided, from the opening line, the unrecognized or dimly apprehended signs of religious and poetical faith.

PART II

Paradise Lost:
Poem of Exile

Me voici restitué à ma rive natale . . . Il n'est d'histoire que de l'âme, il n'est d'aisance que de l'âme.

St.-John Perse, Exil

CHAPTER 4

Princes
of Exile

Summing up his situation, Milton wrote with bitter wit in a letter of 1666: "For what you call *Politica,* but I would rather have you call *loyalty to one's country,*—this particular girl, after enticing me with her fair name, has almost expatriated me, so to speak." But he adds: "one's country is wherever it is well with one"[1]—for Milton, the country of the soul. Doubly exiled from the community of men, first by his loss of eyesight, and then by political isolation, Milton at last found the freedom to write his poem of exile, the last great poem of the European Renaissance, a poem that combines the cool objectivity of Homer, the delicate sensitivity of Vergil, and the strong personal presence of Ovid and the renaissance poets.[2] Standing as it does on the very latest verge of the Renaissance—indeed beyond that verge—the poem looks backward toward the traditional examples of epic narrative; but it also represents a motion forward to the time when the figure of the poet, representing the individual consciousness of man, will become the only organizing center for the long poem, as in Wordsworth's *Prelude,* Whitman's *Song of Myself,* or Pound's *Cantos.*

79

Without ignoring ancient analogies, I would like for a time to
explore the poem's reliance on the individual consciousness by
reading it in the context suggested by a modern analogy, the
poetry of St.-John Perse. The analogy arises in part from the
similarity in the conditions under which the poetry was composed.
Perse too had for many years left poetry for political work, rising
to become secretary general of foreign affairs in the French government. Then in 1940, with the German conquest, all his years of
political effort fell into ruin. He fled into exile in America; im-
poverished, defeated, on the seacoast of New Jersey Perse faced
his dismal situation, and in his poem *Exil,* composed in 1941, he
found to his surprise and comfort that the inner resources of his
poetic power remained (I will quote from the translation by Denis
Devlin):

> And it is no error, O Peregrine,
>   To desire the barest place for assembling on the wastes of exile a
> great poem born of nothing, a great poem made from noth-
> ing. . . .
>   I have built upon the abyss and the spindrift and the sand-
> smoke. I shall lie down in cistern and hollow vessel,
>   In all stale and empty places where lies the taste of great-
> ness. . . .
>   "Where the sands go to their song, there go the Princes of exile,
>   Where there were high taut sails, there goes the wreck more
> silken than a lute-maker's dream,
>   Where there were great military actions, there lies whitening
> now the jawbone of an ass,
>   And the rounding sea rolls her noise of skulls on the shores,
>   And all things in the world to her are in vain, so we heard
>   one night at the world's edge
> From the wind's militias in the sands of exile."
>
> . . . .
>   And morning, for our sake, moves her prophetic finger
> through sacred writings. . . .
>   "O vestiges, O premises,"
> Says the Stranger on the sands, "the whole world is new to me."[3]

One may think of the opening book of *Paradise Lost,* where
another exile arises from the "fiery waves" with his "expanded
wings" and stands upon a "dreary plain" to face his fate with
words that win our admiration:

> Is this the Region, this the Soil, the Clime,
> Said then the lost Arch Angel, this the seat
> That we must change for Heav'n, this mournful gloom
> For that celestial light? Be it so, since hee
> Who now is Sovran can dispose and bid
> What shall be right: fardest from him is best
> Whom reason hath equald, force hath made supream
> Above his equals.   [1.242–49]

This is one response to exile: defiance, hatred of the conqueror, courageous, fierce, and resourceful determination never to submit or yield, however great the cost and pain. But there is another response, and we hear it at the opening of Milton's third book, as the poet intervenes to sing his hymn to light:

> Hail holy light, ofspring of Heav'n first-born . . .
> Thee I re-visit now with bolder wing,
> Escap't the *Stygian* Pool, though long detain'd
> In that obscure sojourn, while in my flight
> Through utter and through middle darkness borne
> With other notes then to th' *Orphean* Lyre
> I sung of *Chaos* and *Eternal Night,*
> Taught by the heav'nly Muse to venture down
> The dark descent, and up to reascend,
> Though hard and rare . . .   [3.1,13–21]

From this standpoint the first two books of Milton's poem come to represent an experience which the poet has endured, and understood, and transcended. Certainly it is true that Satan and his host are permeated with the poet's sympathy, for the poet knows what exile is, and he knows too that the first, spontaneous, inevitable response to defeat is bitterness, dismay, desperation, frustrated anger, hatred of the victor, and emotional refusal to submit or yield; he has dramatized these feelings and attitudes in Satan and Satan's followers, recognizing everywhere the power and the sombre beauty of these figures with all the strength of his immense capacity for imaginative projection:

> All in a moment through the gloom were seen
> Ten thousand Banners rise into the Air
> With Orient Colours waving: with them rose
> A Forrest huge of Spears: and thronging Helms
> Appear'd, and serried Shields in thick array

> Of depth immeasurable: Anon they move
> In perfect *Phalanx* to the *Dorian* mood
> Of Flutes and soft Recorders; such as rais'd
> To highth of noblest temper Hero's old
> Arming to Battel, and in stead of rage
> Deliberate valour breath'd, firm and unmov'd
> With dread of death to flight or foul retreat . . .   [1.544–55]

It wins our admiration, as it should, for we are witnessing here the remnants of a power that derives from the divine creativity. In Milton's view nothing created by God is ever quite destroyed: the remnants of the divine energy still work even in those cast out from light. And so we see the fallen angels rising from that chaos on the burning lake, forming this phalanx, making this music, building a palace, observing a form of government, and engaging in formal parliamentary debate under impressive leadership: thus we see Beelzebub:

> deep on his Front engraven
> Deliberation sat and publick care;
> And Princely counsel in his face yet shon,
> Majestick though in ruin: sage he stood
> With *Atlantean* shoulders fit to bear
> The weight of mightiest Monarchies; his look
> Drew audience and attention still as Night
> Or Summers Noon-tide air, while thus he spake.   [2.302–09]

So Milton encourages our admiration and our pity to play upon the scene; he admits, he insists upon the fading presence of beauty and nobility in Hell. This is particularly clear as the fallen angels disperse to await the results of Satan's mission to earth, and Milton shows us how, while some "with vast *Typhoean* rage" create a "wilde uproar," others sing

> With notes Angelical to many a Harp
> Thir own Heroic deeds and hapless fall
> By doom of Battel; and complain that Fate
> Free Vertue should enthrall to Force or Chance.   [2.548–51]

"Thir song was partial," Milton adds—partial to their own point of view—

> but the harmony
> (What could it less when Spirits immortal sing?)
> Suspended Hell, and took with ravishment

The thronging audience. In discourse more sweet
(For Eloquence the Soul, Song charms the Sense,)
Others apart sat on a Hill retir'd,
In thoughts more elevate, and reason'd high
Of Providence, Foreknowledge, Will, and Fate,
Fixt Fate, free will, foreknowledge absolute,
And found no end, in wandring mazes lost.   [2.552–61]

All this, however "pleasing," Milton adds, is nevertheless "vain," "false," and "fallacious," as Milton then proceeds to show by revealing the full shape of the first two books, which are designed to have the unity of an arch—an arc of insurrection, rising out of that chaos on the burning lake, gradually assuming form and focus, as the legions move in phalanx, and stand before their leader. Then, topping the arch, they build their great palace, where, at the opening of book 2, Satan exalted sits. But after they have engaged in their "great consult" within that palace, the forces of evil fall toward chaos again, in ways that Milton skillfully devises. First Satan departs alone, by his own choice—"this enterprize / None shall partake with me" (2.464–65); and then the fallen angels "disband" their gathered ranks

and wandring, each his several way
Pursues, as inclination or sad choice
Leads him perplext, where he may likeliest find
Truce to his restless thoughts, and entertain
The irksome hours, till his great Chief return.   [2.523–27]

While some choose games or song or philosophical debate, others, in groups of varying size, move out "On bold adventure to discover wide / That dismal World" (2.571–72). And what they find are the rivers of hate, sorrow, lamentation, rage, and oblivion, along with the tortures of heat and cold that await the damned:

Thus roving on
In confus'd march forlorn, th'adventrous Bands
With shuddring horror pale, and eyes agast
View'd first thir lamentable lot, and found
No rest . . .   [2.614–18]

Even their leader, now moving toward the gates of Hell, is forced to recognize with horror his monstrous offspring, Sin and Death, in that allegorical scene where Satan makes his peace with

Death and flatters his daughter Sin, in order to gain his way out of Hell into Chaos. This allegory is an overt step in Satan's degradation in our eyes, a degradation that continues as he moves out into Chaos, where Milton gives a parody of the traditional heroic voyage. Satan, we ought to note, gets through partly by chance, not only by his own efforts:

> all unawares
> Fluttring his pennons vain plumb down he drops
> Ten thousand fadom deep, and to this hour
> Down had been falling, had not by ill chance
> The strong rebuff of som tumultuous cloud
> Instinct with Fire and Nitre hurried him
> As many miles aloft . . .   [2.932–38]

So on he slogs: "behoves him now both Oare and Saile," says the poet sarcastically:

> Ore bog or steep, through strait, rough, dense, or rare,
> With head, hands, wings, or feet pursues his way,
> And swims or sinks, or wades, or creeps, or flyes . . . [2.948–50]

At length he blunders into "a universal hubbub wilde" which represents the storm-center of Chaos, and there from the faltering Anarch manages to find directions toward the newly created world, where Satan at last arrives at the very close of the second book, "like a weather-beaten Vessel"—with "Shrouds and Tackle torn."

Thus Milton's first two books display a self-enclosed form, from Chaos back to Chaos, from stupefaction on the burning lake to floundering through this region of eternal anarchy. Satan's escape is an illusion, as the rest of the poem shows.

II

Satan's sort of insurrection, then, is one way of dealing with the pain of exile. But now, in the prologue to book 3, Milton continues to suggest a better way, despite his blindness:

> Yet not the more
> Cease I to wander where the Muses haunt
> Cleer Spring, or shadie Grove, or Sunnie Hill,
> Smit with the love of sacred song . . .   [3.26–29]

The spring of Helicon, or of Castalia, the grove of the muses, the hill of Parnassus: all this refers to ancient pagan poetry—and yet he calls it sacred; though of course there is more sacred song:

> but chief
> Thee *Sion* and the flowrie Brooks beneath
> That wash thy hallowd feet, and warbling flow,
> Nightly I visit . . .   [3.29–32]

This motif of the singer in darkness returns a few lines later, as the poet compares himself to the nightingale tuning "her nocturnal Note,"[4] and it returns again in the prologues to two later books, where he calls upon the heavenly muse who visits his "slumbers Nightly" (7.29) or "who deignes / Her nightly visitation unimplor'd / And dictates to me slumbring" (9.21–23). He literally composes at night, while he is also living in the night of his blindness; yet, like David the psalmist in Zion, he knows that "the Lord will command his loving-kindness in the daytime, and in the night his song shall be with me" (Ps. 42:8). "Thou hast proved mine heart", says the psalmist, "thou hast visited me in the night" (Ps. 17:3). "I have remembered thy name, O Lord, in the night, and have kept thy law" (Ps. 119:55).

> If I ascend up into heaven, thou art there: if I make
>   my bed in hell, behold, thou art there.
> If I take the wings of the morning, and dwell in the
>   uttermost parts of the sea;
> Even there shall thy hand lead me, and thy right hand shall
>   hold me.
> If I say, Surely the darkness shall cover me; even the night
>   shall be light about me.
> Yea, the darkness hideth not from thee; but the night shineth
>   as the day . . .   [Ps. 139:8–12]

It is this abiding confidence in the presence of God that creates a kind of happiness even within the bounds of his sorrow and lamentation:

> Thus with the Year
> Seasons return, but not to me returns
> Day, or the sweet approach of Ev'n or Morn,
> Or sight of vernal bloom, or Summers Rose,
> Or flocks, or herds, or human face divine;

But cloud in stead, and ever-during dark
Surrounds me, from the chearful waies of men
Cut off . . .   [3.40–47]

As his love of poetry remains undiminished, so his love of natural
beauty remains, even increased by the fact that he now can find
that beauty only in his memory. But most important, his love of
mankind continues, in exalted terms: he speaks of the *human face
divine,* as he remembers it, for he knows that man was made in the
image of God, and that in this image the vestiges of divinity are
still discernible, vestiges of the spiritual beauty that Milton is soon
to show us in his Adam and Eve:

in thir looks Divine
The image of thir glorious Maker shon,
Truth, Wisdome, Sanctitude severe and pure . . .   [4.291–93]

We ought to notice the trinitarian way in which that image is
described, in words that seem to echo Augustine: through the
human countenance shines the Truth of God the Father, the Wisdom of the Son, Word of the Father, and the Sanctity of the Holy
Spirit.[5] But more surprising, perhaps, is the phrase "chearful
waies of men." For the first two books have hardly presented an
altogether cheerful picture of the ways of men. We remember
that long catalogue of the pagan gods in book 1, showing how, as
Milton plainly says:

By falsities and lyes the greatest part
Of Mankind they corrupted to forsake
God their Creator . . .   [1.367–69]

Furthermore, the poet's outbursts of indignation have throughout the first two books cast considerable doubt upon the ways of
men. Thus in book 2, at the end of the satanic parliament, he
cries:

O shame to men! Devil with Devil damn'd
Firm concord holds, men onely disagree
Of Creatures rational, though under hope
Of heavenly Grace; and God proclaiming peace,
Yet live in hatred, enmitie, and strife
Among themselves, and levie cruel warres,
Wasting the Earth, each other to destroy . . .   [2.496–502]

How can we reconcile these harsh utterances with his poignant regret for his loss of the sight of the human face divine and the cheerful ways of men? The contrast may alert us to the vast range of moods and attitudes that the poem represents. Those scenes in Hell have been carefully designed to represent some of the most discouraging ways of men, since it is clear that the fallen angels are being treated as the representatives of human error. Nevertheless the poem includes, even in Hell, some recognition of more cheerful ways. I am not thinking only of the ways in which the fallen angels show that they still retain some rays of their original brightness; but rather of certain subtle ways by which the poem manages to suggest that Satan and his crew are not the only princes of exile. Let us return to see exactly what St.-John Perse meant by that enigmatic phrase. Perse, it appears, is not alluding to anything satanic, when he cries out, "Honour thine exile, O Prince! / And all at once all is power and presence for me, here where the theme of nothingness rises still in smoke" (p. 17). What arises gradually in Perse's poem is a vision of the true princes of exile. Here are some of them, among four brilliant pages of examples, set forth in a Whitmanesque catalogue:

> . . . He who, in the midnight hours, ranges the stone galleries assessing the title-deeds of a beautiful comet; he who, between two wars, watches over the purity of great crystal lenses; he who rises before daylight to clean out the fountains, and the great epidemics are at an end;
>
> . . . . .
>
> he who has the job of consigning incoming ships; and he, too, who discovers one day the very perfume of his soul in the planking of a new sailboat; he who takes over the equinoctial watch on the ramparts of the docks, on the high, sonorous comb of great dams in the mountains and on the great ocean sluices;
>
> . . . . .
>
> He who opens an account in the bank for the researches of the mind; he who enters the arena of his new creation, uplifted in his whole being and, for three days, no one may look upon his silence save his mother, no one may have access to his room save the oldest of the servants;
>
> . . . . .
>
> he who deals, in the town, in such great books as almagesta, portulans and bestiaries; whose solicitude is for the accidents of phone-

tics, the alteration of signs and the great erosions of language; who takes part in the great debates on semantics; who is an authority on the lower mathematics . . .   [pp. 25–33]

"Those are the princes of exile," he concludes, "they have no need of my song." The true princes of exile, then, are those who find a zest in the act of living, those who do their work, out of love for the job, or out of a sense that what they do is significant, although the job may seem menial or trivial, to the great ones of the world. They are the guardians of mankind's past and future. These are the cheerful ways of men which Milton also includes in his poem, through many different devices. Most important is the figure of the poet himself, whose constant presence in the poem provides the most eloquent demonstration that Satan has not succeeded in his efforts to destroy mankind. But there are many others. Some are tucked away in parts of Milton's heroic similes, extraneous, often, to the strict logic of the comparison, but essential as a tacit reassurance that the human face divine has not been utterly lost. We find one in the famous simile of book 1 comparing Satan's shield to the moon:

> whose Orb
> Through Optic Glass the *Tuscan* Artist views
> At Ev'ning from the top of *Fesole,*
> Or in *Valdarno,* to descry new Lands,
> Rivers or Mountains in her spotty Globe.   [1.287–91]

This has sometimes been taken as a premonition of man's search for illegitimate knowledge, but I do not think this is the prime effect. There is here no hint of blame for the astronomer, who is an Artist, a master of his art or science, skilled in his profession; what we feel, rather, is the superiority of his whole situation and effort to that of Satan, though no doubt such artistry might be misused. In another famous simile (1.203–08) one may even feel a certain friendly concern for the pilot of that "small night-founder'd Skiff" who, as seamen tell, mistakes the whale for an island, and in his distress fixes his anchor in the monster's scaly rind and so "Moors by his side under the Lee, while Night / Invests the Sea, and wished Morn delayes." A deceptive anchorage, to be sure, but then Milton does not say that the whale submerged.

Or, as Satan flies toward the gates of Hell, in book 2, we are treated to a glimpse of the faithful voyagers of the earth, in a simile that reminds one of the Portuguese sailors of Camoens:

> As when farr off at Sea a Fleet descri'd
> Hangs in the Clouds, by *Aequinoctial* Winds
> Close sailing from *Bengala,* or the Iles
> Of *Ternate* and *Tidore,* whence Merchants bring
> Thir spicie Drugs: they on the trading Flood
> Through the wide *Ethiopian* to the Cape
> Ply stemming nightly toward the Pole.   [2.636–42]

Here again the mention of drugs may seem to suggest a harmful possibility: but whatever drug-taking may suggest nowadays, the basic meaning of the word "drug" was and still is: a medicinal substance, essential to the healing arts of man, a word "formerly used more widely to include all ingredients used in chemistry, pharmacy, dyeing, and the arts generally."[6] As for "spicie," the word alludes to the fragrant, pleasant aroma of those spices that were much in demand to preserve or make palatable the dreadful food of Milton's day. The implications of the phrase "spicie Drugs" are primarily beneficent and agreeable, though with an undercurrent of possible misuse. So the whole simile provides a rich contrast with Satan's mission, along with a possible parallel.

Best of all, perhaps, is the frequently examined simile at the close of book 4, where, as Satan and the guardian angels are threatening to engage in a combat that might have turned Paradise into ruin, we read that the spears of the good angels ("sharpening in mooned horns / Their phalanx") seemed

> as thick as when a field
> Of *Ceres* ripe for harvest waving bends
> Her bearded Grove of ears, which way the wind
> Swayes them; the careful Plowman doubting stands
> Least on the threshing floore his hopeful sheaves
> Prove chaff.   [4.980–85]

The phrase "careful Plowman doubting" is a little richer in Milton's English than in ours, for "careful" has not only its modern implications of one who is attentive to his work, who takes good care of things, but it also implies a person who is anxious and troubled, full of care; and the word "doubting" implies both a state of uncertainty and also a state of fear lest some disaster happen. The sharpened "horns" of the phalanx, like a sickle, threaten both Satan and earth.[7] It is a superb image of the human condition, again displayed as superior to that of Satan, who, for all his appearance of power, flees abjectly before the sign that God hangs in the heavens. These glimpses of the cheerful ways of the true princes of exile are more frequent than we might think, for sometimes they flash upon us in only a line, or two, or three. Thus in book 9, before the Fall, Satan "works his way"

> As when a Ship by skilful Stearsman wrought
> Nigh Rivers mouth or Foreland, where the Wind
> Veres oft, as oft so steers, and shifts her Saile;
> So varied hee, and of his tortuous Traine
> Curld many a wanton wreath in sight of *Eve*,
> To lure her Eye . . .   [9.513–18]

Similarly, in book 9, Milton somewhat alleviates the effect of the Fall by bringing in his account of the fig tree from which Adam and Eve take those fig leaves:

> not that kind for Fruit renown'd
> But such as at this day to *Indians* known
> In *Malabar* or *Decan* spreds her Armes
> Braunching so broad and long, that in the ground
> The bended Twigs take root, and Daughters grow
> About the Mother Tree, a Pillard shade
> High overarch't, and echoing Walks between;
> There oft the *Indian* Herdsman shunning heate
> Shelters in coole, and tends his pasturing Herds
> At Loopholes cut through thickest shade . . .   [9.1101–10]

It is, no doubt, a barren and grotesque tree, and yet it can be used for man's pleasure and benefit.

Still another way of bringing in these more cheerful glimpses may be found in Milton's use of classical legends and classical history, allusions which are not always treated with some such derogatory tag as "feigned" or "thus they relate, Erring." As Satan is moving in the Serpent's body toward Eve, in book 9, we read this remarkable cluster of the beneficent things of earth:

> pleasing was his shape,
> And lovely, never since of Serpent kind
> Lovelier, not those that in *Illyria* chang'd

Hermione and *Cadmus,* or the God
In *Epidaurus;* nor to which transformd
Ammonian Jove, or *Capitoline* was seen,
Hee with *Olympias,* this with her who bore
Scipio the highth of *Rome.*   [9.503–10]

The story of the changing of Hermione and Cadmus into serpents may seem an ominous and ugly one: Milton uses it thus later
on when he tells how Satan and his host in Hell, glorying in the
fall of man, are changed to serpents. But the story itself is a
curious mixture of implications; it may look ugly, and yet the gods
may here be beneficent after all; it is predominantly a story of
deep human love and ultimate gentleness. Here is the end of it, as
Cadmus feels himself changing into a serpent:

> his cheeks were human,
> And tears ran down them, as he cried: "Come nearer,
> My poor dear wife, while there is something left
> For you to come to; come and touch my hand
> Before I have no hand, am wholly serpent."
> . . . .
> She beat her breast. "O Cadmus,
> Unhappy man," she cried, "remain, put off
> This horrible appearance! What is this?
> Where are your feet, your shoulders, hands, complexion,
> Your—all of you? Why not transform me also,
> Gods of the Heaven, into another serpent?"
> He licked her face, glided between her breasts
> As if he knew them, twined around her neck,
> While all who stood there watching shook in horror.
> But the queen only stroked the serpent neck,
> Crested but smooth, and suddenly there were only
> Two serpents there, entwined about each other,
> And gliding, after a while, to hiding-places
> In the dark woods. Now as before, they never
> Hurt men, nor fear them, for they both remember
> What once they were; they are most gentle serpents.
> [Ovid, *Metamorphoses* 4.582–603, trans. Humphries][8]

What looks bad may indeed be good—or the reverse; but certainly
the reference to the god Aesculapius, the god of healing, and to
his vast sanatorium at Epidaurus—this reference is beneficent,
especially when we recall Ovid's story of how Aesculapius ap-

peared to the Romans who sought his help at Epidaurus in order
to stop the pestilence at Rome:

> the god, all crested
> With gold, in serpent-form, uttered a warning,
> Hissed terribly, a sign that he was coming,
> And all the altars, all the doors, the pavement,
> The roof of gold, the statue, shook and trembled.
> Reared high, he stood there, and he gazed about him
> With fiery eyes, and as the people shuddered,
> The priest, in ceremonial headdress, knew him,
> Calling: "The god! Behold the god! Bow down
> To him in word and spirit, all who stand here!
> That we may see his beauty as our blessing,
> Here at his shrine!"   [15.669–79; trans. Humphries]

And as for the tales that Jove, taking the form of a serpent,
seduced two women: legends say that one son thus produced was
Alexander the Great, who might be dismissed as a mere military
hero—but the other was the man whom Milton here calls the
greatest of all Romans, Scipio Africanus, who conquered Carthage, and yet was also a mystic and a lover of the arts of peace.

Lastly, to sum up this matter of the princes, we should recall the
short introduction to book 11, Milton's preface to his long tale of
human sin and suffering; for it is a passage in which Milton brings
home the redemption of man by comparing Adam and Eve in
prayer with a less ancient pair who, as Ovid tells, had prayed for
the restoration of the human race:

> yet thir port
> Not of mean suiters, nor important less
> Seem'd thir Petition, then when th' ancient Pair
> In Fables old, less ancient yet then these,
> *Deucalion* and chaste *Pyrrha* to restore
> The Race of Mankind drownd, before the Shrine
> Of *Themis* stood devout.   [11.8–14]

"There was no better man than this Deucalion," says Ovid, "No
one more fond of right; there was no woman / More scrupulously
reverent than Pyrrha" (1.322–23; trans. Humphries). So these
reminders of the possibility and the actuality of human restoration grow everywhere in the poem, sometimes arising unexpectedly out of the most appalling context. This poem represents a

shifting, incalculable mixture in which the poet stands ready not only to castigate evil, but also to recognize and celebrate, however briefly, the signs of excellence in the human story. It is this variable, flexible, enigmatic union of opposites that St.-John Perse seems to suggest in several appropriate passages of his own poem of exile:

> And when this day's pale substance had dried into the sands,
> Fragments of beautiful stories adrift in spirals, in the sky full of errors and erring premises, went turning around to the scholiast's delight.   [p. 21]
>
>   . . . . .
>
> And I, from all winged things for which you have no use, composing a language free of usage and pure,
> Now I have once more the design for a great, delible poem.
>   [p. 23]

Voici que j'ai dessein encore d'un grand poème délébile . . . But how can a poem be both *great* and *delible*—that is, *erasable?*

In Perse that strange and rare word *délébile* implies the poet's sense of the precarious nature of all great literary undertakings, the difficulty, indeed the impossibility of fixing human utterance in any form that might be called *in*delible; the poet faces the constantly shifting, evasive, and elusive nature of the human experience that underlies all efforts to set down words, along with the doubt whether, after all the effort, the work can survive "the great erosions of language."

But there is another sense in which a poem may be both great and delible—great because it is delible, great because it is composed in such a way that one aspect of the poem is constantly erasing, or replacing, or altering, or imposing itself upon another part of the poem. *Paradise Lost* is such a poem, with constantly shifting scenes and perspectives and moods and attitudes: it is a poem subject to constant alteration, and even self-contradiction.

This strangely shifting, "delible" quality extends down to the very roots of the poem's style. It is hard to believe that Milton's style could ever have been viewed as a "Chinese Wall,"[9] as though its most remarkable quality were stiffness and rigidity. The style is strange, like that of Perse, remote in many ways from ordinary speech, but it is strange because it is so utterly original in its

shifting, altering, flexible action, its way of breaking down all our
normal expectations of what the English language can do. It
defies grammar, chops out connectives, alters the parts of speech
at will, lays bare the sources of the language; and in short, deals
with the English language in a constantly bold, inventive, unpre-
dictable and unprecedented way. Its syntax has the quality that
Perse calls "syntax of lightning": a flashing mode of utterance,
"pure speech of exile," full of surprise and reverberation.[10] It has
something of the quality that Perse describes in the linguistic passage of "Snows," the last of the poems in his volume *Exile:*

> it is my design, now, to wander among the oldest layers of speech,
> among the farthest phonetic strata: as far as the most far-off lan-
> guages, as far as the most whole and most parsimonious languages,
>   like those Dravidian languages which had no distinct words for
> "yesterday" and "tomorrow" . . . Come and follow us, who have no
> words to say: ascending that pure unwritten delight where runs the
> ancient human phrase, we move about among clear elisions, the
> residues of old prefixes that have lost their initial, and, preceding
> the master works in linguistics, we clear our new ways to those
> unheard-of locutions where the aspiration withdraws behind its
> vowels and the modulation of the breath spreads out, under the
> sway of certain half-voiced labials, in search of pure vocalic finals.
>   And it was at morning, beneath the purest of word-forms, a
> beautiful country without hatred or meanness, a place of grace and
> of mercy for the ascension of the unfailing presages of the mind;
> and like a great *Ave* of grace on our path, the great white rose-
> garden of all the snows all around . . .   [pp. 91–92]

Such a quest through linguistic means for "un beau pays sans
haine ni lésine, un lieu de grace et de merci," is also the design
that lives within the mind of Milton's exiled bard.

The Realms
of Light

Paradise Lost begins with a heavy emphasis upon the last word of
its title, for the words *lost* and *loss,* along with kindred words such
as *ruin,* resound like a hideous dirge throughout books 1 and 2.
This theme is set in the first words of Satan, as he and his mate lie
"weltring" on the burning lake of Hell, and Satan speaks in the
broken, hesitant, veering phrases of torment:

> If thou beest he; But O how fall'n! how chang'd
> From him, who in the happy Realms of Light
> Cloth'd with transcendent brightness didst outshine
> Myriads though bright: If he whom mutual league,
> United thoughts and counsels, equal hope,
> And hazard in the Glorious Enterprize,
> Joynd with me once, now misery hath joynd
> In equal ruin. [1.84–91]

It is a loss so immense that Satan's mind cannot really grasp the
horror; and so, only a few lines later, we find him asking and
declaring:

> What though the field be lost?
> All is not lost; the unconquerable Will,
> And study of revenge, immortal hate,
> And courage never to submit or yield:
> And what is else not to be overcome? [1.105–09]

95

And soon we find "the lost Arch Angel" calling upon "Th' associates and copartners of our loss" to arouse themselves; and at once they arise and come flocking to Satan:

> but with looks
> Down cast and damp, yet such wherein appear'd
> Obscure som glimps of joy, to have found thir chief
> Not in despair, to have found themselves not lost
> In loss it self. [1.522–26]

Yet even in these passages Milton is not presenting simply a lament for loss: the appeal that these opening books have always exerted lies in the fact that they deal with the tenacious effort of these fallen spirits to retain consciousness and hope—to struggle toward the light even when the cause is hopeless and the effort a delusion. Satan cannot become truly wicked in our eyes, cannot become wholly lost, until he is seen to have lost hope, until it is plain that his cause can have no future except in meaningless destruction. There are degrees of Hell, as Satan says in his bitter soliloquy in book 4:

> Which way I flie is Hell; my self am Hell;
> And in the lowest deep a lower deep
> Still threatning to devour me opens wide,
> To which the Hell I suffer seems a Heav'n. [4.75–78]

There are also, in Milton's poem, degrees of Heaven: for there is a Paradise that seems "a Heaven on Earth" and there is also within the poem a bard who can see within his mind glimpses of Heaven. Milton's poem is written to sustain true hope amid a sense of loss, and it is therefore a supremely complex poem with a double plot such as Shakespeare himself never surpassed. One action, begun in books 1 and 2, is the destructive movement that reaches a climax in the ninth book when Eve eats the forbidden fruit and Adam cries, "How art thou lost, how on a sudden lost" (9.900). The second action is a movement of redemption, the action that sustains hope and leads toward man's recovery of the "Realms of Light."

The first action, in books 1 and 2, begins with all the heroic equipment of epic poetry; but at the beginning of book 3 the second action begins quite differently. Or rather, the second action becomes overt here. It has been implicit throughout the first two books, but we have not really been able to see it, so powerful is

Milton's presentation of "heroic" Satan and his peers. This second action now emerges from its "obscure sojourn" as Milton presents the great prologue of book 3, the utterance of a man who suffers blindness but who nevertheless still, in his fashion, sees the light:

> Hail holy light, ofspring of Heav'n first-born,
> Or of th' Eternal Coeternal beam
> May I express thee unblam'd? since God is light,
> And never but in unapproached light
> Dwelt from Eternitie, dwelt then in thee,
> Bright effluence of bright essence increate.
> Or hear'st thou rather pure Ethereal stream,
> Whose Fountain who shall tell?   [3.1–8]

One is struck here by the modesty and humility of this bard's approach to the divine; he is uncertain how to address this holy light and he does not insist upon any one view. He knows only that it is a divine principle which he feels physically now shining upon him, and feels also within himself, mentally and spiritually, in his "love of sacred song," in his love of "the sweet approach of Ev'n or Morn" and of all nature's beauties which he can no longer see; he feels it also in his love of the "human face divine" and of "the chearful waies of men" from whose society his blindness cuts him off, but not without hope and not without the aid of prayer and meditation:

> So much the rather thou Celestial light
> Shine inward, and the mind through all her powers
> Irradiate, there plant eyes, all mist from thence
> Purge and disperse, that I may see and tell
> Of things invisible to mortal sight.   [3.51–55]

At once, as though in answer to that prayer, the poem makes in effect a new start, as we move to the scene in Heaven. The effect of a new beginning is reinforced by the echoes of the heavenly conferences that occur in the opening book of the *Odyssey* between Zeus and Athena, in the opening book of the *Aeneid* between Jupiter and Venus, and also in the opening book of the *Metamorphoses,* as angry Zeus consults with all the gods about the destruction of the human race and its regeneration. Here Milton presents the theological principles from which the redemptive action of his poem proceeds.[1] And here we meet the most puzzling and disconcerting passage in the entire poem, a passage that

has annoyed a good many readers, the speech where the Almighty
Father views all his works and, seeing Satan now emerged from
Hell, declares that man will succumb to Satan's "glozing lyes"

> And easily transgress the sole Command,
> Sole pledge of his obedience: So will fall
> Hee and his faithless Progenie: whose fault?
> Whose but his own? ingrate, he had of mee
> All he could have; I made him just and right,
> Sufficient to have stood, though free to fall. [3.94–99]

Whose fault? Milton has composed the speech in a way that tends to
set our teeth on edge and to make us cry out rebelliously, "Whose
but your own? You made us insufficient to have stood, decreed to
fall." Perhaps the speech is designed to have a neutral quality, but
it seems impossible to read this passage aloud without creating
either a harsh defensive tone or a tone of grieved lament.[2] But
now, as though realizing the problems that his words have raised,
Milton's God goes on to argue patiently the reasonableness of his
procedure:

> Such I created all th' Ethereal Powers
> And Spirits, both them who stood & them who faild;
> Freely they stood who stood, and fell who fell.
> Not free, what proof could they have givn sincere
> Of true allegiance, constant Faith or Love,
> Where onely what they needs must do, appeard,
> Not what they would? what praise could they receive?
> What pleasure I from such obedience paid,
> When Will and Reason (Reason also is choice)
> Useless and vain, of freedom both despoild,
> Made passive both, had servd necessitie,
> Not mee. [3.100–11]

The tone is better here. Milton's God is pleading with mankind,
perhaps a little too anxiously, to understand the gift of freedom.
God's apparent lack of control over Satan, we can now begin to
see, represents part of God's view of every creature's freedom to
break the bounds that are prescribed, not forced upon us. The
same problem is soon to be presented when Satan overleaps the
walls of Paradise and lands on his feet within those guarded pre-
cincts. Why bother to set up the walls and provide that angelic

guard, we may well ask? But again, these arrangements indicate the ideal, the desired order of being, somewhat as human laws attempt to indicate the desired limits of human self-will.

Milton is wrestling here, and allowing us to wrestle, with a problem of almost intolerable tension. Milton believes, with all the force of his religious being, that there is an omnipotent God who rules the universe with perfect justice; and he also believes, with all the force of his humanistic self, that human beings have freedom of the will: the freedom to choose. So, as the divine plan of redemption is now unfolded, the main point lies in the recovery and sustaining of man's freedom of the will. God says that after the Fall he will renew man's "lapsed powers" so that "once more he shall stand / On even ground against his mortal foe" (3.178–79). *On even ground:* the whole poem depends upon this promise. Milton here solves the controversial problem of grace in a very delicate way.[3] At first Milton may sound Calvinistic when he has God say, "Some I have chosen of peculiar grace / Elect above the rest; so is my will" (3.183–84). That is to say, some individuals will be given special grace which makes them preeminent in virtue and especially chosen for salvation: individuals such as St. Paul, St. Augustine, or, perhaps, John Milton—but this does not mean, Milton adds, that the rest of mankind will be damned, as the strict Calvinists were asserting. Milton will have none of this doctrine, for his God says, "I will cleer thir senses dark, / What may suffice" (3.188–89); man will have what may suffice to achieve his salvation. And God promises that he will "soft'n stonie hearts / To pray, repent, and bring obedience due" (3.189–90). To stress the beneficent nature of this promise, he repeats the wording: "To prayer, repentance, and obedience due, / Though but endevord with sincere intent, / Mine eare shall not be slow, mine eye not shut" (3.191–93). If we will only *try* to pray, repent, and be obedient, even though we cannot in ourselves achieve these aims, the effort in itself will be sufficient for salvation. He also promises that he

> will place within them as a guide
> My Umpire *Conscience,* whom if they will hear,
> Light after light well us'd they shall attain,
> And to the end persisting, safe arrive.   [3.194–97]

The opportunity to regain the realms of light, then, is open to *all,* and only those who neglect or scorn the opportunity will be excluded from mercy. The Son offers to sacrifice himself in order to insure that God's grace will remain available to *all* mankind:

> And shall grace not find means, that finds her way,
> The speediest of thy winged messengers,
> To visit all thy creatures, and to all
> Comes unprevented, unimplor'd, unsought,
> Happie for man, so coming . . .   [3.228–32]

Then God goes on to explain the workings of his mercy in a subtly challenging way:

> Be thou in *Adams* room
> The Head of all mankind, though *Adams* Son.
> As in him perish all men, so in thee
> As from a second root shall be restor'd,
> As many as are restor'd, without thee none.   [3.285–89]

That guarded phrase, "As many as are restor'd," stands as both a warning and a promise; not all mankind will be restored to happiness, but the number of the restored remains within the choice of man. Milton, in this crucial part of his poem, where he is taking every possible care to make his theology absolutely clear, will not predict (as he does so strongly in books 11 and 12) that only a few shall be restored. Instead, he insists that the possibility of restoration lies open for every man to choose.

At the outset of the scene, Milton has deliberately evoked the full weight of every ultimate question about God's justice; then he has clearly and patiently offered the answers to those doubts; and now, at the very close, the voice of the poet, mankind's representative, seems to join in the angelic chorus of praise:

> Hail Son of God, Saviour of Men, thy Name
> Shall be the copious matter of my Song
> Henceforth, and never shall my Harp thy praise
> Forget, nor from thy Fathers praise disjoine.   [3.412–15]

That phrase, "Hail Son of God," may recall the opening line of the book: "Hail holy light, ofspring of Heav'n first-born."[4] For the Son of God said, in the Gospel of John: "I am the light of the world: he that followeth me shall not walk in darkness, but shall

have the light of life" (8:12). In this way the prologue and the
scene in Heaven tend to become inseparably one.

Thus far, then, a burst of light out of the darkness; but now,
exactly in the middle of book 3, the scene shifts back into darkness
as Satan is presented walking on the outward shell of the round
universe, in a place "Dark, waste, and wild, under the frown of
Night / Starless expos'd" (3.424–25). As though realizing a human
need to descend from abstract light to concrete earth, Milton now
gives one of the most detailed of all his epic similes, a simile filled
to overflowing with the varied activities of animals and of human
beings, activities set in landscapes that range from snowy ridge to
fertile springs to barren plains:

> As when a Vultur on *Imaus* bred,
> Whose snowie ridge the roving *Tartar* bounds,
> Dislodging from a Region scarce of prey
> To gorge the flesh of Lambs or yeanling Kids
> On Hills where Flocks are fed, flies toward the Springs
> Of *Ganges* or *Hydaspes, Indian* streams;
> But in his way lights on the barren plaines
> Of *Sericana,* where *Chineses* drive
> With Sails and Wind thir canie Waggons light.   [3.431–39]

It is a glimpse of a broad range of human possibilities: predatory,
with "the roving *Tartar*"; pastoral, on those "Hills where Flocks
are fed"; or ingeniously mechanical, as with those delightful sail-
driven wagons. Then, abruptly and savagely, Milton reminds us
that many men will turn these possibilities to folly as he presents
his surprising version of Limbo, reminiscent of Ariosto's Paradise
of Fools on the moon. By thus so obviously bringing in a motif
derived from a poet of the Italian Renaissance, Milton illustrates
pointedly how far he will range from the epic examples set by
Homer and Vergil. Already, by bringing in that Spenserian and
Ovidian allegory of Sin and Death near the end of book 2, and by
his unusually personal and intimate prologue to book 3, Milton
has shown that this poem will never abide by any ancient example,
or any modern example, as we now see from his treatment of
Limbo. Milton brings the poem down to earth by reminding us of
the violent religious quarrels of the Reformation, and by bringing

in the harsh voice of controversy which Milton so often uses in his prose treatises:

> then might ye see
> Cowles, Hoods and Habits with thir wearers tost
> And flutterd into Raggs, then Reliques, Beads,
> Indulgences, Dispenses, Pardons, Bulls,
> The sport of Winds: all these upwhirld aloft
> Fly o're the backside of the World farr off
> Into a *Limbo* large and broad, since calld
> The Paradise of Fools, to few unknown
> Long after . . .   [3.489–97]

Milton views this comical catastrophe of his opponents with a fierce revolutionary relish, while in his mention of the "few" we have more than a hint that most of mankind may perish. But there is something more important here than the satire in itself. The passage serves to bring back intimately the voice of the bard, to develop the personality of the singer within whose mind the poem's action from now on will clearly be performed.[5] Not only is he a blind and devout man, as we have learned from his prologue to book 3; he is also a political activist, a man deeply concerned with the immediate ecclesiastical issues in his own world.

Meanwhile, a new mode of construction is being introduced into the poem, in accord with this vast enlargement of the poet's voice and personality. The old epic mode of narration pursued superbly in books 1 and 2, with Satan as the apparent epic hero, is now dropped; and a quite different mode of operation is adopted, a mode that I should like to describe by the phrase "panels of action."[6] Book 3 seems to be composed of four panels: first, the prologue, bringing us to the center of the poet's mind; secondly, the objective consultation in Heaven; thirdly, the return of the intimate voice, with a different tone, in the darkness of Limbo; and fourthly, a panel that returns us to the realms of light. These panels, with harsh colloquial satire set sharply against the abstract theological language of the heavenly conclave, and set also against the devotional intimacy of the prologue, may suggest the many ways in which Milton includes within the major form of the classical epic certain examples of what Kenneth Burke calls minor form.[7] For the poem seems to contain at least one example of

almost every literary kind known to man. The first two books
provide examples of the oration and of formal allegory. Book 4
presents examples of the dramatic soliloquy in Satan's self-
addresses, along with scenes of pastoral and a love-song, sung by
Eve to Adam. In book 5 we have a psalm, sung by Adam and Eve
to their Creator. Book 7 gives a meditation on the first chapter of
Genesis. The opening portion of book 9 offers a short scene of
domestic comedy, as Adam attempts to persuade Eve not to go off
by herself, while the elements of a Greek tragedy will be found in
the whole treatment of the Fall in this book.[8] In book 10 we have
the formal "complaint" of Adam along with another tale of Ovidian metamorphosis, as Satan and his host are turned into serpents. And lastly, in books 11 and 12, we have a long, long example of the popular, didactic poem of biblical paraphrase. All this
within a poem that constantly maintains its touch with the heroic
mode of Homer and Vergil, along with reminiscences of Ovid,
Tasso, Ariosto, Camoens, and Spenser. It is indeed an immense
baroque edifice—a unique construction made by the technique of
arranging adjacent and contrasting panels.

II

After the panel of Limbo, the poem again undergoes a
metamorphosis, from dark to light, as Satan views the stairs that
lead to heaven—stairs that symbolize the promise of God's
everpresent grace, as Milton goes on to suggest by several beneficent comparisons:

> The Stairs were such as whereon *Jacob* saw
> Angels ascending and descending, bands
> Of Guardians bright, when he from *Esau* fled
> To *Padan-Aram* in the field of *Luz,*
> Dreaming by night under the open Skie,
> And waking cri'd, This is the Gate of Heav'n.   [3.510–15]

A few lines later, Satan looks down into the bright interior of the
universe and sees

> A passage down to th' Earth, a passage wide,
> Wider by farr then that of after-times
> Over Mount *Sion,* and, though that were large,

> Over the *Promis'd Land* to God so dear,
> By which, to visit oft those happy Tribes
> On high behests his Angels to and fro
> Pass'd frequent, and his eye with choice regard
> From *Paneas* the fount of *Jordans* flood
> To *Bëersaba,* where the *Holy Land*
> Borders on *Aegypt* and the *Arabian* shoare . . .   [3.528–37]

It is an image of the promised action of grace within the fallen world. And with such intimations of God's future favor toward mankind, we should not be surprised to find Satan's "wonder" at the beauty of the world, a few lines later, recorded through a most benign simile:

> As when a Scout
> Through dark and desert wayes with peril gone
> All night; at last by break of chearful dawne
> Obtains the brow of some high-climbing Hill,
> Which to his eye discovers unaware
> The goodly prospect of some forein land
> First seen, or some renownd Metropolis
> With glistering Spires and Pinnacles adornd,
> Which now the Rising Sun guilds with his beams.   [3.543–51]

Some things of the fallen world, then, are cheerful and goodly; and the Scout, while perhaps the forerunner of a military force, may, on the other hand, be another of the princes of exile: a good man doing his job on a journey of exploration. His response to the scene is clearly distinguished from Satan's:

> Such wonder seis'd, though after Heaven seen,
> The Spirit maligne, but much more envy seis'd
> At sight of all this World beheld so faire.   [3.552–54]

The Scout may still be one of those who choose to be restored.

Even those who fail, it seems, are not always to be blamed quite as harshly as we might expect from Milton's outburst against the follies of Limbo. As Satan flies to the sun, and in that place "beyond expression bright" (3.591) adopts the disguise of a stripling cherub, it proves to be a disguise which all the light of the sun itself cannot reveal, and which all the brilliant vision of Uriel, angel of the sun, cannot penetrate. This the poet explains in one of his most familiar asides, a familiarity which is now growing

THE REALMS OF LIGHT

rapidly in the poem, stressing and sustaining the presence of the
bard in all its action:

> For neither Man nor Angel can discern
> Hypocrisie, the only evil that walks
> Invisible, except to God alone,
> By his permissive will, through Heav'n and Earth:
> And oft though wisdom wake, suspicion sleeps
> At wisdoms Gate, and to simplicitie
> Resigns her charge, while goodness thinks no ill
> Where no ill seems: Which now for once beguil'd
> *Uriel*, though Regent of the Sun, and held
> The sharpest sighted Spirit of all in Heav'n.   [3.682–91]

How, then, can we be expected to blame Eve very harshly when
she fails to penetrate Satan's disguise?

Indeed, pity for mankind is soon to become the dominant feeling of book 4, following naturally from the divine charity and pity
that the Son of God has just expressed in Heaven. We may grasp
this change very clearly if we set books 1 and 2 against books 3 and
4 and see them paired in an essential contrast. Books 1 and 2 are
books of loss that turn to books of hate; books 3 and 4 are books of
recovery that turn to books of love. Books 1 and 2 are inseparably
paired, as book 1 moves into book 2 with hardly a break, while at
the center of the junction Satan sits exalted on his throne:

> and from despair
> Thus high uplifted beyond hope, aspires
> Beyond thus high, insatiate to pursue
> Vain Warr with Heav'n, and by success untaught
> His proud imaginations thus displaid.   [2.6–10]

Book 3 discards these "proud imaginations" and begins the new
movement of the poem into the realms of light; at the end of book
3, we stand on the radiance of the Sun itself. And then book 3
flows on almost without a break into book 4, while at the center of
this junction, at the opening of book 4, we find the bard speaking
in an attitude of deepest pity and concern for all mankind:

> O for that warning voice, which he who saw
> Th' *Apocalyps*, heard cry in Heav'n aloud,
> Then when the Dragon, put to second rout,
> Cam furious down to be reveng'd on men,

Wo to the inhabitants on Earth! that now,
While time was, our first Parents had bin warnd
The coming of thir secret foe, and scap'd
Haply so scap'd his mortal snare; for now
Satan, now first inflam'd with rage came down,
The Tempter ere th' Accuser of man-kind,
To wreck on innocent frail man his loss
Of that first Battel, and his flight to Hell.   [4.1–12]

This cry will of course be answered in part when God sends the angel Raphael down to inform Adam and Eve of their danger. Yet the poet seems to have become so deeply immersed in the present action that he is unaware of that plan. He speaks in the human voice of one who does not wholly know what lies ahead and who waits for the muse to prompt his "unpremeditated verse." In the act of creation he discovers the nature of his own response, as he explores the way toward Eden. But what shall we make of the bard's sympathy for the plight of *innocent frail man* before the Fall? Are we really to regard man as "ill secur'd" in his happiness, as Satan says (4.370), unable to penetrate hypocrisy, *frail,* yet somehow made sufficient by God to have stood? The voice of pity here seems to draw out all the implications of that word *frail:* not simply the basic meaning, "liable to break or to be broken" ("free to fall"), but all the weight of all the other meanings of the word: "easily crushed or destroyed," "weak, subject to infirmities; wanting in power, easily overcome," or worse yet, "morally weak; unable to resist temptation; habitually falling into transgression."[9] We may well ask: how can a man be made sufficient to have stood, though frail? But the prime impact here is not theological, and the paradox may well pass unnoticed, for the main effect of the outcry is to stress the singer's presence, to tell us of his love and pity, so different from Satan's hate and envy.

Another contradiction immediately follows, as the poet describes the Hell that rages now within the breast of Satan: "Now conscience wakes despair / That slumberd, wakes the bitter memorie / Of what he was" (4.23–25). Satan with a conscience? This seems not quite in accord with the theology that has just been explained, for Milton has given in book 3 the traditional view that

Satan will never be granted grace, and thus, presumably, could never have a conscience. For conscience, we have been told, is the umpire that God will place within man's breast after the Fall, as a divinely given guide that may lead man from light to light toward his salvation. Then Milton goes on to create a more striking unorthodoxy[10] as he reveals a Satan who still seems to possess the power of choice, a Satan who starts to curse God and then turns to curse himself, "since against his thy will / Chose freely what it now so justly rues" (4.71–72). It even seems to Satan that a way out might still remain in repentance: "O then at last relent," he cries, that is, repent, give up your obstinate course: "is there no place / Left for Repentance, none for Pardon left?" (4.79–80). Milton is boldly raising here another of his ultimate questions: would not a just God prefer to see Satan repent, and give him the chance to repent? Milton seems to leave the question open by showing that Satan's pride would never have accepted the chance, and that therefore God has not offered it: "This knows my punisher," says Satan, "therefore as farr / From granting hee, as I from begging peace" (4.103–04). The effect of Satan's whole soliloquy at the outset of book 4 is this: Satan, like any mortal man, seals his own doom by making a deliberate choice of evil. Milton leaves us with the feeling that Satan somehow has the power, if he had only used it, to make a better choice.

Something very important is accomplished by this humanization of Satan, this treatment of his psychology as resembling that of fallen man. The effect is to place him on the same plane, "on even ground," with man. Satan constantly boasts that he is God's adversary, but it seems he is really fighting only man, whom God has placed on equal terms with Satan, giving man *what may suffice* even after the Fall. Though the poet, in his distress, has called man *frail*, man does not appear quite as frail as Satan appears in this soliloquy. For Milton has designed Satan's hymn to light, Satan's address to the sun, Satan's prologue to his life on earth, in such a way that we are bound to compare it, point by point, with the feelings and attitudes expressed by the poet in his great prologue to book 3. Satan's soliloquy begins as a poem of loss, quickly turns to a hymn of hate, and then to an expression of despair. Satan at the outset addresses not the Eternal nor the abstract

essence that is God, but simply addresses the physical planet in
terms that convey an implicit paganism, sun-worship:

> O thou that with surpassing Glory crownd,
> Look'st from thy sole Dominion like the God
> Of this new World; at whose sight all the Starrs
> Hide thir diminisht heads; to thee I call,
> But with no friendly voice, and add thy name
> O Sun, to tell thee how I hate thy beams
> That bring to my remembrance from what state
> I fell, how glorious once above thy Spheare . . .   [4.32–39]

We cannot fail to recall how the warmth of the sun shining on the
blind poet had brought to his remembrance his continuing love of
poetry, of nature, and of the human face divine.

Thus a contrast is set that will continue throughout the fourth
book; and then, after the interlude of the middle books, will return with redoubled intensity in book 9. Constantly, this fourth
book works through a contrast of what I have called panels of
action: the poet's love, the devil's hate. It is sometimes said that
books 4 and 9 represent the action of three main characters,
Adam and Eve and Satan; but there is a fourth character, in some
ways more important than any of these: the poet, whose tacit
presence and open intervention remind us that the freedom of
the human will is not all lost, but indeed remains in a voice of the
most remarkable beauty and power.

Thus as Satan fares on toward Eden, we gain our view of
Paradise through a moving camera-eye; but it is not wholly true to
say that we see Paradise through Satan's eyes.[11] Alongside Satan,
or behind him, or looking over his shoulder, we have the broader
vision of the poet, who includes Satan within his view, counteracts
Satan's envy, and promises Satan's defeat in the very fact that this
one fallen man, at least, can still love God's goodness to mankind.
We have at first the illusion of moving in with Satan's eyes:

> And of pure now purer aire
> Meets his approach, and to the heart inspires
> Vernal delight and joy, able to drive
> All sadness but despair.   [4.153–56]

It is not Satan whose heart feels vernal delight and joy in the

scene, but the poet, or any normal human being, as Milton goes
on to make clear in one of his most effective similes:

> As when to them who sail
> Beyond the *Cape of Hope,* and now are past
> *Mozambic,* off at Sea North-East windes blow
> *Sabean* Odours from the spicie shoare
> Of *Arabie* the blest, with such delay
> Well pleas'd they slack thir course, and many a League
> Cheard with the grateful smell old Ocean smiles.   [4.159–65]

Satan has truly sailed beyond the Cape of Hope into the despair of
his soliloquy; but such a choice is not the only way, as the rest of
the simile implies. Here again is Milton's reminder of the true
princes of exile: those who appreciate the beauties of the creation,
express their love of God's bounty, and carry on their work in
cheerful ways.

So, in alternating scenes, we have the poet's admiring presentation of Adam and Eve, in passages clearly distinguished from
Satan's view by the poet's commentary, while Satan, mouthing his
bitter soliloquies, can only cry out, "O Hell! what doe mine eyes
with grief behold" (4.358). It is essential to stress the many ways in
which the poet's panels of delighted vision are distinguished from
Satan's panels of hate. For here, "where the Fiend / Saw undelighted all delight" (4.285–86), Milton presents his views of
Paradise and of Adam and Eve with continuous inclusion of us as
audience, to whom the poet addresses a continuous commentary
on the scene. Thus as Satan first approaches this "delicious
Paradise" (an echo of the Vulgate's *in paradiso voluptatis*)[12] Adam
is called "our general Sire" and the Tree of Knowledge is called
"our Death."[13] From this kind of *our* the whole manner of the
poet's address proceeds, including us within his many comparisons, his allusions to the world we know, whether in myth and
legend or by contrast and analogy with daily life. Thus when the
poet describes our first view of Adam and Eve, his commentary
includes the beauty as well as the shame of our world: "Then was
not guiltie shame, dishonest shame / Of natures works," he says,
and his voice rises, while the direction of the sentence changes:

> honor dishonorable,
> Sin-bred, how have ye troubl'd all mankind
> With shews instead, meer shews of seeming pure,

> And banisht from mans life his happiest life,
> Simplicitie and spotless innocence.
> So passd they naked on, nor shund the sight
> Of God or Angel, for they thought no ill:
> So hand in hand they passd, the lovliest pair
> That ever since in loves imbraces met,
> *Adam* the goodliest man of men since born
> His Sons, the fairest of her Daughters *Eve*.   [4.313–24]

In the last two lines, through the peculiarities of Milton's syntax, the shame of man is in some measure ameliorated by the fact that goodly men and fair daughters are still derived from Adam and Eve.

All these comments and familiar interventions of the bard prepare the way for his longest internal intervention (internal as distinguished from the great prologues, but indeed it is as long as some of the prologues) which occurs about three-quarters of the way through book 4 (736–75). It is Milton's famous celebration of wedded love in Paradise, uttered as the poet watches Adam and Eve enter their bower for the night. Milton proceeds to tell us plainly what he thinks about the facts of married life,[14] both before the Fall and after:

> nor turnd I weene
> *Adam* from his fair Spouse, nor *Eve* the Rites
> Mysterious of connubial Love refus'd:
> Whatever Hypocrites austerely talk
> Of purity and place and innocence,
> Defaming as impure what God declares
> Pure, and commands to som, leaves free to all.   [4.741–47]

For God commanded in Genesis: "Be fruitful and multiply." And with this thought Milton takes issue with St. Paul's advice concerning marriage and celibacy in I Corinthians, where St. Paul regards marriage as second best, though not sinful (7:38). Milton would have noticed that St. Paul offers this as his own opinion, saying that he has "no commandment of the Lord: yet I give my judgment, as one that hath obtained mercy of the Lord to be faithful" (7:25). Milton, following the Protestant tradition, thinks that St. Paul was simply mistaken here; the judgment of John Milton, as one who also has, he hopes, obtained mercy of the Lord, says quite otherwise:

> Our Maker bids increase, who bids abstain
> But our Destroyer, foe to God and Man?
> Haile wedded Love, mysterious Law, true sourse
> Of human ofspring, sole proprietie,
> In Paradise of all things common else.   [4.748–52]

Wedded Love, he goes on to say, still stands as an island of purity in the fallen life of exile:

> By thee adulterous lust was driv'n from men
> Among the bestial herds to raunge, by thee
> Founded in Reason, Loyal, Just, and Pure,
> Relations dear, and all the Charities
> Of Father, Son, and Brother first were known.
> Farr be it, that I should write thee sin or blame,
> Or think thee unbefitting holiest place,
> Perpetual Fountain of Domestic sweets,
> Whose Bed is undefil'd and chast pronounc't,
> Present or past, as Saints and Patriarchs us'd.   [4.753–62]

Here indeed, he adds, is the place where the god of love truly reigns, and he transfers to this place the attributes of the pagan Cupid: "Here Love his golden shafts imploies, here lights / His constant Lamp, and waves his purple wings, / Reigns here and revels" (4.763–65). *Revels:* a dangerous word, but for Milton not inappropriate in a garden which the Latin Bible calls the *Paradise of Delight.* Other kinds of "love" and "revelry" surround and threaten the married state, as he continues:

> Reigns here and revels; not in the bought smile
> Of Harlots, loveless, joyless, unindeard,
> Casual fruition, nor in Court Amours
> Mixt Dance, or wanton Mask, or Midnight Bal,
> Or Serenate, which the starv'd Lover sings
> To his proud fair, best quitted with disdain.   [4.765–70]

So much for those Petrarchan sonneteers; Adam and Eve had better music than Astrophel and Stella: "These lulld by Nightingales imbraceing slept, / And on thir naked limbs the flourie roof / Showrd Roses, which the Morn repair'd" (4.771–73).

Then the poet concludes the first view of Paradise by pronouncing a benediction upon the wedded pair, a conclusion that forms, in its rhetorical construction, an implicit contrast with the ending of Satan's last soliloquy of hate, where he snarled, "Live while ye may, / Yet happie pair; enjoy, till I return, / Short pleasures, for long woes are to succeed" (4.533–35). But now the bard blesses and implores, "Sleep on, / Blest pair; and O yet happiest if ye seek / No happier state, and know to know no more" (4.773–75).

Milton's frank discussions of paradisal sexuality have embarrassed some people, including C. S. Lewis[15] and the angel Raphael, but these discussions lie at the very center of his view of human nature. It seems that Adam and Eve, before the Fall, are not so utterly different from fallen man as might at first be thought. For Milton, life in Paradise is not without its problems, nor is life for fallen man without its joys. We have not only the heritage of that original sin; there is also a continuity of grace between us and our Grand Parents.

In all these ways, books 3 and 4 are designed as a unit to counteract the thrust of Hell in the first two books. The unified action of the two opening books, as I have said in the preceding chapter, may be described as an arc, an arch, moving upward from Chaos and then downward, back to Chaos. How should one describe the utterly different action that grows from the introduction of light in book 3? It is an action of illumination that continues with hardly a pause throughout most of book 4; and then, after a strongly shaded contrast at the close of book 4, resumes its action of light in the first, pastoral half of book 5; then runs again into heavy shadow through the war in Heaven, but emerges in triumphant light at the close of book 6 as the Son of God goes forth to win his victory:

> And the third sacred Morn began to shine
> Dawning through Heav'n: forth rush'd with whirl-wind sound
> The Chariot of Paternal Deitie,
> Flashing thick flames . . .   [6.748–51]

That victory of light is an image of the Resurrection on the morning of Easter Day, and also an image of the fearful light of the Last Judgment. Thus the varied action of books 3, 4, 5, and 6 is bound together into one enormous panel, composed of many subpanels, moving from the merciful promise of the Son of God in book 3 to the merciful and terrifying judgment by the same Son of God at the close of book 6. Considering all this, we might speak, using

Milton's own term, of an *irradiated* action, an action of light and shade, as in some painting by Poussin, moving over a vast and peopled landscape,[16] spreading out from the poet's prayer for the gift of inner light, and accompanied by the light of his presence.

In the first two books the poet has allowed his presence to remain relatively minor, while we watch the arc of insurrection soar and fade. In book 3 the poet emerges into prominence, and the light of God floods the scene, illuminating Satan's blackness, his inner torment, his fading strength; then revealing his flight before the sign of power that God hangs in the heavens, and later telling of Satan's defeat in the heavenly war. Meanwhile, although the presence of Satan so frequently shadows the scene, we are encouraged to appreciate the goodness of the gifts given to Adam and Eve, gifts that still, in sufficient measure, remain to man in his exile from Eden. Man has what will suffice to enable him to choose his own salvation.

This, I think, is the meaning of the way in which Milton has framed this sequence of four books (3, 4, 5, 6) between two of his great prologues. In the prologue to book 3 the poet emerges from the darkness of Hell into the light of Heaven; and in the prologue to book 7 he prays that he may be allowed to return now to his native earth, even though life there for him has become a painful life of exile, "In darkness, and with dangers compass round" (7.27). The poem's basically baroque structure could not be more clearly defined than by the placement of these prologues. It is under firm control, while allowing room for the most elaborate variations, an inner plenitude of panels in "various style."

We should note, finally, one of the benefits of Milton's original ten-book division: for the long seventh book of 1667, devoted to the story of the Creation, is the only book framed (or guarded) between two of Milton's great prologues; and it is a book in which Satan does not set his foot. It is as though the poet had at last made his way out of Hell and Chaos into some bright and gracious sanctuary at the center of the mind. Like the blind Orion of Poussin's famous painting, he has penetrated to the farthest East, where his sight is miraculously restored.

CHAPTER 6

The Diffusion
of Good

Milton's conception of an expanding universe, motivated by the ever-creative goodness of God, is clearly represented in the movement from destruction to creation that occurs in books 6 and 7. As the numerological critics have pointed out, the manifestation of the chariot of the Son covers the exact center of the poem, which occurs in the sixth book of 1667 between lines 761 and 762, or at line 766 in the second edition.[1] Whichever version one is reading, everyone is bound to sense that this triumphal appearance is presented in the very middle of the poem, a fact especially evident in the twelve-book division of 1674. Yet it would be wrong, I think, to feel that after this manifestation of the Son's triumphant power the poem moves "downward", except in a physical sense.[2] The poem moves to earth, a movement enforced by Milton's great prologue to book 7; but, as the angels tell us in their hymn at the close of that book, the Son's act of creation is greater than his conquest of the rebellious angels:

> Creation and the Six dayes acts they sung,
> Great are thy works, *Jehovah,* infinite
> Thy power; what thought can measure thee or tongue
> Relate thee; greater now in thy return
> Then from the Giant Angels; thee that day
> Thy Thunders magnifi'd; but to create
> Is greater then created to destroy.   [7.601–07]

If we compare this long hymn with the briefly reported praise sung by the same angels at the Son of God's return from victory over the "Giant Angels," we can sense how subtly Milton is preparing the way for the great vision of creative power soon to appear:

> Sole Victor from th' expulsion of his Foes
> *Messiah* his triumphal Chariot turnd:
> To meet him all his Saints, who silent stood
> Eye witnesses of his Almightie Acts,
> With Jubilie advanc'd; and as they went,
> Shaded with branching Palme, each order bright,
> Sung Triumph, and him sung Victorious King,
> Son, Heire, and Lord, to him Dominion giv'n,
> Worthiest to Reign: he celebrated rode
> Triumphant through mid Heav'n, into the Courts
> And Temple of his mightie Father Thron'd
> On high; who into Glorie him receav'd,
> Where now he sits at the right hand of bliss.   [6.880–92]

We do not hear the song itself; Milton is waiting for a greater occasion to recite the angels' hymn of praise. For the present, the reported celebration serves to complete the symbolism that has marked his ending of the war in Heaven, which has mingled suggestions of the victory of Christ at the Resurrection with suggestions of his victory at the Day of Judgment. Thus the allusion in the closing line above ("Where now he sits at the right hand of bliss") evokes the Ascension of Christ as related in Hebrews (1:3) and fulfills the implications of God's stress upon the fact that the Son will come forth to win his victory at the dawning of the third day:

>   two dayes are past,
> Two dayes, as we compute the dayes of Heav'n
> . . . .
> Two dayes are therefore past, the third is thine
> . . . .
> And the third sacred Morn began to shine
> Dawning through Heav'n: forth rush'd with whirl-wind sound
> The Chariot of Paternal Deitie . . .   [6.684–85,699,748–50]

Meanwhile the constant use of the word "saints" to describe the good angels as they battle in book 6 suggests the triumph of more earthly "saints," that is, the just, in the common puritan usage. Thus the Son appears in his chariot:

> Attended with ten thousand thousand Saints,
> He onward came, farr off his coming shon,
> And twentie thousand (I thir number heard)
> Chariots of God, half on each hand were seen:
> Hee on the wings of Cherub rode sublime
> On the crystallin Skie, in Saphir Thron'd.
> Illustrious farr and wide, but by his own
> First seen, them unexpected joy surpriz'd,
> When the great Ensign of *Messiah* blaz'd
> Aloft by Angels born, his Sign in Heav'n:
> Under whose Conduct *Michael* soon reduc'd
> His Armie, circumfus'd on either Wing,
> Under thir Head imbodied all in one.   [6.767–79]

The allusion here to "the sign of the Son of man" in Matthew (24:27–30) combines with a later allusion to Christ's prediction of the separation of the sheep from the goats (6.856–57; Matthew 25:31–33) to carry on the apocalyptic implications of the prophecy in Jude (14–15): "Behold, the Lord cometh with ten thousands of his saints, To execute judgment upon all." But most important here is the clear indication of God's immense reserves of power: he has held back a half of his angels to accompany the Son (though not to fight) in his victory; this is clear from the way in which Michael and his army see the "ten thousand thousand Saints" approaching from afar. This allocation of forces (half of the good angels equalling the third that has fallen) has been set forth from the outset of the battle; it is hard to see why some readers do not accept what seems to be the clear sense of what God is saying:[3]

> *Gabriel,* lead forth to Battel these my Sons
> Invincible, lead forth my armed Saints
> By Thousands and by Millions rang'd for fight;
> Equal in number to that Godless crew
> Rebellious . . .   [6.46–50]

Equal in number they must be, for if the loyal angels were *twice* as numerous as Satan's host, how could we ever explain the remarkable strength of the rebellious angels in holding the fight to a destructive draw? In accordance with his theology Milton has the angels, like man, placed "on even ground" with the forces of evil, as a test of faith. God makes the point a second time when, addressing the Son, he describes the "Equal" strength of the two forces:

> sore hath been thir fight,
> As likeliest was, when two such Foes met arm'd;
> For to themselves I left them, and thou knowest,
> Equal in their Creation they were form'd.   [6.687–90]

In this way Milton has created an allegory of the spiritual combat fought by God's "saints" on earth: a "sore" combat in which the just are rescued, first, by the atonement of the Crucifixion, and last, by the judgment of the Son at the Day of Doom. The vast reserve forces are of course not needed for these victories, which the Son performs alone, while the "saints," as Milton says at the close of the war in Heaven, "silent stood / Eye witnesses of his Almightie Acts," and only after his return sing jubilee.

But in the acts to follow in book 7 the angels begin to celebrate the Creation as soon as they hear the command given to the Son; they sing here a version of the Gloria sung by the angels at the birth of Jesus; here is the first incarnation:

> Glorie they sung to the most High, good will
> To future men, and in thir dwellings peace:
> Glorie to him whose just avenging ire
> Had driven out th' ungodly from his sight
> And th' habitations of the just; to him
> Glorie and praise, whose wisdom had ordain'd
> Good out of evil to create, in stead
> Of Spirits maligne a better Race to bring
> Into thir vacant room, and thence diffuse
> His good to Worlds and Ages infinite.   [7.182–91]

The diffusion of good may be disturbed, as in the war in Heaven, but its onward impulse cannot be stopped, as Milton now proceeds to show, beginning with a brilliant contrast with the scene in book 2 where Hell's gates open upon Chaos "With impetuous recoile and jarring sound . . . and on thir hinges grate / Harsh Thunder," while "like a Furnace mouth" they "Cast forth redounding smoak and ruddy flame"(2.880–81,888–89).

Now in book 7 the Son of God again goes forth in all his majesty, to perform the greater act of diffusing good:

> About his Chariot numberless were pour'd
> Cherub and Seraph, Potentates and Thrones,
> And Vertues, winged Spirits, and Chariots wing'd,
> From the Armoury of God . . .
> Heav'n op'nd wide
> Her ever during Gates, Harmonious sound
> On golden Hinges moving, to let forth
> The King of Glorie in his powerful Word
> And Spirit coming to create new Worlds.   [7.197–200,205–09]

The contrast with Satan's voyage in book 2 is stressed by a glimpse of "the vast immeasurable Abyss / Outrageous as a Sea, dark, wasteful, wilde" (7.211–12). But the Son of God rides out over the "surging waves" with absolute command in word and act:

> Silence, ye troubl'd waves, and thou Deep, peace,
> Said then th' Omnific Word, your discord end:
> Nor staid, but on the Wings of Cherubim
> Uplifted, in Paternal Glorie rode
> Farr into *Chaos,* and the World unborn;
>
> . . . .
> and in his hand
> He took the golden Compasses, prepar'd
> In Gods Eternal store, to circumscribe
> This Universe, and all created things:
> One foot he center'd, and the other turn'd
> Round through the vast profunditie obscure,
> And said, thus farr extend, thus farr thy bounds,
> This be thy just Circumference, O World.   [7.216–20,224–31]

Then after earth has been hung "self-ballanc't on her Center," and after light "Ethereal, first of things, quintessence pure" has been created, the angelic hosts again burst into song:

> with joy and shout
> The hollow Universal Orb they fill'd,
> And touch't thir Golden Harps, & hymning prais'd
> God and his works, Creatour him they sung,
> Both when first Eevning was, and when first Morn.   [7.256–60]

It seems that they thus celebrate the action of each day of Creation, for after the second day we hear: "So Eev'n / And Morning *Chorus* sung the second Day" (7.274–75). But it is not clear whether the angels or evening and morning form that chorus: the two are fused. Thereafter only "Eev'n and Morn" record, or crown, or solemnize, the days, until the sixth day is "accomplish't" and the Creator returns to the Heaven of Heavens:

> Followd with acclamation and the sound
> Symphonious of ten thousand Harpes that tun'd
> Angelic harmonies :
> . . . .
> Open, ye everlasting Gates, they sung,
> Open, ye Heav'ns, your living dores; let in
> The great Creator from his work returnd
> Magnificent, his Six days work, a World;
> Open, and henceforth oft; for God will deigne
> To visit oft the dwellings of just Men
> Delighted, and with frequent intercourse
> Thither will send his winged Messengers
> On errands of supernal Grace.   [7.558–60,565–73]

And the echo of Psalm 24 shows that the prophecy of grace will be fulfilled on earth.

Then, as the "Filial Power" rejoins the Father (from whom he has never been separated) the angels celebrate the seventh day with a service filled with pomp and gold, appropriate to Heaven, if not to earth:

>   the Harp
> Had work and rested not, the solemn Pipe,
> And Dulcimer, all Organs of sweet stop,
> All sounds on Fret by String or Golden Wire
> Temper'd soft Tunings, intermixt with Voice
> Choral or Unison; of incense Clouds
> Fuming from Golden Censers hid the Mount.   [7.594–600]

And the celebration concludes with the thirty-line hymn to God's creative power, beginning with the lines that I have quoted at the outset of this chapter, and continuing on with triumphant praise of God's creative bounty diffused to worlds and multitudes as yet unknown:

>   Who seekes
> To lessen thee, against his purpose serves
> To manifest the more thy might: his evil
> Thou usest, and from thence creat'st more good.

Witness this new-made World, another Heav'n
From Heaven Gate not farr . . .   [7.613–18]

Here, then, at the close of book 7, or, in the first edition, in the middle of book 7, is the climax of one strand in the poem's twofold plot: the strand of redemption, showing the irresistible flowing forth of God's creative goodness,[4] which man's fall, like the war in Heaven, may disturb, but never stop. There is a continuity between this Creation and the creative light that still can work within the vision of the redeemed man. Milton's vision of Creation proves that the apprehension of God's goodness can still be recovered, with love and gratitude, by fallen man. Here is the paradise within.

II

The climactic nature of this vision is stressed in the first edition by the length of the original seventh book, with its 1290 lines forming the longest book thus far in the poem. It is all one book of Creation, for Adam has still to tell his memories of his first "upspringing" and the story of the creation of Eve. Yet, despite the advantage of this emphasis, Milton's division of the latter half of this long book into a new book 8 is highly effective and appropriate. For this eighth book of the second edition has essentially a different theme from the preceding account of the six days of Creation. Book 7 in the new division is one sustained hymn of praise to God's creative bounty. The new book 8 reveals the presence of what Milton here calls "doubt." The word "doubt" here performs in exactly the ambiguous way that the words "frail," "wanton," or "error" have performed in the scenes before the Fall:[5] they are words wholly innocent, not "noxious" in this paradisal context—but they imply the presence of certain qualities inherent in the Creation that will lead to man's fall, qualities inherent in the gift of freedom and the gift of reason.

This shift of basic theme is made plain at the outset of book 8 as Adam thanks the angel for allaying his desire to know "Of things above his World," to learn what Raphael calls "the secrets of another world, perhaps / Not lawful to reveal"—though for man's good, the angel adds, "This is dispenc't"(5.455,569–71). But

Adam's thirst for knowledge is not yet satisfied, despite his gratitude:

> What thanks sufficient, or what recompence
> Equal have I to render thee, Divine
> Hystorian, who thus largely hast allayd
> The thirst I had of knowledge, and voutsaf't
> This friendly condescention to relate
> Things else by me unsearchable, now heard
> With wonder, but delight, and, as is due,
> With glorie attributed to the high
> Creator; some thing yet of doubt remaines,
> Which only thy solution can resolve.   [8.5–14]

There is of course no doubt of God's goodness; the doubt is only uncertainty about how to interpret God's ways. Adam proceeds to ask, in larger terms, much the same question that Eve had asked in book 4, when, after her echoing love-song, she so abruptly changed her tone to ask why the stars shine while the two of them are sleeping: "But wherfore all night long shine these, for whom, / This glorious sight, when sleep hath shut all eyes?"(4.657–58). Adam beautifully explains that the stars have their duty "to Nations yet unborn," that their influence helps to temper or nourish all things that grow on earth, and that even if mankind did not exist, "Millions of spiritual Creatures walk the Earth / Unseen, both when we wake, and when we sleep" (4.677–79).

   Nevertheless, as he looks upon the entire universe, Adam is led to wonder why such an immense and intricate creation of stars should have been designed only to provide light for the earth, "in all thir vast survey / Useless besides;"

>   reasoning I oft admire,
> How Nature wise and frugal could commit
> Such disproportions, with superfluous hand
> So many nobler Bodies to create,
> Greater so manifold to this one use . . .   [8.24–29]

Reasoning, we see, is not infallible in its conclusions, for, although Raphael says, "To ask or search I blame thee not," (66) he makes it clear that Adam's question has carried man beyond the range of legitimate searching; and the angel predicts the "quaint opinions" that Adam's descendants will put forth as a result of just this kind of "reasoning." He concludes by urging Adam not to pursue this kind of study, but to concentrate his thoughts on "what he gives to thee, this Paradise / And thy fair *Eve*":

> Heav'n is for thee too high
> To know what passes there; be lowlie wise:
> Think onely what concernes thee and thy being . . . [8.171–74]

Then Adam, "cleerd of doubt," declares himself fully satisfied, once again, and says that he now understands that man should live without "perplexing thoughts" and "anxious cares"—which he says will "not molest us, unless we our selves / Seek them with wandring thoughts, and notions vaine"(8.179–87). But there is the problem, as Adam realizes when he contemplates his own and Eve's interior motions:

> But apte the Mind or Fancie is to roave
> Uncheckt, and of her roaving is no end;
> Till warn'd, or by experience taught, she learn
> That not to know at large of things remote
> From use, obscure and suttle, but to know
> That which before us lies in daily life,
> Is the prime Wisdom . . .   [8.188–94]

Adam is recognizing here the inherent, created tendency of the "Fancie" which he has described to Eve at the outset of book 5, while reassuring her that her disturbing dream, though containing evil thoughts, has left "No spot or blame behind." When Reason is asleep or at rest, he has explained,

> Oft in her absence mimic Fansie wakes
> To imitate her; but misjoyning shapes,
> Wilde work produces oft, and most in dreams,
> Ill matching words and deeds long past or late.   [5.110–13]

Adam is not limiting the "wilde work" of fancy to the state of dreaming; the tendency toward such roving or wildness is a part of man's created perfection. Only warning or experience will teach mankind how to control such roving of his "unexperienc't thought."

But even when abstruse studies are given up and the mind is devoted to the problems of daily life in Paradise, the doubts arise, "yet sinless." Adam now goes on to tell the story of the workings of his reason upon his first upspringing, when he rightly understood that he could not have been self-created:

> Not of my self; by some great Maker then,
> In goodness and in power praeeminent;
> Tell me, how may I know him, how adore,
> From whom I have that thus I move and live,
> And feel that I am happier then I know.   [8.278–82]

Then he shows his dignity and his boldness as he tells how he has reasoned with God over man's need for a mate, winning the divine approbation for his request:

> Thus farr to try thee *Adam,* I was pleas'd,
> And finde thee knowing not of Beasts alone,
> Which thou hast rightly nam'd, but of thy self,
> Expressing well the spirit within thee free,
> My Image, not imparted to the Brute,
> Whose fellowship therefore unmeet for thee
> Good reason was thou freely shouldst dislike,
> And be so minded still; I, ere thou spak'st,
> Knew it not good for Man to be alone,
> And no such companie as then thou saw'st
> Intended thee, for trial onely brought,
> To see how thou could'st judge of fit and meet:
> What next I bring shall please thee, be assur'd,
> Thy likeness, thy fit help, thy other self,
> Thy wish, exactly to thy hearts desire.   [8.437–51]

Well and good; but, Adam goes on to say, a problem has arisen from this so desirable gift of God, for Adam admits that he feels a "Commotion strange" whenever he looks at Eve—*Commotion strange,* a charming euphemism that perfectly suggests the combination of dignity and innocence in our grand parents. Milton insists on bringing out the whole difficult problem: Adam himself asks the embarrassing question, since he finds himself "here onely weake / Against the charm of Beauties powerful glance":

> Or Nature faild in mee, and left some part
> Not proof enough such Object to sustain
> Or from my side subducting, took perhaps
> More then enough; at least on her bestow'd
> Too much of Ornament . . .

"For well I understand," Adam says, that she is supposed to be inferior to me intellectually,

> yet when I approach
> Her loveliness, so absolute she seems
> And in her self compleat, so well to know
> Her own, that what she wills to do or say,
> Seems wisest, vertuousest, discreetest, best;

(Adam's confusion here seems to have produced Milton's worst line!)

> All higher knowledge in her presence falls
> Degraded, Wisdom in discourse with her
> Looses discount'nanc't, and like folly shewes;
> Authoritie and Reason on her waite,
> As one intended first, not after made
> Occasionally . . .   [8.532–56]

All this questioning of "nature" amounts to saying that perhaps God has made a mistake in creating Adam and Eve in this fashion. Thus the angel rebukes Adam sharply, "with contracted brow," pointing out at length that man was made for higher purposes than "carnal pleasure." But Adam is only "half abash't" at this stern rebuke, and he defends himself by saying that what most attracts him about Eve are the "decencies" that he finds in her— "decencies" in the old sense of qualities of fitness and harmony:

> those graceful acts,
> Those thousand decencies that daily flow
> From all her words and actions, mixt with Love
> And sweet compliance, which declare unfeign'd
> Union of Mind, or in us both one Soule:
> Harmonie to behold in wedded pair
> More grateful then harmonious sound to the eare.   [8.600–06]

The link with Milton's earlier praise of wedded love in book 4 makes Adam's defense here very strong. And after all, Adam cleverly asks, don't the angels in heaven also love? Here the angel gives his famous blush, "Celestial rosie red, Loves proper hue," and answers, in effect, yes, we are happy, and yes, we do love, but I've got to be getting on home now, for it's sunset, and remember,

> take heed least Passion sway
> Thy Judgement to do aught, which else free Will
> Would not admit; thine and of all thy Sons
> The weal or woe in thee is plac't; beware.
> I in thy persevering shall rejoyce,
> And all the Blest: stand fast; to stand or fall
> Free in thine own Arbitrement it lies.
> Perfect within, no outward aid require;
> And all temptation to transgress repel.   [8.635–43]

Perfect within—all the preceding doubts have been allowed and caused by the nature and conditions of man's perfection. Sexuality, under reason's control, is justified by the example of the angels, and attractive reluctance, modesty, and blushing in Eve (as in the angel) are all part of that perfection before the Fall:

> She heard me thus, and though divinely brought,
> Yet Innocence and Virgin Modestie,
> Her vertue and the conscience of her worth,
> That would be woo'd, and not unsought be won,
> Not obvious, not obtrusive, but retir'd,
> The more desirable, or to say all,
> Nature her self, though pure of sinful thought,
> Wrought in her so, that seeing me, she turn'd;
> I follow'd her, she what was Honour knew,
> And with obsequious Majestie approv'd
> My pleaded reason. To the Nuptial Bowre
> I led her blushing like the Morn . . .   [8.500–11]

It is passages such as this that have led some readers, perhaps most readers, to feel that Milton is having difficulty in distinguishing between fallen and unfallen sexuality and that indeed, as Tillyard has put it, Milton is constantly "faking" in his account of paradisal life by "attributing to Eve and Adam feelings which though nominally felt in the state of innocence are actually not compatible with it." Both, he says, "are virtually fallen before the official temptation has begun." Poetically and dramatically, he argues, Milton could not have done otherwise.[6]

But the issue should be put another way, as J. M. Evans has shown in his demonstration that in Milton's view "Man's innocence was not 'effortless,' " was not "a condition of stability." "The perfection of Adam and Eve no less than the perfection of the garden they inhabit is nothing if not conditional, for it requires their constant vigilance to preserve the balance of forces on which it depends."[7] The poem, then, means exactly what it seems to say: that Adam and Eve, before the Fall, were very much like their descendants, that the difference between the fallen and the unfallen state does not reside in any change of the essential human qualities: free will, and the power of choice. The change is only in the non-essential conditions of life: in the presence of pain, sorrow, and temporal death (for ultimate immortality is not denied), and in the outward conditions of life: harshness of climate, sweat of the brow to provide food and shelter—all non-essential to man's happiness in Milton's view. For happiness resides in the love of God: in gratitude and praise for the gifts that God still showers upon fallen man through the vestiges of God remaining in the Creation and in the bounty of his grace.

CHAPTER 7

The Power
of Choice

Adam and Eve, before the Fall, have all our basic psychological
qualities: they are "frail" in the sense that their power of choice
may wrongly choose; choice is difficult because "wandring
thoughts" and passions and the wild work of fancy are all part of
the broad field in which human choice must operate. Adam and
Eve find it difficult to choose rightly because they are so "unexperienc't"; their descendants find it difficult to choose because they
have so much experience, see so many possibilities, dangers, and
advantages. Yet in Milton's universe the power of choice is essential to man's perfection and man's happiness, whether fallen or
unfallen. That is why the words "choice" and "choose" ring
throughout *Paradise Lost*, from the opening words of Satan, "and
in my choyce / To reign is worth ambition though in Hell . . ."
(1.261–62) through the words of God declaring "Reason also is
choice," on to the famous closing lines where Adam and Eve must
learn "where to choose / Thir place of rest" (12.646–47).[1]

As in these instances, so in book 8 these crucial words are placed
in an emphatic position, at the end of a line, when Adam recalls
the divine prohibition in the very phrase that Satan has used in
book 1:

127

> Sternly he pronounc'd
> The rigid interdiction, which resounds
> Yet dreadful in mine eare, though in my choice
> Not to incur . . .   [8.333–36]

The power of choice, then, is essential to Milton's view of the dynamic, progressive, eternal expansion of God's goodness; by warning and experience man must learn to manage the gift of freedom, and seek his happiness beyond the limitations of the flesh.

Nothing could stress the essential humanity of Adam and Eve more strongly than the scene that opens book 9, after Satan has uttered his Euripidean, or Senecan prologue to the tragedy of the Fall (99–178). Here Milton brings our grand parents closer to us than we have thus far seen them. This is not done suddenly: it has been a gradual process from their first appearance in book 4. The more we see of them and the more we hear them talk, the more they seem like us. In book 5, for example, Adam and Eve have already begun to drop the formal modes of address that marked their speeches in book 4. When Adam sees the angel approaching his door he calls to Eve, who is within "due at her hour" preparing dinner,

> Haste hither *Eve*, and worth thy sight behold
> Eastward among those Trees, what glorious shape
> Comes this way moving . . .
>   But goe with speed,
> And what thy stores contain, bring forth and poure
> Abundance, fit to honour and receive
> Our Heav'nly stranger . . .   [5.308–10,313–16]

Eve is amused at Adam's abrupt and excited concern for her "stores" and she answers in a leisurely and stately way (one can imagine her quiet smile):

>   *Adam*, earths hallowd mould,
> Of God inspir'd, small store will serve, where store,
> All seasons, ripe for use hangs on the stalk;
> Save what by frugal storing firmness gains
> To nourish, and superfluous moist consumes:
> But I will haste and from each bough and break,
> Each Plant & juciest Gourd will pluck such choice
> To entertain our Angel guest, as hee

Beholding shall confess that here on Earth
God hath dispenst his bounties as in Heav'n.
      So saying, with dispatchful looks in haste
She turns, on hospitable thoughts intent
What choice to chuse for delicacie best . . .   [5.321–33]

Thus Eve shows her command of the household affairs, using her
reason wittily to pun before going forth to exercise her power of
choice in the preparation of that elegant vegetarian meal.[2]

The sense of comedy here, enforced by Milton's own quiet wit
in regarding this pastoral feast—"No fear lest Dinner coole"—is
carried on in the early part of book 9, where, though Milton has
said that he must now change his notes to tragic, the first act of his
tragedy might well be described as a domestic comedy. Here at the
outset the grand titles of address are completely dropped, and
Adam and Eve are introduced simply as the "human pair." "And
Eve first to her Husband thus began," without any of those words
about "My Author and Disposer," "Unargu'd I obey," and so on,
such as we heard in book 4. Eve opens her speech here in what
might be called a normal wifely fashion: *Adam*," she says, quite
informally—

  Adam, well may we labour still to dress
This Garden, still to tend Plant, Herb and Flour.
Our pleasant task enjoyn'd, but till more hands
Aid us, the work under our labour grows,
Luxurious by restraint; what we by day
Lop overgrown, or prune, or prop, or bind,
One night or two with wanton growth derides
Tending to wilde.   [9.205–212]

We must believe that Eve is truly concerned about her work
here, and not simply fishing for a compliment, for Milton's whole
account of life in Paradise has stressed the importance of this
element of labor.[3] Milton is placing a special stress upon the words
of Genesis where God says to Adam and Eve: "Be fruitful and
multiply, and replenish the earth, and subdue it," along with the
later statement that "the Lord God took the man, and put him
into the garden of Eden to dress it and to keep it," with man's
duties clarified by the statement that before this "there was not a
man to till the ground" (Gen. 1:28; 2:5, 15). Eve's concern for the

results of their "labour" of dressing and re-dressing is one of the problems raised by the whole Creation's "wanton" tendency to be fruitful and multiply, even to the extent of "tending to wilde." Nature's vitality, whether in vegetation or in man and woman, is not easy to "subdue" and keep in reasonable order.

The point has been clearly made in book 5 as Milton describes the angel's approach to Adam's door:

> through Groves of Myrrhe,
> And flouring Odours, Cassia, Nard, and Balme;
> A Wilderness of sweets; for Nature here
> Wantond as in her prime, and plaid at will
> Her Virgin Fancies, pouring forth more sweet,
> Wilde above rule or art; enormous bliss.   [5.292–97]

Here again the words "wantond" and "wilde" give the clue to the inherent problem: things unconfined and unrestrained tend to become "luxurious", tend to run beyond the rule and art of reason. Man's duty is to bring these "Virgin Fancies" of nature under the control of reason, for fancy, we recall, can make "wilde work". Eve is therefore completely right to show concern over the way in which their labors seem ineffective. Adam himself has explained to Eve the importance of their labor in book 4, as they retire to their blissful bower:

> When *Adam* thus to *Eve:* Fair Consort, th' hour
> Of night, and all things now retir'd to rest
> Mind us of like repose, since God hath set
> Labour and rest, as day and night to men
> Successive, and the timely dew of sleep
> Now falling with soft slumbrous weight inclines
> Our eye-lids; other Creatures all day long
> Rove idle unimploid, and less need rest;
> Man hath his daily work of body or mind
> Appointed, which declares his Dignitie,
> And the regard of Heav'n on all his waies;
> While other Animals unactive range,
> And of thir doings God takes no account.   [4.610–22]

The word "account" tells us to take the divine "regard" on all man's ways in two senses: God holds man's ways in high regard, with affection and respect—but also, the eye of God is watching all man's ways, and will take account of how he performs his ap-

pointed tasks. Therefore, Adam adds, at dawn "we must be ris'n /
And at our pleasant labour," which he then proceeds to describe
with exactly the conditions that are worrying Eve in book 9:

> to reform
> Yon flourie Arbors, yonder Allies green,
> Our walks at noon, with branches overgrown,
> That mock our scant manuring, and require
> More hands then ours to lop thir wanton growth . . .
>
> [4.624–29]

There again is the word "wanton", along with the witty play on the
Latin base of *manuring*—working with the hands, for such work is
surely needed: "Those Blossoms also, and those dropping
Gumms, / That lie bestrowne unsightly and unsmooth, / Ask rid-
dance, if we mean to tread with ease . . ." (4.630–32).

Thus Eve is right to be concerned over the results of their labor,
and right to consider ways of improving its effect:

> Thou therefore now advise
> Or hear what to my mind first thoughts present,
> Let us divide our labours, thou where choice
> Leads thee, or where most needs, whether to wind
> The Woodbine round this Arbour, or direct
> The clasping Ivie where to climb, while I
> In yonder Spring of Roses intermixt
> With Myrtle, find what to redress till Noon . . .   [9.212–19]

She suggests this division of labor because, she adds, when they
are together they waste too much time in looking at each other
and smiling and talking, and thus "th' hour of Supper comes
unearn'd" (9.225).

"To whom mild answer *Adam* thus return'd," maintaining something of that earlier formality of address, along with some measure of masculine condescension:

> Sole *Eve*, Associate sole, to me beyond
> Compare above all living Creatures deare,
> Well hast thou motion'd, wel thy thoughts imploy'd
> How we might best fulfill the work which here
> God hath assign'd us, nor of me shalt pass
> Unprais'd: for nothing lovelier can be found
> In woman, then to studie houshold good,
> And good workes in her Husband to promote.   [9.227–34]

Adam sounds here as though he had observed hundreds of women: clearly Adam is becoming Everyman. But, he adds, life in Eden is not supposed to be so arduous. It is quite all right for us to look and smile at each other while we work; and then he makes man's first strategic error, for he goes on to say:

> But other doubt possesses me, least harm
> Befall thee sever'd from me; for thou knowst
> What hath bin warn'd us, what malicious Foe
> Envying our happiness, and of his own
> Despairing, seeks to work us woe and shame
> By sly assault . . .   [9.251–56]

Considering this danger, then, Adam advises,

>   leave not the faithful side
> That gave thee being, stil shades thee and protects.
> The Wife, where danger or dishonour lurks,
> Safest and seemliest by her Husband staies,
> Who guards her, or with her the worst endures.   [9.265–69]

Here again, Adam is speaking with the voice of Everyman in the daily world, foreshadowing his decision to eat the apple and with her the worst endure. Eve in her reply becomes Everywoman, too, as she withdraws to her earlier mode of formal address:

> To whom the Virgin Majestie of *Eve*,
> As one who loves, and some unkindness meets,
> With sweet austeer composure thus reply'd.
> Ofspring of Heav'n and Earth, and all Earths Lord . . .
>   [9.270–73]

She goes on to say that she knows all about this enemy, for Adam has told her about Satan, and she has overheard the warning of the departing angel. Thus she is shocked to think that Adam would mistrust her:

> But that thou shouldst my firmness therfore doubt
> To God or thee, because we have a foe
> May tempt it, I expected not to hear . . .
> Thoughts, which how found they harbour in thy brest,
> *Adam*, missthought of her to thee so dear?
> To whom with healing words *Adam* reply'd.
> Daughter of God and Man, immortal *Eve* . . .
>   [9.279–81,288–91]

I do trust you, he says, I do, but—and then he flounders into a very unconvincing argument: I am only trying to prevent the dishonor that lies in the fact of being tempted. Then he tries a stronger point, which one wishes that he had tried first. I cannot get along without you, he says, I will be stronger in your presence: "I from the influence of thy looks receave / Access in every Vertue, in thy sight / More wise, more watchful, stronger . . ." (9.309–11). And now Milton tells us very plainly what he is about, for by his introductory phrasing he places the scene in our own world:

> So spake domestick *Adam* in his care
> And Matrimonial Love, but *Eve*, who thought
> Less attributed to her Faith sincere,
> Thus her reply with accent sweet renewd.
>   If this be our condition, thus to dwell
> In narrow circuit strait'nd by a Foe,
> Suttle or violent, we not endu'd
> Single with like defence, wherever met,
> How are we happie, still in fear of harm?
>   . . . .
> Fraile is our happiness, if this be so,
> And *Eden* were no *Eden* thus expos'd.   [9.318–26,340–41]

This is not what Adam has been saying: they are not confined to a narrow circuit; they can go anywhere together. And this idea that they are made, or ought to be made, to meet temptation singly— this represents, as Milton's whole poem before this has made clear, a misunderstanding of the nature of the universe, where nothing stands alone, but everything lives best in the linked universe of love, with respect for those above and care for those below. This is why Adam at last replies "fervently," exclaiming:

> O Woman, best are all things as the will
> Of God ordaind them, his creating hand
> Nothing imperfet or deficient left
> Of all that he Created . . .   [9.343–46]

The meaning of Eden, he says, has nothing to do with this idea of complete personal independence. The freedom of the will, Adam goes on to explain, exercises its power of choice within a universe of interdependent and mutual responsibility: "Not then mistrust, but tender love enjoynes, / That I should mind thee oft, and mind thou me" (9.357–58). "Mind" here does not mean simply "obey", but rather means "Pay attention to," "be mindful" of one another's best interests and advice. Then Adam goes on to make the choice very plain: "Wouldst thou approve thy constancie, approve / First thy obedience;" (9.367–68) that is, obedience to what is clearly Adam's wish and best advice. He leaves it up to her to choose, saying: "But if thou think" (and clearly he does not think so)

> trial unsought may finde
> Us both securer then thus warnd thou seemst,
> Go; for thy stay, not free, absents thee more . . .   [9.370–72]

Adam seems to be telling her that if she thinks that staying together, not seeking trial, may create a sense of false security, then it is better for her to go, since she will be staying with him against her will.

To some readers Adam has seemed weak here, but the question is highly debatable, for it may well seem that Adam is only carrying out here the view of the workings of free will that the poem has over and over again explained to us and to Adam. He has made it plain that he does not wish her to go; he has asked for her obedience to this wish. His respect for human reason makes it impossible for him to detain her by force and his love for Eve makes it impossible for him to speak more harshly. It is true that later on, after the Fall, in that unpleasant scene of domestic bickering, Eve snaps back at Adam with the bitter reproach:

> why didst not thou the Head
> Command me absolutely not to go,
> Going into such danger as thou saidst?
> Too facil then thou didst not much gainsay,
> Nay, didst permit, approve, and fair dismiss.
> Hadst thou bin firm and fixt in thy dissent,
> Neither had I transgress'd, nor thou with mee.   [9.1155–61]

But here she is angrily distorting the effect of Adam's earlier speech, where Adam seems to hope that by this evidence of his respect for her intelligence, she will come round to his point of view:

> Go in thy native innocence, relie
> On what thou hast of vertue, summon all,
> For God towards thee hath done his part, do thine.   [9.373–75]

With this meagre compliment, Adam reminds Eve that her part is to be mindful of Adam's best advice. And Adam still seems to hope that Eve will choose to take his advice.

"So spake the Patriarch of Mankinde," says Milton, but the Patriarch soon suffers the fate of his sons:

> but *Eve*
> Persisted, yet submiss, though last, repli'd.
> With thy permission then . . .   [9.376–78]

Has he really given her permission to go? It would be more accurate to say that he has given her permission to disobey his wishes if she chooses to do so, and this is exactly the permission that God himself allows the freedom of the will. God, to be sure, has laid down his commandment absolutely, but it is not, I think, valid to argue from this that Adam should have been equally absolute. Even in Milton's day, the relation between husband and wife could not have been regarded as precisely analogous to the relation between God and man. Of course we think of Milton's earlier statement in book 4:

> Hee for God only, shee for God in him:
> His fair large Front and Eye sublime declar'd
> Absolute rule . . .   [4.299–301]

But this at once is followed by the passage where he adds that Eve's "subjection" must be "requir'd with gentle sway." It is this gentle sway that Adam is attempting to exert here, but Eve, insisting on her own right to choose, makes the wrong choice. That is, the consequences prove her wrong, but neither of them can possibly know that she will fall. And we notice that Milton does not, as she departs, subject Eve to any very strong condemnation. Instead, he describes her situation and her beauty in terms that draw our strong sympathies toward her unprotected state, her utterly innocent beauty, her earnest work, her good intentions. She means no harm, and she really does have the welfare of her garden at heart. Anyhow, she is not going far—only to that rose

garden over there, yonder, as she says: they can see the spot from
where they are standing.

Now, as she ominously withdraws her hand from her husband's
hand, Milton surrounds her with a fragrant cloud of pagan
myths—all of them concerned with attractive, beneficent spirits
and deities of nature:

> and like a Wood-Nymph light
> *Oread* or *Dryad*, or of *Delia's* Traine,
> Betook her to the Groves, but *Delia's* self
> In gate surpass'd and Goddess-like deport,
> Though not as shee with Bow and Quiver armd,
> But with such Gardning Tools as Art yet rude,
> Guiltless of fire had formd, or Angels brought.
> To *Pales*, or *Pomona*, thus adornd,
> Likest she seemd, *Pomona* when she fled
> *Vertumnus*, or to *Ceres* in her Prime,
> Yet Virgin of *Proserpina* from *Jove*.   [9.386–96]

Everyone has felt an ominous undercurrent here, as in the phrase
"Guiltless of fire," the allusion to Pomona and her persistent
wooer, Vertumnus, or the oblique reference to the sorrows of
Ceres, through the loss of her daughter to the prince of Hades.
But the dominant effect of all these myths is quite favorable to
Eve: Delia is Diana, and by using twice the unusual name Delia,
Milton reminds us of her birth, along with Apollo, on the pure
and sacred island of Delos. Pales, ancient Roman goddess of flocks
and herds, was a beneficent deity, worshipped by rites of purifica-
tion. As for the story of Pomona, Milton has given the allusion an
ominous twist by referring to the time when, he says, she "fled
Vertumnus." Yet in Ovid's *Metamorphoses* this is quite an amusing
and harmless story, where Pomona provides a true original for
Milton's Eve:

> Gardens and fruit were all her care; no other
> Was ever more skilled or diligent. Woods and rivers
> Were nothing to her, only the fields, the branches
> Bearing the prosperous fruits. She bore no javelin,
> But the curved pruning-hook, to trim the branches,
> Check too luxuriant growth, or make incision
> For the engrafted twig to thrive and grow in.
> She would not let them thirst: the flowing waters

> Poured down to the roots. This was her love, her passion.
> Venus was nothing to her . . .

But all the rustic gods try to win her, especially Vertumnus, who tries every possible disguise, every possible verbal manoeuvre, for over a hundred lines of Ovid, with no effect at all on the cool maiden. So at last, in desperation, he throws off his latest disguise

> and stood before her
> In the light of his own radiance, as the sun
> Breaks through the clouds against all opposition.
> Ready for force, he found no need; Pomona
> Was taken by his beauty, and her passion
> Answered his own. [*Met.* 14.624–34,767–71, trans. Humphries]

Such is the atmosphere of purity and harmlessness that Milton gives to Eve.

When the poet bursts out in his own voice with his commentary, he cannot bring himself quite to blame her, though it looks at first as though he is going to do so: "O much deceav'd, much failing, hapless *Eve*," he cries, but then the sentence bends over the line, in Milton's metamorphic way and assumes a different meaning, for it appears that the poet is saying only that she is deceived in thinking that she will return to Adam by noon, in time to have Adam's lunch ready. Her failing, we see, is her failing to return to Adam as she now promises:

> And all things in best order to invite
> Noontide repast, or Afternoons repose.
> O much deceav'd, much failing, hapless *Eve*,
> Of thy presum'd return! event perverse!
> Thou never from that houre in Paradise
> Foundst either sweet repast, or sound repose . . .   [9.402–07]

Notice that Milton does not say "perverse woman" but simply "perverse event," that is to say, outcome contrary to her and Adam's expectations. Thus the poet's sympathy and pitying admiration play over the figure of Eve as she works among her roses:

> them she upstaies
> Gently with Mirtle band, mindless the while,
> Her self,

(that is, not attentive to herself, with all her mind focused on the flowers)

> though fairest unsupported Flour
> From her best prop so farr, and storm so nigh.   [9.430–33]

Then, as we watch the serpent crawling "Among thick-wov'n Arborets and Flours . . . the hand of *Eve*," we realize that her gardening labors have already produced here an effect that, Milton says, surpasses the "feigned" gardens of Adonis, or the Gardens of King Alcinous in the *Odyssey*, or that true garden described in the Song of Solomon. Finally, to cap the climax of this mood of sympathy and admiration, Milton brings forward his greatest tribute to the beauty of the earth, as tended and inhabited now by fallen man and woman:

> As one who long in populous City pent,
> Where Houses thick and Sewers annoy the Aire,
> Forth issuing on a Summers Morn to breathe
> Among the pleasant Villages and Farmes
> Adjoynd, from each thing met conceaves delight,
> The smell of Grain, or tedded Grass, or Kine.
> Or Dairie, each rural sight, each rural sound;
> If chance with Nymphlike step fair Virgin pass,
> What pleasing seemd, for her now pleases more,
> She most, and in her looks summs all Delight.
> Such Pleasure took the Serpent to behold
> This Flourie Plat, the sweet recess of *Eve*
> Thus earlie, thus alone; her Heav'nly forme
> Angelic, but more soft, and Feminine,
> Her graceful Innocence, her every Aire
> Of gesture or lest action overawd
> His Malice, and with rapine sweet bereav'd
> His fierceness of the fierce intent it brought . . .   [9.445–62]

The effects of this great pastoral moment seem to be double. First, it throws our sympathy overwhelmingly toward Eve: so beautiful, so talented, so innocent: how unfair it seems that she should be permitted to undergo temptation by such an adversary, whose hypocrisy we know that she can never penetrate. Even Uriel, the regent of the sun, we recall, could not penetrate the disguise of that youthful cherub in book 3. At the same time the comparison suggests that Satan's design will not be wholly success-

ful. He has not utterly destroyed God's Paradise of Delight, since
the poet here still delights in these man-made scenes of farm and
village, and in feminine beauty, almost as much as he delights in
this imagined garden and in Eve herself.

The same kind of sympathy is thrown toward Adam before his
fall, and thus much argument has raged over whether or not
Adam is justified in his anguished, intuitive, passionate decision to
eat the fruit and die with Eve:

> How can I live without thee, how forgoe
> Thy sweet Converse and Love so dearly joyn'd . . . [9.908–09]

Yet the poet, in his abstract assertions after the Fall, and in his
picture of the painful bickering of Adam and Eve, leaves no doubt
that we are supposed to condemn them both. The trouble is that
Milton's sympathetic presentation makes it difficult to condemn
them very firmly. As Waldock sees the problem: "the poem asks
from us, at one and the same time, two incompatible responses. It
requires us . . . with the full weight of our minds to believe that
Adam did right, and simultaneously requires us with the full
weight of our minds to believe that he did wrong. The dilemma is
as critical as that, and there is no way of escape." Exactly, this is the
effect of book 9, but Waldock then goes on to see this as, in some
sense, a failure in Milton's total design: "*Paradise Lost* cannot take
the strain at its centre, it breaks there, the theme is too much for it.
. . . if the net effect of all [Milton's] labour is to justify man's ways
against God's ways: well, that was one of the risks, inherent in the
venture, that he did not see."[4]

But it is hard to believe that Milton, long choosing and beginning late, after a lifetime of theological study and speculation, did
not understand all the risks of his venture. It seems too easy a way
out to say that Milton's unconscious sympathies have led him to
give a more favorable portrait of Adam and Eve than he meant to
give; or that his desire to write an interesting poem led him to
undermine his theological purpose; or that Milton was not really
interested in the Fall so much as in portraying human nature as he
knew it.

The two incompatible responses that Waldock describes result
from Milton's ultimate, climactic presentation of the problems

inherent in the power of choice. With Eve, vanity, ambition, and the illusions fostered by Satan lead to her disastrous choice; but such tendencies to wild are part of her perfection: she must learn by experience, since warning has not sufficed, to manage herself better, to use her reason more wisely. With Adam, passion for Eve has overcome his reason; and he too must now learn from experience to use his reason with better effect. What Milton is stressing above all is his view that there is *not a break* between the unfallen and the fallen state; there is a *continuity* implicit in the irresistible diffusion of God's goodness. God's plan was to make us as we are. Thus Eve's unruly tendencies, Adam's commotion strange, and that domestic argument where Eve chooses to go off alone—such things do not represent a couple *fallen* before the Fall, but a couple *perfectly human* before the Fall, truly the "human pair." By its constant emphasis on man's "perfection" before the Fall, the poem asks us to revise and expand our easy notions of what constituted that original innocence and perfection.[5]

Strong emotions, Milton implies, are a part of man's perfection. The tug and pull of two reasoning minds, the disagreement between two individuals who both possess the freedom of the will— this too is part of man's perfection, for how could freedom otherwise exist and how could life be of the slightest interest without that freedom? All these qualities, Milton makes clear, must of course be kept under the gentle sway of reason—but then, as Milton insists in that remarkable parenthesis of book 3, "Reason also is choice." Strange as it may seem, the problem of making the right choice, the problem of the right exercise of freedom, is shown to be as difficult before the Fall as it is afterwards. We must remember the chief point of that heavenly dialogue in book 3: that the power of choice remains essentially the same in man, whether before or after the Fall. Before the Fall, Milton's God insists, man was made "sufficient to have stood"; after the Fall, Milton's God still insists, man has "what may suffice." Man's power of choice will be renewed by grace, and the universal link of love will be made evident to man through his knowledge that the Son of God became man and died to save mankind.

Milton's view of Adam and Eve, from the moment of their creation, emphasizes the growing, kinetic, dynamic quality of their awareness. They are born in a state of perfection which involves the ability to learn from experience and instruction. Thus Eve in book 4 is led by the divine voice to leave her "watry image" and to look upon Adam, and then, as she turns to flee, she is brought back by Adam's plea to her proper place as Adam's mate. Milton's view of man's "perfection" is never static or passive: man's dignity depends upon the power of choice, which inevitably includes the right to err as well as the right to make amends for error. To Milton man's "perfection" lies in man's ability to grow, however painfully, in wisdom and understanding.

CHAPTER 8

The Winding up of the Action

The tenth book of *Paradise Lost*, Addison remarks, "has a greater variety of Persons in it than any other in the whole Poem. The Author upon the winding up of his Action introduces all those who had any Concern in it, and shews with great Beauty the influence which it had upon each of them. It is like the last Act of a well written Tragedy, in which all who had a part in it are generally drawn up before the Audience, and represented under those Circumstances in which the determination of the Action places them."[1] Thus Milton binds his poem into unity by elements of reprise that begin with the bard's re-assertion of the power of choice in his brief prologue to book 10:

> for what can scape the Eye
> Of God All-seeing, or deceave his Heart
> Omniscient, who in all things wise and just,
> Hinder'd not *Satan* to attempt the minde
> Of Man, with strength entire, and free Will arm'd,
> Complete to have discover'd and repulst
> Whatever wiles of Foe or seeming Friend.
> For still they knew, and ought to have still remember'd
> The high Injunction not to taste that Fruit,
> Whoever tempted; which they not obeying,
> Incurr'd, what could they less, the penaltie,
> And manifold in sin, deserv'd to fall. [10.5–16]

"What could they less?"—again, as at the outset of book 4, the bard has entered into the center of the action, but here he checks our human sympathy with the fall of "innocent frail man." However strong that sympathy may be, the facts of God's justice and mercy set forth so clearly in book 3 must be remembered: man was not "frail" except in the basic sense of being "liable to fall or break." "With strength entire, and free Will arm'd" man's perfection held the power to make a better choice. Then follows a heavenly conclave that overtly recalls the prophecies and doctrines of the similar conclave in book 3, including a memory of the promise that the Son of God will restore man's freedom. Thus the heavenly conclave at the outset of book 10 plays its part in what Addison calls "the determination" or "the winding up" of the action, while at the same time creating the effect of starting a new action—the action of redemptive grace, counteracting chaos in the moral realm, just as the Son of God had defeated Satan's forces in book 6 and made way for the acts of Creation in book 7.

Milton ties all these actions of the Son together by the lines of book 10 that recall the Son's resplendent light, as described in two previous revelations of his triumphant glory:

> So spake the Father, and unfoulding bright
> Toward the right hand his Glorie, on the Son
> Blaz'd forth unclouded Deitie; he full
> Resplendent all his Father manifest
> Express'd, and thus divinely answer'd milde.   [10.63–67]

>   Mean while the Son
> On his great Expedition now appeer'd,
> Girt with Omnipotence, with Radiance crown'd
> Of Majestie Divine, Sapience and Love
> Immense, and all his Father in him shon.   [7.192–96]

> He said, and on his Son with Rayes direct
> Shon full, he all his Father full exprest
> Ineffably into his face receiv'd . . .   [6.719–21]

Now, as the Son begins the action of tempering justice with mercy, he announces that he will descend without the bright "Attendance" and the glorious "Train" that accompanied his first two epiphanies. He comes almost in human guise, "the mild Judge and Intercessor both," as the language of the poem descends from the grand style toward a biblical humility based upon the words of Genesis and many other biblical passages. In the poem's opening panel (which ends at line 228) there are no epic similes, no classical allusions, while latinity of diction is notably reduced in the conversation with the fallen pair, except in Adam's words when he repeats the satanic excuse of "necessity, the tyrant's plea," and declares,

> strict necessitie
> Subdues me, and calamitous constraint,
> Least on my head both sin and punishment,
> However insupportable, be all
> Devolv'd . . .   [10.131–35]

Latinity of diction has its role to play in the poem's action. We may sympathize with current efforts to diminish the number of alleged latinisms in the poem—if by *latinisms* we mean words used only, or primarily, in a Latin sense, or with a witty awareness of the Latin root.[2] Still, such latinisms are the outworks of Milton's latinity: they serve to make us aware of the various degrees of latinity present in various parts of the poem, with significant effect. Thus the latinity in the preceding passage, by temporarily "raising" the style, seems to suggest an element of hollowness and pretence in Adam's excuse, preparing for the shameful evasion that follows, in simpler language, but still highly suspended syntax:

> This woman whom thou mad'st to be my help,
> And gav'st me as thy perfet gift, so good,
> So fit, so acceptable, so Divine,
> That from her hand I could suspect no ill,
> And what she did, whatever in it self,
> Her doing seem'd to justifie the deed;
> Shee gave me of the Tree, and I did eate.   [10.137–43]

The reminiscence of Adam's conversation with Raphael, where Adam confessed that her beauty seemed to possess a superior power over him, reinforces the innuendo that the fall is really God's own fault.

The Son repeats the response that Raphael had given then with "contracted brow", though now the voice is milder in its firm reproach:

> Adornd
> She was indeed, and lovely to attract
> Thy Love, not thy Subjection, and her Gifts
> Were such as under Government well seem'd,
> Unseemly to beare rule, which was thy part
> And person, had'st thou known thy self aright.   [10.151–56]

Then Milton utterly turns the tables upon Adam by showing that
Eve has none of this bluster and evasion, but knows her self and
her guilt, which she confesses in a simple, biblical pentameter:
"The Serpent me beguil'd and I did eate" (10.162).

That simple phrasing sets the tone and manner for what follows, as the Son proceeds to judgment and Milton adapts many
biblical words:[3]

> then pittying how they stood
> Before him naked to the aire, that now
> Must suffer change, disdain'd not to begin
> Thenceforth the forme of servant to assume,
> As when he wash'd his servants feet, so now
> As Father of his Familie he clad
> Thir nakedness with Skins of Beasts, or slain,
> Or as the Snake with youthful Coate repaid;
> And thought not much to cloath his Enemies:
> Nor hee thir outward onely with the Skins
> Of Beasts, but inward nakedness, much more
> Opprobrious, with his Robe of righteousness,
> Araying cover'd from his Fathers sight.   [10.211–23]

The last four lines are based on Isaiah's "robe of righteousness"
(61:10), while the latinate word "Opprobrious" stands forth in
emphatic position as a sign of theological interpretation.

Then, after the Son has ascended to rejoin the Father, the central panel of the book opens with syntax that foretells a drastic
change in style and subject:

> Meanwhile, ere thus was sin'd and judg'd on Earth,
> Within the Gates of Hell sate Sin and Death,
> In counterview within the Gates, that now
> Stood open wide, belching outrageous flame
> Farr into *Chaos*, since the Fiend pass'd through . . . [10.229–33]

The ironies and linkages are clear: the "outrageous flame"

belched into Chaos once more forms the strongest possible contrast with the perfect circle of Creation drawn by the Son of God
with his golden compasses; and the implications of an Unholy
Trinity are reinforced by our memory of their first appearance in
book 2.

Now the epic style of the opening book reappears in a stiffened,
hardened form that suggests a subtle parody of the grandeur that
one has admired in the poem's beginning. The three panels of
book 10 present the action of redemptive love at beginning and
end, while the central panel re-enacts the fallen images and pos-
tures of the first two books. Sin and Death here bring with them a
series of similes and classical allusions, presented with a gradual
rise in the concentration of latinity. That rise is felt in the opening
speech of Sin, as "connatural" (246) prepares the way for the strict
latinism of "impassable, *impervious*" (254), where Milton cleverly
stresses the inflation of the style by preceding the latinism with its
definition! This leads on into the latinate pair "for intercourse /
Or transmigration" (260–61) and the redundancy of the concluding "attraction and instinct" (263).

Such language leads the way toward the re-introduction of the
heroic simile when Death snuffs "the smell / Of mortal change on
Earth":

>   As when a flock
> Of ravenous Fowl, though many a league remote,
> Against the day of Battel, to a Field,
> Where Armies lie encampt, come flying, lur'd
> With sent of living Carcasses design'd
> For death, the following day, in bloodie fight.
> So sented the grim Feature, and upturn'd
> His Nostril wide into the murkie Air,
> Sagacious of his Quarrey from so farr.   [10.272–81]

Feature is a brilliant piece of etymological wit, for the word carries
backward through Middle English and Old French to the original
Latin of *factura:* a formation, a thing produced; while *Sagacious*
carries back to the root *sagire:* to perceive or discern quickly or
acutely. Thus latinate diction supports the heroic simile on every
side. Meanwhile the simile itself recalls the way in which Satan has
landed on the created universe like a vulture on Imaus bred, and

has sat upon the Tree of Life "like a Cormorant", in wait for the "living Carcasses" of Adam and Eve after their mortal change.

With such preparation Milton now proceeds to display another heroic work of building, traditional in epic, as in the building of Pandaemonium or Carthage; and he does so, as Tillyard long ago pointed out,[4] by suggesting a bitter parody of the account of the Creation, when

> on the watrie calme
> His brooding wings the Spirit of God outspred,
> And vital vertue infus'd, and vital warmth
> Throughout the fluid Mass, but downward purg'd
> The black tartareous cold infernal dregs
> Adverse to life . . .   [7.234–39]

Now the cold infernal dregs return from Hell to build their work, not upon a "calme", but out of raging anarchy:

> Then Both from out Hell Gates into the waste
> Wide Anarchie of *Chaos* damp and dark
> Flew divers, & with Power (thir Power was great)
> Hovering upon the Waters; what they met
> Solid or slimie, as in raging Sea
> Tost up and down, together crowded drove
> From each side shoaling towards the mouth of Hell.
>   [10.282–88]

Hovering upon the Waters: the phrase evokes not only the biblical words, "And the Spirit of God moved upon the face of the waters" (Genesis 1:2), but also Milton's adaptation of that sentence in the opening of his poem, where he prays for inspiration from the same creative power that performed the original Creation:

> Thou from the first
> Wast present, and with mighty wings outspread
> Dove-like satst brooding on the vast Abyss
> And mad'st it pregnant: What in me is dark
> Illumine, what is low raise and support . . .   [1.19–23]

For the poet himself is about to embark upon his own heroic work of building. Furthermore, the placement of the phrase *Hovering upon the Waters*, in this context, may recall a similar placement of the word *Hovering* back in the scene in Hell where Satan and Death confront each other:

> and such a frown
> Each cast at th' other, as when two black Clouds
> With Heav'ns Artillery fraught, come rattling on
> Over the *Caspian*, then stand front to front
> Hov'ring a space, till Winds the signal blow
> To joyn thir dark Encounter in midair . . .   [2.713–18]

Now in book 10 another dark encounter is accompanied with another simile involving winds in a Russian setting, though this time farther north, in keeping with the action of these cold infernal dregs:

> As when two Polar Winds blowing adverse
> Upon the *Cronian* Sea, together drive
> Mountains of Ice, that stop th' imagin'd way
> Beyond *Petsora* Eastward, to the rich
> *Cathaian* Coast.   [10.289–93]

This structure is not only a bridge between Hell and earth, but is also an obstruction that blocks the way toward a rich realm of promise, whether in Heaven or in Paradise on earth.[5]

Then a heavy infiltration of latinate diction combines with inverted syntax and a cluster of classical allusions to give an "heroic" grandeur to the scene:

> The aggregated Soyle
> Death with his Mace petrific, cold and dry,
> As with a Trident smote, and fix't as firm
> As *Delos* floating once; the rest his look
> Bound with *Gorgonian* rigor not to move,
> And with *Asphaltic* slime; broad as the Gate,
> Deep to the Roots of Hell the gather'd beach
> They fasten'd, and the Mole immense wraught on
> Over the foaming deep high Archt, a Bridge
> Of length prodigious joyning to the Wall
> Immoveable of this now fenceless world
> Forfeit to Death; from hence a passage broad,
> Smooth, easie, inoffensive down to Hell.   [10.293–305]

Inoffensive, like *impervious* earlier, stresses the inflation of the style, being used in the Latin sense of *inoffensus*: without hindrance, unobstructed; while the syntax itself seems to collapse under the strain. The second and fourth in the heavy series of posterior adjectives do not in fact modify their preceding nouns: *Mole im-*

mense is not in parallel with *deep high Archt*, for *high Archt* really modifies *Mole*. Likewise *length prodigious* is not in parallel with *Wall Immoveable*, for the wall of "this now fenceless world" has, alas, been removed: it is the *Bridge* (three lines before) which is now *Immoveable*. But *world* and *Forfeit* are all too exactly now allied. At the same time this subtle displacement of the adjectives creates a mimetic movement of construction from one side of the abyss to the other.

Milton then opens his next heroic simile with a phrase reminiscent of both Vergil (*Georgics* 4.176) and Ovid (*Met.* 5.416–17): "So, if great things to small may be compar'd. . . ."[6] That phrase has been used in the poem twice before. First, in book 2, as Satan stands poised on the brink of Chaos:

> Nor was his eare less peal'd
> With noises loud and ruinous (to compare
> Great things with small) then when *Bellona* storms,
> With all her battering Engines bent to rase
> Som Capital City . . .   [2.920–24]

And again in book 6 as prelude to the combat of Michael and Satan:

> from each hand with speed retir'd
> Where erst was thickest fight, th' Angelic throng,
> And left large field, unsafe within the wind
> Of such commotion, such as to set forth
> Great things by small, if Natures concord broke,
> Among the Constellations warr were sprung,
> Two planets rushing from aspect maligne
> Of fiercest opposition in mid Skie,
> Should combat, and thir jarring Sphears confound.   [6.307–15]

So here in book 10 the phrase foreshadows the destruction of Paradise and the breaking of nature's concord soon to be shown in the shifting of the planets, while the simile itself suggests Satan's effort to "yoke" man's liberty, as he voyaged from his palace of Pandaemonium:[7]

> So, if great things to small may be compar'd,
> *Xerxes*, the Libertie of *Greece* to yoke,
> From *Susa* his *Memnonian* Palace high
> Came to the Sea, and over *Hellespont*

> Bridging his way, *Europe* with *Asia* joyn'd,
> And scourg'd with many a stroak th' indignant waves.
>
> [10.306–11]

Indignant suggests a Vergilian usage, "disdaining to bear": "pontem indignatus Araxes" (*Aeneid* 8.728), along with the favorite Ovidian usage, "unable to endure": "fretaque indignantia miscent" (*Met.* 11.491). Both meanings suggest the retribution to follow.

Finally, the latinity reaches its outrageous climax in one enormous pun that derides the pretensions of every Roman pontifex:

> Now had they brought the work by wondrous Art
> Pontifical, a ridge of pendent Rock
> Over the vext Abyss, following the track
> Of *Satan*, to the self same place where hee
> First lighted from his Wing, and landed safe
> From out of *Chaos* to the outside bare
> Of this round World . . .   [10.312–18]

The pun is reinforced by the reference to "this new wondrous Pontifice" a few lines later (348). We may recall that it was at exactly this spot of Satan's landing that Milton had located his Limbo in book 3, the place where popish follies, as Milton sees them, "Fly o're the backside of the World."

It was here too, on this outer shell of the World, that Satan in book 3 had seen the juncture of the stairs let down from heaven with a "passage down to th' earth," a juncture full of beneficent overtones. But now in book 10 an ominous *trivium* has been formed by this new pontifice, this "stupendious" and "portentous" bridge, which Satan's "faire Inchanting Daughter" now hails as the result of her parent's "magnific deeds", by which God's "Quadrature" is parted from Satan's "Orbicular World," where Sin and Death, as Satan declares, will reign "Plenipotent on Earth" and "No detriment need feare" (10.351–409).

After this new work of satanic building we return with Satan to the scene of Pandaemonium, here appropriately introduced with an heroic simile combining a frozen setting with military desolation caused by warfare between barbaric armies:

> As when the *Tartar* from his *Russian* Foe
> By *Astracan* over the Snowie Plaines

Retires, or *Bactrian* Sophi from the hornes
Of *Turkish* Crescent, leaves all waste beyond
The Realme of *Aladule*, in his retreate
To *Tauris* or *Casbeen*.   [10.431–36]

It is an image of defeat that underlies the "false glitter" of Satan's
inflated account of his heroic exploit, with its old familiar pomp
again echoing the glories of heaven: "Thrones, Dominations,
Princedoms, Vertues, Powers." But he is answered by that "dismal
universal hiss" as, like Cadmus in Ovid's tale,[8]

His Visage drawn he felt to sharp and spare,
His Armes clung to his Ribs, his Leggs entwining
Each other, till supplanted down he fell
A monstrous Serpent on his Belly prone . . .   [10.511–14]

Supplanted: with sardonic memory of the Latin root, *supplantare*,
"to trip up by the heels." Meanwhile the whole assembly is transformed:

dreadful was the din
Of hissing through the Hall thick swarming now
With complicated monsters, head and taile,
Scorpion and Asp, and *Amphisboena* dire,
Cerastes hornd, *Hydrus*, and *Ellops* drear,
And *Dipsas* (Not so thick swarm'd once the Soil
Bedrop with blood of *Gorgon*, or the Isle
Ophiusa) but still greatest hee the midst,
Now Dragon grown, larger then whom the Sun
Ingenderd in the *Pythian* Vale on slime,
Huge *Python*, and his Power no less he seem'd
Above the rest still to retain . . .   [10.521–32]

The memory of the change of Cadmus and Hermione seems to
have evoked the memory of other Ovidian tales: the story of Perseus' flight over Libya with the dripping head of the Gorgon,
the story of the Python defeated by Apollo, [9] and, with special
relevance, the story of the Cerastae, with its reference to
"Ophiusiaque arva":

Outraged by these impious sacrifices [of guests], fostering Venus
was preparing to desert her cities and her Ophiusian plains; 'but,'
she said, 'wherein have these pleasant regions, wherein have my
cities sinned? What crime is there in them? Rather let this impious

race pay the penalty by exile or by death, or by some punishment
midway betwixt death and exile. And what other can that be than
the penalty of a changed form?' [*Met.* 10.228–34; trans. Miller]

The whole scene of metamorphosis in book 10 evokes the earlier
tale of change that Sin related in Hell, as she told of her transformation from a beauteous shape into that monstrous shape resembling Ovid's Scylla. Thus the themes of Ovidian metamorphosis
tie the middle of book 10 with the ending of book 2, playing an
essential part in the winding up of the action.

But the metamorphosis of Satan and his host here forecasts a
sadder change, as the planets change their motions to "noxious
efficacie" and "synod unbenigne" and earth begins its stormy
changes:

> Now from the North
> Of *Norumbega*, and the *Samoed* shoar
> Bursting thir brazen Dungeon, armd with ice
> And snow and haile and stormie gust and flaw,
> *Boreas* and *Caecias* and *Argestes* loud
> And *Thrascias* rend the Woods and Seas upturn . . .
>
> [10.695–700]

So from discord in the winds and seasons we move on to see the
beasts devouring one another, "to graze the Herb all leaving," and
from there to the center of this discord, Adam, where he now lies
"in a troubl'd Sea of passion tost," as Satan once lay confounded
upon that burning lake.

With Adam's "complaint" (a set piece in the tradition of Ovid's
Heroides or the tormented soliloquies of the *Metamorphoses*)[10] the
third panel of the book begins, at line 720, and concludes with the
scene of penitence almost 400 lines later. This panel of redemption matches the first in style and theme, but greatly exceeds it in
length and in dramatic power. First we watch the workings of
Adam's free will as he makes his way through all his questions and
excuses toward a reasoned conclusion utterly different from that
reached in Satan's soliloquy of book 4 ("Evil, be thou my Good"),
for Adam's reason brings him, by relentless facing of the facts, to
the conviction of his own guilt:

> Him after all Disputes
> Forc't I absolve: all my evasions vain
> And reasonings, though through Mazes, leads me still

> But to my own conviction: first and last
> On mee, mee onely, as the sourse and spring
> Of all corruption, all the blame lights due;
> So might the wrauth.   [10.828–34]

Then follows that reconciliation of Adam and Eve, so well explained by Tillyard and Summers.[11] Now Adam, unlike the Adam at the opening of book 9, holds firm control. His power of reason now makes the right choices, refusing Eve's suggestions that they remain childless, or commit suicide. He chooses trust in God, patience, and the better fortitude of using their creative powers to offset the changed conditions of life:

>   such Fire to use,
> And what may else be remedie or cure
> To evils which our own misdeeds have wrought,
> Hee will instruct us praying, and of Grace
> Beseeching him, so as we need not fear
> To pass commodiously this life, sustain'd
> By him with many comforts, till we end
> In dust, our final rest and native home.   [10.1078–85]

The relatively simple language of this ending represents the state of "humiliation meek" that Adam and Eve have reached. The entire final panel shows not a single epic simile, not a single overt classical allusion. Reason, acting under grace, needs no such aids from ancient epic. Even the element of latinity is considerably reduced: there is plenty of the latinity normal to the writing of a renaissance humanist, but there is none of that sense of inflated style caused by pompous latinisms and strained inversions. The mode of the ancient complaint is turned into a rigorous self-examination, leading to confession of guilt, while at the very close an elaborate expansion of the classical rhetoric of repetition is turned into an emphasis upon the "contrite heart" of Psalm 51:[12]

> What better can we do, then to the place
> Repairing where he judg'd us, prostrate fall
> Before him reverent, and there confess
> Humbly our faults, and pardon beg, with tears
> Watering the ground, and with our sighs the Air
> Frequenting, sent from hearts contrite, in sign
> Of sorrow unfeign'd, and humiliation meek . . .
>   So spake our Father penitent, nor *Eve*
> Felt less remorse: they forthwith to the place

Repairing where he judg'd them prostrate fell
Before him reverent, and both confess'd
Humbly their faults, and pardon beg'd, with tears
Watering the ground, and with thir sighs the Air
Frequenting, sent from hearts contrite, in sign
Of sorrow unfeign'd, and humiliation meek.
                              [10.1086–92,1097–1104]

The technique of repetition may remind us of an earlier example, more intricately composed, with reversal and a rounded insistence on the word "sweet"—Eve's great love-song to Adam in book 4 (641–56). The less artful, more straightforward repetitions here may suggest a different state of mind—an awareness of a higher love without which life could not be endured.

Yet they have still much to learn. Adam's hope to pass this life "commodiously" must be qualified by the bitter scenes of misery to follow in the closing books, while his assumption that they will find their "final rest" in the dust must be altered to belief that an immortal home with God is still open to those who rightly choose.

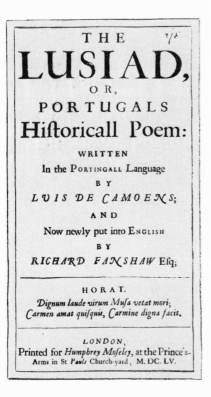

THE LUSIAD, OR, PORTUGALS Hiftoricall Poem:

WRITTEN

In the PORTINGALL Language

BY

LVIS DE CAMOENS;

AND

Now newly put into ENGLISH

BY

RICHARD FANSHAW Efq;

HORAT.

Dignum laude virum Mufa vetat mori;
Carmen amat quifquis, Carmine digna facit.

LONDON,
Printed for Humphrey Mofeley, at the Prince's-
Arms in St Pauls Church-yard, M. DC. LV.

CHAPTER 9

"A Poem Written in Ten Books"

If we share Addison's view that book 10 represents "the winding up of the action," it seems almost inevitable that the remainder of the poem will turn to aftermath and epilogue. But I cannot agree with Prince that in reading long poems and novels we are bound to experience a flagging of interest in "the last stretch."[1] At least, the *Aeneid* and the *Lusiad* do not seem to me to end in this way, nor do *Tom Jones*, *Ulysses*, and *The Wings of the Dove*. Some better explanation or defence of Milton's ending must be found—and many have been offered, effectively explaining the theological design that underlies this ending.[2] But these explanations do not often touch upon the problem of the lowered style, so low in places that Milton seems to become almost an ordinary versifier of biblical history.

It is a gradual lowering, for there is no sudden falling-off in the grandeur and force of Milton's high style. The first half of book 11, up through the grand roll call of empires, shows Milton's poetical powers at their strongest; but gradually, with the visions and responses in the latter half of book 11, and then for most of book 12, the style works downward, with occasional flashes of power, until in the last twenty-five lines the grand style reappears in all its sinuous complexity and power.

Like many other readers, I expressed, in *The Paradise Within*, considerable disappointment with Milton's performance in his finale, and I do not now wish wholly to retract that adverse view, although the present chapter and the next will suggest several different ways of approaching these problems. That adverse view, contained in tempered, chastened form within the next chapter, may at least help to clarify the reasons why so many readers have expressed such disappointment, beginning with Dryden and Addison.[3] But, as always, it is unwise to be severe with Milton: he has a way of defeating all his critics. It now seems likely to me that this lowered style is designed to create a number of ironical contrasts in the context of literary tradition. First, a contrast with the military action in the last book of the *Aeneid*. Next, a contrast, enforced by an ironical parallel in structure, with the history of the rise of Rome that Ovid presents in the closing books of the *Metamorphoses*, a contrast in particular with the inflated style that Ovid uses in his last, fifteenth book, as he praises the glories of Augustan Rome. And thirdly, a contrast with the last, tenth book of an epic strongly influenced by Ovid: the *Lusiad* of Camoens, where the tenth book is devoted to delineating the past and future glories of the Portuguese empire.

Reserving discussion of Ovid's example for a later section, I should like to turn first to the analogies that seem to exist between the *Lusiad* and *Paradise Lost*. These analogies may take on added strength when we recall that Richard Fanshawe's translation, *The Lusiad, or, Portugals Historicall Poem*, the first of many English versions, appeared in London in 1655. We may well believe that this translation would have caught the attention of Milton, for several reasons. It was issued by the same publisher, Humphrey Moseley, who had published Milton's minor poems in 1645. Milton had been for many years a strong admirer of Tasso, and Fanshawe at the outset of his dedication stresses Tasso's admiration for the poem: "for he was heard to say (his great *Jerusalem* being then an Embrio) *He feared no man but Camoens*: Notwithstanding which, he bestow'd a Sonet in his praise." And, most important, Milton was at this very time embarking upon the sustained composition of his own epic, the fulfillment of the great work that he had been contemplating from his youth.

But the epic on the Fall of Man that appeared at last in 1667 was far different from the poem that Milton had envisioned in his early years. From many indications it is clear that Milton originally hoped to write a patriotic epic on a British theme—something to do with Britain's legendary past or Britain's dimly historical kings. In the Trinity manuscript Milton had jotted down, at about the age of thirty, no less than thirty-three different subjects from British legend or history as possible topics for tragedy or, in at least one case, for "A Heroicall Poem" on the subject of King Alfred.[4] In 1639, in his Latin poem written to Manso, Tasso's patron, Milton wrote of his hope that he might "recall in song my native kings, and Arthur setting wars in motion even beneath the earth."[5] Then a year later, in the Latin elegy upon the death of his friend Diodati, he expressed at length a similar hope, mentioning several ancient British legends and vowing that his pastoral pipe "shall be left dangling on some old pine tree far away and quite forgotten by me; or else, quite changed, you shall shrill forth a British theme to your native Muses."[6] And in 1641, in *The Reason of Church-government*, he wrote the famous passage in which he tells of all his many poetical hopes and plans—including his hopes of writing an epic on a national theme.[7]

We can see, then, why the *Lusiad* might hold a natural appeal for the young Milton. But we have no external evidence that Milton actually read the *Lusiad*, in Fanshawe's version or in any other form. All we can say is that in view of Milton's remarkable command of languages, including Latin, French, Italian, and Spanish, it seems likely that he could have made his way through the original. And in any case, long before Fanshawe's version appeared, there were available to Milton translations of the poem into Spanish, and even into Latin. As an omnivorous reader, and as a poet especially concerned with the patriotic, historical epic, Milton, I believe, could hardly have been prevented from reading this poem praised by Tasso.

We do, however, have evidence of another kind, and it lies in *Paradise Lost* itself.[8] Milton's interest in the subject of the Portuguese epic is reflected in the allusions to African places associated with Portuguese voyages and conquests, in the middle of the enormous catalogue of empires that Milton presents in book 11:

> *Mombaza*, and *Quiloa*, and *Melind*,
> And *Sofala* thought *Ophir*, to the Realme
> Of *Congo*, and *Angola* fardest South . . .   [11.399–401]

And then there are the two great similes referring to those who voyage round "the *Cape of Hope*," "Close sailing from *Bengala*, or the Iles / Of *Ternate* and *Tidore*" (2.636–42,4.159–65).

But by far the most interesting evidence lies in the fact that Milton first published his poem in 1667 as "A Poem Written in Ten Books." Seven years later, for the second edition, Milton gave his poem the Vergilian number of books by the simple expedient of dividing the two longest, 7 and 10, into two books apiece. This redivision was so easy to perform, and Milton's aim to emulate Vergil is so clear throughout the first two books, that we inevitably wonder why Milton ever produced his poem with ten books in the first place. Indeed, the symmetry of dividing the poem into two halves of six books apiece, after Vergil's model, leaps to the eye and is strongly enforced by Milton's prologue to the seventh book, when he says:

> Half yet remaines unsung, but narrower bound
> Within the visible Diurnal Spheare . . .   [7.21–22]

And it is approximately half the poem in number of lines and pages. Yet in 1667 Milton chose to present the second half in an asymmetrical division into four books. This deliberate violation of the obvious Vergilian expectation suggests that Milton, after all those many years of planning his epic, must have had some compelling design in mind when he offered us this poem in ten books.

Several suggestions have been made. First, that the ten books imply some kind of five-act division, according to the epic theories of the time—two books per act.[9] It is true that the first four books of Milton's poem fall very neatly into two acts of two books each. But thereafter the division becomes more and more uneven. Books 7 and 8 (1667), according to this theory, ought to form the fourth act, but in fact these books are not paired; they are clearly

Paradise loft.

A
POEM

N: Cooke
Coll: Regal: Soc:
1738

John Lucius Dampier the gift of
Mary Cooke
1835, Written in

TEN BOOKS

By JOHN MILTON.

Licenfed and Entred according
to Order.

LONDON

Printed, and are to be fold by *Peter Parker*
under *Creed* Church neer *Aldgate*; And by
Robert Boulter at the *Turks Head* in *Bifhopfgate-ftreet*;
And *Matthias Walker*, under St. *Dunftons* Church
in *Fleet-ftreet*, 1667.

split off from each other by the great prologue to book 8 (1667) in which Milton says that he must change his notes to tragic and treat of

> foul distrust, and breach
> Disloyal on the part of Man, revolt,
> And disobedience: On the part of Heav'n
> Now alienated, distance and distaste,
> Anger and just rebuke, and judgement giv'n,
> That brought into this World a world of woe,
> Sinne and her shadow Death, and Miserie
> Deaths Harbinger . . .   [9.6–13]

Thus the five-act structure suggested at the outset has been dissolved, just as the latent twelve-book division has been dissolved.

Perhaps Milton's rejection of Homeric or Vergilian divisions is a way of expressing his rejection of traditional epic themes, a way of implying that his poem has an utterly different mode of inspiration and hence of organization. But why then ten books? Why not thirteen, or seventeen, or any untraditional number? But Milton could never be so untraditional. I believe that certain scholars are right in arguing that Milton saw a special significance in the number ten, which was in ancient theory regarded as the perfect number.[10] At the same time the division into ten books would serve to suggest that we are to compare this poem with certain epics of the Renaissance, Tasso's epic in twenty cantos, or the epic of Camoens in ten cantos. Indeed, the *Lusiad* is the only important epic before *Paradise Lost* that was thus divided into ten parts; hence it seems possible that the appearance of Fanshawe's translation in 1655 may have had some influence upon Milton's decision to issue his poem with a ten-book division.

In any case, it is essential to notice that in both the *Lusiad* and *Paradise Lost* (1667) the tenth book is the longest book of the poem, and in each epic this final book consists mainly of visions and descriptions of the future course of history: for Camoens the glorious history of Portuguese conquest after da Gama, for Milton, the sad history of the human race after the Fall. The ironical significance of this parallel was long ago pointed out by Bowra, when he noted the place-names that evoked the memory of Portuguese conquests in Milton's catalogue in book 11. In particular Bowra notes the echo of Camoens's line "De Quiloa, de Mombaça, e de Sofala" (*Lusiad,* 1, st.54) in Milton's line *"Mombaza,* and *Quiloa,* and *Melind"* (11.399). And he then sums up the meaning of this parallel: the world that da Gama sees

> is to be in some sense the heritage of the Portuguese; it is at least the scene of many of their glorious exploits. The world which Adam sees belongs to all mankind, and while the rolling names show how great a possession it is, they are only a preliminary to the dismal history that follows. For Milton, as for Camoens, geography has its romance, but, so far from finding satisfaction in the great world which lies before him, Adam is called to see what havoc his descendants will make of it and what a need there is for real devotion and courage.[11]

That is, for a kind of devotion and courage quite different from the qualities displayed by the great explorers and conquerors, "hitherto the onely Argument Heroic deem'd."

We should note a further detail which will reinforce the truth of Bowra's view. This prophecy by Camoens, like the final view of human history in *Paradise Lost,* is divided into two parts: one presented in narrative and the other presented in vision. In Camoens's tenth book a nymph first narrates in song the exploits of the Portuguese heroes; then the queen of the nymphs takes da Gama and his followers up to the top of a high mountain, and there, using a strange model of the universe, shows to them the vast regions of the earth that lie open for Portuguese exploration.[12] Milton has reversed the order of vision and narration, but the two-part division of this finale suggests a pointed parallel, particularly when we consider one important aspect of the *Lusiad's* final book. Perhaps the most striking aspect of Camoens's technique here lies in his sonorous, magical roll of geographical names: exotic names that evoke the mystery and lure of the East, beckoning the conqueror on with the promise of both glory and material reward. As the place-names roll forth, stanza after stanza, Camoens creates the impression of the vast, wondrous, inexhaustible variety of the earth that still remains to be won (I quote from Fanshawe's version, where the old typography gives the place-names a special prominence):

> See the *Cape* call'd of old AROMATA,
> But GUARDAFU which now the *Dwellers* call;

Where the RED-SEA (so famous) doth Embay,
Dy'd with her Bottome's shade! This is the *Wall*
Or running *Boundarie*, which ASIA
Divides from AFFRICK: And the principal
    Cities, that on the *Affrick-side* are seen,
    Are ARCHICHO, MACUA, and (chief) SUANQUEN.   [st.97]

See *heer*, where *Nature* prodigall hath bin,
The *Kingdom* of ULCINDE; and the long
Bay of JAQUETE, where the Waves flow in
With speed incredible, as fast out-throng!
CAMBAYA see, where this *Gulph* doth begin,
In *wealth* and *people* infinite and strong!   [st.106]

Behold the City of TAVAY, with which
The spatious *Empire* of SIAN begins!
TENESSERI! QUEDA: with pepper rich
For which the praise she from all other wins!
MALACCA see before, where *ye* shall pitch
Your great *Emporium*, and your *Magazins* . . .   [st.123]

Through all these *Orientall* Seas behold,
Sown infinite of *Isles* that have no name!
TIDORE see! TERNATE, whence are roll'd
(Holding black *Night* a Torch) thick *Plumes* of *Flame*!   [st.132]

Such lists of names have of course a strong precedent in Hesiod, Homer, and Vergil, and especially in Ovid; nevertheless, the placing of certain Portuguese conquests in the middle of Milton's heroic catalogue seems to evoke the glorious prediction of Camoens, along with Greek and Roman models.

His Eye might there command wherever stood
City of old or modern Fame, the Seat
Of mightiest Empire, from the destind Walls
Of *Cambalu*, seat of *Cathaian Can*
And *Samarchand* by *Oxus*, *Temirs* Throne.
To *Paquin* of *Sinoean* Kings, and thence
To *Agra* and *Lahor* of great *Mogul*
Down to the golden *Chersonese*, or where
The *Persian* in *Ecbatan* sate, or since
In *Hispahan*, or where the *Russian Ksar*
In *Mosco*, or the Sultan in *Bizance*,
Turchestan-born; nor could his eye not ken
Th' Empire of *Negus* to his utmost Port
Ercoco and the less Maritine Kings
Mombaza, and *Quiloa*, and *Melind* . . .   [11.385–99]

Then, with a terrible irony, Milton spreads out before Adam, by vision and narration, the fearful story of mankind's misdeeds, beginning with the sin of Cain. Among these horrors, the exploits of the military conquerors rank high:

> Where Cattel pastur'd late, now scatterd lies
> With Carcasses and Arms th' ensanguind Field
> Deserted: Others to a Citie strong
> Lay Siege, encampt; by Batterie, Scale, and Mine,
> Assaulting; others from the Wall defend
> With Dart and Jav'lin, Stones and sulfurous Fire;
> On each hand slaughter and gigantic deeds . . .
> *Adam* was all in tears, and to his guide
> Lamenting turnd full sad; O what are these,
> Deaths Ministers, not Men, who thus deal Death
> Inhumanly to men, and multiply
> Ten thousand fould the sin of him who slew
> His Brother; for of whom such massacher
> Make they but of thir Brethren, men of men?
> [11.653–59,674–80]

Are these the "nobler sights" that have been promised (11.411)? But Milton has a further irony in store: the truly noble sights are those that hint of man's possible salvation even in the midst of such horrors, a possibility represented by the appearance of figures such as Enoch, Noah, Moses, and Abraham, and finally, by the narration of the birth and death of Christ. These are the nobler sights that Michael will reveal for the purpose of teaching Adam the lesson that he learns at the very close:

> Henceforth I learne, that to obey is best,
> And love with feare the onely God, to walk
> As in his presence, ever to observe
> His providence, and on him sole depend . . .   [12.561–64]

The contrast, then, between the final books of these two poems has a powerful function. For Milton seems to be saying here that all the hopes of the Renaissance as suggested by Tasso, or Camoens, or Spenser were illusory: especially the hope that a single great nation might lead the world toward true Christian greatness, the hope that Milton himself, in 1644, expressed in a famous passage of his *Areopagitica*:

> Lords and Commons of England, consider what Nation it is
> wherof ye are, and wherof ye are the governours: a Nation not slow
> and dull, but of a quick, ingenious, and piercing spirit, acute to
> invent, suttle and sinewy to discours, not beneath the reach of any
> point the highest that human capacity can soar to. . . . Why else
> was this Nation chos'n before any other, that out of her as out of
> *Sion* should be proclam'd and sounded forth the first tidings and
> trumpet of Reformation to all *Europ*. . . . Now once again by all
> concurrence of signs, and by the generall instinct of holy and de-
> vout men . . . God is decreeing to begin some new and great
> period in his Church, ev'n to the reforming of Reformation it self:
> what does he then but reveal Himself to his servants, and as his
> manner is, first to his English-men . . .[13]

It was, presumably, upon this hope that Milton based his early
plans for a national epic of England that would be "doctrinal and
exemplary" to a nation of such a destiny—a poem that might do
for England what Camoens had done for the history of his own
small seafaring nation. But it could not be done, after the failure
of the Puritan Commonwealth had broken Milton's faith in national glory and military power. Viewed in the context of Camoens's epic, Milton's tenth book in 1667 represents a bitter
commentary upon his own earlier hopes and the hopes of the
Renaissance. Milton's epic, and especially the last book of his epic,
constitutes a fulfillment of the bitter lament of the old man at the
close of Camoens's fourth canto, that lament and denunciation
uttered as da Gama's fleet sets sail:

> Oh, the folly of it, this craving for power, this thirsting after the
> vanity we call fame, this fraudulent pleasure known as honour that
> thrives on popular esteem! When the vapid soul succumbs to its
> lure, what a price it exacts, and how justly, in perils, tempests,
> torments, death itself! It wrecks all peace of soul and body, leads
> men to forsake and betray their loved ones, subtly yet undeniably
> consumes estates, kingdoms, empires. Men call it illustrious, and
> noble, when it merits instead the obloquy of infamy; they call it
> fame, and sovereign glory, mere names with which the common
> people delude themselves in their ignorance . . . O unhappy race,
> true heirs of that madman, whose sin and disobedience not only
> doomed you to gloomy exile from paradise but drove you from that
> other divine state of simple, tranquil innocence, the golden age,
> condemning you in its place to this age of iron and instruments of
> destruction! [4.st.95–98, trans. Atkinson][14]

Nevertheless, as this passage shows, the difference between the epic of Portuguese conquest and the epic of the Fall of Man is far from absolute. The great power of each epic lies in the fact that each can include its opposite. Thus Milton makes his Satan so attractively heroic in the first two books of *Paradise Lost* that many readers since the time of Blake have felt that Satan was the true hero of the poem;[15] and in the same complex fashion, Camoens's poem gains strength from the recognition that the achievements it sets out to celebrate may be corrupted in their very enactment.

Each poet's method is particularly clear in the seventh book of his epic, where the arrival at a land of promise is flanked on either side by warnings of possible or certain failure to make proper use of that promise. The seventh canto of the *Lusiad* relates the longed-for arrival at India, the completion of the heroic voyage and the beginning of Portugal's empire:

> And now land was close at hand, the land so many others had longed to reach, that lay between the Ganges, sprung from the earthly paradise, and the Indus. Take courage, my brave men, who have set your hearts on the victor's palm. You have arrived: the land of wealth abounding lies before you. [7.st.1; p.161]

Yet the glorious promise of the arrival has already been qualified at the very end of canto 6, as the poet warns that a special kind of hero and a special kind of virtue are required to make the proper use of this achievement:

> Their goal is such honours as their stout right arm may win them and they may justly call their own. Ever on guard, girt with tempered steel, exposed to storms and tempestuous seas . . . it is thus that there is bred in the human breast a callous, ennobling contempt for honours and wealth, the honours and wealth that come by fortune's whim and not as the reward of virtue and endurance. It is thus that, with understanding deepened and matured by experience, there are revealed to one, as from a commanding eminence, all the pettiness and futility of ordinary life. [6.st.97–99; pp.159–60]

Then stanzas 4–14 of the seventh canto itself are given over to a furious denunciation of all the other nations of Europe for fighting one another, instead of conquering the infidel. Only Portugal, through such voyages as those of da Gama, has overcome the folly of all the rest of Europe: "Madmen that you are, thirsting in your blindness for the blood of your own! But here at least, in this small land of Portugal, there will not lack those who will do and dare for Christendom" (7.st.14; p.163). One may well feel the danger that even Portugal's best may not be able to overcome the folly of other Christians.

Then, after the wonders and treacheries of Calicut have been revealed, at the very close of the seventh canto, Camoens breaks off abruptly to utter a lament on the unhappy plight of the poet himself, plagued by poverty and injustice, and showing now a full awareness of the corruption that has already beset the Portuguese empire:

> And still, O Nymphs, it was not enough that I should be hounded by such an enormity of woes. It remained for me to see my verses rewarded as they were by those whose deeds I sang. Where I had looked for leisure and laurel wreaths, they found me instead new refinements of toil and condemned me to an existence harsher than before.
>
> Reflect, Nymphs, on what a breed of stalwarts it is your Tagus nurtures, that are incapable of higher esteem than this, or other favours, for him who gives them glory through his song . . .
>
> Fear not, Muses, that I shall sing the grave and honest-seeming man who accepts office at his monarch's instance, only thereafter to rob and despoil the poor; nor the man who holds it right and just that royal decrees should be observed with all severity, yet will admit neither the fairness nor the considerateness of paying the worker for the sweat of his brow; nor him who, lacking a fund of experience, would base a claim to prudence on the ingenuity of his grounds for taxing with greedy rapacity the labours of others, from which he stands aside. [7.st.81–86; pp.176–77]

It is clear now that da Gama's band constituted a rare breed, achieving an ideal of heroic action that their successors have found difficult to maintain. And lest we misunderstand the idealized nature of the vision of empire represented in the tenth canto, the poet at the very close reveals his deep dejection and his prayer of hope that the king will, in spite of all bad auguries, achieve a further action of the honorable fame that this poem celebrates:

> And now, my Muse, let there be an end: for my lyre is no longer attuned and my voice grows hoarse, not from my song but

from seeing that those to whom I sing are become hard of hearing and hard of heart. This country of mine is made over to lusting greed, its sense of values eclipsed in an austerity of gloom and depression: there is no longer to be had from it that recognition which fans the flame of genius as nothing else can. And I know not by what turn of destiny it should have lost the sense of joyous pride and pervasive pleasure that buoys up man's spirit to face toils and travails with unfailing cheerfulness.

I appeal to you, my King, who occupy your throne in further-ance of the divine will. Look round at other peoples and reflect on the excellence of these vassals who call you their lord . . .

Prepared for any sacrifice in your service, unswerving in obedi-ence to their so distant king, receiving with a ready and unquestion-ing alacrity your every command, however harsh: with the knowl-edge that your eye is upon them they will attack in your name the very devils of hell, and I doubt not but they will make you the victor, not the vanquished, in the struggle. [10.st.145–48; p.247]

Thus the poet's voice in the *Lusiad* casts a sombre doubt upon the very exploits he has celebrated. In the same way, the poet's voice in *Paradise Lost* places the beginning of man's life amid the gloomiest of predictions. Book 7 of *Paradise Lost*, in its original version, presents Milton's account of the beauties of the new Crea-tion, including Adam and Eve, newly formed. But at the begin-ning and the end of this account of the entire Creation, Milton has placed his sombre view of his own life and the world he knows. The prologue to book 8 (1667) declares: "I now must change / Those Notes to Tragic." The prologue to book 7 is also potentially tragic in its view of the poet's personal situation, blind, sur-rounded by enemies, and living in grave danger after the fall of the Commonwealth: yet the poet can still address his Heavenly Muse, while recalling an ominous Ovidian tale:

> Standing on Earth, not rapt above the Pole,
> More safe I Sing with mortal voice, unchang'd
> To hoarce or mute, though fall'n on evil dayes,
> On evil dayes though fall'n, and evil tongues;
> In darkness, and with dangers compast round,
> And solitude; yet not alone, while thou
> Visit'st my slumbers Nightly, or when Morn
> Purples the East: still govern thou my Song,
> *Urania*, and fit audience find, though few.
> But drive farr off the barbarous dissonance

> Of *Bacchus* and his Revellers, the Race
> Of that wilde Rout that tore the *Thracian* Bard
> In *Rhodope*, where Woods and Rocks had Eares
> To rapture, till the savage clamor dround
> Both Harp and Voice; nor could the Muse defend
> Her Son. So fail not thou, who thee implores:
> For thou art Heav'nlie, shee an empty dreame.   [7.23–39]

The voice of the bard, full of trouble and hope and personal opinion, thus plays an essential part in the meaning and in the success of both these epics. For in each the poet stands forth as the representative of an ideal, spoken by a human being who has suffered the woes of mankind and who yet believes that man can overcome his woe.[16] Thus in the tenth canto of the *Lusiad* we hear the poet's voice:

> And here, Calliope, in this my final labour, I invoke your aid again. Grant me, I beseech of you, in return for what I now seek to write, and seek perhaps in vain, that I may recover the joy of writing, that is beginning to fail me. The years are closing in about me, and soon summer must give way to autumn. Fate's chill hand is descending on my muse, that I no longer boast of with pride, nor can even rely upon. The buffetings of fortune sweep me on towards the dark river of oblivion and eternal sleep. Enable me, great Queen of the Muses, still to accomplish my desire towards my native land. [10.st.8–9; p.219]

So too, in *Paradise Lost*, we hear the voice of the bard speaking at the outset of his eighth book (1667), as he scorns the military trappings of earlier epics:

> The skill of Artifice or Office mean,
> Not that which justly gives Heroic name
> To Person or to Poem. Mee of these
> Nor skilld nor studious, higher Argument
> Remaines, sufficient of it self to raise
> That name, unless an age too late, or cold
> Climat, or Years damp my intended wing
> Deprest, and much they may, if all be mine,
> Not Hers who brings it nightly to my Ear.   [9.39–47]

In this combination of suffering and hope, anguish at mankind's failures and faith in his own version of heroic virtue, the poet creates an epic in which he becomes an actor in his own poem and himself becomes, in his own way, an example of true heroic fortitude.

CHAPTER 10

Trials
of Faith

The parallels that the preceding chapter has drawn between the
final books of *Paradise Lost* and the *Lusiad* may help us toward a
clearer understanding of the lower style that Milton has chosen to
follow in his ending. For Milton's lowered style refuses to be
heroic: the style itself scorns the distentions of empire and leads
toward the firm and quiet closing words of Adam and the angel:

> Henceforth I learne, that to obey is best,
> And love with feare the onely God, to walk
> As in his presence, ever to observe
> His providence, and on him sole depend,
> Merciful over all his works, with good
> Still overcoming evil, and by small
> Accomplishing great things, by things deemd weak
> Subverting worldly strong, and worldly wise
> By simply meek;
> . . . .
> This having learnt, thou hast attained the summe
> Of wisdom; hope no higher, though all the Starrs
> Thou knewst by name, and all th' ethereal Powers,
> All secrets of the deep, all Natures works,
> Or works of God in Heav'n, Air, Earth, or Sea,
> And all the riches of this World enjoydst,
> And all the rule, one Empire . . .   [12.561–69,575–81]

Thus the theological design should work hand in hand with the poetical, stylistic design, perhaps after the manner suggested by John Dryden in 1682, in his preface to *Religio Laici*:

> The Expressions of a Poem, design'd purely for Instruction, ought to be Plain and Natural, and yet Majestick: for here the Poet is presum'd to be a kind of Law-giver, and those three qualities which I have nam'd are proper to the Legislative style. The Florid, Elevated and Figurative way is for the Passions; for Love and Hatred, Fear and Anger, are begotten in the Soul by shewing their Objects out of their true proportion; either greater than the Life, or less; but Instruction is to be given by shewing them what they naturally are. A Man is to be cheated into Passion, but to be reason'd into Truth.[1]

What Milton has achieved in the passages just quoted seems to be something very close to what Dryden here calls "the Legislative style"—a manner that is "Plain and Natural, and yet Majestick," a style that avoids the cheats of passion and attempts to reason Adam and his descendants into truth. Elsewhere, the style at times becomes florid and elevated, when Adam is shown those scenes that stir his horror, fear, or delight; but the legislative explanations of his divine instructor always follow to reveal the cheat and show what these things naturally are, by reason and by theological truth.

The clue to the theological design[2] is given in book 11 with the opening words of "the Father, without Cloud, serene":

> I at first with two fair gifts
> Created him endowd, with Happiness
> And Immortalitie: that fondly lost,
> This other serv'd but to eternize woe;
> Till I provided Death; so Death becomes
> His final remedie, and after Life
> Tri'd in sharp tribulation, and refin'd
> By Faith and faithful works, to second Life,
> Wak't in the renovation of the just,
> Resignes him up with Heav'n and Earth renewd.   [11.57–66]

Death thus becomes a benefit, not only a penalty, since death ends all woe for the just man and "resignes him up"—that is, releases him, into a second life in the new heaven and new earth prophesied in the second epistle of Peter (3:13). But this will happen only after a life tested ("tri'd") in sharp tribulation, and purified ("refin'd") by "Faith and faithful works." Mankind is to be "justified," in the protestant sense, by faith, accompanied by works flowing from faith, works of love and gratitude.

In this mingled tone of severity and mercy, the Father then calls upon Michael to "drive out the sinful Pair" from Paradise "without remorse"—but he adds an instruction that sets forth a temperate and merciful mode of banishment:

> Yet least they faint
> At the sad Sentence rigorously urg'd,
> For I behold them soft'nd and with tears
> Bewailing thir excess, all terror hide.
> If patiently thy bidding they obey,
> Dismiss them not disconsolate; reveale
> To *Adam* what shall come in future dayes,
> As I shall thee enlighten, intermix
> My Cov'nant in the Womans seed renewd;
> So send them forth, though sorrowing, yet in peace . . .
>   [11.108–17]

Certainly Adam's restored faith needs tempering, for he sees the process of salvation as lacking all bitterness and tribulation:

> *Eve*, easily may Faith admit, that all
> The good which we enjoy, from Heav'n descends
> But that from us ought should ascend to Heav'n
> So prevalent as to concerne the mind
> Of God high-blest, or to incline his will,
> Hard to belief may seem; yet this will Prayer,
> Or one short sigh of humane breath, up-borne
> Ev'n to the Seat of God. For since I saught
> By Prayer th' offended Deitie to appease,
> Kneel'd and before him humbl'd all my heart,
> Methought I saw him placable and mild,
> Bending his eare; perswasion in me grew
> That I was heard with favour; peace return'd
> Home to my brest, and to my memorie
> His promise, that thy Seed shall bruise our Foe;
> Which then not minded in dismay, yet now
> Assures me that the bitterness of death
> Is past, and we shall live. Whence Haile to thee
> *Eve* rightly call'd, Mother of all Mankind,
> Mother of all things living, since by thee
> Man is to live, and all things live for Man.   [11.141–61]

The vagueness of Adam's phrasing allows a hope that perhaps the entire penalty has been annulled: that not only the "bitterness" in the process of death is past, but that the threatened death itself has been revoked, "and we shall live," perhaps forever? But the echo of the words of Agag just before his terrible death at the hands of Samuel (I Samuel 15:32–33) shows the bitter fallacy of this easy hope, while the foreshadowing of the Annunciation implies the sorrow and suffering by which man lives.

Eve too picks up the optimistic strain, saying that labor in Paradise can never be onerous:

> while here we dwell,
> What can be toilsom in these pleasant Walkes?
> Here let us live, though in fall'n state, content.   [11.178–80]

Such hopes are quickly dashed by the grim epic omens:

> The Bird of *Jove*, stoopt from his aerie tour,
> Two Birds of gayest plume before him drove:
> Down from a Hill the Beast that reigns in Woods,
> First Hunter then, pursu'd a gentle brace,
> Goodliest of all the Forrest, Hart and Hinde . . .
>
> [11.185–89]

The pitying admiration of the last line here is quite appropriate to the subtle manner in which Michael and his military angels are now presented:

> A glorious Apparition, had not doubt
> And carnal fear that day dimm'd *Adams* eye.
> Not that more glorious, when the Angels met
> *Jacob* in *Mahanaim*, where he saw
> The field Pavilion'd with his Guardians bright;
> Not that which on the flaming Mount appeerd
> In *Dothan*, cover'd with a Camp of Fire,
> Against the *Syrian* King, who to surprize
> One man, Assassin-like had levied Warr,
> Warr unproclam'd.   [11.211–20]

These allusions to the beneficent presence of divine power, as experienced by Jacob and Elisha (Genesis 32:1–2; 2 Kings 6:17), foreshadow Michael's assurance of God's omnipresence, and thus serve proleptically to moderate the effect of horror with which Adam and Eve receive the word of their exile. For the two fall

from the excess of optimism into the excess of despair, Adam
being "Heart-strook with chilling gripe of sorrow," while Eve utters her piercing lament:

> O flours,
> That never will in other Climate grow,
> My early visitation, and my last
> At Eev'n, which I bred up with tender hand
> From the first op'ning bud, and gave ye Names,
> Who now shall reare ye to the Sun, or ranke
> Your Tribes, and water from th' ambrosial Fount?
> Thee lastly nuptial Bowre, by mee adornd
> With what to sight or smell was sweet; from thee
> How shall I part, and whither wander down
> Into a lower World, to this obscure
> And wilde, how shall we breath in other Aire
> Less pure, accustomd to immortal Fruits?   [11.273–85]

The passage is a tissue of ironies, for flowers will grow in that
lower world, and later Eves will breed them up from the first
opening buds, call the flowers by name, place them in rows, and
water them—though not from an ambrosial fount. And botanists
will rank their tribes in the proper species. Other nuptial bowers
will be adorned by other Eves. True, all will be "lower" in excellence, but even now, outside of Paradise, the flowers and shrubs
and trees described in book 7 are awaiting the touch of mankind's
cultivation. Her thoughtless reference to "immortal Fruits" reminds us that it was her "mortal taste" of that forbidden fruit
which now compels her to go forth to gather mortal fruits and
flowers in the lower world.

The tone of the angel's reply to these laments is perfectly tempered: he is firm, but "milde," performing his mission "with regard benigne" (11.286, 334). The poem, it seems, is to end in a
delicate poise, a balance of attitudes, where the sense of loss is
subtly qualified by a sense of gain. Though the chief actors are
condemned to death, we are to sense a restoration of the world to
order, though at heavy cost.

It is such an assurance of restoration that Michael now gives, in
answer to Adam's crushed and hopeless lament for the expected
loss of God's presence:

> This most afflicts me, that departing hence,
> As from his face I shall be hid, depriv'd
> His blessed count'nance; here I could frequent,
> With worship, place by place where he voutsaf'd
> Presence Divine, and to my Sons relate;
> On this Mount he appeerd, under this Tree
> Stood visible, among these Pines his voice
> I heard, here with him at this Fountain talk'd . . .
> In yonder nether World where shall I seek
> His bright appearances, or footstep trace?   [11.315–22,328–29]

As with the earlier allusions to Jacob and Elisha, the phrasing of Adam's lament itself implies the continued presence of God with the sons of Adam: Moses and Elijah will hear the voice of the Lord upon a Mount; the Lord or his angel will appear to Gideon and Zechariah under an oak or myrtle tree; and the woman of Samaria will speak with Jesus as he sits by Jacob's well. Thus Michael assures Adam, in terms of the Augustinian tradition, that the *vestigia*, the traces, the footsteps of God will be everywhere present:

> *Adam*, thou know'st Heav'n his, and all the Earth,
> Not this Rock onely; his Omnipresence fills
> Land, Sea, and Aire, and every kinde that lives,
> Fomented by his virtual power and warmd:
> All th' Earth he gave thee to possess and rule,
> No despicable gift; surmise not then
> His presence to these narrow bounds confin'd
> Of Paradise or *Eden* . . .   [11.335–42]

The power manifested in the original Creation will remain as "virtual power," inward, essential, life-giving power, for Adam and his sons to enjoy:

> Yet doubt not but in Vallie and in Plaine
> God is as here, and will be found alike
> Present, and of his presence many a signe
> Still following thee, still compassing thee round
> With goodness and paternal Love, his Face
> Express, and of his steps the track Divine.   [11.349–54]

"Which that thou mayst beleeve, and be confirmd," the angel adds—invoking the protestant doctrine of confirmation, by which a mature intelligence confirms his faith—[3]

>   know I am sent
> To shew thee what shall come in future dayes
> To thee and to thy Ofspring; good with bad
> Expect to hear, supernal Grace contending
> With sinfulness of Men, thereby to learn
> True patience, and to temper joy with fear
> And pious sorrow . . .   [11.355–62]

Such is the wholly benevolent aim of the scenes to follow.

II

As Adam now ascends the hill to see the visions of the future,
Milton skillfully brings in the means of redemption, through alluding to Christ's temptation in the wilderness and using an ambiguous syntax that for a time allows us to see the kingdoms of the
world through the eyes of both the second Adam and the first:[4]

> Not higher that Hill nor wider looking round,
> Whereon for different cause the Tempter set
> Our second *Adam* in the Wilderness,
> To shew him all Earths Kingdomes and thir Glory.
> His Eye might there command wherever stood
> City of old or modern Fame, the Seat
> Of mightiest Empire . . .   [11.381–87]

And so for over twenty lines we have the gorgeous roll of names,
with Milton manifesting all the power of his high style, recalling in
one final burst of grandeur the epic panoply of the opening book.
And all to excellent purpose here: for, as the allusion to the second Adam indicates, these are all "glories" of the fallen world, as
they were in book 1, though we were then inclined to place their
worth higher, despite their setting in the flames of Hell. The
obvious excess of the grand roll of empires here carries the mind
back through the whole poem to the building of Pandaemonium
and the roll call of fallen angels, and makes a deliberate judgment
of those "heroic" scenes: "but to nobler sights / *Michael* from
Adams eyes the Filme remov'd" (11.411–12).

We know what those nobler sights will be: sights that prove the
constant presence of God in the world of men, his "goodness and
paternal Love"—although Michael has also warned Adam to ex-

pect a mixture of "good with bad," as divine grace contends with man's sinfulness. Nevertheless, the first vision creates an effect of shock, in us, in Adam, and in Michael, as the scene of the murder of Abel is expanded with grim details:

> Whereat hee inlie rag'd, and as they talk'd,
> Smote him into the Midriff with a stone
> That beat out life; he fell, and deadly pale
> Groand out his Soul with gushing bloud effus'd.
> Much at that sight was *Adam* in his heart
> Dismai'd, and thus in haste to th' Angel cri'd.
>   O Teacher, some great mischief hath befall'n
> To that meek man, who well had sacrific'd;
> Is Pietie thus and pure Devotion paid?
>   T' whom *Michael* thus, hee also mov'd, repli'd.
> These two are Brethren, *Adam*, and to come
> Out of thy loyns; th' unjust the just hath slain,
> For envie that his Brothers Offering found
> From Heav'n acceptance; but the bloodie Fact
> Will be aveng'd, and th' others Faith approv'd
> Loose no reward, though here thou see him die,
> Rowling in dust and gore. To which our Sire.
>   Alas, both for the deed and for the cause!
> But have I now seen Death? Is this the way
> I must return to native dust? O sight
> Of terrour, foul and ugly to behold,
> Horrid to think, how horrible to feel!   [11.444–65]

That vision may at first seem not quite in accord with God's direction to Michael: "all terror hide," but that direction, it now appears, was meant to apply only to the demeanour of Michael and his military angels: they are not to appear in a terrifying way. But with the visions of human life a sense of terror is required, if faith is to be confirmed. Adam must now believe that the crime will be avenged, "and th' others Faith approv'd / Loose no reward," however horrible his death. For the present, however, Michael's teaching seems to have no effect in diminishing Adam's horror. Nor is Adam's equanimity restored by the grim vision that follows:

>   wherein were laid
> Numbers of all diseas'd, all maladies
> Of gastly Spasm, or racking torture, qualmes

> Of heart-sick Agonie, all feavorous kinds,
> Convulsions, Epilepsies, fierce Catarrhs,
> Intestin Stone and Ulcer, Colic pangs,
> Dropsies, and Asthma's, and Joint-racking Rheums.
>
> [11.479–85]

Such is the scene in Milton's first edition; in the revised edition of 1674 he extended the range and increased the horror by inserting these lines between the last two given above:

> Daemoniac Phrenzie, moaping Melancholie
> And Moon-struck madness, pining Atrophie,
> Marasmus, and wide-wasting Pestilence . . .

It is powerfully done; no wonder Adam weeps and cries out in anguish, asking why life should be given on these terms, and why the Image of God should be subjected to such deformities. But the appalling effectiveness of the scene receives from Michael a sharp didactic explanation that is hard to square with human experience, which tells us that many temperate men suffer the kinds of painful illness above described:

> Thir Makers Image, answerd *Michael*, then
> Forsook them, when themselves they villifi'd
> To serve ungovern'd appetite, and took
> His Image whom they serv'd, a brutish vice,
> Inductive mainly to the sin of *Eve*.
> Therefore so abject is thir punishment,
> Disfiguring not Gods likeness, but thir own,
> Or if his likeness, by themselves defac't
> While they pervert pure Natures healthful rules
> To loathsom sickness, worthily, since they
> Gods Image did not reverence in themselves.   [11.515–25]

Nevertheless Adam gives the answer proper to faith: "I yield it just, said *Adam*, and submit." He is moving through the process of his confirmation: Milton is writing a theological paradigm of the workings of faith, as his frequent repetition of the word in book 12 makes plain.[5]

Milton's following account of the gradual decline of the temperate man into old age helps to moderate Michael's didactic rigor, but as Milton proceeds into the next vision, where the grave Sons of God are seduced by the "Beavie of fair Women," Michael's tone becomes sententious, harsh, and at the close sarcastic:

For that fair femal Troop thou sawst, that seemd
Of Goddesses, so blithe, so smooth, so gay,
Yet empty of all good wherein consists
Womans domestic honour and chief praise;
Bred onely and completed to the taste
Of lustful appetence, to sing, to dance,
To dress, and troule the Tongue, and roule the Eye.
To these that sober Race of Men, whose lives
Religious titl'd them the Sons of God,
Shall yeild up all thir vertue, all thir fame
Ignobly, to the traines and to the smiles
Of these fair Atheists, and now swim in joy,
(Erelong to swim at larg) and laugh; for which
The world erelong a world of tears must weepe.   [11.614–27]

Meanwhile the promised consolation in the last third of book
11 resides primarily in a series of allusions to the vain attempts of
the "one just Man alive" to stem the tide of evil:

The onely righteous in a World perverse,
And therefore hated, therefore so beset
With Foes for daring single to be just,
And utter odious Truth . . .   [11.701–04]

We may argue that this has been foreshadowed in the figure of
Abdiel, but the parallel, undoubtedly designed with care, serves
here to show how far Milton has departed from his allegory of the
War in Heaven. For in this allegory of the spiritual combat, as
fought from the revolt of the angels until the Day of Doom, Abdiel is indeed the only righteous in the perverse band of Satan—
but he returns to join the two-thirds of the angels that have remained faithful. Milton's just man on earth has no one to join on
earth, for

all shall turn degenerate, all deprav'd,
Justice and Temperance, Truth and Faith forgot;
One Man except, the onely Son of light
In a dark Age . . .   [11.806–09]

In this way life on earth is here explicitly equated with the life of
Satan's host, whereas in the opening books the association of earth
with evil has been developed by implication only: implication that
provides the setting for a redemptive movement. The strict equa-

tion of earth with evil produces an unsettling effect in book 11, a feeling that, somehow, Milton is retreating from his earlier assertions and demonstrations that man's free will suffices to offer the possibility of recovering that paradise within.

But Milton has a careful plan, well explained by Summers when he says that we are to see "this pattern of destruction followed by a new and greater creation."[6] This aim is clearly set forth in the lines that Milton added when he divided the original book 10 into two books:

> As one who in his journey bates at Noone,
> Though bent on speed, so heer the Archangel paus'd
> Betwixt the world destroy'd and world restor'd . . .   [12.1–3]

The symbolical visions of the world of sin, we see, are only half the story: the world of consolation remains. The design is even more strongly emphasized in the Argument to book 12, written after the first edition had appeared:[7]

> *The Angel* Michael *continues from the Flood to relate what shall succeed; then, in the mention of* Abraham, *comes by degrees to explain, who that Seed of the Woman shall be, which was promised* Adam *and* Eve *in the Fall; his Incarnation, Death, Resurrection, and Ascension; the state of the Church till his second Coming.* Adam *greatly satisfied and recomforted by these Relations and Promises descends the Hill with* Michael; *wakens* Eve, *who all this while had slept, but with gentle dreams compos'd to quietness of mind and submission.* Michael *in either hand leads them out of Paradise, the fiery Sword waving behind them, and the Cherubim taking thir Stations to guard the Place.*

What happens in the poetry is something different. First of all, Milton changes the poetic method from vision to narration:

> but I perceave
> Thy mortal sight to faile; objects divine
> Must needs impaire and wearie human sense:
> Henceforth what is to com I will relate . . .   [12.8–11]

The basic reason for the change is perhaps clear enough: the process of redemption through the sacrifice of Christ involves the most complex and controversial of theological issues; to provide adequate explanation Michael must be allowed to enfold the action of history within a carefully woven network of accurate and

precise theology. Thus Milton devotes his last book primarily to a
rational account of the theology of the remnant, as developed by
the protestant reformers under the strong influence of Augustine's later writings on the problem of grace. As the current theology of the remnant begins to dominate the poem's world, its tone
and manner move farther and farther away from the poise and
tempering of attitudes promised by Michael and God at the outset
of book 11.

As a result the effects and proportions implied by the Argument to book 12 are not fulfilled. The last half of the Argument,
with its comforting and reassuring emphasis, describes what happens only in the last hundred lines of this book of 649 lines. And
the first half of the Argument, with its emphasis on the coming of
the "Seed of the Woman," is also greatly out of proportion with
what actually happens in the poem. It is not until line 360 that we
come to the birth of the Messiah, and then his whole career from
Incarnation to Ascension is dealt with in less than a hundred lines,
and these for the most part filled with theological explanation.
Milton declines to represent the gospel story in any kind of extended vision: the chief events are simply mentioned, in lines that
do not amount to more than fifteen in all, of which these are the
most detailed:

> yet at his Birth a Starr
> Unseen before in Heav'n proclaims him com,
> And guides the Eastern Sages, who enquire
> His place, to offer Incense, Myrrh, and Gold;
> His place of birth a solemn Angel tells
> To simple Shepherds, keeping watch by night;
> They gladly thither haste, and by a Quire
> Of squadrond Angels hear his Carol sung.   [12.360–67]

That Carol, we remember, has been sung in Milton's poem by the
angels before the Creation: it is not sung now.

For Milton is not here concerned with celebration or with affectionate meditation: he is "expounding a doctrine," as Madsen has
very well said, and the exposition is admirably performed, in lines
that "have their own kind of intellectual energy":[8]

> The Law of God exact he shall fulfill
> Both by obedience and by love, though love

> Alone fulfill the Law . . .
> For this he shall live hated, be blasphem'd,
> Seis'd on by force, judg'd, and to death condemnd
> A shameful and accurst, naild to the Cross
> By his own Nation, slaine for bringing Life;
> But to the Cross he nailes thy Enemies,
> The Law that is against thee, and the sins
> Of all mankinde, with him there crucifi'd,
> Never to hurt them more who rightly trust
> In this his satisfaction . . .   [12.402–04,411–19]

This abstract account of salvation is set within the section of 550 lines in which Michael tells the sombre history of the world from after the Flood through the Day of Doom: it is a threefold process of corruption and renewal, each part of the process re-enacting the story of the world from the Creation to the Flood. The third cycle closes with Milton's denunciation of the corruptions and persecutions of the Church after the time of the apostles down to the bitter sufferings of the just in Milton's own day and in later ages:

> the rest, farr greater part,
> Will deem in outward Rites and specious formes
> Religion satisfi'd; Truth shall retire
> Bestuck with slandrous darts, and works of Faith
> Rarely be found: so shall the World goe on,
> To good malignant, to bad men benigne,
> Under her own waight groaning, till the day
> Appear of respiration to the just,
> And vengeance to the wicked . . .   [12.533–41]

Book 12 thus presents a twofold problem, both theological and poetical. First, the stern doctrine of the remnant seems to depart from the promise set forth by God himself in book 3, implied in the recovery of Adam and Eve in book 10, set forth again by God at the beginning of book 11, carried on by Michael's words of reassurance to Adam early in book 11, and asserted once more in the Argument to book 12. Grace is freely offered to all—but few will choose to accept that gift. Is this, then, what it means to be placed "on even ground" with Satan, sufficient to have stood, though free to fall? It is a paradox beyond any human explanation, but for Milton, his own experience seems to have proved it true:

> Standing on Earth, not rapt above the Pole,
> More safe I Sing with mortal voice, unchang'd
> To hoarce or mute, though fall'n on evil dayes,
> On evil dayes though fall'n, and evil tongues;
> In darkness, and with dangers compast round,
> And solitude; yet not alone, while thou
> Visit'st my slumbers Nightly, or when Morn
> Purples the East: still govern thou my Song,
> *Urania*, and fit audience find, though few.   [7.23–31]

Looking back now we can see that warnings of this tragic paradox have been given from time to time early in the poem. In book 1, before the catalogue of devils disguised as pagan deities, we heard how these devils wandered "ore the Earth / Through Gods high sufferance for the tryal of man," and how

> By falsities and lyes the greatest part
> Of Mankind they corrupted to forsake
> God their Creator, and th' invisible
> Glory of him, that made them, to transform
> Oft to the Image of a Brute, adorn'd
> With gay Religions full of Pomp and Gold . . .   [1.365–72]

Those religions, for Milton, surely include the pomp and gold of Roman or Laudian ceremony.[9] Thus book 1 foretells the decline of the Church narrated in book 12. Then in book 3, just after the promise of universal grace has been given in Heaven, we come upon that Limbo of Vanity "to few unknown / Long after."

We have been warned—the paradox of mankind's preference for evil over goodness has been with us from the outset of the poem—and yet the power of Adam and Eve's recovery in book 10 is so moving that we are bound to believe that such a choice lies open to all mankind. The resolution of this paradox is made more difficult, not easier, by Milton's insistence upon the doctrine of the freedom of the will as a principle that he cannot bear to renounce. It may well seem, as it sometimes seems to Adam, that only a faulty piece of workmanship or planning on the part of God could have led to such an overwhelming number of wrong choices. Milton's last book forces the cruel paradox upon us.

One is left with a trial of faith.[10] We must regard the survival of the just, few though they may be, as a fulfillment of the divine plan of redemption. The way is open to all. If few choose to follow that way, human beings have only themselves to blame. The theological principle is clear: only those of little or no faith will doubt its justice.

The starkness of the choice here is related to the lowering of style in book 12, as evidenced in the long stretches of biblical paraphrase, where Milton seems to have deliberately withheld his full poetical powers, leaving the facts of biblical history to speak for themselves, without embellishment, except for the web of theological interpretation (as in the emphasis here on the word "Faith"):

> I see him, but thou canst not, with what Faith
> He leaves his Gods, his Friends, and native Soile
> *Ur* of *Chaldoea*, passing now the Ford
> To *Haran*, after him a cumbrous Train
> Of Herds and Flocks, and numerous servitude;
> Not wandring poor, but trusting all his wealth
> With God, who call'd him, in a land unknown.
> *Canaan* he now attains, I see his Tents
> Pitcht about *Sechem*, and the neighbouring Plaine
> Of *Moreh*; there by promise he receaves
> Gift to his Progenie of all that Land . . .   [12.128–38]

By the plain style the plain truth will appear. Such a deliberate humbling of the high style, bringing it gradually down to the lowest range of the "Legislative style," would indeed be congruent with the moral principle expressed by Adam and the angel at the close of the world's history: "by small / Accomplishing great things, by things deemd weak / Subverting worldly strong." To tell of the grandest truth in a humble style may be seen as an act of piety and devotion. The lowering of the style, then, is an act of *ascesis* such as we are to see performed at length in *Paradise Regain'd*. But in book 12 Milton is having some difficulty in thus lowering his style, for there are clumsy, awkward moments:

> the like shall sing
> All Prophecie, That of the Royal Stock
> Of *David* (so I name this King) shall rise
> A Son, the Womans Seed to thee foretold,
> Foretold to *Abraham*, as in whom shall trust
> All Nations, and to Kings foretold, of Kings
> The last, for of his Reign shall be no end.   [12.324–30]

Milton has not yet learned how to handle this lower style with assurance; perhaps his long practice in the high style has made his hand unsteady here. In any case, there can be little doubt that the lowering is done as part of his total design, however the words may stumble now and then.

Milton's total design in the last book of his poem is to convey the ultimate message of the biblical prophets and of the entire New Testament: nothing abides, nothing has true value, except the spiritual bond between Jehovah and his people. The very remoteness and abstractness of Jehovah places an almost unbearable strain upon humanity. Hence the continual temptation of mankind, shown throughout books 1 and 12, to worship false gods tangibly rooted in the cults of earth. Milton's reliance on abstraction in his account of the coming joy presents us with the problem that the prophets faced: how to persuade an audience of unbelievers or half-believers that a god remote and unseeable deserves an absolute faith.[11] His "legislative" mission has, for a time, taken precedence over his full poetical powers.[12] But then, in the closing lines, that power re-emerges in all its vitality, as Milton at the close defines the heroism of those who can admit their fault, declare their faith, and go forward to face the complex life of the world we know.

CHAPTER 11

The
Solitary
Way

"In my end is my beginning," T. S. Eliot wrote in *East Coker,* "In my beginning is my end"—adapting an ancient motto said to belong to Mary, Queen of Scots. I should like, in concluding this part, to think of *Paradise Lost* from this standpoint, as a poem where the end returns to the beginning. Such an approach is implicit in the closing lines of the poem, which tell of Adam and Eve's departure from Paradise. I use the word *departure* instead of the more traditional term *expulsion*, for Milton's ending moderates the stark and threatening words of Genesis: "so he drove out the man; and he placed at the east of the garden of Eden cherubims, and a flaming sword which turned every way, to keep the way of the tree of life."

Milton's presentation also differs greatly from the usual pictorial representations of the Expulsion in renaissance or baroque art, as in the design of Milton's earliest illustrator (1688: see illustration above).[1] Here the stern-faced angel with his left hand grasps Adam firmly by the shoulder, as though partly pushing and partly steadying an Adam whose hands cover his face and

185

whose body seems about to drop to the ground with anguish. Meanwhile, in his right hand the angel holds a sword toward Adam's leg, threatening any effort at return. Or consider Michelangelo's Expulsion, on the Sistine Chapel ceiling, where the angel seems to hold the point of his sword against the back of Adam's neck, while Adam strikes a gesture of fear and pleading, with an expression of poignant regret and remorse, and Eve cowers at his side. Or, farthest of all from Milton's conception, recall Masaccio's fresco in the church of the Carmine at Florence, where Eve expresses by her ragged, open mouth a cry of grief almost beyond bearing.

But Milton, as always, does things in his own way. He has shown the horror of the Fall throughout his last two books, with their oppressive tale of human wickedness, which evokes Adam's cry when he sees the murder of Abel:

> O sight
> Of terrour, foul and ugly to behold,
> Horrid to think, how horrible to feel!   [11.463–65]

Milton will not end his poem in such a mood. The angel does not hold a sword, and he does not drive the human pair, but rather saves them from a burning residence, as the angels in the Book of Genesis (chapter 19) escort Lot and his family from the doomed city of Sodom, taking them by the hand; or as Aeneas in a different fashion escorts his son and his father from burning Troy. Milton carefully places the guardian cherubim, with the flaming sword "before them," at a distance from Adam and Eve, as the procession of cherubim descends "from the other Hill:"

> High in Front advanc't,
> The brandisht Sword of God before them blaz'd
> Fierce as a Comet; which with torrid heat,
> And vapour as the *Libyan* Air adust,
> Began to parch that temperate Clime ;   [12.632–36]

"whereat," Milton continues—at the sight of the blazing sword approaching—the angel grasps Adam by one hand and Eve by the other, and he leads them to safety through the east gate of Paradise and down to the plain of Eden that lies below the mount of Paradise:

In either hand the hastning Angel caught
Our lingring Parents, and to th' Eastern Gate
Led them direct, and down the Cliff as fast
To the subjected Plaine; then disappeer'd.   [12.637–40]

This is an act of rescue, a sign of mercy, and it does not evoke
horror or terror in our first parents:

They looking back, all th' Eastern side beheld
Of Paradise, so late thir happie seat,
Wav'd over by that flaming Brand, the Gate
With dreadful Faces throng'd and fierie Armes:
Som natural tears they drop'd, but wip'd them soon;
The World was all before them, where to choose
Thir place of rest, and Providence thir guide:
They hand in hand with wandring steps and slow,
Through *Eden* took thir solitarie way.   [12.641–end]

And they will find a place of rest, as Milton has implied by a
complex simile that he has placed earlier within this ending, the
simile in which he compares the assembling cherubim to the evening mist that a field-laborer sees as he returns home from work
in the English countryside:

So spake our Mother *Eve*, and *Adam* heard
Well pleas'd, but answer'd not; for now too nigh
Th' Archangel stood, and from the other Hill
To thir fixt Station, all in bright array
The Cherubim descended; on the ground
Gliding meteorous, as Ev'ning Mist
Ris'n from a River o're the marish glides,
And gathers ground fast at the Labourers heel
Homeward returning.   [12.624–32]

One may feel something ominous in this glowing mist, for
meteors were traditionally regarded as ominous; but there is
much more in the simile than dread. There is here the sense of a
fertile river valley in which the mist counteracts the effects of
threatening fire and parching heat; and there is the promise of a
peaceful homecoming after a hard day of labor. All this provides
an implicit answer to the question: what lies ahead for Adam and
Eve? The emphasis has fallen on that word *choose*, in the lines
"The World was all before them, where to *choose* / Thir place of
rest, and Providence thir guide." The word *choose* not only re-

ceives a special stress here by coming at the end of the line; it also
seems to govern the word *Providence*. That is to say, Providence
will be their guide if they choose to accept the guidance. One
notices too a paradox in the word *solitarie*: they are a solitary *pair*,
hand in hand, and they may if they choose also have the presence
of Providence to be their guide. Furthermore, those final two
words of the poem, *solitarie way*, and the word *wandring*, despite
their apparent gloom and bleakness, are lighted with some hope
in their full context of allusion, for these words echo Psalm 107,
speaking of the Hebrew people:

>   They *wandered* in the wilderness in a *solitary way*;
> They found no city to dwell in.
> Hungry and thirsty,
> Their soul fainted in them.
> Then they cried unto the Lord in their trouble,
> And he delivered them out of their distresses.
> And he led them forth by the right way,
> That they might go to a city of habitation.
> Oh that men would praise the Lord for his goodness,
> And for his wonderful works to the children of men!

The total context of that phrase *solitarie way* is thus one of hope
and faith. And that sentence of the psalm, "Oh that men would
praise the Lord for his goodness, And for his wonderful works to
the children of men," is repeated three more times in this psalm,
so that one cannot miss the meaning. It is, then, in this setting of
hope and faith and love that Adam and Eve begin their life in the
fallen world, while at the same time the phrases "torrid heat" and
"fierie Armes," along with the imagery of meteor, blazing comet,
and "*Libyan* Air adust," draw us back to the poem's opening
books, as though Adam and Eve were on the verge of entering
into the kind of world therein displayed.

To grasp this circular effect one needs to reconsider the double
movement of the first four books: from Satan and the fallen
angels in Hell upward through Chaos toward the light of Heaven
and then on toward the vision of Paradise on earth. Literally, as
we follow Satan's voyage, we may seem to perform a journey
forward in time, moving from Hell to the new earth. Yet from
another standpoint, we are performing a more significant journey

backward in time, from the fallen world of the first two books toward the pristine, earlier world of book 4. This journey backward is also a journey inward, from the fallen world of everyday toward that center of remembrance where, as Milton's colleague, Peter Sterry, said, the soul may experience "an awakening by reason of the primitive Image of pure Nature raising it self by degrees, and sparkling through the *Rubbish*, the confusions of the present state."[2]

This effect of a journey backward and inward is created largely by the imagistic action of the opening books, notably in that immense roll call of evil that dominates the middle of the first book. Milton's device of calling the roll of fallen angels under the names of the later false gods has the effect of gradually dissolving our consciousness of Hell as any special place, and instead we find ourselves watching the operations of evil as it spreads out over the face of the earth:

> First *Moloch*, horrid King besmear'd with blood
> Of human sacrifice, and parents tears,
> Though for the noyse of Drums and Timbrels loud
> Their childrens cries unheard, that past through fire
> To his grim Idol. Him the *Ammonite*
> Worshipt in *Rabba* and her watry Plain,
> In *Argob* and in *Basan*, to the stream
> Of utmost *Arnon* . . .
> Next *Chemos*, th' obscene dread of *Moabs* Sons,
> From *Aroer* to *Nebo*, and the wild
> Of Southmost *Abarim*; in *Hesebon*
> And *Horonaim*, *Seons* Realm, beyond
> The flowry Dale of *Sibma* clad with Vines,
> And *Eleale* to th' *Asphaltick* Pool.   [1.392–99,406–11]

Every name here has its concrete, evocative identity in the Old Testament, including even here some promise of redemption, for every name connotes the victory of Jehovah over some pagan deity.[3] Yet the names create their major effect without recognition of their specific biblical context: they locate the action in the world of watery plains and flowery dales and vines and slimy pools. Milton gives in this roll call a summation of human vice, depravity, and irreligion, enacted in the landscapes of the earth.

It is the world we know, the world conveyed with equal vividness through the working of Milton's epic similes, whose subtle inter-relations with his theme and action have been successfully shown by many critical readings.[4] Thus in the great cluster of comparisons (1.286–313) that comes just before the roll call of devils, the name *"Vallombrosa"* adumbrates the valley of the shadow of death; and *"Orion* arm'd" suggests the retributive justice of God, whose power is immediately after this displayed by reference to the destruction of the Egyptian host in the Red Sea. These are the tentacles of association and implication by which the forces of evil are bound to earth; and these ties are essential in maintaining the unity of the poem. Yet, curiously, these ties, having performed their function, are not the matters that remain foremost in mind after the reading: what vividly remains is the sometimes tenuously relevant allusion to the actual world. It is not some vague astronomer who views that moon resembling Satan's shield: it is the famous *"Tuscan* Artist," viewing the moon "from the top of *Fesole,* / Or in *Valdarno."* It is not simply some tall pine to which Satan's spear is compared: it is a pine "Hewn on *Norwegian* hills, to be the Mast / Of some great Ammiral." The fallen angels on the lake are not simply compared with fallen autumnal leaves, but with those leaves "that strow the Brooks / In *Vallombrosa,* where th' *Etrurian* shades / High overarch't imbowr." These details cling to the mind long after the basis for their introduction has been forgotten.

The ultimate effect of all these similes is simple and sensuous: they serve, like the roll call, to settle us within a world we know, as in the brilliant simile that appears in book 2, just as the Satanic parliament is adjourning:

> Thus they thir doubtful consultations dark
> Ended rejoycing in thir matchless Chief:
> As when from mountain tops the dusky clouds
> Ascending, while the North wind sleeps, o'respread
> Heavn's chearful face, the lowring Element
> Scowls ore the dark'nd lantskip Snow, or showre;
> If chance the radiant Sun with farewell sweet
> Extend his ev'ning beam, the fields revive,
> The birds thir notes renew, and bleating herds
> Attest thir joy, that hill and valley rings.   [2.486–95]

The action moves, suddenly, to the world we know; and thus the similes of the first two books come to include the varied land-scapes of the earth, and all the world's activities. They include war and the literature of war, as when Satan stands before his host in pride and Milton compares this army with the "Heroic Race . . . That fought at *Theb's* and *Ilium*" and recalls everything that re-sounds

> In Fable or *Romance* of *Uthers* Son
> Begirt with *British* and *Armoric* Knights;
> And all who since, Baptiz'd or Infidel
> Jousted in *Aspramont* or *Montalban*,
> *Damasco*, or *Marocco*, or *Trebisond*,
> Or whom *Biserta* sent from *Afric* shore
> When *Charlemain* with all his Peerage fell
> By *Fontarabbia*.   [1.580–87]

The similes include the superstitions of the English peasant, with his moonlight elves, the barbarian hordes that overran the Roman Empire, and the great fleets that carry the world's trade.

To all these comparisons one must add the impact of those huge symbolic scenes of worldly activity: the building of the baroque palace of Pandaemonium; the council of Satan and his peers, with all the familiar political manoeuvres; and the arts and exploits displayed by the fallen angels after the council adjourns: feats of "Olympian Games," music of harp and song, philosophic reasoning "Of Providence, Foreknowledge, Will, and Fate," ex-peditions of discovery "O're many a Frozen, many a Fierie Alpe."[5]

These images, whether in epic simile or in literary allusion or in metaphorical tableau, succeed in creating a double action for the first four books. Literally, the action moves from Hell, through Chaos in book 2, to Heaven in book 3, and then at last to earth in book 4. But more deeply, more essentially, the action moves from the world we know toward the inward Light by which man is enabled to see a Paradise that lies within the center of the poem and within the center of the mind and memory. It is a brilliant poetical strategy. The eyes of the imagination, looking back over the first two books from the vantage point of Paradise, can see a thousand varied images of the fallen world, imbedded in a "darkness visible," licked on all sides by flame, " 'Twixt upper, nether, and surrounding Fires." Thus the literal, initial impact of these opening books becomes subtly inverted. Literally, we may say, these images from the fallen world are used to describe Hell and the fallen angels, to give them body and actuality. But essentially this whole fiery setting in Hell becomes a vast metaphor by which Milton interprets the actions of the world we know. It is from this world that Milton's bard performs a journey backward and inward, toward the Light.

Thus Milton's poem comes to assume a form that might be described in visual terms as a picture with a dark border but a bright center. The opening books and the closing books present the dark border of the world we know, in flames, in ruins: but the center holds, for at the center the voice of the bard has performed a journey backward and inward to discover the springing center of creativity described by Peter Sterry:

> as Paradise, so the *pure Image* of God in the Soul, seems to some not to be *lost* or destroyed, but *hid* beneath the ruines of the fall. Thus *Knowledge* springing in the Soul, seems to be a *remembrance,* the Life of all good, an awakening by reason of the primitive Image of pure Nature raising it self by degrees, and sparkling through the *Rubbish,* the confusions of the present state.[6]

II

Adam and Eve, as they walk through the fallen world "with wandring steps and slow," may remind us that there are in Milton's poem two other figures that move in a "solitarie way." The first of these is Satan,[7] who, after his expulsion from the Heavenly Paradise, makes what one might call a pseudo-pilgrimage from Hell to earth—and certainly in his case the word *expulsion* is appropriate:

>   Him the Almighty Power
> Hurld headlong flaming from th' Ethereal Skie
> With hideous ruine and combustion down
> To bottomless perdition, there to dwell
> In Adamantine Chains and penal Fire,
> Who durst defie th' Omnipotent to Arms.   [1.44–49]

The contrast between the treatment of fallen angel and fallen man could hardly be more pointed. Yet Satan undertakes a pilgrimage of sorts, for Satan offers the pretense that he is making his journey from Hell to earth in order that he may rejoice in the wonderful works of the Lord—and this is the meaning of the word *pilgrimage*: "a journey (usually of considerable duration) made to some sacred place, as an act of religious devotion."[8] Such is the motivation that Satan in book 3 offers to Uriel, the angel of the sun, after Satan has adopted his disguise of a traveling cherub, looking like an angel in a renaissance painting:

> Under a Coronet his flowing haire
> In curles on either cheek plaid, wings he wore
> Of many a colourd plume sprinkl'd with Gold,
> His habit fit for speed succinct, and held
> Before his decent steps a Silver wand. [3.640–44]

It is a ludicrous and ironical scene, if we remember the enormous size and baleful, blazing eyes of Satan in Hell. But here he has "His habit fit for speed succinct"—his clothing is tied up or close-fitting so that he can make all speed in his pilgrimage. And in this neat and humble garb he addresses Uriel, in the very attitude of Psalm 107:

> Unspeakable desire to see, and know
> All these his wondrous works, but chiefly Man,
> His chief delight and favour, him for whom
> All these his works so wondrous he ordaind
> Hath brought me from the Quires of Cherubim
> Alone thus wandring. [3.662–67]

His way is bleakly solitary; yet he uses the language found in Psalm 107 and in a score of other places in the psalms or other books of the Bible where we find that phrase "wonderful works" or "wondrous works." Uriel is taken in and replies happily, also using the language and the lesson of the psalms:

> Faire Angel, thy desire which tends to know
> The works of God, thereby to glorifie
> The great Work-Maister, leads to no excess
> That reaches blame, but rather merits praise
> The more it seems excess, that led thee hither

> From thy Empyreal Mansion thus alone,
> To witness with thine eyes what some perhaps
> Contented with report heare onely in heav'n:
> For wonderful indeed are all his works,
> Pleasant to know, and worthiest to be all
> Had in remembrance alwayes with delight.   [3.694–704]

The last three lines contain a clear echo of Psalm 111, verse 4: "He hath made his wonderful works to be remembered." But of course Satan's pilgrimage is hardly one of love and delight, for, as we come to see, he envies the beauty of the earth and he sees "undelighted all delight" (4.286).

There is, however, another figure in this poem who walks a solitary way; he is introduced plainly at the opening of book 3, although in fact he has been with us from the very first line of the poem and he will remain until the last. He is the singer in darkness who tells this tale, and who, though blind, sees things invisible to mortal sight. Through his blindness, he says, he is now cut off from seeing the wondrous works of God, and yet with the eyes of the mind he makes his pilgrimage to paradise—revealing in his own response the delight in God's works that Satan cannot feel. It is a journey of remembrance, using all the aids that divine grace and human knowledge can provide, in accord with the principle of memory set forth by Augustine in his *De Trinitate*, as he takes pains to remove any implications of Platonic *anamnesis*. The human mind, Augustine explains,

> . . . has indeed no memory of its own blessedness; for that was once and is no longer, and the mind has totally forgotten it, so that no reminder can bring it back. It can only believe, on the faith of the Scriptures of its God, written by his prophet, the story of a happiness of paradise and the account conveyed in narrative form of man's original good and evil. But it has the memory of the Lord its God. For he ever is . . . And he is everywhere in his wholeness; so that in him the mind lives and moves and has its being, and therefore has the power to remember him. Not that it recollects having once known him in Adam, or anywhere else before this bodily life, or at its first making and planting in this body. Of none of these things has it any memory whatsoever: all of them are buried in oblivion. But it can be so reminded as to turn again unto the Lord, who is the light by which even in its turning away from him it was still somehow touched.[9]

Under the inspiration of this light a rising tide of irresistible creative power runs from the outset of book 3 on through the accounts of Paradise and Creation. The alternations here between the poet's praise and Satan's hatred create what might be called a battle between light and dark, framed between two angelic psalms in praise of Creation—psalms that foreshadow and complete the imperfect human apprehension of Paradise that lies between these two angelic poems. The first of these angelic hymns is that spoken by Uriel at the very close of book 3:

> I saw when at his Word the formless Mass,
> This worlds material mould, came to a heap:
> Confusion heard his voice, and wilde uproar
> Stood rul'd, stood vast infinitude confin'd;
> Till at his second bidding darkness fled,
> Light shon, and order from disorder sprung:
> Swift to thir several Quarters hasted then
> The cumbrous Elements, Earth, Flood, Aire, Fire,
> And this Ethereal quintessence of Heav'n
> Flew upward, spirited with various forms,
> That rowld orbicular, and turnd to Starrs
> Numberless, as thou seest, and how they move;
> Each had his place appointed, each his course,
> The rest in circuit walles this Universe.   [3.708–21]

The angel places the stress on order, rule, form, design, purpose, and thus on the wondrous power of God to control such plenitude, such rich fertility of being. Perfect beauty exists within a powerful design; the bounty of the material universe is beautiful only within an orderly and appointed plan.

Book 7 of *Paradise Lost* represents the detailed fulfillment of that vision, told by another angel, Raphael, whose long psalm of praise reveals all the richness of the six days of creation, and then concludes with these words:

> So Ev'n and Morn accomplish't the Sixt day:
> Yet not till the Creator from his work
> Desisting, though unwearied, up returnd
> Up to the Heav'n of Heav'ns his high abode,
> Thence to behold this new created World
> Th' addition of his Empire, how it shew'd
> In prospect from his Throne, how good, how faire,
> Answering his great Idea.   [7.550–57]

Milton is celebrating here the pure idea of beauty—the Platonic idea of Creation that existed in the mind of God and is now recreated here within the poet's mind and in our own minds, as we read. But this idea, in its full grandeur and power, Milton allows the two angels to tell; it is beyond human vision, except, of course, for a divinely inspired poet and prophet.

By contrast, in books 4 and 5, we watch the human singer attempting to grasp and to convey a glimpse of that divine idea of perfect beauty; we watch Adam's descendant, in his own imperfect way, attempting to fulfill the original impulse of joy and gratitude which Adam himself remembers as his earliest emotion:

> Thou Sun, said I, faire Light,
> And thou enlight'nd Earth, so fresh and gay,
> Ye Hills and Dales, ye Rivers, Woods, and Plaines
> And ye that live and move, fair Creatures, tell,
> Tell, if ye saw, how came I thus, how here?
> Not of my self; by some great Maker then,
> In goodness and in power praeeminent;
> Tell me, how may I know him, how adore,
> From whom I have that thus I move and live,
> And feel that I am happier then I know.   [8.273–82]

So every part in this portion of the poem, extending from the hymn to light at the outset of book 3 to this address to light by Adam in book 8, is held together by the voice of praise, which rises above the satanic voice of hate. This contrast is especially evident in book 4, as Adam's descendant, the modern singer, struggles to express his love and wonder at this answer to his journey of remembrance, while Satan becomes a foil to the redeemed vision of the bard, who now, overcome with delight and joy, is able to create a vision of the earthly Paradise out of his knowledge of the Bible and of human history and mythology.[10] Throughout we have a subtle distinction between Satan's point of view and that of the *human* viewer:

> Beneath him [Satan] with new wonder now he views
> To all delight of human sense expos'd
> In narrow room Natures whole wealth, yea more,
> A Heaven on Earth . . .   [4.205–08]

The wonder that Satan feels here is not the wonder of the psalms;

Satan feels amazement, astonishment, but not delight. Such delight is reserved for "human sense" in the vision of the redeemed man.[11]

But here the problem is, he goes on to say, how to deal with something that lies beyond the limits of art:

> But rather to tell how, if Art could tell,
> How from that Saphire Fount the crisped Brooks,
> Rowling on Orient Pearl and sands of Gold,
> With mazie error under pendant shades
> Ran Nectar, visiting each plant, and fed
> Flours . . .   [4.236–41]

What kind of flowers? Simply, "Flours worthy of Paradise." The poet at this point seems unable to imagine any further detail than this, and he ends his scene with a summary: "Thus was this place / A happy rural seat of various view." He has throughout proceeded by such humanizing touches: embedding this account in a specific geographical place amidst the events of human history; imaging the mount of Paradise as a sort of human organism with thirst and veins; and then, after admitting the limitations of art, coming to rest in the image of a happy English country estate— not, of course, an adequate image (nothing is), but at least it is a vestige of Paradise. It is something man has made by art out of nature—though here in Paradise is a scene that surpasses all the efforts of human imagination in gardening or architecture. The main effect is simply this: here is one of us trying to tell the story—impossible to tell.[12] "Not that fair field / Of *Enna*," nor "that sweet Grove / Of *Daphne* by *Orontes*," "nor that *Nyseian* Isle," "Nor where *Abassin* Kings thir issue Guard," none of these, says the singer, "might with this Paradise / Of *Eden* strive." The description does not matter. The very admission of the speaker's inadequacy indicates his gratitude for the gift. What matters is his love for the Creator as conveyed by his love for all created things. The expression of this love is the goal of the speaker's pilgrimage, and he conveys it all as he joins with Adam and Eve in their morning hymn in praise of the wondrous works of God:[13]

> These are thy glorious works Parent of good,
> Almightie, thine this universal Frame,

> Thus wondrous fair; thy self how wondrous then!
> . . . .
> Joyn voices all ye living Souls, ye Birds,
> That singing up to Heaven Gate ascend,
> Bear on your wings and in your notes his praise;
> Yee that in Waters glide, and yee that walk
> The Earth, and stately tread, or lowly creep;
> Witness if I be silent, Morn or Eeven,
> To Hill, or Valley, Fountain, or fresh shade
> Made vocal by my Song, and taught his praise.
> Hail universal Lord, be bounteous still
> To give us onely good; and if the night
> Have gathered aught of evil or conceald,
> Disperse it, as now light dispels the dark.   [5.153–55,197–208]

As long as a living poet can sing that song, the continuity between human beings, nature, and God will persist, and each human being may reach the proper goal of his solitary way—which is of course solitary only in the sense that it must be followed in accordance with each individual's deepest inner being. But Satan is truly solitary, cut off by his pride even from his followers: "this enterprize," he says as he departs from Hell upon his pilgrimage of hate, "this enterprize / None shall partake with me" (2.465–66). Milton's Hell is populated by individuals isolated by their crimes against Creation.

For humankind, in Milton's view, the way need not be solitary in this literal, single sense. The rich paradox and ambiguity of Milton's ending has nowhere been captured better than in William Blake's two great drawings of Adam and Eve leaving Paradise. In both drawings a sorrowing angel leads Adam and Eve forth gently by the hand. In both drawings Blake presents a sheet of flame behind the human pair, with terrifying effect. Hand in hand with the angel, Adam and Eve step forward toward us, their descendants. In one of Blake's drawings (see illustration here) they look upward, with considerable apprehension and uncertainty. In the other version (see frontispiece) they look downward at the serpent writhing between them on the ground, and their look is one of horror, fear, and repugnance. Will they go the way of Satan, they seem to be asking. Behind them, in both drawings, the four staring figures on horseback present no answer to that question. Their eyes are full of enigma and mystery. They look into a future that Adam and Eve must choose to make.

William Blake, "Expulsion from Paradise," Henry E. Huntington Library and Art Gallery.

PART III

Paradise Lost:
Figurations of Ovid

In nova fert animus mutatas dicere formas
corpora; di, coeptis (nam vos mutastis et illas)
adspirate meis primaque ab origine mundi
ad mea perpetuum deducite tempora carmen!

Metamorphoses, *1. 1–4*

CHAPTER 12

The
Anti-heroic
Epic

Milton's daughter Deborah, in her old age, recalled how she and her sisters had read to their father the works of three favorite authors. "Isaiah, Homer, and Ovid's metamorphoses," John Ward reports, "were books, which they were often called to read to their father; and at my desire she [Deborah] repeated a considerable number of verses from the beginning of both these poets with great readiness"—"both these poets" evidently meaning Homer and Ovid, as distinguished from the prophet Isaiah.[1] The omission of Vergil is surprising, and it is quite possible that Deborah, speaking many years after the event, simply failed to remember the reading of Vergil.[2] Yet the thought comes to mind: has the twelve-book division of *Paradise Lost* in the second edition led us somewhat to overestimate the example of Vergil, in comparison with Homer and Ovid? But it is enough to learn from Milton's daughter that, during the years when Milton was composing his epic, Ovid's *Metamorphoses* was still one of his best loved books. With this thought in mind I should like to explore the possibility that Ovid's example extended far beyond the many mythological allusions and parallels,[3] that the presence of Ovid may be found both in minute figurations of detail and in the larger figurations of structure and form.

Over the past twenty years classical scholars have gradually recovered the view of Ovid's *Metamorphoses* which Quintilian seems to have taken as generally understood in the generation following Ovid's death: that his long poem belongs to the epic genre. Ovid's choice of hexameter verse, his frequent and overt echoes of Vergilian phrases and motifs, the vast scope of his poem, and his efforts to spin "an unbroken thread of verse" all point toward a poem of epic ambitions. Yet, if this *carmen perpetuum* is to be regarded as epic, our definition of the genre must be expanded far beyond the terms that will include the epics of Homer and Vergil. In what sense, for example, could the *Metamorphoses* be called "heroic"? It was a problem that clearly bothered Quintilian when, considering Ovid in the context of Homer, Vergil, Lucretius, Ennius, and Lucan, he found a quality that he called *lascivus*—playful, sportive, indecent, excessively ornamented—even when Ovid was writing in the heroic mode. "Ovid has a lack of seriousness even when he writes epic and is unduly enamoured of his own gifts," Quintilian said, but, he added, "portions of his work merit our praise." ("Lascivus quidem in herois quoque Ovidius et nimium amator ingenii sui, laudandus tamen in partibus.")[4] How can we account for the frequently witty episodes, the archness of tone, the showy rhetoric, and above all, how can the *Metamorphoses* be said to grow into a unity of action and theme?

Recent studies of Ovid have brought us a great way toward a solution of these problems. Brooks Otis, in his controversial, stimulating *Ovid as an Epic Poet*, finds a strong element of unity in Ovid's careful arrangement of his materials in parallel and contrasting "panels;" while Robert Coleman has stressed the subtlety of Ovid's "inset technique."[5] Charles Segal has found another element of unity in the skillfully patterned scenes of landscape, the *loci amoeni*, that occur throughout the poem.[6] And Karl Galinsky, among others, has found yet another kind of unity in the constant presence of the poet as narrator,[7] a presence culminating in the remarkable assertion of poetic immortality at the very close:

Iamque opus exegi, quid nec Iovis ira nec ignis
nec poterit ferrum nec edax abolere vetustas.
cum volet, illa dies, quae nil nisi corporis huius
ius habet, incerti spatium mihi finiat aevi:
parte tamen meliore mei super alta perennis
astra ferar, nomenque erit indelebile nostrum,
quaque patet domitis Romana potentia terris,
ore legar populi, perque omnia saecula fama,
siquid habent veri vatum praesagia, vivam.

And now my work is done, which neither the wrath of Jove, nor
fire, nor sword, nor the gnawing tooth of time shall ever be able to
undo. When it will, let that day come which has no power save over
this mortal frame, and end the span of my uncertain years. Still in
my better part I shall be borne immortal far beyond the lofty stars
and I shall have an undying name. Wherever Rome's power extends over the conquered world, I shall have mention on men's lips,
and, if the prophecies of bards have any truth, through all the ages
shall I live in fame. [15.871–end, trans. Miller]

The creative consciousness of man, Ovid seems to be saying, will
survive all his other achievements, even the achievements of empire. All history, all myth, all religion will find the only hope of
immortality in the records left by the creative mind of the *vates*,
bard and prophet, who in this poem speaks the last word, *vivam*.[8]
Thus the entire immense narration of fifteen books is suffused
with the voice of the narrator, who weaves his stories together by
witty, sometimes absurdly contrived transitions, by constant repetition and cross-reference, by holding story within story, by landscape, by chronology, by "panels," and by the continuous, over-
arching themes of love and passion: the *amor* of Venus, the *furor*
of Bacchus.[9] In order to see how the peculiar qualities of the
Metamorphoses may be reflected in *Paradise Lost*, it is essential here
to explore certain aspects of Ovid's poem.

I

One should first consider the problems raised by those "panels"
in which Ovid is clearly emulating the high heroic style of Homer
and Vergil, particularly in the narration of battles. As Otis has
shown, such episodes stand out with special emphasis, by being

flanked on either side by amatory panels which form a strong contrast in theme and manner with the heroic central panel. It may be that Otis goes too far in attempting to work out parallels and contrasts in detail, but it seems clear that significant arrangements in panels are being made, in the manner illustrated at the outset by the placing of the Phaeton episode:

Apollo-Daphne (*ab*)   Jupiter-Callisto (*b′c′*)
                          Phaeton Panel
Jupiter-Io (*bc*)   Apollo-Coronis (*a′b′*)

As Otis explains, the episodes on either side of the Phaeton panel show a chiastic relation of *amores* by Jove and Apollo, an effect reinforced by cross-references within the episodes. Similarly, the epic tale of Perseus occupies a central position between two kinds of episodes:

Vengeance Episodes (Actaeon, Semele, Narcissus-Echo, Pentheus
    First Amatory Frame: Love-tales of the Minyades
            Epic Central Panel (Perseus-Andromeda-Phineus)
    Second Amatory Frame: Love-tales of the Muses (Proserpina)
Vengeance Episodes (Arachne, Niobe, Lycian Peasants, Marsyas)

Furthermore, Otis argues, the arrangements show more than simple symmetry: there is also progression: "Though the episodes after each central panel correspond to those before it, they also reveal a significant change, a change which almost insensibly prepares the reader for the next major section." In this way Ovid controls "the poem's restless variety and movement."[10]

This kind of arrangement finds a parallel in the tenth book of *Paradise Lost*, where, as I have shown in chapter 8, a long central panel of "heroic" action is set between panels with a different style and theme:

Condemnation   "Triumph" of   Reconciliation
of Adam and Eve   Sin, Death, and Satan   of Adam and Eve

That central panel contains an explicit, extended example of Ovidian metamorphosis—matching the other extended example of Ovidian metamorphosis: the transformation of Sin into a resemblance of Scylla in book 2. It seems quite possible that Milton

would have sensed in the *Metamorphoses* something of the structure that Otis has discerned, for at least the placement of the
heroic panels in Ovid is clear enough. But Milton's central panel
here is mock-heroic, inflated, and in the end, deflated. Can Ovid's
heroic panels be interpreted as similar parodies of the heroic
manner?

A number of classical scholars have recently argued for this
point of view.[11] The story of Phaeton (1.750–79,2.1–328), epic in
its manner, hardly tells a story of heroic courage: the poor foolish
boy is frightened to death. And there are elements in the Perseus
panel that considerably deflate the epic pretensions of the
episode.[12] For example, the heroic effect in Perseus' rescue of
Andromeda is undercut by the way in which, as the monster approaches, Perseus pauses to strike a bargain with the parents!
Indeed the following passage is full of phrases that detract from
the heroic mode: Andromeda's parents offer wailings "befitting
the occasion"—*dignos tempore fletus*: a proper introduction to a
carefully negotiated bargain under stress:

> Then speaks the stranger: "There will be long time for weeping by
> and by; but time for helping is very short. If I sought this maid as
> Perseus, son of Jove and that imprisoned one whom Jove filled with
> his life-giving shower; if as Perseus, victor over Gorgon of the snaky
> locks, and as he who has dared to ride the winds of heaven on
> fluttering wings, surely I should be preferred to all suitors as your
> son-in-law. But now I shall try to add to these great gifts the gift of
> service, too, if only the gods will favour me. That she be mine if
> saved by my valour is my bargain." The parents accept the
> condition—for who would refuse?—and beg him to save her, prom-
> ising him a kingdom as dowry in addition. [4.695–705, trans. Mil-
> ler]

Quis enim dubitaret? The narrator's wry interjection stresses the
absurdity of the situation, just as earlier his way of telling about
Perseus' love at first sight gives a comic touch: "Smitten by the
sight of her exquisite beauty, he almost forgot to move his wings
in the air" (4.676–77, trans. Miller). Then Andromeda, despite
her terrible situation, "bound by the arms to a rough cliff," follows
the social customs for young maidens when Perseus speaks to her:
"She was silent at first, for, being a maid, she did not dare address

a man; she would have hidden her face modestly with her hands but that her hands were bound" (4.681–83, trans. Miller). This smacks of social comedy rather than epic. Then, after all this, the fight with the monster is presented in heroic style, full of similes and accompanied by applause from the gods above. With such a prelude, the heroic action is bound to seem a bit inflated, though still a good example of how well Ovid can imitate the heroic manner when he wishes to do so.

In book 5 the battle of Perseus with Phineus and his crowd is told in a curious way that seems to mix parody with serious epic effect. Phineus, after starting the fight, takes refuge behind the altar, while his followers die in ways that seem excessively ingenious, outdoing Homer:

> Then Phorbas of Syene, Metion's son, and Libyan Amphimedon, eager to join in the fray, slipped and fell in the blood with which all the floor was wet. As they strove to rise the sword met them, driven through the ribs of one and through the other's throat.
>
> But Eurytus, the son of Actor, who wielded a broad, two-edged battle-axe, Perseus did not attack with his hooked sword, but lifting high in both hands a huge mixing-bowl heavily embossed and ponderous, he hurled it crashing at the man. The red blood spouted forth as he lay dying on his back, beating the floor with his head. . . .
>
> Phineus did not dare to come to close combat with his enemy, but hurled his javelin. This was ill-aimed and struck Idas, who all to no purpose had kept out of the fight, taking sides with neither party. [5.74–91, trans. Miller]

Finally Perseus stands alone as "Phineus and a thousand followers close round him." Somehow this number is whittled down to two hundred, in ways that Ovid declines to explain, saying only: "It would take too long to tell the names of the rank and file who perished. Two hundred men survived the fight; two hundred saw the Gorgon and turned to stone." Then, amid the grotesque statues of his two hundred followers, the cowardly Phineus emerges begging for his life, and for an answer is allowed to decorate the house of Perseus's father-in-law: "I will make of you," says the hero, "a monument that shall endure for ages; and in the house of my father-in-law you shall always stand on view, that so my wife may find solace in the statue of her promised lord

. . . And now in marble was fixed the cowardly face, the suppliant look, the pleading hands, the whole cringing attitude" (5.157–58, 207–09,227–29,234–35, trans. Miller).

What shall one make of this mode of heroic story-telling? Is Ovid simply writing badly, because his heart is not in the heroics?[13] But it seems likely that so skillful a poet would be fully aware of his effects, and that he has deliberately composed this battle in a way that will not allow us to take it with complete solemnity. Readers sometimes speak of Ovid's addiction to cruelty, his delight in blood and brutality.[14] But is it not possible to find in these extravagant modes of death a revulsion against cruelty and brutal slaughter? No one stresses the horrors of war more fiercely than the advocates of peace.

The whole problem comes to a head in the battle of the Lapiths and the Centaurs, in book 12, where Ovid's invention of ingenious ways of slaughter goes far beyond anything in the Phineus episode and very far beyond anything in Homer or Vergil. Nestor, the narrator of this episode, is supposedly telling the tale of Caenis-Caeneus; but, with the garrulity of his old age, Nestor spends 250 lines on the battle of the Lapiths and the Centaurs before he comes at last to the role of Caeneus, whose burying under a mountain of uprooted trees forms the climax of several dozen bizarre ways of dying. These increase in ingenuity and in size of weapons used, from a mixing vat to a chandelier to a "huge altar, fire and all," "a threshold-stone, a weight for a team of oxen," an oak tree, a "rock torn from the mountain side," "a log which two yokes of cattle could scarce move" (12.260–61,281–82,341,432). Finally the Centaurs, frustrated and enraged (like Achilles) when Caeneus proves invulnerable to their spears and swords, respond to the cry: "Come then, let us heap stones and tree-trunks on him, mountains at a time! let's crush his stubborn life out with forests for our missiles!"

> saxa trabesque super totosque involvite montes
> vivacemque animam missis elidite silvis!   [12.507–08]

And so before long "Othrys was stripped of trees and Pelion had lost his shade" (513; trans. Miller).

Milton, then, could have found in Ovid considerable precedent for parodic treatment of heroic warfare, which some readers have come to see as an essential element in Milton's account of the war in Heaven.[15] As in Ovid, Milton's narration is done in a mixed style, for both poets are showing their skill in imitating Homer—while at the same time suggesting the ultimate futility of such heroic exploits. "Warr wearied hath perform'd what Warr can do," says Milton's God, as he watches the warring angels, in the climax of their fight:

> They pluckt the seated Hills with all thir load,
> Rocks, Waters, Woods, and by the shaggie tops
> Up lifting bore them in thir hands: Amaze,
> Be sure, and terrour seis'd the rebel Host,
> When coming towards them so dread they saw
> The bottom of the Mountains upward turn'd,
> Till on those cursed Engins triple-row
> They saw them whelmd, and all thir confidence
> Under the weight of Mountains buried deep . . .
> So Hills amid the Air encountered Hills
> Hurl'd to and fro with jaculation dire . . .   [6.644–52,64–65]

Milton's account of the hurling of hills is partly derived from Hesiod's account of the war against the Titans,[16] but we can hardly fail to think also of Ovid's account of the burying of Caeneus under that great mountain of uprooted trees. The difficulties that critics have had with Milton's war in Heaven are quite similar to those encountered by readers of Ovid's epic panels: is the writing simply awkward and inflated and unsure, or is it a deliberate creation of heroic parody? The taunting and jesting of Satan and Beelzebub, along with the throwing about of mountains, leads me to feel that the element of parody in Milton's war is paramount and holds the whole narration under control, as in Ovid. Consider too the strategic placing of Milton's war in Heaven: a long heroic panel set in between two episodes of pastoral: Paradise before, and the whole Creation after. Milton seems to have combined the device of the recollected narrative (modelled on the *Aeneid* and the *Odyssey*) with the Ovidian technique of placing episodes of heroic parody within contrasting panels—the structural principle followed by Milton in book 10.

Thus, throughout *Paradise Lost*, Milton has intermingled struc-

tures and motifs from what we may call the four great classical
epics: the *Iliad*, the *Odyssey*, the *Aeneid*, and the *Metamorphoses*.
Ovid's great poem, by its consistent transmutation of epic materials, has helped to show Milton many ways in which he might
transcend the Aonian mount.

II

Milton's prologue to book 1 shows a subtle blending of motifs
from the epics of Homer and Vergil, and properly so, for the first
two books of *Paradise Lost* are predominantly modelled upon the
heroic aspects of those three epics—along with the imitators of
Homer and Vergil in the heroic mode: Claudian, Apollonius,
Statius, Lucan, and others. Milton, then, begins his poem with
transcendent emulation of that heroic mode. Yet echoes of Ovid,
recessive at first, become more and more resonant, until, in the
middle of book 2, Ovidian motifs begin openly and powerfully to
mingle with the old heroic mode. Even in the opening prologue
the shade of Ovid is perhaps not utterly absent, for he too, though
not "first," taught "In the Beginning how the Heav'ns and Earth /
Rose out of *Chaos*" (1.9–10). Ovid of course does not begin his epic
in medias res: he begins at the beginning:

> Before the sea was, and the lands, and the sky that hangs over all,
> the face of Nature showed alike in her whole round, which state
> have men called chaos: a rough, unordered mass of things, nothing
> at all save lifeless bulk and warring seeds of ill-matched elements
> heaped in one. No sun as yet shone forth upon the world, nor did
> the waxing moon renew her slender horns; not yet did the earth
> hang poised by her own weight in the circumambient air, nor had
> the ocean stretched her arms along the far reaches of the lands.
> And, though there was both land and sea and air, no one could
> tread that land, or swim that sea; and the air was dark. No form of
> things remained the same; all objects were at odds, for within one
> body cold things strove with hot, and moist with dry, soft things
> with hard, things having weight with weightless things. [1.5–20,
> trans. Miller]

Milton's echoes of this passage, along with other aspects of
Ovid's account of Creation, have been carefully studied by Davis
Harding,[17] who shows that Milton is recalling Ovid's account in

exact detail in books 2, 3, and 7 of *Paradise Lost*, especially in this passage of book 2:

> a dark
> Illimitable Ocean without bound,
> Without dimension, where length, breadth, and highth,
> And time and place are lost; where eldest Night
> And *Chaos*, Ancestors of Nature, hold
> Eternal *Anarchie*, amidst the noise
> Of endless warrs, and by confusion stand.
> For hot, cold, moist, and dry, four Champions fierce
> Strive here for Maistrie, and to Battel bring
> Thir embryon Atoms . . .
>   Into this wilde Abyss,
> The Womb of nature and perhaps her Grave,
> Of neither Sea, nor Shore, nor Air, nor Fire,
> But all these in thir pregnant causes mixt
> Confus'dly, and which thus must ever fight,
> Unless th' Almighty Maker them ordain
> His dark materials to create more Worlds . . .
>   [2.891–900,910–16]

One point should be added to Harding's fine analysis. As Satan flounders through this "crude consistence," Milton seems to have caught up the root meanings of *instabilis tellus*, *innabilis unda*, "earth on which one cannot stand," "wave in which one cannot swim" (*Met.* 1.16)—to create his parody of an heroic voyage, as Satan "swims or sinks, or wades, or creeps, or flyes" (2.950).

Paradise Lost moves overtly from Chaos to Creation at the juncture of books 2 and 3, as we travel with Satan through Chaos, and then, with the guidance of the bard, enter the realms of light. But we have in fact been reading a version of chaos and creation throughout book 1, as Satan and his crew at first lie "weltering," stunned, and without distinct form, in the burning lake, and Satan views his "dismal Situation waste and wilde":

> A Dungeon horrible, on all sides round
> As one great Furnace flam'd, yet from those flames
> No light, but rather darkness visible
> Serv'd only to discover sights of woe,
> Regions of sorrow, doleful shades, where peace
> And rest can never dwell, hope never comes
> That comes to all; but torture without end

> Still urges, and a fiery Deluge, fed
> With ever-burning Sulphur unconsum'd . . .   [1.60–69]

The ambiguous, shifting syntax, or melting down of syntax, seems in itself a version of chaos. "Dungeon horrible" may seem at first to be in apposition to "dismal Situation," but the phrase veers about to become the subject of the verb "flam'd"—or perhaps "flam'd" is a participle modifying "Furnace." "No light" seems to promise a firm start, but the phrase is quickly revised to "darkness visible," and both phrases then together become the implausible subject of "Serv'd only to discover." "Torture" seems at first to refer back to "comes," but then goes forward to link with "urges." This is the sort of shifting, evasive syntax that we have seen in book 10, as Sin and Death build their bridge across Chaos (10.299–304). But soon a sort of order begins to appear as Satan gradually brings his words into the form of an oration, pulls himself together to fly upward from this "abject" posture, marshalls his forces in military array, and finally builds the palace and capital of Pandaemonium. All this constitutes a process of mock-creation, factitious order arising out of chaos and assuming the illusion of a parliamentary government in Satan's "great Consult." Yet in the middle of book 2 this illusion of order gradually dissolves, ending with the revelation of a region worse than Chaos, for there is here not even the possibility of good:

> A Universe of death, which God by curse
> Created evil, for evil only good,
> Where all life dies, death lives, and nature breeds,
> Perverse, all monstrous, all prodigious things,
> Abominable, inutterable, and worse
> Then Fables yet have feign'd, or fear conceiv'd,
> *Gorgons* and *Hydra's*, and *Chimera's* dire.   [2.622–28]

Such is the close of the heroic promise delivered in the preceding portion of the first two books, an illusion delivered in terms inherited from Homer and Vergil, replete with heroic building (like that of Vergil's Carthage), heroic speeches of encouragement (such as Aeneas gave his forces after the great storm in Vergil's opening book), an heroic catalogue (of fallen angels), heroic debate of leaders, and the start of what seems to be an heroic voyage.

But now, with this breeding of monstrous things, worse than any known to Greek fables, the mode of narration undergoes a transformation into what I have called (in chapter 5) "panels of action"—a phrase that I had been using in lectures on Milton before coming upon Otis's use of the term "panels" to describe Ovid's mode of construction. This coincidence of terms may help to reinforce the validity of the analogies between Ovid and Milton that I am here proposing.

The presence of Ovid has been quite subdued in the first book and a half of Milton's poem, though sometimes emerging in collaboration with echoes of Homer and Vergil and others. Thus the reference to the myth of Typhon (1.199–200), and the following description of volcanic eruptions from mount Pelorus and mount Aetna (230–37) together evoke the memory of the stories told in Ovid about the giant Typhoeus (*Met.* 5.346–58); but Milton's description is equally indebted to Vergil's account of the rumblings of Aetna, caused by the writhings of another giant, Enceladus (*Aeneid* 3.570–82).

Another, and a more subtle blending of echoes, this time from Homer, Vergil, and Ovid, is found in Milton's account of Satan's spear:

> His Spear, to equal which the tallest Pine
> Hewn on *Norwegian* hills, to be the Mast
> Of some great Ammiral, were but a wand,
> He walkt with to support uneasie steps
> Over the burning Marle . . .   [1.292–96]

Homer describes the huge club or staff of Polyphemus, made of olive wood, and compares it with a mast (*Odyssey* 11.322); Vergil describes the Cyclops as carrying "the trunk of a pine tree to guide and support him walking" (*Aeneid* 3.659); while Ovid combines all these elements of Milton's comparison, as he speaks of "the pine tree, large enough to carry a ship's rigging, which served him as a staff" (13.782–83, trans. Innes). But these and similar allusions in book 1 of *Paradise Lost* are relatively slight, and while the change of the giant angels into less than smallest dwarfs at the close of book 1 may suggest a metamorphosis of the Ovidian kind, the only extended allusion to Ovid before the episode of Sin and Death is found near the middle of book 2:

> As when *Alcides* from *Oechalia* [18] Crown'd
> With conquest, felt th' envenom'd robe, and tore
> Through pain up by the roots *Thessalian* Pines,
> And *Lichas* from the top of *Oeta* threw
> Into th' *Euboic* Sea.   [2.542–46]

The details match closely the account of Ovid (9.136–219), thus
preparing our minds for the drastic change in mode of narration
marked by the strong reminiscences of Ovid that we find in the
account of Sin and her transformation.

Milton turns our minds toward Ovid at the outset of the
episode when he says:

> about her middle round
> A cry of Hell Hounds never ceasing bark'd
> With wide *Cerberean* mouths full loud . . .   [2.653–55]

for Ovid draws the analogy with Cerberus:

> et corpus quaerens femorum crurumque pedumque
> Cerbereos rictus pro partibus invenit illis . . .

> and, feeling for her thighs, her legs, her feet, she finds in place of
> these only gaping dogs'-heads, such as a Cerberus might have.
> [14.64–65, trans. Miller]

Five lines later Milton's reference to the dogs that "Vex'd *Scylla*
bathing in the sea" recalls an essential feature of Ovid's story:
Scylla's habit of bathing in a certain cove, where jealous Circe
caused the hideous change:

> There was a little pool, curving into a deep bow, a peaceful place
> where Scylla loved to come . . . This pool, before the maiden's
> coming, the goddess befouls and tinctures with her baleful poisons.
> . . . Then Scylla comes and wades waist-deep into the water; when
> all at once she sees her loins disfigured with barking monster-
> shapes. [14.51–61, trans. Miller]

And the following allusion to the "Night-Hag" (662–66) recalls
Circe's use of "Hecateia carmina" (14.44) while mixing her
poisonous herbs. With our minds thus directed to Ovid's story, a
subtle series of parallels may occur. Sin's narration of her own
change reminds one of the several times Ovidian characters tell
the tales of their own transformations, just as Glaucus,
passionately in love with Scylla, here tells to her the story of his

change from man into sea-god. Then at the close of Sin's narration her horrified efforts to flee from her fatal offspring Death may suggest Scylla's efforts to flee from the barking monsters: "And at the first, not believing that these are parts of her own body, she flees in fear and tries to drive away the boisterous, barking things. But what she flees she takes along with her" (14.61–63, trans. Miller).

> At last this odious offspring whom thou seest
> Thine own begotten, breaking violent way
> Tore through my entrails, that with fear and pain
> Distorted, all my nether shape thus grew
> Transform'd: but he my inbred enemie
> Forth issu'd, brandishing his fatal Dart
> Made to destroy: I fled, and cry'd out *Death*;
> Hell trembl'd at the hideous Name, and sigh'd
> From all her Caves, and back resounded *Death*.
> I fled, but he pursu'd . . .   [2.781–90]

The repetition is a characteristic device of Ovidian rhetoric:[19] thus at the end of the story of Narcissus and Echo we find a similar matching of words at the ends of the lines:

> indoluit, quotiensque puer miserabilis "eheu"
> dixerat, haec resonis iterabat vocibus "eheu";
> cumque suos manibus percusserat ille lacertos,
> haec quoque reddebat sonitum plangoris eundem.

and as often as the poor boy says "Alas!" again with answering utterance she cries "Alas!" and as his hands beat his shoulders she gives back the same sounds of woe. [3.495–98, trans. Miller]

The reminiscences of Ovid here are thus dominant (though they are combined with many other echoes, from Spenser, Homer, and Vergil), and they may lead us on to feel that echoes of the *Metamorphoses*, in story, in rhetoric, in structure, are helping to weave Milton's poem into a *carmen perpetuum*, interfused with echoes of other epics, ancient and modern. Ovid's voice is only one of many voices that we hear within Milton's "various style," but I believe that it deserves to be recognized as equal in importance to any other voice from Greek or Roman poetry.

So now, as Satan moves into Chaos, Ovid's account of Chaos provides the ground, *instabilis*, *innabilis*, upon which Milton inter-weaves his many echoes of earlier heroic poems by Homer, Vergil, Lucan, Statius, Apollonius Rhodius, and Spenser—all cohering within a context that quite diminishes the heroic effect. For Satan is utterly lost, as he half admits to Chaos:

> I come no Spie,
> With purpose to explore or to disturb
> The secrets of your Realm, but by constraint
> Wandring this darksome desart, as my way
> Lies through your spacious Empire up to light,
> Alone, and without guide, half-lost, I seek
> What readiest path leads where your gloomie bounds
> Confine with Heav'n . . .   [2.970–77]

And from Chaos he receives a diminishing answer: "I know thee, stranger, who thou art" (990)—words that echo a biblical passage in which Jesus casts out a devil who says, "I know thee who thou art" (Luke 4:33–36): "And they were all amazed, and spake among themselves, saying, What a word is this! for with authority and power he commandeth the unclean spirits, and they come out." This is the authority and power that have caused the rout that Chaos now describes:

> I know thee, stranger, who thou art,
> That mighty leading Angel, who of late
> Made head against Heav'ns King, though overthrown.
> I saw and heard, for such a numerous host
> Fled not in silence through the frighted deep
> With ruin upon ruin, rout on rout,
> Confusion worse confounded . . .   [2.990–96]

With all these implications of Satan's weakness, the heroic echoes turn to parody, in another example of a panel of "heroic" style, set in between two panels of quite different mode: the allegorical, metamorphic panel of Satan's encounter with Sin and Death, and the prologue to book 3, where the bard, far from Satan's "weather-beaten" state, revisits "safe" the "holy light,"

> Escap't the *Stygian* Pool, though long detain'd
> In that obscure sojourn, which in my flight
> Through utter and through middle darkness borne
> With other notes then to th' *Orphean* Lyre
> I sung of *Chaos* and *Eternal Night* . . .   [3.14–18]

"With other notes," because the Orphean lyre represents creative power, whereas Milton's first two books, by Milton's phrasing here completely included within the realm of Chaos and Eternal Night, have presented a process of illusory creation.[20] What true creation means we are soon to learn, when we come to view the panels of Paradise.

CHAPTER 13

Pastoral Love: Versions and Subversions

Thus we are prepared for a mutation from the old heroic mode into a new mode composed by one who, like Ovid, is "Not sedulous by Nature to indite / Warrs, hitherto the onely Argument / Heroic deem'd" (9.27–29). This new mutation moves on in book 4 to tell of the first human lovers; and that love-tale begins with an allusion to Ovidian myth. When Eve tells to Adam the story of her first awakening, and of her vision of herself reflected in a lake, the reminiscence of Ovid's story of Narcissus has been felt by every reader.[1] The tale in Milton is all the more Ovidian because Milton sets it in the kind of *locus amoenus* that Ovid so often presents as the scene of a metamorphosis:

> That day I oft remember, when from sleep
> I first awak't, and found my self repos'd
> Under a shade on flours, much wondring where
> And what I was, whence thither brought, and how.
> Not distant far from thence a murmuring sound
> Of waters issu'd from a Cave and spread
> Into a liquid Plain, then stood unmov'd
> Pure as th' expanse of Heav'n; I thither went
> With unexperienc't thought, and laid me downe

219

On the green bank, to look into the cleer
Smooth Lake, that to me seemd another Skie.
As I bent down to look, just opposite,
A Shape within the watry gleam appeerd
Bending to look on me . . .   [4.449–62]

There was a clear pool with silvery bright water, to which no
shepherds ever came, or she-goats feeding on the mountain-side, or
any other cattle; whose smooth surface neither bird nor beast nor
falling bough ever ruffled. Grass grew all around its edge, fed by
the water near, and a coppice that would never suffer the sun to
warm the spot. Here the youth, worn by the chase and the heat, lies
down, attracted thither by the appearance of the place and by the
spring. While he seeks to slake his thirst another thirst springs up,
and while he drinks he is smitten by the sight of the beautiful form
he sees. He loves an unsubstantial hope and thinks that substance
which is only shadow. [*Met.* 3.407–17, trans. Miller]

Narcissus pines away with vain desire, but Eve, with her thought
now less "unexperienc't," yields to Adam's call and touch, sees and
knows his grace and wisdom, using her reason to make a choice:
the poem's first evidence (as Burden has well said) of the human
workings of the freedom of the will.[2]

Yet how "frail" its proper workings may be is at once suggested
by a glimpse of Eve's voluptuous beauty and by an ironical allusion to two deities whose jealous quarrels continually disrupt the
world of Ovidian myth:

                    half her swelling Breast
Naked met his under the flowing Gold
Of her loose tresses hid: he in delight
Both of her Beauty and submissive Charms
Smil'd with superior Love, as *Jupiter*
On *Juno* smiles, when he impregns the Clouds
That shed *May* Flowers; and press'd her Matron lip
With kisses pure . . .   [4.495–502]

It is a happy scene, but we know the escapades and impregnations
that lie behind that jovial smile.

Satan then shatters the peaceful scene with his long soliloquy of
envy, but, after the angelic guard is seen alert to aid, we return to
the peaceful scene, and Eve sings her echoing song of love, a
remarkable show-piece that concentrates in sixteen lines certain

techniques of repetition and reversal that are reminiscent of the
Ovidian style:

> Sweet is the breath of morn, her rising sweet,
> With charm of earliest Birds; pleasant the Sun
> When first on this delightful Land he spreads
> His orient Beams, on herb, tree, fruit, and flour,
> Glistring with dew; fragrant the fertil earth
> After soft showers; and sweet the coming on
> Of grateful Eevning milde, then silent Night
> With this her solemn Bird and this fair Moon,
> And these the Gemms of Heav'n, her starrie train:
> But neither breath of Morn when she ascends
> With charm of earliest Birds, nor rising Sun
> On this delightful land, nor herb, fruit, floure,
> Glistring with dew, nor fragrance after showers,
> Nor grateful Evening mild, nor silent Night
> With this her solemn Bird, nor walk by Moon,
> Or glittering Starr-light without thee is sweet.   [4.641–56]

Brief examples of this sort of repetitive technique are scattered
throughout the *Metamorphoses*.[3] One of the most striking occurs
only a few hundred lines after the tale of Narcissus, a position
especially suggestive, since the tale of Narcissus is set within the
tale of Echo; and thus a virtuoso series of echo-words and phrases
abound on either side of the Narcissus panel. Then early in book
4 Ovid tells another story of passionate love, the tale of Salmacis
and Hermaphroditus, again associated with a beautiful pool in a
typical Ovidian landscape:

> Here he saw a pool of water crystal clear to the very bottom. No
> marshy reeds grew there, no unfruitful swamp-grass, nor spiky
> rushes; it is clear water. But the edges of the pool are bordered with
> fresh grass, and herbage ever green. A nymph dwells in the pool,
> one that loves not hunting, nor is wont to bend the bow or strive
> with speed of foot. She only of the naiads follows not in swift Di-
> ana's train. Often, 'tis said, her sisters would chide her: 'Salmacis,
> take now either hunting-spear or painted quiver, and vary your
> ease with the hardships of the hunt.' But she takes no hunting-
> spear, no painted quiver, nor does she vary her ease with the hard-
> ships of the hunt; but at times she bathes her shapely limbs in her
> own pool; often combs her hair with a boxwood comb, often looks
> in the mirror-like waters to see what best becomes her. Now,

wrapped in a transparent robe, she lies down to rest on the soft grass or the soft herbage. Often she gathers flowers; and on this occasion, too, she chanced to be gathering flowers when she saw the boy and longed to possess what she saw. [4.297–316, trans. Miller]

Salmacis, like Eve, uses the waters as a mirror; and like Eve she would rather carry flowers than weapons. In this context, the technique of negative repetition in the middle of the passage becomes especially significant for Eve's love-song, with its turn to "nor," "nor":

> "Salmaci, vel iaculum vel pictas sume pharetras
> et tua cum duris venatibus otia misce!"
> nec iaculum sumit nec pictas illa pharetras,
> nec sua cum duris venatibus otia miscet . . .   [4.306–09]

At the same time, we might recall the words that Vertumnus speaks to Pomona in Ovid:

> tu primus et ultimus illi
> ardor eris, solique suos tibi devovet annos.
> adde, quod est iuvenis, quod naturale decoris
> munus habet formasque apte fingetur in omnes,
> et quod erit iussus, iubeas licet omnia, fiet.
> quid, quod amatis idem, quod, quae tibi poma coluntur,
> primus habet laetaque tenet tua munera dextra!
> sed neque iam fetus desiderat arbore demptos
> nec, quas hortus alit, cum sucis mitibus herbas
> nec quicquam nisi te . . .

You will be his first love and his last, and to you alone he will devote his life. Consider also that he is young, blest with a native charm, can readily assume whatever form he will, and what you bid him, though without stint you bid, he will perform. Moreover your tastes are similar, and the fruit which you so cherish he is the first to have and with joyful hands he lays hold upon your gifts. But neither the fruit of your trees, nor the sweet, succulent herbs which your garden bears, nor anything at all does he desire save you alone. [14.682–91, trans. Miller]

Again we have the turn near the close, with the use of "neque," "nec," "nec"; while the ending, *nec quicquam nisi te*—"nothing without you"—in the context of fruit and herbs, provides a particularly close and suggestive parallel.

But the deeper roots of Eve's technique of repetition lie in the

pastoral tradition, as my colleague Gordon Williams has pointed
out to me. At the close of Vergil's seventh eclogue—from which
Milton took the motto for his volume of 1645—we find an example of this technique along with the ancient pastoral *topos* in which
the "sweetness" of herb, tree, fruit, and flower arises from or is
surpassed by the beloved:

> Corydon
> Populus Alcidae gratissima, vitis Iaccho,
> formosae myrtus Veneri, sua laurea Phoebo;
> Phyllis amat corylos; illas dum Phyllis amabit,
> nec myrtus vincet corylos, nec laurea Phoebi.
> Thyrsis
> Fraxinus in silvis pulcherrima, pinus in hortis,
> populus in fluviis, abies in montibus altis;
> saepius at si me, Lycida formose, revisas,
> fraxinus in silvis cedat tibi, pinus in hortis.

Hercules loves poplars best of all; Bacchus prefers the vine;
Venus, the Queen of Beauty, loves the myrtle best; and Apollo his
own bays. Phyllis is fond of hazels. As long as Phyllis likes them best,
neither the myrtle nor Apollo's bays shall take a higher place than
hazels.

The ash in forests is the loveliest tree; the pine in gardens; the
poplar by the river's bank; and the fir-tree on the mountain-
heights. But if you, my handsome Lycidas, will spend more time
with me, the ash in her own forest and the pine-tree in the garden
must give place to you.   [7.61–68; trans. Rieu]

The hints of Vergilian pastoral in Eve's song, perhaps assisted
by the reference to Lycidas, would not have come to Milton un-
mediated. Gordon Williams has also pointed out some striking
parallels in Calpurnius Siculus, probably writing in Nero's reign,
and in Nemesianus, of the third century A.D.—poets whose eclogues were well known in the Renaissance, and who carried on
the Vergilian tradition while combining it with the intricate
rhetoric of Ovid.[4] Thus in the third eclogue of Calpurnius we
hear another Lycidas singing these lines as part of a long love-
song for Phyllis:

> te sine, vae misero, mihi lilia nigra videntur
> nec sapiunt fontes et acescunt vina bibenti.
> at si tu venias, et candida lilia fient
> et sapient fontes et dulcia vina bibentur.

> ille ego sum Lycidas, quo te cantante solebas
> dicere felicem . . .

Without you (poor wretch that I am!), lilies seem black to me, fountains lose their taste and wine as I drink turns sour. But if you come, lilies will grow white again, fountains taste aright and wine be sweet to drink. I am that Lycidas at whose singing you used to declare your joy . . .   [3.51–56; trans. Duff][5]

Then in the second eclogue of Nemesianus we find an imitation of both Calpurnius and Vergil which strikes even nearer to the love-song of Eve:

> te sine, vae misero, mihi lilia fusca videntur
> pallentesque rosae nec dulce rubens hyacinthus,
> nullos nec myrtus nec laurus spirat odores.
> at si tu venias, et candida lilia fient
> purpureaeque rosae, et dulce rubens hyacinthus;
> tunc mihi cum myrto laurus spirabit odores.
> nam dum Pallas amat turgentes unguine bacas,
> dum Bacchus vites, Deo sata, poma Priapus,
> pascua laeta Pales, Idas te diligit unam.

Without you (poor wretch that I am!), lilies seem grey to me and roses pale, and the hyacinth has no sweet blush, nor do myrtle or laurel breathe any fragrance; but if you come, lilies will grow white once more, the roses be red, and the hyacinth regain its sweet blush; then for me will laurel with myrtle breathe fragrance forth. For while Pallas loves the olive-berries that swell with fatness, while Bacchus loves the vines, Deo her crops, Priapus his fruits and Pales the joyous pastures, Idas loves you alone.   [2.44–52; trans. Duff][6]

"Without thee"—so pastoral art lives in Milton's Paradise where the poet's vision shows the possibility of recovering the pristine love of nature, man, and God that stands as the healing center for mankind's heavy loss.

An interesting rhetorical analogy of another kind occurs in one of the best known passages in Ovid, the account of how the trees gather round at the song of Orpheus. This famous passage, like Eve's love-song, covers sixteen lines, and like Eve's song it is divided into sections of nine and seven lines, with a reversal of syntax at the tenth line:

> umbra loco venit: non Chaonis afuit arbor,
> non nemus Heliadum, non frondibus aesculus altis,

nec tiliae molles, nec fagus et innuba laurus,
et coryli fragiles et fraxinus utilis hastis
enodisque abies curvataque glandibus ilex
et platanus genialis acerque coloribus inpar
amnicolaeque simul salices et aquatica lotos
perpetuoque virens buxum tenuesque myricae
et bicolor myrtus et bacis caerula tinus.
vos quoque, flexipedes hederae, venistis et una
pampineae vites et amictae vitibus ulmi
ornique et piceae pomoque onerata rubenti
arbutus et lentae, victoris praemia, palmae
et succincta comas hirsutaque vertice pinus,
grata deum matri, siquidem Cybeleius Attis
exuit hac hominem truncoque induruit illo.   [10.90–105]

A literal translation, adapting the Loeb version, will make clear
the shift that occurs in the tenth line of this catalogue:

> shade came to the place: nor was the Chaonian tree absent, nor the
> grove of the Heliades, nor the oak with its deep foliage, nor the soft
> linden, nor the beech and the virgin laurel, and the brittle hazel,
> and the ash suitable for spear-shafts, and the smooth silver-fir, and
> the ilex bending with acorns, and the pleasant plane-tree, and the
> many-colored maple, and likewise the river-haunting willows, and
> the lotus, lover of pools, and the ever-green boxwood, and the
> slender tamarisk, and the double-colored myrtle, and the viburnum
> with its dark blue berries.

"After this amazing list of 18 trees," says Anderson, "Ovid stops to
take a breath, then plunges on. He begins this second sequence
with an apostrophe to ivy and a unique epic epithet *flexipedes*":[7]

> You also, pliant-footed ivy, came, and along with you tendrilled
> grapes, and the elm-trees draped with vines and the mountain-ash,
> and the pitch-pines, and the wild strawberry-tree loaded with ruddy
> fruit, and the pliant palm, prize of victory, and the bare-trunked
> pine with broad leafy top, pleasing to the mother of the gods, since
> Attis, dear to Cybele, exchanged for this his human form and stif-
> fened in its trunk.

The catalogue, the dimensions of the piece, and the shift in
movement at line ten all suggest a tantalizing parallel—the kind of
creative imitation that the renaissance school-boy was trained to
make, adapting the devices of Ovidian rhetoric to a quite different
subject from the original.[8] No single passage in ancient poetry,

then, lies behind the remarkable technique of Eve's love-song; it is a complex blending of many pastoral and Ovidian devices.

These Ovidian echoes serve as a reminder that a host of other echoes run throughout book 4 and the first half of book 5—the "pastoral" scenes of *Paradise Lost*. Brooks of nectar run over sands of gold (4.237–40), reminding us of Ovid's *saturnia regna* (1.111) and of his story concerning Midas and the river Pactolus (11.142–45). There are "Groves whose rich Trees wept odorous Gumms and Balme" (4.248), reminding us of the weeping tree that was Myrrha and the weeping trees that were the Heliades (*Met.* 2.340–66; 10.489–502). And the *locus amoenus* gathers up details from a dozen Ovidian settings:

> Another side, umbrageous Grots and Caves
> Of coole recess, o're which the mantling Vine
> Layes forth her purple Grape, and gently creeps
> Luxuriant; mean while murmuring waters fall
> Down the slope hills, disperst, or in a Lake,
> That to the fringed Bank with Myrtle crownd,
> Her chrystall mirror holds, unite thir streams.   [4.257–63]

Meanwhile "Universal *Pan* / Knit with the *Graces* and the *Hours* in dance / Led on th' Eternal Spring" (4.266–68), evoking the legend of Zephyrus and Chloris-Flora referred to overtly at the outset of book 5 (16)—the legend made famous by Botticelli and told by Ovid in his *Fasti* (5.195–220). The thought of eternal spring leads on to that scene in Ovid near the walls of Enna where there is a lake named Pergus—a scene of *perpetuum ver*:

> A ring of trees encircles the pool, clothing the lakeside all around, and the leaves of the trees shelter the spot from Phoebus' rays, like a screen. Their boughs afford cool shade, and the lush meadow is bright with flowers. There it is always spring. In this glade Proserpine was playing, picking violets or shining lilies. With childlike eagerness she gathered the flowers into baskets and into the folds of her gown, trying to pick more than any of her companions. Almost at one and the same time, Pluto saw her, and loved her, and bore her off—so swift is love. [5.388–96, trans. Innes]

Dis (to use Ovid's term) was there, we may recall, because the heavings of the giant Typhoeus, described by Ovid a few lines

earlier, had made him worry that his nether kingdom might be
opened to the light, and therefore he had come up above ground
to inspect the surface of Sicily. So we come to the well-known
passage in Milton:

> Not that faire field
> Of *Enna*, where *Proserpin* gathring flours
> Her self a fairer Floure by gloomie *Dis*
> Was gatherd, which cost *Ceres* all that pain
> To seek her through the world . . .   [4.268–72]

But all that pain of Ceres is not told in the *Metamorphoses*: it is told
in Ovid's other, and longer version of the story in his *Fasti*
(4.420–620). Thus both of Ovid's great treasuries of ancient myth
tend to cohere within the context of Milton's allusions, as in the
earlier reference to the legend of Chloris. This allusion to the
rape of Proserpine is the most significant mythological reference
in the entire fourth book, perhaps in the entire poem, since it
foreshadows the seduction of Eve by the Prince of the underworld
and links directly with the scene in book 9, where, shortly after the
cluster of allusions to Pomona, Ceres and Proserpine (9.393–96),
Satan in the form of the serpent spies Eve alone in a "spot more
delicious" than any *locus amoenus* ever before described:

> Veil'd in a Cloud of Fragrance, where she stood,
> Half spi'd, so thick the Roses bushing round
> About her glowd, oft stooping to support
> Each Flour of slender stalk, whose head though gay
> Carnation, Purple, Azure, or spect with Gold,
> Hung drooping unsustained, them she upstaies
> Gently with Mirtle band, mindless the while,
> Her self, though fairest unsupported Flour,
> From her best prop so farr, and storm so nigh.   [9.425–33]

In book 4, after the long imitation of the Narcissus tale and the
love-song of Eve, we come to the "blissful bower," so different
from Spenser's Bower of Bliss; a bower woven together out of
flowers and shrubs filled with a mythological redolence: the laurel
of Daphne, the myrtle of Venus, and other plants and flowers
associated with Ovidian metamorphoses: violet, crocus, and

hyacinth.[9] These associations are then reinforced and coalesced as Milton sums up the Ovidian atmosphere:

> In shadier Bower
> More sacred and sequesterd, though but feignd,
> *Pan* or *Silvanus* never slept, nor Nymph,
> Nor *Faunus* haunted. Here in close recess
> With Flowers, Garlands, and sweet-smelling Herbs
> Espoused *Eve* deckt first her Nuptial Bed . . .   [4.705–10]

Thus too the "silvan lodge" where Adam and Eve receive the angel "like *Pomona's* Arbour smil'd / With flourets deck't and fragrant smells" (5.378–79), while the reference to Pomona links with the earlier passage in book 5 where Adam and Eve hasten "to thir mornings rural work"

> Among sweet dewes and flours; where any row
> Of Fruit-trees overwoodie reachd too farr
> Thir pamperd boughes, and needed hands to check
> Fruitless imbraces: or they led the Vine
> To wed her Elm; she spous'd about him twines
> Her mariageable arms, and with her brings
> Her dowr th' adopted Clusters, to adorn
> His barren leaves.   [5.212–19]

The last five lines here adapt the passage in Ovid where Vertumnus, disguised as an old woman, attempts to win Pomona's love:

> There was an elm tree opposite, a lovely sight to see, with its bunches of shining grapes, and this the god praised, and its companion vine no less. 'But,' he said, 'if this tree trunk stood by itself, and was not wedded to the vine, it would be of no interest to anybody, except for its leaves. Moreover, the vine is supported by the elm to which it has been united, whereas if it had not been so married, it would lie trailing on the ground. And yet you are unmoved by the example of this tree! You shun marriage, and do not care to wed.' [14.661–68, trans. Innes]

The earlier part of Milton's passage echoes Ovid's preceding account of Pomona's cultivation of her fruit-trees, as with her pruning knife "she would cut away growth that was too luxurious, and prune back branches that were spreading in different directions" ("qua modo luxuriem premit et spatiantia passim / bracchia conpescit": 14.629–30, trans. Innes).

All these allusions to Ovidian myth in the pastoral scenes of *Paradise Lost* combine to warn of the imminence of change in Paradise: for Ovid himself has adapted the *locus amoenus* from the tradition of pastoral poetry, and then has used it (as Charles Segal has shown)[10] to invert, or subvert, the pastoral values of Theocritus and Vergil. In the idylls and eclogues the pastoral settings of pools, streams, fountains, caves, flowers, grass, and trees provide the cool recesses and shady bowers from which the pastoral vision can view the troubles of the world from a distance, in a purifying perspective. But in Ovid, these peaceful settings are deceptive haunts of violence; their *otium* invites the sexual ravages of self-love, rape or seduction by the gods; even Vertumnus is "ready to use force" (14.770). Pastoral *otium* creates a sense of security within the fragile peace of the pastoral moment, but Ovidian *otium* creates a sense of underlying, uncontrollable danger arising from the passionate energies that dominate the earth.

The deceptive beauty of these Ovidian scenes is summed up in the horror of Dryope's innocent plucking of the water-lotus—the plant in whose shape the nymph Lotis had found refuge "while fleeing from Priapus' vile pursuit" (9.346–48; trans. Miller). The transformation of Dryope into a tree occurs beside "a pool whose shelving banks take the form of sloping shores, the top of which a growth of myrtle crowns" ("est lacus, adclivis devexo margine formam / litoris efficiens, summum myrteta coronant": 9.334–35)—lines that Milton seems to evoke in a passage quoted earlier (4.260–63). The fatal flower is full of beautiful promise: "Near the margin of the pool a plant of the water-lotus grew full of bright blossoms, the harbingers of fruit. To please her little son the mother plucked some of these blossoms, and I was in the act to do the same [says her sister] when I saw drops of blood falling from the flowers and the branches shivering with horror" (9.340–45; trans. Miller). Thus Ovid's persistent subversion of pastoral values serves as a warning that the threat of destructive power lurks everywhere in Milton's Eden.

The illustration here reproduced was designed by Carlotta Petrina as a frontispiece for book 4 of *Paradise Lost;* but it could serve almost as well as an illustration for book 4 of Ovid's *Metamorphoses,* with its tale of Salmacis and Hermaphroditus. The artist has

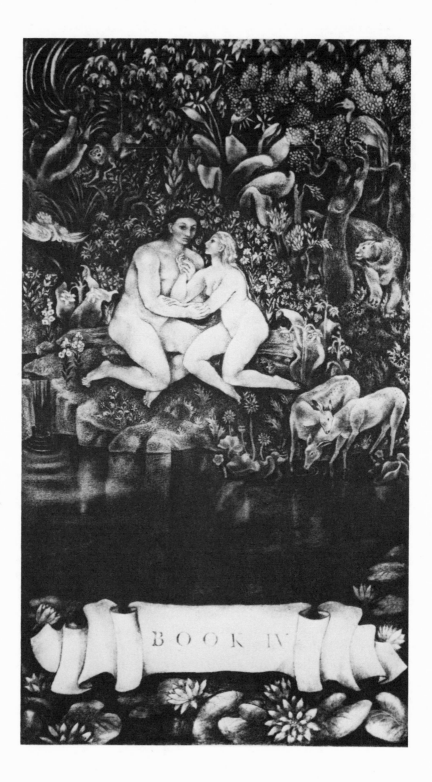

caught the Ovidian implications of Milton's pastoral. The female figure making the advances could almost be the nymph Salmacis, and the passive, bemused male figure staring outward could almost be the unresponsive Hermaphroditus: "When the nymph begged and prayed for at least a sister's kiss, and was in [the] act to throw her arms round his snowy neck, he cried: 'Have done, or I must flee and leave this spot—and you'" (4.334–36). One can glimpse here also something like the mulberry tree, "full of snow-white berries," beside the "cool spring" in the tale of Pyramus and Thisbe (4.89–90), while the varied flowers (including suggestions of the water-lotus?), birds, and animals might be seen as allusions to the metamorphoses that so often overtake the mortal lovers in Ovid's myths of passion. And it is such passion—of revenge, ambition, envy, and love—that will destroy this pastoral of Paradise.

These allusions to Ovidian myth, then, are far more than decorations, or acknowledgment of an epic predecessor; they lie at the very heart of Milton's purpose: to show how this greatest of changes brought in all other forms of change and changing forms, and then to show how Ovid's sense of endless change may be converted into change that has a higher, a teleological design.

CHAPTER 14

The
Ultimate
Design

Awareness of Milton's ultimate design is maintained throughout *Paradise Lost* by the voice of the bard, the narrator, or the authorial presence, as it is sometimes called—that presence recognized in so many recent studies and frequently remarked in the preceding section of this book.[1] Such a presence, so different from the objectivity of Homer, may in part derive from Vergil's "subjective style" in the *Aeneid*. But the presence of Vergil's narrator is subtle and usually tacit, though now and then, infrequently, emerging in open exclamations of sympathy or revulsion. Ovid appears to have picked up this mode of presence from Vergil, and to have carried it several steps further in the *Metamorphoses*.[2] It may well be that Ovid's example encouraged the epic poets of the Renaissance to carry the process of authorial intervention even further, reaching a final stage in the remarkably long interventions of Camoens, Spenser, and Milton.[3] Ovid's interventions are usually quite brief, but they are persistent and pervasive in a way that may remind us of the constant presence of the narrative voice in *Paradise Lost*. A few examples from Ovid may help to suggest a

232

general similarity in technique, while illustrating the differences in tone and attitude.

In the tale of Deucalion and Pyrrha the voice of the narrator at first emerges almost imperceptibly as Deucalion suggests that they should throw the stones:

> Coniugis augurio quamquam Titania mota est,
> spes tamen in dubio est: adeo caelestibus ambo
> diffidunt monitis; sed quid temptare nocebit?

Although Pyrrha is moved by her husband's surmise, yet hope still wavers; so distrustful are they both as to the heavenly command. But what harm will it do to try? [1.395–97, trans. Miller]

This resembles the Vergilian mode of presence, entering into the minds of the characters and expressing their inmost thoughts. Then Ovid returns to objective narration, but for only two lines:

> descendunt: velantque caput tunicasque recingunt
> et iussos lapides sua post vestigia mittunt.
> saxa (quis hoc credat, nisi sit pro teste vetustas?)
> ponere duritiem coepere suumque rigorem
> mollirique mora mollitaque ducere formam.

They go down, veil their heads, ungird their robes, and throw stones behind them just as the goddess had bidden. And the stones—who would believe it unless ancient tradition vouched for it?—began at once to lose their hardness and stiffness, to grow soft slowly, and softened to take on form. [1.398–402]

The skeptical interjection, with the appeal to tradition, is constantly recurring in the poem, sometimes in a phrase: "si modo credimus," "si credere dignum est," "prior edidit aetas," "fama est," or simply a word such as "dicitur," "fertur," "ferunt," "memorant," or "dicunt"—all meaning something like "they say"—"I don't myself vouch for it, but this is what I have heard." Such words and phrases have a great cumulative effect in creating the impression of a single controlling presence.

Then, after this strong interjection, Ovid returns to the objective manner—but again, for only two lines:

> mox ubi creverunt naturaque mitior illis
> contigit, ut quaedam, sic non manifesta videri
> forma potest hominis, sed uti de marmore coeptis
> non exacta satis rudibusque simillima signis . . .

> Then, when they had grown in size and become milder in their
> nature, a certain likeness to the human form, indeed, could be seen,
> still not very clear, but such as statues just begun out of marble
> have, not sharply defined, and very like roughly blocked-out im-
> ages. [1.403–06]

The comparison with something that the author seems to be recalling from his own observation is characteristic of Ovid's constant
comparisons with everyday things.[4] This tendency is carried to the
extreme in his simile of the raising of a curtain in the Roman
theater (3.111–14), or his mock-hesitant comparison of the homes
of the highest gods to the Palatine: "hic locus est, quem, si verbis
audacia detur, / haud timeam magni dixisse Palatia caeli" (1.175–
76).

Ovid concludes his account of the stones with a gesture of piety:
"And in a short time, through the operation of the divine will, the
stones thrown by the man's hand took on the form of men, and
women were made from the stones the woman threw." Then the
passage is rounded off with a characteristic *sententia*: "Hence come
the hardness of our race and our endurance of toil; and we give
proof from what origin we are sprung."

> inque brevi spatio superorum numine saxa
> missa viri manibus faciem traxere virorum
> et de femineo reparata est femina iactu.
> inde genus durum sumus experiensque laborum
> et documenta damus qua simus origine nati.   [1.411–15]

More dramatic examples may be found in quite a different kind
of episode—the story of Tereus and Philomela, where Ovid enfolds the beginning of the fearful tale within a continuous commentary, addressing the reader in a familiar fashion, interpreting
overtly every act and emotion, setting the tale within the reader's
apprehension by everyday allusions (translation adapted from
Miller and Innes):

> ecce venit magno dives Philomela paratu,
> divitior forma; quales audire solemus
> naidas et dryadas mediis incedere silvis,
> si modo des illis cultus similesque paratus.
> non secus exarsit conspecta virgine Tereus,

> quam si quis canis ignem supponat aristis
> aut frondem positasque cremet faenilibus herbas.

Behold, Philomela entered, attired in rich apparel, but richer still in beauty. She was like the descriptions that one often hears of the naiads and the dryads who haunt the depths of the woodlands, if only they wore ornaments and garments such as hers. The moment he saw the maiden Tereus was inflamed with love, just as if some person should set fire to ripe grain, or dry leaves, or hay stored away in the mow. [6.451–57]

The series of comparisons at the close serves to enforce the authorial interpretation of Tereus. But more open interpretation follows, at length: "Her beauty, indeed, was worth it; but in his case his own passionate nature stirred him on, and, besides, the people of his region are quick to respond to the promptings of Venus: his own fault and his nation's burnt in him."

> digna quidem facies; sed et hunc innata libido
> exstimulat, pronumque genus regionibus illis
> in Venerem est: flagrat vitio gentisque suoque.   [6.458–60]

"There was nothing which he would not do or dare, smitten by this mad passion. His heart could scarce contain the fires that burnt in it."

> et nihil est, quod non effreno captus amore
> ausit, nec capiunt inclusas pectora flammas.   [6.465–66]

Then the narrator's indignation at the shameful lies and hypocrisy of Tereus bursts out violently:

> pro superi, quantum mortalia pectora caecae
> noctis habent! ipso sceleris molimine Tereus
> creditur esse pius laudemque a crimine sumit.

O gods above, what blind night rules in the hearts of men! In the very act of pushing on his shameful plan Tereus gets credit for a kind heart and wins praise from wickedness. [6.472–74]

Milton, then, could have found in the *Metamorphoses* ample precedent for enfolding his own story within the consciousness of his own fictive presence. It is not the presence of John Milton as a person, though some of his personal attributes and experiences are there—but rather, as in Ovid, the presence of a creative, remembering, sympathizing, judging mind that holds under control materials that include and then exceed even the vast range of Ovidian mythology. For all of ancient myth must now be transcended by the new religion that was arising in Ovid's day, and was soon to offer a new faith to fill the place of the gods that were dying (while still living in affectionate memory) within the skeptical consciousness of Ovid's poem. Milton's allusions to Ovidian myth, and to the same or other myths preserved by other classical authors, combine with biblical story to create a rich remembrance of the vast world of ancient religions, some horrible, as the worship of Moloch, some beautiful, as the worship of Thammuz, some almost irresistible, as the worship of Venus and Bacchus, but all remembered and included, sometimes with reproach, sometimes with full appreciation of their beauty. Milton's poem stands as a vast memorial to the deep religious needs and purposes of mankind, fulfilled, as Milton believes, in the dynamic inclusiveness of his own faith.

II

The nature of that fulfillment is recorded in Milton's "historical" conclusion, the tenth book of the first edition, the eleventh and twelfth books of the second edition, where Milton seems to evoke an ironical memory of the closing books of Ovid's epic. In the eleventh book of the *Metamorphoses*, after the migration of Bacchus and his followers to Tmolus, the story of Midas, and the brief account of the founding of Troy, the portion of the poem devoted mainly to tales of love and passion concludes on a gentler, more beneficent note, with the story of Peleus and Thetis and the long tale of the true love of Ceyx and Alcyone. The opening of book 12 marks the movement into another theme, with the introduction of Priam, Hector, and Paris, and the thousand ships of the Greeks who sailed in vengeance. The last four books are clearly differentiated from the preceding portion of the poem; the brief account of Troy in book 11 is buried amidst Bacchic and amorous tales and cannot be taken to mark the beginning of the poem's "historical" movement—though, in Ovid's way, it foreshadows that movement. But now, in books 12–15, we turn to the story of Troy, the story of Aeneas, the story of Rome, and the glories of the Roman empire under Augustus. Up through book 11 all is myth; after that the thread of the tale is "history"—the legendary history of Troy and Rome and the actual history of Ovid's own day, interspersed, and sometimes overwhelmed, with myths—the battle of the Lapiths and Centaurs, or the love tales of Acis, Galatea, and Polyphemus, Scylla, Glaucus, and Circe, Pomona and Vertumnus.

Critics of Ovid have had much the same problems in dealing with Ovid's concluding "historical" books that critics of Milton have had in dealing with the last two books of *Paradise Lost*, where Milton turns away from the story of the Fall to recount the history of mankind. Critics have called Ovid's performance in his last four books perfunctory, "prosy," and lacking in continuity with the preceding books—except for the brilliantly told fables that constantly interrupt the "history." [5] So too critics of Milton have often viewed the last two books of *Paradise Lost* as a weak epilogue, with occasional flashes of power. But perhaps in both cases we are not catching the interplay of the poet's lowered style against the higher style that he elsewhere displays. Some classical scholars seem to be turning toward the view that Ovid's "perfunctory" account of Aeneas is an indication that Ovid will not attempt to compete with Vergil on his own ground. Ovid will recount the "history," drily and quickly, while using it to provide a "liaison" for the fables of love and passion that are his chief concern. [6] Under such circumstances the exalted praise of Julius Caesar and Augustus at the close is bound to seem inflated (though not necessarily meant to seem so by the author). Ovid's example here may have provided Milton with an opportunity to create a subtle series of ironies.

At the outset of Milton's history of the fallen world, the example of Ovid may be evoked by the grand catalogue of earth's empires that Michael shows to Adam (11.385–411). Although that catalogue is indebted to Homer, Vergil, or Camoens, still the catalogues of those poets are not usually so condensed and compact as Milton's glorious roll of proper names. For models of such compact catalogues one may turn to Ovid, since he is notorious for exactly such lists of names, places, and things. [7] We have read the catalogue of the trees that gathered around Orpheus, and to this one should add the catalogue of mountains burned during the ride of Phaeton (2.217–26), followed by the even longer catalogue of rivers (2.242–59). There is also the catalogue of Actaeon's dogs (3.206–25), the enormous list of comparisons and possessions sung by Polyphemus (13.789–820), and the heaping of place-names in the last book of the *Metamorphoses* (15.700–718), where Ovid tells of the journey of Aesculapius to Rome:

> Romethiumque legit Caulonaque Naryciamque
> evincitque fretum Siculique angusta Pelori
> Hippotadaeque domos regis Temesesque metalla
> Leucosiamque petit tepidique rosaria Paesti.
> inde legit Capreas promunturiumque Minervae
> et Surrentino generosos palmite colles
> Herculeamque urbem Stabiasque et in otia natam
> Parthenopen et ab hac Cumaeae templa Sibyllae.

[He] skirted Romethium and Caulon and Narycia; then passed the Sicilian sea and Pelorus' narrow strait, sailed by the home of Hippotades, past the copper mines of Temesa, and headed for Leucosia and mild Paestum's rose gardens. Thence he skirted Capreae, Minerva's promontory, and the hills of Surrentum rich in vines; thence sailed to Herculaneum and Stabiae and Parthenope, for soft pleasure founded, and from there to the temple of the Cumaean Sibyl (15.705–12, trans. Miller).

Such passages seem to resound within Milton's lines:

> *Mombaza*, and *Quiloa*, and *Melind*,
> And *Sofala* thought *Ophir*, to the Realme
> Of *Congo*, and *Angola* fardest South;
> Or thence from *Niger* Flood to *Atlas* Mount
> The Kingdoms of *Almansor*, *Fez* and *Sus*,
> *Marocco* and *Algiers*, and *Tremisen* . . .   [11.399–404]

Both Camoens and Milton have learned some lessons from Ovid.

Such Ovidian catalogues of course are not limited to the *Metamorphoses*: one thinks of the catalogue of places visited or viewed by Ceres in her search for Proserpine (*Fasti* 4.469–80,563–72), especially the second of these lists, with its witty, self-mocking conclusion:

> nam modo turilegos Arabas, modo despicit Indos,
> hinc Libys, hinc Meroë siccaque terra subest;

> nunc adit Hesperios Rhenum Rhodanumque Padumque
>   teque, future parens, Thybri, potentis aquae.
> quo feror?

For now she looked down on the incense-gathering Arabs, and now on the Indians: beneath her lay on one side Libya, on the other side Meroe, and the parched land. Now she visited the western rivers, the Rhine, the Rhone, the Po, and thee, Tiber, future parent of a mighty water. Whither do I stray? [4.569–73, trans. Frazer]

"Where am I going in such a rush?" Nothing could show more clearly that here is *Ovidius lascivus*, playing a witty game with sound and versification, as in the earlier outrageous line "Himeraque et Didymen Acragantaque Tauromenumque" (*Fasti* 4.475).

Milton too in his way is playing a game with his catalogue in book 11, not the "solemn game" that Eliot once saw there,[8] but a fierce, sardonic game by which he inflates the "glories" of empire just before showing their crimes and follies. Then in book 12 Milton gives, by contrast, another list of places, presented in a lower, simpler style, without rhetorical flourishes, almost clumsy in its manner, as Michael describes to Adam the places that Abraham and his seed will inhabit:

> *Canaan* he now attains, I see his Tents
> Pitcht about *Sechem*, and the neighbouring Plaine
> Of *Moreh*; there by promise he receaves
> Gift to his Progenie of all that Land;
> From *Hamath* Northward to the Desert South
> (Things by thir names I call, though yet unnam'd)
> From *Hermon* East to the great Western Sea,
> Mount *Hermon*, yonder Sea, each place behold
> In prospect, as I point them; on the shoare
> Mount *Carmel*; here the double-founted stream
> *Jordan*, true limit Eastward; but his Sons
> Shall dwell to *Senir*, that long ridge of Hills.
> This ponder, that all Nations of the Earth
> Shall in his Seed be blessed . . .   [135–48]

The Holy Land has no need of classical rhetoric to reveal its meaning. Just as Ovid's "Aeneid" serves as "a bare narrative framework"[9] within which delightful fables are woven, so Milton's bare account of biblical history in book 12 serves as a framework within which high points revealing God's power are enhanced.

After his grand catalogue of empires, Milton's history of mankind falls into two parts—and so does Ovid's final book, in a way that may have suggested a two-part finale to both Camoens and Milton. The first half is given over to philosophical instruction involving the origins and primaeval years of the human race, while the second half tells of Roman myths and the glories of Roman history. King Numa "was not content with learning the rites of the Sabine race, but conceived a grander project, to inquire into the nature of the universe" (15.5–6, trans. Innes). Desiring such knowledge, he left his native town and went to Crotona, where Pythagoras was living in exile from Samos. There Numa learns the teachings of Pythagoras, whose situation, political views, and achievements are described by Ovid in a way very close to the attitudes, the hopes, and the aims of John Milton:

> There was a man here, Samian born, but he
> Had fled from Samos, for he hated tyrants
> And chose, instead, an exile's lot. His thought
> Reached far aloft, to the great gods in Heaven,
> And his imagination looked on visions
> Beyond his mortal sight. All things he studied
> With watchful eager mind, and he brought home
> What he had learned and sat among the people
> Teaching them what was worthy, and they listened
> In silence, wondering at the revelations,
> How the great world began, the primal cause,
> The nature of things, what God is, whence the snows
> Come down, where lightning breaks from, whether wind
> Or Jove speaks in the thunder from the clouds,
> The cause of earthquakes, by what law the stars
> Wheel in their courses, all the secrets hidden
> From man's imperfect knowledge. [15.60–72, trans. Humphries]

One passage in the Latin is especially evocative, when applied to Milton: "quae natura negabat / visibus humanis, oculis ea pectoris hausit"—"what nature denied to human sight he feasted upon with the eyes of the mind" (15.63–64).

Ovid then delivers the teachings of Pythagoras in the form of a four-hundred-line speech by the sage himself (15.75–478). It begins with a warning against the eating of animal food, an act which led to the corruption of mankind's original innocence: "O mortals, do not pollute your bodies with a food so impious!"[10] Such a practice, he declares, was not known in the golden age, "blessed with the fruit of the trees and the herbs which the ground sends forth" (97–98). Then "all things were free from treacherous snares, fearing no guile and full of peace" (102–03). But after someone, setting a bad example, "whoever he was, envied the food of lions, and thrust down flesh as food into his greedy stomach, he opened the way for crime [fecit iter sceleri]" (104–06); then "further impiety grew out of that [longius inde nefas abiit]" (111).

> inde (fames homini vetitorum tanta ciborum est!)
> audetis vesci, genus o mortale! quod, oro,
> ne facite, et monitis animos advertite nostris!

Thence (so great is man's lust for forbidden food!) do you dare thus to feed, O race of mortals! I pray you, do not do it, but turn your minds to these my words of warning.   [138–40]

Then Pythagoras proceeds to reveal the secrets of the universe: "Great matters, never traced out by the minds of former men, things that have long been hidden, I will sing" (146–47). He tells how "our souls are deathless" (158) and live by constant transmigration into other bodies: "All things are changing; nothing dies. The spirit wanders, comes now here, now there, and occupies whatever frame it pleases. From beasts it passes into human bodies, and from our bodies into beasts, but never perishes" (165–68). That is why Pythagoras abhors the eating of flesh: "Therefore, lest your piety be overcome by appetite, I warn you as a seer, do not drive out by impious slaughter what may be kindred souls, and let not life be fed on life" (173–75).

This principle, *omnia mutantur, nihil interit* (165), operates throughout the world: "All things are in a state of flux, and everything is brought into being with a changing nature. . . . For that which once existed is no more, and that which was not has come to be; and so the whole round of motion is gone through again" (177–78,183–85). So landscape changes, so decaying carcasses produce animal life, so great cities and empires are ever-changing:

> . . . some nations putting on new strength and others falling into weakness. So was Troy great in wealth and men, and for ten years was able to give so freely of her blood; but now, humbled to earth, she has naught to show but ancient ruins, no wealth but ancestral tombs. Sparta was at one time a famous city; great Mycenae flourished, and Cecrops' and Amphion's citadels. Sparta is now a worthless countryside, proud Mycenae has fallen; and what is the Thebes of Oedipus except a name? . . . And now fame has it that Dardanian Rome is rising, and laying deep and strong foundations by the stream of Tiber sprung from the Apennines. She therefore is changing her form by growth, and some day shall be the capital of the boundless world! [421–35]

Then he briefly recalls the prophecy that Aeneas will found a new city in a foreign land—thus recalling the whole compass of the *Aeneid*, with its celebration of the glories of *Roma Aeterna*, as in Vergil's sixth book. Ovid will go on, in the latter half of his final book, to celebrate those glories—but he will not here call that city or that empire immortal, though he has done so in the *Fasti* (3.72). Ovid's celebration of Rome is qualified by the long speech of Pythagoras, for Rome too will decay, if the lesson of Pythagoras is right.[11] Individual heroes, such as Julius Caesar and Augustus, will be transmuted into gods—but Rome itself cannot avoid the universal process of change. Only poetry will endure.

The whole speech of Pythagoras evokes analogies with the instruction of Adam by the two angels: instruction by Raphael in the secrets of the universe, in the middle books, with the stern warnings against transgressing the divine prohibition; and finally, Michael's story of the turning of man toward evil, the sad history of the crimes of the human race, down to Milton's own day and beyond.

But Milton's poem is designed to include, transcend, and contradict teachings like those of Pythagoras, for in Milton's universe eternal flux exists only in Chaos. When the elements have entered into forms created by God their circular movement plays a part in a teleological plan in which all created things prove to be

> yet regular
> Then most, when most irregular they seem:
> And in their motions harmonie Divine
> So smooths her charming tones, that Gods own ear
> Listens delighted.   [5.623–27]

Thus, although within each creature the four elements may re-
volve in their circular way, the creatures themselves are designed
in a scale that looks upward, each creature having an allegiance
toward the divine, as Raphael explains in his great organic images:

> So from the root
> Springs lighter the green stalk, from thence the leaves
> More aerie, last the bright consummate floure
> Spirits odorous breathes: flours and thir fruit
> Mans nourishment, by gradual scale sublim'd
> To vital Spirits aspire, to animal,
> To intellectual, give both life and sense,
> Fansie and understanding, whence the soule
> Reason receives, and reason is her being . . .   [5.479–87]

Raphael goes on to suggest the possibility of an even higher ascension, saying that perhaps

> Your bodies may at last turn all to Spirit,
> Improv'd by tract of time, and wingd ascend
> Ethereal, as wee, or may at choice
> Here or in Heav'nly Paradises dwell;
> If ye be found obedient . . .   [5.497–501]

Even disobedience cannot wholly interrupt that upward movement: Milton's conclusion, with its sad and bitter story of the
cycles of mankind's growth and decay, nevertheless moves toward
the day when the just will receive immortal joy and time will cease.
Milton's *carmen perpetuum* records a changing movement, under
the freedom of the will, not without purpose, not without end. In
adapting the Pythagorean and Ovidian theory of change, Milton
thus invalidates its central principle, as the Jupiter who saved
Deucalion and Pyrrha from the flood is transformed into the God
of Milton:

Such grace shall one just Man find in his sight,
That he relents, not to blot out mankind,
And makes a Covenant never to destroy
The Earth again by flood, nor let the Sea
Surpass his bounds, nor Rain to drown the World
With Man therein or Beast; but when he brings
Over the Earth a Cloud, will therein set
His triple-colour'd Bow, whereon to look
And call to mind his Cov'nant: Day and Night,
Seed time and Harvest, Heat and hoary Frost
Shall hold thir course, till fire purge all things new,
Both Heav'n and Earth, wherein the just shall dwell.

[11.890–end]

PART IV

The Chosen Sons

But when we have to do with things which we behold with the mind, that is, with the intelligence and with reason, we speak of things which we look upon directly in the inner light of truth which illumines the inner man and is inwardly enjoyed.

Augustine, De Magistro

CHAPTER 15

Paradise Regain'd:
The Interior
Teacher

In the search for universals, said Augustine, "we do not listen to anyone speaking and making sounds outside ourselves. We listen to Truth which presides over our minds within us, though of course we may be bidden to listen by someone using words. Our real Teacher is he who is so listened to, who is said to dwell in the inner man, namely Christ, that is, the unchangeable power and eternal wisdom of God."[1] Milton shared this Augustinian view of "wisdom" speaking within the mind. The "prophetic function" of Christ, he said, "has two parts, one external and one internal. The first is the revelation of divine truth, the second the illumination of the mind."[2] The two roles of course cannot be separated, but it seems fair to say that *Paradise Lost,* in keeping with its epic decorum, presents the Son of God primarily in his external function, as in the revelation of his majestic power in book 6; whereas *Paradise Regain'd* shows the Son in his second, his internal function. Through a process of renunciation *Paradise Regain'd* gradually reveals the voice of Truth speaking within the illuminated mind.

A mode of renunciation is implicit in the basic style of *Paradise Regain'd*: a ground-style that Milton carefully announces in his

247

opening lines and maintains with strong consistency throughout
the first book:

> I who e're while the happy Garden sung,
> By one mans disobedience lost, now sing
> Recover'd Paradise to all mankind,
> By one mans firm obedience fully tri'd
> Through all temptation, and the Tempter foil'd
> In all his wiles, defeated and repuls't,
> And *Eden* rais'd in the wast Wilderness.

The allusion to *Paradise Lost* here asks us to recall that poem, and
to note how different this new poem will be in its theme and hence
in its style. We need only recall the latinate suspension and compression of that first enormous sentence of *Paradise Lost* to feel the
contrast with the normal movement and scope of educated English speech in *Paradise Regain'd*. It is a simple "I" who sings this
new poem, a plain man without his bardic "robes." The voice of
the narrator now speaks in a style appropriate to a poem
prompted, not by emulation of the epic Muse, but purely by the
"Spirit who ledst this glorious Eremite / Into the Desert." Leaving behind the poem that dealt with an argument

> Not less but more Heroic than the wrauth
> of stern *Achilles* on his Foe pursu'd
> Thrice Fugitive about *Troy* Wall . . .   [*PL* 9.14–16]

this poem turns "to tell of deeds / Above Heroic, though in secret
done" (*PR* 1.14–15).

"In secret"—the phrase suggests its Latin original, *in secreto:* "in
solitude, in a solitary place, in retirement," along with the English
meaning, "in private." Thus the prologue foresees the final line:
"Home to his Mothers house private return'd."

Hence the trappings of *Paradise Lost* recede from view in book 1
of *Paradise Regain'd*: as the opening lines prophesy, the syntax will
tend to display the normal, supple, easy movement of an educated
mind. Furthermore, when we recall the vast range of elaborate
epic similes in the opening book of *Paradise Lost,* it is significant to
notice that the opening book of *Paradise Regain'd* contains not a
single simile of this kind; indeed it contains no classical allusions
whatsoever, except near the close of the book, where the pagan

oracles are mentioned only in order to announce their demise, as Jesus says to Satan:

> No more shalt thou by oracling abuse
> The Gentiles; henceforth Oracles are ceast,
> And thou no more with Pomp and Sacrifice
> Shalt be enquir'd at *Delphos* or elsewhere,
> At least in vain, for they shall find thee mute.
> God hath now sent his living Oracle
> Into the World, to teach his final will,
> And sends his Spirit of Truth henceforth to dwell
> In pious Hearts, an inward Oracle
> To all truth requisite for men to know.   [1.455–64]

The firm and quiet manner of these lines, dignified, yet modest, is representative of the ground-style laid down in book 1 of *Paradise Regain'd* as a central principle of the whole poem's action. To be sure, the difference from *Paradise Lost* is not complete. The language is less obviously latinate, though there is still plenty of latinity, since this is part of the renaissance heritage. And there are still a good many of those peculiar Miltonic compressions, transcending and defying grammar. The style, in short, reminds us, at a distance, of the manner of *Paradise Lost*: but it is all deliberately muted, thoroughly absorbed into another texture of writing:

> So spake our Morning Star then in his rise,
> And looking round on every side beheld
> A pathless Desert, dusk with horrid shades;
> The way he came not having mark'd, return
> Was difficult, by humane steps untrod;
> And he still on was led, but with such thoughts
> Accompanied of things past and to come
> Lodg'd in his brest, as well might recommend
> Such Solitude before choicest Society.
> Full forty days he pass'd, whether on hill
> Sometimes, anon in shady vale, each night
> Under the covert of some ancient Oak,
> Or Cedar, to defend him from the dew,
> Or harbour'd in one Cave, is not reveal'd . . .   [1.294–307]

We can recognize the voice and the manner as Miltonic: but the language is essentially that of any educated man. This effect, both common and peculiar, suggests the phrase by which Hopkins de-

fined the language of poetry: "current language heightened"—
heightened here by a voice that belongs to a uniquely gifted individual and yet is still the voice of a man searching inwardly in
common ways for the common bond of mankind. The muted,
chastened style[3] thus announced in the first book of *Paradise Regain'd* seems appropriately chosen to pursue a work that bears
some relation to the venerable line of meditations on a Gospel
text.

From beginning to end of this poem the mind of the narrator
roams freely over the past, present, and future life of its hero. We
begin, after the brief prologue, with a memory of the scene at
Jordan during the baptism of Jesus by John: a scene that Satan
recapitulates only forty lines later when he warns his Council that
he has heard "the Sov'raign voice" at Jordan pronounce this man
"my Son." And only forty lines after this (130–67) we hear the
"Sov'raign voice" itself, addressing Gabriel in Heaven, and summing up the whole life of the Son, from the mission of Gabriel at
the Annunciation, through the coming temptation in the Wilderness, where the hero will "lay down the rudiments / Of his great
warfare"—the basic principles of the warfare that will destroy the
power of Sin and Death "By Humiliation and strong Sufferance."
Thus prepared by the Father's own summation of the Son's
career, we now come to "the Son of God" himself:

> Mean while the Son of God, who yet some days
> Lodg'd in *Bethabara* where *John* baptiz'd,
> Musing and much revolving in his brest,
> How best the mighty work he might begin
> Of Saviour to mankind, and which way first
> Publish his God-like office now mature,
> One day forth walk'd alone, the Spirit leading;
> And his deep thoughts, the better to converse
> With solitude, till far from track of men,
> Thought following thought, and step by step led on,
> He entred now the bordering Desert wild,
> And with dark shades and rocks environ'd round,
> His holy Meditations thus persu'd.   [1.183–95]

The period of temptation, we see, is primarily a mental
retirement—"thought following thought"—and what follows now
(196–293) is a meditation on the entire life of Jesus, given in the

person of the hero himself, as he meditates on the meaning of his existence:

> O what a multitude of thoughts at once
> Awakn'd in me swarm, while I consider
> What from within I feel my self, and hear
> What from without comes often to my ears,
> Ill sorting with my present state compar'd.

He recalls his childhood, his visit to the Temple, his early aspirations when "victorious deeds / Flam'd in my heart, heroic acts";

> Yet held it more humane, more heavenly first
> By winning words to conquer willing hearts,
> And make perswasion do the work of fear;
> At least to try . . .

Then he recalls how his mother had "inly rejoyc'd" at his youthful thoughts, how she had informed him that he was the son of Heaven's Eternal King, how she had told him of the Annunciation and the Nativity: when

> a glorious Quire
> Of Angels in the fields of *Bethlehem* sung
> To Shepherds watching at their folds by night,
> And told them the Messiah was now born,
> Where they might see him, and to thee they came;
> Directed to the Manger where thou lais't,
> For in the Inn was left no better room . . .

A biblical simplicity is thus interwoven with the subdued Miltonic and latinate idiom of this poem. And we learn of the Wise Men, of Simeon and Anna, and how Jesus, pondering these things, along with the Scriptures, came to realize he was the promised Messiah:

> this chiefly, that my way must lie
> Through many a hard assay even to the death,
> E're I the promis'd Kingdom can attain,
> Or work Redemption for mankind, whose sins
> Full weight must be transferr'd upon my head.

Then finally, after this glimpse of the Passion, he remembers the central scene at Jordan:

> But as I rose out of the laving stream,
> Heaven open'd her eternal doors, from whence

> The Spirit descended on me like a Dove,
> And last the sum of all, my Father's voice,
> Audibly heard from Heav'n, pronounc'd me his,
> Me his beloved Son, in whom alone
> He was well pleas'd; by which I knew the time
> Now full, that I no more should live obscure,
> But openly begin, as best becomes
> The Authority which I deriv'd from Heaven.
> And now by some strong motion I am led
> Into this wilderness, to what intent
> I learn not yet, perhaps I need not know;
> For what concerns my knowledge God reveals.

This poem, then, first of all concerns the self-discovery of the hero: what it means to be pronounced the Son of God. And indeed, as we read and re-read this poem, we are struck by the way in which that phrase "Son of God" resounds throughout the poem as the chief title by which Milton alludes to the hero. The phrase "Son of God" occurs no less than thirty-nine times; ten times in book 1 and twenty-one times in the concluding book. A few statistics may be in order here to make an important point. Milton calls his hero Jesus only six times; he calls him Savior twenty-one times, Messiah seven times—but he never once calls his hero by the name of Christ. This is not simply because he prefers to use the Hebrew equivalent, Messiah, for as I have said, this term is not used often, nor does he use the translated title "Anointed" more than once.

Why not use the term *Christ*? I think Milton avoids the term here because he is not writing only about the life of Christ, that unique being, Prophet, Priest, and King; he is writing about a composite generalized being whom he calls the Son of God in such an insistent way as to recall the opening of John's Gospel: "But as many as received him, to them gave he power to become the sons of God" (1:12); or the promise of Paul in Romans 8:14: "For as many as are led by the Spirit of God, they are the sons of God." Or, best of all, the words of John's first Epistle (3:1–3): "Behold, what manner of love the Father hath bestowed upon us, that we should be called the sons of God: therefore the world knoweth us not, because it knew him not. Beloved, now are we the sons of God, and it doth not yet appear what we shall be: but we know that, when he shall appear, we shall be like him; for we shall see him as he is. And every man that hath this hope in him purifieth himself, even as he is pure."

After tantalizing us with the phrase throughout the poem, Milton finally clarifies the issues for us at the very close, as Satan is about to make his last desperate effort: the temptation of the pinnacle. Here, with a wonderful irony, Milton matches the opening meditation of the hero by giving now Satan's own sardonic commentary on the Gospel story, Satan's version of what it means to be the Son of God:

> To whom the Fiend now swoln with rage reply'd:
> Then hear, O Son of *David*, Virgin born;
> For Son of God to me is yet in doubt,
> Of the Messiah I have heard foretold
> By all the Prophets; of thy birth at length
> Announc't by *Gabriel* with the first I knew,
> And of the Angelic Song in *Bethlehem* field,
> On thy birth-night, that sung thee Saviour born.
> From that time seldom have I ceas'd to eye
> Thy infancy, thy childhood, and thy youth,
> Thy manhood last, though yet in private bred;
> Till at the Ford of *Jordan* whither all
> Flock'd to the Baptist, I among the rest,
> Though not to be Baptiz'd, by voice from Heav'n
> Heard thee pronounc'd the Son of God belov'd.
> Thenceforth I thought thee worth my nearer view
> And narrower Scrutiny, that I might learn
> In what degree or meaning thou art call'd
> The Son of God, which bears no single sence;
> The Son of God I also am, or was,
> And if I was, I am; relation stands;
> All men are Sons of God; yet thee I thought
> In some respect far higher so declar'd.   [4.499–521]

He has not long to wait, for true relation stands: placed on the pinnacle and faced with the final temptation, the hero answers in the words of the Bible: "Tempt not the Lord thy God, he said and stood. / But Satan smitten with amazement fell." Into those brief words, "Tempt not the Lord thy God," Milton has packed a trinity of meanings: they bear no single sense.[4] First of all, in the traditional interpretation, the words give the answer that any man might give: that is, one must not ask God for unreasonable help,

one must not ask for unnecessary evidence of divine favor. But
secondly, in Milton's strategic placing of the words, they show why
Satan fell, stupefied, "strook with dread and anguish," filled with
"Ruin, and desperation, and dismay." Satan is confounded by the
revelation that he has been tempting divinity incarnate. And
thirdly, we may take the words to indicate the full self-realization
of the hero: he understands now what he has not known earlier,
or has known by glimpses only: that he is himself divine.

Certainly the critics are right who have said that this invulnerable hero makes it very difficult to produce a dramatic development in the poem.[5] Satan is "aghast" from the opening and feels
his forces shattered from the outset; his "motivation" for the
temptations seems to be the curiosity of desperation rather than
any real hope of victory. How, then, can the poem sustain our
interest? I believe the answer lies in watching the movements of
the narrating mind as it defines the nature of the Son of God. The
whole poem presents a mind that uses the "characters" to explore
the problems and besetting sins of any potential Son of God
among men: a mind that conveys the process of temptation by
creating what might be called a contest of styles. The ground of
this great warfare is laid down, stylistically, in book 1; what we feel
here, I think, is the presence of a mind engaged in an immense
effort at self-control, a mind held in leash, poised, tense, alert,
watching any tendency toward elaboration, luxury, self-
indulgence: alert to control any temptation that might lead away
from the ground that is set, ethically, theologically, and stylistically, at the end of book 1, in answer to Satan's opening manoeuvres:

> To whom our Saviour with unalter'd brow.
> Thy coming hither, though I know thy scope,
> I bid not or forbid; do as thou find'st
> Permission from above; thou canst not more.

Book 1 is a prelude: it draws the scene; it establishes the
ground-style; it sets the problems to be explored, and foresees
their conclusion. The action proper begins with book 2, where the
life of Jesus is considered from many different perspectives. First,
from the viewpoint of the new-born Christians who had been

baptized at Jordan—Andrew, Simon Peter, and others, whom we meet in a pastoral setting, with a clear echo of the opening line of Spenser's *Shepheardes Calender*—"A Shepeheards boye (no better doe him call)":

> Then on the bank of *Jordan,* by a Creek:
> Where winds with Reeds, and Osiers whisp'ring play
> Plain Fishermen, no greater men them call,
> Close in a Cottage low together got
> Thir unexpected loss and plaints out breath'd.   [2.25–29]

From this base in pastoral diction they speak in language that moves gracefully out of the biblical toward the latinate:

> our eyes beheld
> Messiah certainly now come, so long
> Expected of our Fathers; we have heard
> His words, his wisdom full of grace and truth,
> Now, now, for sure, deliverance is at hand,
> The Kingdom shall to *Israel* be restor'd:
> Thus we rejoyc'd, but soon our joy is turn'd
> Into perplexity and new amaze . . .   [2.31–38]

But they end with simple faith: "Soon we shall see our hope, our joy return."

From these we turn to "Mother *Mary*" (2.60), whom we find pondering in her heart all the major events in her son's life to this point: the Annunciation, the Nativity—

> In such a season born when scarce a Shed
> Could be obtain'd to shelter him or me
> From the bleak air; a Stable was our warmth,
> A Manger his . . .

the flight into Egypt, his acknowledgment as Son at Jordan, the prophecy of Simeon, and that time when Jesus visited the Temple:

> when twelve years he scarce had seen,
> I lost him, but so found, as well I saw
> He could not lose himself; but went about
> His Father's business . . .

And now as Mary "with thoughts / Meekly compos'd awaited the fulfilling," we have a glimpse of her son, at the center of the poem's inward action, as he,

> tracing the Desert wild,
> Sole but with holiest Meditations fed,
> Into himself descended . . .   [2.109–11]

After all these humble, inward scenes, so frequently marked by
a biblical simplicity of phrasing, the process of temptation now
bursts upon us in the high oratorical style of *Paradise Lost*, as we
hear Satan addressing his host of devils and consulting with them
over how to proceed in the face of such dangerous self-mastery:

> Princes, Heavens antient Sons, Aethereal Thrones,
> Demonian Spirits now, from the Element
> Each of his reign allotted, rightlier call'd,
> Powers of Fire, Air, Water, and Earth beneath . . .   [2.121–24]

That touch of the old fallen oratory leads us quickly down to the
lowest level of sensuality, as Belial moves to suggest that the Son of
God be tempted by sexual appetite. Thus Milton skillfully manages to include in his poem an aspect of human weakness that
could not be associated with Jesus. Milton has Satan reject Belial's
suggestion in such a way as to remind us of lust's long history,
bringing in the first strong coloring from classical mythology that
has been allowed thus far in the poem:

> Before the Flood thou with thy lusty Crew,
> False titl'd Sons of God—

note how Milton keeps the problem ever before us: what it means
to be a Son of God—

> roaming the Earth
> Cast wanton eyes on the daughters of men,
> And coupl'd with them, and begot a race.
> Have we not seen, or by relation heard,
> In Courts and Regal Chambers how thou lurk'st,
> In Wood or Grove by mossie Fountain side,
> In Valley or Green Meadow to way-lay
> Some beauty rare, *Calisto, Clymene,*
> *Daphne,* or *Semele, Antiopa,*
> Or *Amymone, Syrinx,* many more
> Too long, then lay'st thy scapes on names ador'd,
> *Apollo, Neptune, Jupiter,* or *Pan,*
> Satyr, or Fawn, or Silvan?   [2.178–91]

That brilliant cluster of old Ovidian myths, rejected here even by Satan, prepares us for the combat that will now develop in a long contest of styles, as the rich, sensuous coloring and the high rhetoric of the world rise up against the "frugal" ground-style set in book 1: a style which represents the way of temperance struggling against the self-indulgence of an elaborate style.

Thus the vision of the Banquet now arises (2.337–66) in an effort to obliterate the hero's self-control. It is a step upward from Belial's sensuality, but it includes a touch of Belial's suggestion in the vision of

> Nymphs of *Diana's* train, and *Naiades*
> With fruits and flowers from *Amalthea's* horn,
> And Ladies of th' *Hesperides* . . .

Its appeal to hunger of course relates back to the preliminary temptation of book 1, while the whole scene looks forward to the following temptations of wealth and regal power; for it is "A Table richly spred, in regal mode." Milton is offering a Roman banquet to all the quickened senses:

> And at a stately side-board by the wine
> That fragrant smell diffus'd, in order stood
> Tall stripling youths rich clad, of fairer hew
> Then *Ganymed* or *Hylas* . . .

The worlds of classic myth and medieval romance are ransacked for physical allurement and brought to a climax in those superbly overwrought lines of Spenserian motif and alliteration, carrying the appeal of sound to its furthest poetical extreme:

> And Ladies of th' *Hesperides,* that seem'd
> Fairer then feign'd of old, or fabl'd since
> Of Fairy Damsels met in Forest wide
> By Knights of *Logres,* or of *Lyones,*
> *Lancelot* or *Pelleas,* or *Pellenore* . . .

We return with a shock to the frugal ground-style, as Jesus rejects the offer, renouncing imagery in favor of irony—except for a brief suggestion of the communion table:

> To whom thus Jesus temperately reply'd:
> Said'st thou not that to all things I had right?

> And who withholds my pow'r that right to use?
> Shall I receive by gift what of my own,
> When and where likes me best, I can command?
> I can at will, doubt not, as soon as thou,
> Command a Table in this Wilderness,
> And call swift flights of Angels ministrant
> Array'd in Glory on my cup to attend . . .   [2.378–86]

So the central contest, the full excitement, of the poem lies in the movements, the fluctuations, of the narrating mind itself. It is an inward combat created by Milton's brilliant manipulation of styles, a contest in which the flights of poetic splendor are consistently drawn back by the prevailing net of a frugal style to the ground of renunciation and temperance.[6] The way in which this ground-style represents the controlling ideal of the poem is clearly shown now in the speech of Jesus that closes book 2, in answer to the temptation of wealth. Here Milton gives, exactly in the center of the poem, a definition of true Kingship, true Sonship. Jesus first alludes to Gideon, Jephthah, and David, and then places them beside certain men "Among the Heathen" who are also "Worthy of Memorial": "*Quintius, Fabricius, Curius, Regulus.*" This colloca-tion of Roman and biblical heroes of the simple life points the way toward the association of Job with Socrates that is soon to follow in book 3, as Jesus rejects the temptation of glory by praising higher conquests won

> By deeds of peace, by wisdom eminent,
> By patience, temperance; I mention still
> Him whom thy wrongs with Saintly patience born,
> Made famous in a Land and times obscure;
> Who names not now with honour patient *Job*?
> Poor *Socrates* (who next more memorable?) . . .   [3.91–96]

Anticipating this open praise of Socrates, the great ethical speech of the Son ending book 2 proceeds to show how the Socra-tic reliance on the inner man (Socrates' "discovery of the soul," as Cornford has called it)[7] leads onward into the Christian concept of highest kingship: we note the quiet implication of the "wreath of thorns" and the "burden" of Second Isaiah:

> What if with like aversion I reject
> Riches and Realms; yet not for that a Crown,

> Golden in shew, is but a wreath of thorns,
> Brings dangers, troubles, cares, and sleepless nights
> To him who wears the Regal Diadem,
> When on his shoulders each mans burden lies;
> For therein stands the office of a King,
> His Honour, Vertue, Merit and chief Praise,
> That for the Publick all this weight he bears.
> Yet he who reigns within himself, and rules
> Passions, Desires, and Fears, is more a King;
> Which every wise and vertuous man attains:
> And who attains not, ill aspires to rule
> Cities of men, or head-strong Multitudes,
> Subject himself to Anarchy within,
> Or lawless passions in him which he serves.
> But to guide Nations in the way of truth
> By saving Doctrine, and from errour lead
> To know, and knowing worship God aright,
> Is yet more Kingly, this attracts the Soul,
> Governs the inner man, the nobler part,
> That other o're the body only reigns,
> And oft by force, which to a generous mind
> So reigning can be no sincere delight.
> Besides to give a Kingdom hath been thought
> Greater and nobler done, and to lay down
> Far more magnanimous, then to assume.   [2.457–83]

"To lay down"—with his careful placing of those words at the end of a line, Milton forces us to pause and complete the phrase in the familiar words of the Gospel of John:

> As the Father knoweth me, even so know I the Father: and I lay down my life for the sheep.
> And other sheep I have, which are not of this fold: them also I must bring, and they shall hear my voice; and there shall be one fold, and one shepherd.
> Therefore doth my Father love me, because I lay down my life, that I might take it again.
> No man taketh it from me, but I lay it down of myself. I have power to lay it down, and I have power to take it again. This commandment have I received of my Father.   [John 10:15–18]
> Greater love hath no man than this, that a man lay down his life for his friends.   [John 15:13]

Thus the Greek virtue of magnanimity is redefined in Christian terms, as expounded by Milton in his *De Doctrina* (2.9): "High-mindedness is shown when in seeking or not seeking riches, advantages or honors, in avoiding them or accepting them, a man behaves himself as befits his own dignity, rightly understood" (trans. Carey).[8] It is important that thus, in the middle of the poem, Milton should pay tribute to classic virtue and classic thought, for the tribute helps to qualify the renunciation of Greek culture that follows in book 4.

From this steadfast center of the poem, a center defined both by concept and by style, Satan now attempts to move the hero by rhetorical and imagistic elaborations that gradually rise toward the height of Milton's grand style. The temptation of glory begins on a higher pitch of rhetorical insinuation than anything we have seen earlier, especially in contrast with the long, straightforward, temperate speech we have just heard:

> I see thou know'st what is of use to know,
> What best to say canst say, to do canst do;
> Thy actions to thy words accord, thy words
> To thy large heart give utterance due, thy heart
> Conteins of good, wise, just, the perfect shape.
>   . . . wherefore deprive
> All Earth her wonder at thy acts, thy self
> The fame and glory, glory the reward
> That sole excites to high attempts the flame
> Of most erected Spirits, most temper'd pure
> Aetherial, who all pleasures else despise,
> All treasures and all gain esteem as dross,
> And dignities and powers all but the highest?   [3.7–30]

In line with such artifice and convolution the first half of the third book is devoted to abstract argument at a very high level of rhetorical elaboration and oratorical prowess.

Jesus answers this challenge with a burst of oratory that has puzzled many readers, since the harshness here seems out of line with the charity of a Savior, seems rather to voice the bitter disillusionment of John Milton himself, who had once tried to win a victory of the Just with the help of the many, and had seen the whole effort fail:

> For what is glory but the blaze of fame,
> The peoples praise, if always praise unmixt?

And what the people but a herd confus'd,
A miscellaneous rabble, who extol
Things vulgar, & well weigh'd, scarce worth the praise,
They praise and they admire they know not what;
And know not whom, but as one leads the other;
And what delight to be by such extoll'd,
To live upon thir tongues and be thir talk,
Of whom to be disprais'd were no small praise?
His lot who dares be singularly good.
Th' intelligent among them and the wise
Are few, and glory scarce of few is rais'd.
This is true glory and renown, when God
Looking on the Earth, with approbation marks
The just man, and divulges him through Heaven
To all his Angels, who with true applause
Recount his praises . . .   [3.47–64]

We are right, I think, if we hear in these words the voice of the old
Cromwellian, elected even in defeat. But is it a flaw in the fabric of
the poem? Is it a flaw like that which Arnold Stein has seen in
Milton's later description of the Parthian power, where he feels
that "Milton has tampered with the perspective," so that a "narrative voice seems to have intruded without warrant"?[9] But that
narrative voice has been in control of the action from the poem's
outset, where we met at the first word the "I" whose thoughts
enact the poem. In a pure drama, properly so called, it would
indeed be a flaw if one felt another voice coming through instead
of the voice appropriate to a given character in that drama. But in
this inward speaking of the narrative mind, all "characters," all
speeches, are enveloped within, and suffused with, the controlling
voice of the narrator himself. That mind is exploring its own
problems, as well as those of mankind, through the speeches of
the "characters," who have indeed no separate existence, whose
very function is to take upon themselves the voice of the narrator.

That is why the poem never shows any extended effort to present a drama of characters in the usual sense. Satan and the Son of
God in this poem speak within the mind of one who hopes to be
himself a Son of God; both these actors use the human voice that
this particular possible Son of God, John Milton, possesses. So I
think it is hardly valid to object that this poem does not present
the Christ of the Gospels. For this is not a rehearsal of the Gos-

pels; it is rather (as Hopkins would say) a rehearsal of the self, where the voice of the inner man discovers what a true Son of God ought to reply to such temptations.

Thus earlier we have heard Satan speak, as it might seem, "out of character," when he rebukes Belial for suggesting a temptation through female beauty:

> or should she confident,
> As sitting Queen ador'd on Beauties Throne,
> Descend with all her winning charms begirt
> To enamour, as the Zone of *Venus* once
> Wrought that effect on *Jove,* so Fables tell;
> How would one look from his Majestick brow
> Seated as on the top of Vertues hill,
> Discount'nance her despis'd, and put to rout
> All her array; her female pride deject,
> Or turn to reverent awe? for Beauty stands
> In the admiration only of weak minds
> Led captive; cease to admire, and all her Plumes
> Fall flat and shrink into a trivial toy . . .   [2.211–23]

If this strikes us as more Miltonic than Satanic,[10] it need not worry us: the "characters" of this poem exist, not for their own points of view, but as occasions, as channels, by which the narrative voice can make its way.

Now, after this brilliant battle of rhetoric has ended with the defeat of worldly glory, so, in another mode of temptation, Milton moves onward, in the second half of book 3, to show a richer, higher style arising out of the temperate ground. It is a significant touch that Milton should have the grand tableau of Parthian power, with its echoes of the grand style of *Paradise Lost*, literally rise up from a pastoral plain:

> With that (such power was giv'n him then) he took
> The Son of God up to a Mountain high.
> It was a Mountain at whose verdant feet
> A spatious plain out strech't in circuit wide
> Lay pleasant; from his side two rivers flow'd,
> Th' one winding, the other strait and left between
> Fair Champain with less rivers interveind,
> Then meeting joyn'd thir tribute to the Sea:
> Fertil of corn the glebe, of oyl and wine,

> With herds the pastures throng'd, with flocks the hills,
> Huge Cities and high towr'd, that well might seem
> The seats of mightiest Monarchs . . .   [3.251–62]

And so we come to those grandly over-wrought displays of proper names that sum up worldly power and empire:

> *Ecbatana* her structure vast there shews,
> And *Hecatompylos* her hunderd gates,
> There *Susa* by *Choaspes*, amber stream,
> The drink of none but Kings; of later fame
> Built by *Emathian*, or by *Parthian* hands,
> The great *Seleucia, Nisibis,* and there
> *Artaxata, Teredon, Tesiphon* . . .   [3.286–92]

> From *Arachosia*, from *Candaor* East,
> And *Margiana* to the *Hyrcanian* cliffs
> Of *Caucasus*, and dark *Iberian* dales,
> From *Atropatia* and the neighbouring plains
> Of *Adiabene, Media,* and the South
> Of *Susiana* to *Balsara's* hav'n.   [3.316–21]

It is appropriate, I think, that near the close of all this splendid panoply, Milton should bring in (at line 329) the poem's outstanding example of a pompous and affected latinism: "Chariots or Elephants *endorst* with Towers." And it is even more appropriate that at the very end of the vision we should meet the poem's first example of an epic comparison, one that clearly reminds us of the allusions to chivalric romance in the opening book of *Paradise Lost* (582–87, 763–66):

> Such forces met not, nor so wide a camp,
> When *Agrican* with all his Northern powers
> Besieg'd *Albracca*, as Romances tell;
> The City of *Gallaphrone,* from thence to win
> The fairest of her Sex *Angelica*
> His daughter, sought by many Prowest Knights,
> Both *Paynim*, and the Peers of *Charlemane*.
> Such and so numerous was thir Chivalrie . . .   [3.337–44]

This great passage on the Parthians demonstrates, as the banquet scene has earlier shown, that this writer is still at the peak of his powers. All the strength of *Paradise Lost* is still there; he can use it when he chooses; but here the Son of God condemns the grand

vision as "argument / Of human weakness rather then of
strength."

As the fourth book opens, Milton announces the imminent
climax of the grand style by introducing a cluster of similes. They
are not quite heroic similes; they are rather subdued echoes of the
heroic mode; but they serve to prepare for the epic manner of the
following tableau of Rome, where Milton bends his heroic bow
still further, carrying the compressed richness of his high style to
its absolute and appropriate limit:

> Thence to the gates cast round thine eye, and see
> What conflux issuing forth, or entring in,
> Pretors, Proconsuls to thir Provinces
> Hasting or on return, in robes of State;
> Lictors and rods the ensigns of thir power,
> Legions and Cohorts, turmes of horse and wings:
> Or Embassies from Regions far remote
> In various habits on the *Appian* road,
> Or on the *Aemilian,* some from farthest South,
> *Syene,* and where the shadow both way falls,
> *Meroe Nilotic* Isle, and more to West,
> The Realm of *Bocchus* to the Black-moor Sea;
> From the *Asian* Kings and *Parthian* among these,
> From *India* and the golden *Chersoness,*
> And utmost *Indian* Isle *Taprobane,*
> Dusk faces with white silken Turbants wreath'd:
> From *Gallia, Gades,* and the *Brittish* West,
> *Germans* and *Scythians,* and *Sarmatians* North
> Beyond *Danubius* to the *Tauric* Pool.   [4.61–79]

This vision of Rome is more than the climax of the high style: it is
a culmination of all the many threads of temptation that have
been weaving their way toward this highest "grandeur and majestic show / Of luxury," of "wealth and power, / Civility of Manners,
Arts, and Arms." For the Son's answer recalls the Banquet scene
of book 2:

> though thou should'st add to tell
> Thir sumptuous gluttonies, and gorgeous feasts
> On *Cittron* tables or *Atlantic* stone;
> (For I have also heard, perhaps have read)
> Their wines of *Setia, Cales,* and *Falerne,*
> *Chios* and *Creet,* and how they quaff in Gold,
> Chrystal and Myrrhine cups imboss'd with Gems

> And studs of Pearl, to me should'st tell who thirst
> And hunger still . . .   [4.113–21]

It has all been one sustained temptation,[11] from the point where
Belial first spoke of sexual appetite, up through the more refined
appetites of the banquet, and onward to this moment of final
rejection for these kingdoms of the flesh, the world, and the devil.

For this, we must note, is the end of Satan's kingdoms,[12] as
Satan himself three times says: first, in concluding his vision of
Rome:

> These having shewn thee, I have shewn thee all
> The Kingdoms of the world, and all thir glory.   [4.88–89]

Next, in his answer to the Son's rejection, where Milton concludes
the whole sequence by bringing in the ending of the second temptation in Luke's account: "The Kingdoms of the world to thee I
give . . . if thou wilt fall down, / And worship me"; with the
answer: "Get thee behind me . . ." (4.163–67, 193–94). And
thirdly, by way of prologue to the next vision:

> Therefore let pass, as they are transitory,
> The Kingdoms of this world; I shall no more
> Advise thee, gain them as thou canst, or not.   [4.209–11]

But just as he had offered the sexual suggestion of Belial, before
the temptation of the Kingdoms, properly so called, here Milton
adds another temptation. What implications lie in this placing of
the final tableau of Greek culture outside of the Kingdoms of the
World? First of all, we should note, with some relief, perhaps, that
these realms of Greek culture do not lie within Satan's gift: he
does not control them, he does not offer to give them. Satan can
only urge the Son of God to use Greek culture on the wrong
terms, that is, to value Greek learning and art beyond the bounds
proper to a Son of God. Thus: shall the Son of God concede that
Athens is truly "Mother of Arts / And Eloquence," that her
Tragedians are "teachers best / Of moral prudence," "High actions, and high passions best describing"? Shall the Son of God
concede that Socrates was really "Wisest of men" and that Greek
thought is all in all because "These rules will render thee a King
Compleat / Within thy self"?

The Son has already anticipated his answer in the long speech

at the end of book 2. The Son of God can never rest within the
ideal of being "compleat / Within thy self." This, he has implied, is
a right beginning, but the Son of God must look beyond himself to
the thorns, the burden, the weight of mankind's incompleteness.

The Son's answer at first should cause us no discomfort: he does
not at first deny the value of Greek culture: he says only that it is
not necessary to the good life:

> To whom our Saviour sagely thus repli'd.
> Think not but that I know these things, or think
> I know them not; not therefore am I short
> Of knowing what I aught: he who receives
> Light from above, from the fountain of light,
> No other doctrine needs, though granted true . . .   [4.285–90]

Milton could have avoided all our modern worries over this scene
if he had only had the consideration to stop here; but, as in Satan's
scorn of sexual weakness, or in Jesus' denunciation of glory, so
here the personal involvement of the narrator runs beyond the
bounds of an easy propriety. For the Christian humanist and
platonist this is the greatest challenge: can he be brought to say
that truth resides in Greek achievements, in and by themselves?[13]
The Son of God is thus driven to make, at this point, a judgment
more drastic and more violent than that made by the rest of the
poem. For the whole poem qualifies and moderates this fierce
renunciation, while at the same time this particular episode shows
the speaker's readiness to make the ultimate sacrifice, if it should
be demanded. The tone is tense, vehement, almost savage in
places:

> But these are false, or little else but dreams,
> Conjectures, fancies, built on nothing firm.
> The first and wisest of them all profess'd
> To know this only, that he nothing knew;
> The next to fabling fell and smooth conceits . . .
> Alas what can they teach, and not mislead;
> Ignorant of themselves, of God much more,
> And how the world began, and how man fell
> Degraded by himself, on grace depending?
> Much of the Soul they talk, but all awrie,
> And in themselves seek vertue, and to themselves
> All glory arrogate, to God give none . . .   [4.291–315]

And as for learning the "secret power / Of harmony" and "moral prudence" from Greek poetry:

> All our Law and Story strew'd
> With Hymns, our Psalms with artful terms inscrib'd,
> Our Hebrew Songs and Harps in *Babylon*,
> That pleas'd so well our Victors ear, declare
> That rather *Greece* from us these Arts deriv'd;
> Ill imitated, while they loudest sing
> The vices of thir Deities, and thir own
> In Fable, Hymn, or Song, so personating
> Thir Gods ridiculous, and themselves past shame.
> Remove their swelling Epithetes thick laid
> As varnish on a Harlots cheek, the rest,
> Thin sown with aught of profit or delight,
> Will far be found unworthy to compare
> With *Sion's* songs, to all true tasts excelling,
> Where God is prais'd aright, and Godlike men,
> The Holiest of Holies, and his Saints;
> Such are from God inspir'd, not such from thee;
> Unless where moral vertue is express't
> By light of Nature not in all quite lost.   [4.334–52]

The violence of the charge, followed by the curt qualification, suggests that here is the hardest renunciation of all; but if necessary, the Son of God is prepared to lay down all. It is the same action that Milton's older contemporary, Nicholas Ferrar, performed on his deathbed, where, as the scene has come down to us, he said at last to his brother:

> When you have measured out the place for my grave, then goe and take out of my Study, those three great Hampers full of Bookes that have stood there locked up these many yeares: They were not many scores but many Hundreths in all kind of Languages, which he had in all places gotten with great search, and some cost. They were Comedies, Tragedies, Love-Hymns, Heroicall Poems, and such like. Carry (sayd he) those Hampers to the place of my grave, and upon it, see you burn them all: and this he spake with some vehemency and passion of Indignation. Goe, Let it be done, Let it be done . . .

And after the books had been burned, John Ferrar returned to his brother's bedside and "told him, all was done, as he had required." "Then he suddenly lifting up himself, sat up in his Bed, gave God hearty thanks, and called for Pen, Inke, and Paper," and wrote out the following document:

> November 28th 1637. I. H. S. In the name of God, Amen.
>
> In as much as all the Comedyes, Tragedyes, Pastoralls etc: and all those they call Heroicall Poems, none excepted; and like wise all the Bookes of Tales, which they call Novells, and all feigned Historyes written in Prose, all Love Hymns, and all the like Bookes are full of Idolatry, and especially tend to the Overthrow of Christian Religion, undermining the very Foundations thereof, and corrupt and pollute the minds of the Readers, with filthy lusts, as, woe is me, I have proved in my self. In this regard therefore, to shew my detestation of them to the World, and that all others may take warning, I have burned all of them, and most humbly have, and doe beseech God, to forgive me all my mispent time in them, and all the sinns that they have caused in me, which surely, but for his infinite Grace, had carryed my soule down into Hell long ere this . . . I beseech all that truly feare God, that love Jesus Christ, to consider these things well. Amen, Amen, Amen.[14]

So Milton's Son of God must also enact this final renunciation: a stern demand, but just, in terms of the whole poem; for what has the poem been saying if it has not said that the myths and elaborations of classical literature are unnecessary, dangerous, and unreliable? Milton has constantly affirmed this in the ground-style of his poem, where "swelling Epithetes" are removed, and a basic idiom is achieved approaching the "majestic unaffected stile" that Milton here praises in the Hebrew prophets. "So spake the Son of God" and Satan finds himself now "Quite at a loss, for all his darts were spent."

With those words (4.366) Milton marks the close of his long analysis of human temptation. What remains is prophecy, epiphany, and praise, which Milton gives in three symbolic scenes. First Satan arouses a tremendous storm which shadows forth the Passion and the Resurrection, as Milton makes clear by having Satan allude to the future sufferings of Jesus immediately before and after the storm (4.386–88, 477–83). Next comes the full revelation of divine power, suggesting the Day of Judgment, as the Son of God stands on the pinnacle, and Satan falls, accompanied to his doom by a pair of true epic similes which drive home the absolute finality of the defeat. And then at once the angels transport the Son of God to a pastoral valley, where the "Angelic Quires" sing their concluding hymn of praise, which Milton phrases in a way that allows the Son of God in this poem to suggest the restored Image of God in man, the Paradise within.

> True Image of the Father whether thron'd
> In the bosom of bliss, and light of light
> Conceiving, or remote from Heaven, enshrin'd
> In fleshly Tabernacle, and human form,
> Wandring the Wilderness, whatever place,
> Habit, or state, or motion, still expressing
> The Son of God, with Godlike force indu'd
> Against th' Attempter of thy Fathers Throne,
> And Thief of Paradise; him long of old
> Thou didst debel, and down from Heav'n cast
> With all his Army, now thou hast aveng'd
> Supplanted *Adam,* and by vanquishing
> Temptation, hast regain'd lost Paradise . . .
> For though that seat of earthly bliss be fail'd,
> A fairer Paradise is founded now
> For *Adam* and his chosen Sons, whom thou
> A Saviour art come down to re-install.
> Where they shall dwell secure, when time shall be
> Of Tempter and Temptation without fear.   [4.596–617]

For Adam and his *chosen* Sons. Milton has never before in his poetry used the word *chosen* in quite so bare and unguarded a way. "Some I have chosen of peculiar grace / Elect above the rest," the voice of God has said in *Paradise Lost,* but, we are reassured, "The rest shall hear me call, and oft be warnd / Thir sinful state," while "offerd grace" will invite all men to repent: "for I will cleer thir senses dark / What may suffice" (3.183–89). And the subtle analysis of the doctrine of Election in his *De Doctrina* (1.4) makes it plain that although equal grace is not offered to all, still sufficient grace is offered to everyone. "Of one thing, then, we may be absolutely positive," says Milton: God "excludes no man from the way of penitence and eternal salvation, unless that man has continued to reject and despise the offer of grace, and of grace sufficient for salvation, until it is too late" (trans. Carey).[15] Can it be that now, at the close of one of his latest poems, Milton is reverting to a sterner doctrine of the chosen? Is this paradise within regained only for a chosen few?

Perhaps such a sterner possibility may lie within the ambiguous opening of *Paradise Regain'd*:

> I who e're while the happy Garden sung,
> By one mans disobedience lost, now sing
> Recover'd Paradise to all mankind . . .

Is Paradise recovered "to all mankind," or is this poet singing to all mankind the story of a Paradise recovered—for the chosen few? Why then sing the story to all mankind? But no one can know whether he is truly one of the chosen: in the terms of traditional puritan theology, all who hear the story must search within themselves for the signs of saving faith. *Paradise Regain'd,* with its rigorous denunciation of the "people" and its stern rejection of the modes of pagan culture, may seem to lend itself to such an interpretation.

Yet the presence of *Samson Agonistes* as the "companion poem"[16] in this volume reassures us that Milton has not indeed engaged in such a Calvinistic rejection of the freedom of the will that lies at the heart of *Paradise Lost.* As Mary Ann Radzinowicz has shown in her recent admirable study,[17] *Samson Agonistes* represents the process of regeneration at work in the individual soul and demonstrates the way in which the chosen one "Elect above the rest" may lead the rest to understand the ways of God and maintain their faith in a degree that will suffice for salvation.

Paradise Regain'd has made the withdrawal to the desert, has denounced the culture of cities in a way characteristic of the biblical prophets, has declined to acknowledge an open alliance with any of the classical genres, has indeed shown a willingness to reject classical culture after the manner of the proto-puritan Father, Tertullian:

> What indeed has Athens to do with Jerusalem? What concord is there between the Academy and the Church? . . . Our instruction comes from "the porch of Solomon," who had himself taught that "the Lord should be sought in simplicity of heart." Away with all attempts to produce a mottled Christianity of Stoic, Platonic, and dialectic composition! We want no curious disputation after possessing Christ Jesus . . .[18]

But *Samson Agonistes* shows a further stage of action beyond the "private" workings of grace in the soul of man: this drama fashioned after the manner of the Greeks (with the help of the modern Italians) will show how a poet can absorb the lessons of the past and treat the ancients in the manner sanctioned by the great Alexandrian humanist, Clement:

> Thus philosophy was necessary to the Greeks for righteousness, until the coming of the Lord. . . . For God is the source of all good things; of some primarily, as of the old and new Testaments; of others by consequence, as of philosophy. But it may be, indeed, that philosophy was given to the Greeks immediately and primarily, until the Lord should call the Greeks. For philosophy was a "schoolmaster" to bring the Greek mind to Christ, as the Law brought the Hebrews. Thus philosophy was a preparation, paving the way towards perfection in Christ.[19]

Appropriately, then, Milton has chosen an ancient form, developed as part of a public religious occasion, to demonstrate the workings of free will and grace within the community of mankind. Thus, near the end of his career, Milton conveys his lifelong belief that "the holiness and wisdom in both word and deed of many of the heathens" show that "some traces of the divine image still remain in us."[20]

CHAPTER 16

Samson Agonistes:
The Breath
Of Heaven

> *Sam.* A little onward lend thy guiding hand
> To these dark steps, a little further on;
> For yonder bank hath choice of Sun or shade,
> There I am wont to sit, when any chance
> Relieves me from my task of servile toyl,
> Daily in the common Prison else enjoyn'd me,
> Where I a Prisoner chain'd, scarce freely draw
> The air imprison'd also, close and damp,
> Unwholsom draught: but here I feel amends,
> The breath of Heav'n fresh-blowing, pure and sweet,
> With day-spring born; here leave me to respire.

This is an opening rich with implications, for the situation suggests the opening of Sophocles' redemptive tragedy, *Oedipus at Colonus,* where the blind Oedipus is led on stage by his daughter Antigone. We know that Samson will also be accepted by the divine power, as Oedipus was at last accepted and transfigured by the divine powers at the close of that Greek play. At the same time Milton's phrasing in these opening lines contains a redemptive overtone drawn from the first chapter of the Gospel of Luke, where Zacharias prophesies the redemption of God's people: "Through the tender mercy of our God; whereby the *dayspring* from on high hath visited us, to give light *to them that sit in darkness* and in the shadow of death, *to guide our feet* into the way of peace." So the guiding hand that Samson speaks of here is a human hand, literally, and the breath of Heaven that he enjoys is a physical breeze, literally; but this opening, with Milton's characteristic mingling of classical and Christian evocations, will suggest the presence of a higher power, still to be revealed.

Samson's long prologue here displays a remarkable combination of self-control and turbulent emotional power.[1] Although he bitterly laments his captivity and his loss of sight, he refuses the temptation to blame God for his fate:

> Promise was that I
> Should *Israel* from *Philistian* yoke deliver;
> Ask for this great Deliverer now, and find him
> Eyeless in *Gaza* at the Mill with slaves,
> Himself in bonds under *Philistian* yoke;
> Yet stay, let me not rashly call in doubt
> Divine Prediction; what if all foretold
> Had been fulfilld but through mine own default,
> Whom have I to complain of but my self? [38–46]

But as his agony swells out, the temptation returns, and is again refused:

> God, when he gave me strength, to shew withal
> How slight the gift was, hung it in my Hair.
> But peace, I must not quarrel with the will
> Of highest dispensation, which herein
> Happ'ly had ends above my reach to know:
> Suffices that to me strength is my bane,
> And proves the sourse of all my miseries;
> So many, and so huge, that each apart
> Would ask a life to wail, but chief of all,
> O loss of sight, of thee I most complain!
> Blind among enemies, O worse then chains,
> Dungeon, or beggery, or decrepit age! [58–69]

And so on into that famous lamentation where the steady flow of the blank verse breaks under the strain and is transformed into a lyric utterance of short and long lines, ebbing and flowing with the speaker's almost unbearable pain:

> O dark, dark, dark, amid the blaze of noon,
> Irrecoverably dark, total Eclipse
> Without all hope of day!
> O first created Beam, and thou great Word,
> Let there be light, and light was over all;
> Why am I thus bereav'd thy prime decree?
> The Sun to me is dark
> And silent as the Moon,
> When she deserts the night
> Hid in her vacant interlunar cave.   [80–89]

How poorly the chorus understands this man, as they enter now, judging him only by outward appearances. "Can this be hee?" they ask, recalling the physical grandeur of his exploits:

> Can this be hee,
> That Heroic, that Renown'd,
> Irresistible *Samson*? whom unarm'd
> No strength of man, or fiercest wild beast could withstand;
> Who tore the Lion, as the Lion tears the Kid,
> Ran on embattelld Armies clad in Iron
> And weaponless himself,
> Made Arms ridiculous, useless the forgery
> Of brazen shield and spear, the hammer'd Cuirass,
> *Chalybean* temper'd steel, and frock of mail
> Adamantean Proof.   [124–34]

But more deeply, Samson's prologue has shown him to be a man whose mind and character still retain a great potential. The function of the various episodes that we now watch is to release and develop that deep potential.

In the first episode the "Consolation" of the chorus does not lead Samson to blame God or lose his faith in God's justice, although the "Counsel" offered by Samson's friends is full of painful queries:

> *Chor.* Tax not divine disposal, wisest Men
> Have err'd, and by bad Women been deceiv'd;
> And shall again, pretend they ne're so wise.
> Deject not then so overmuch thy self,
> Who hast of sorrow thy full load besides;

> Yet truth to say, I oft have heard men wonder
> Why thou shouldst wed *Philistian* women rather
> Then of thine own Tribe fairer, or as fair,
> At least of thy own Nation, and as noble.   [210–18]

But Samson defends his first Philistine marriage on the grounds that he "knew / From intimate impulse" that it was ordained by God for Israel's deliverance: "The work to which I was divinely call'd." And he adds that he "thought" the same was true for Dalila—though there is a tacit admission of possible error here, perhaps an error of self-deception caused by the "specious" charms of Dalila.[2]

The chorus wryly concedes Samson's ability "to provoke" the Philistines—but to what end? "Yet *Israel* still serves with all his Sons." Here, surprisingly, Samson leaps to defend both himself and God. In spite of his weaknesses, he declares, Israel had many opportunities to throw off the Philistine yoke, if they had supported him on many different occasions:

> *Sam.* That fault I take not on me, but transfer
> On *Israel's* Governours, and Heads of Tribes,
> Who seeing those great acts which God had done
> Singly by me against their Conquerours
> Acknowledg'd not, or not at all consider'd
> Deliverance offerd.   [241–46]

With the memory of his deeds and the grandeur of his language Samson convinces the chorus that the fault is indeed in the Israelites, who have before this deserted their heroes. Milton skillfully conveys the distance between such heroes and the ordinary man by a curiously deflating use of rhyme at the close of this choric response:

> *Chor.* Thy words to my remembrance bring
> How *Succoth* and the Fort of *Penuel*
> Thir great Deliverer contemn'd,
> The matchless *Gideon* in pursuit
> Of *Madian* and her vanquisht Kings:
> And how ingrateful *Ephraim*
> Had dealt with *Jephtha,* who by argument,
> Not worse then by his shield and spear
> Defended *Israel* from the *Ammonite,*

Had not his prowess quell'd thir pride
In that sore battel when so many dy'd
Without Reprieve adjudg'd to death,
For want of well pronouncing *Shibboleth*.   [277–89]

One of the astonishing things about Milton's art in this whole
drama is the way in which he has, it seems, deliberately played
down the choruses in the middle of the drama, refusing to give
the chorus very good lines, except toward the beginning (where
they are uplifted by the memory of Samson's physical prowess),
and toward the end (where they are strengthened by Samson's
recovery and ultimate victory). After each of the first three
episodes, Milton has given the chorus words that are, for the most
part, dry and commonplace, often surprisingly flat, as here at the
end of the first episode:

Yet more there be who doubt his ways not just,
As to his own *edicts,* found contra*dicting,*
Then give the rains to wandring thought,
Regardless of his glories *diminution:*
Till by thir own perplexities *involv'd*
They ravel more, still less *resolv'd,*
But never find self-satisfying *solution.*
    As if they would confine th' interminable,
And tie him to his own *prescript,*
Who made our Laws to bind us, not himself,
And hath full right to *exempt*
Whom so it pleases him by *choice*
From National obstriction, without *taint*
Of sin, or legal *debt;*
For with his own Laws he can best *dispence.*   [300–14]

The rhymes and partial rhymes here (which I have italicized)
create by their "jingling" an effect of something like triviality in
the chorus; and since Milton elsewhere in the play writes so very
well, we are bound to ask whether there is not some deliberate
effect in thus making the chorus speak so flatly.[3] Indeed, the
heavy-handed use of rhyme and partial rhyme here seems almost
to mirror the contempt for rhymed verse that Milton had expressed several years earlier in the prefatory note to *Paradise Lost:*[4]

The Measure is *English* Heroic Verse without Rime, as that of
Homer in *Greek,* and of *Virgil* in *Latin;* Rime being no necessary

Adjunct or true Ornament of Poem or good Verse, in longer Works especially, but the Invention of a barbarous Age, to set off wretched matter and lame Meeter; grac't indeed since by the use of some famous modern Poets, carried away by Custom, but much to thir own vexation, hindrance, and constraint to express many things otherwise, and for the most part worse then else they would have exprest them.

Rhyme, he declares, is "a thing of it self, to all judicious eares, triveal and of no true musical delight," which cannot be found "in the jingling sound of like endings." The choric stanzas that I have just quoted seem to prove the point. Is this an instance of Milton's sardonic humor—to give the chorus stanzas of deliberate flatness? At the very least it would appear that Milton's use of rhyme here has the effect of lowering the tone of high seriousness and making impossible any great dignity in this choric speech. The effect is thus to stress, by contrast, the grandeur of Samson, the glory of his poetry, the greatness of his mind: his difference from ordinary men.

This difference also appears by contrast with his father Manoa, who now enters to begin the second episode. Manoa complains bitterly to his son and seems so deeply involved in his own grief that he cannot think about the effect that his words may have upon Samson:

> Nay what thing good
> Pray'd for, but often proves our woe, our bane?
> I pray'd for Children, and thought barrenness
> In wedlock a reproach; I gain'd a Son,
> And such a Son as all Men hail'd me happy;
> Who would be now a Father in my stead?
>
> . . . .
>
> Alas methinks whom God hath chosen once
> To worthiest deeds, if he through frailty err,
> He should not so o'rewhelm, and as a thrall
> Subject him to so foul indignities,
> Be it but for honours sake of former deeds.   [350–55, 368–72]

But Samson is far from being shaken by these moans; he has faced all this long ago; and he answers with self-control and dignity:

> Appoint not heavenly disposition, Father,
> Nothing of all these evils hath befall'n me

> But justly; I my self have brought them on,
> Sole Author I, sole cause . . .   [373–76]

And he ends, as in his great prologue, with a surge of immense
vitality, though turned against himself:

> O indignity, O blot
> To Honour and Religion! servil mind
> Rewarded well with servil punishment!
> The base degree to which I now am fall'n,
> These rags, this grinding, is not yet so base
> As was my former servitude, ignoble,
> Unmanly, ignominious, infamous,
> True slavery, and that blindness worse then this,
> That saw not how degeneratly I serv'd.   [411–19]

The distance between Samson and ordinary men is at once
emphasized by Manoa, as he proceeds to ignore the power of
Samson's self-castigation and answers at first with a querulous (and,
to the reader, half-comic) understatement: "I cannot praise thy
Marriage choises, Son, / Rather approv'd them not;" and this is
followed by obvious doubt of his son's divine inspiration in these
matters:

> but thou didst plead
> Divine impulsion prompting how thou might'st
> Find some occasion to infest our Foes.
> I state not that; this I am sure; our Foes
> Found soon occasion thereby to make thee
> Thir Captive, and thir triumph; thou the sooner
> Temptation found'st, or over-potent charms
> To violate the sacred trust of silence
> Deposited within thee.   [420–29]

Then Manoa, returning to his self-centered complaint, adds, "A
worse thing yet remains": the Philistines are today celebrating
Dagon's victory in delivering Samson into their hands (one may
hear the voice of aged self-pity):

> So *Dagon* shall be magnifi'd, and God,
> Besides whom is no God, compar'd with Idols,
> Disglorifi'd, blasphem'd, and had in scorn
> By th' Idolatrous rout amidst thir wine;
> Which to have come to pass by means of thee,

> *Samson,* of all thy sufferings think the heaviest,
> Of all reproach the most with shame that ever
> Could have befall'n thee and thy Fathers house.   [440–47]

Here again, Samson acknowledges his fault with dignity and rational power, but he goes beyond his earlier self-denunciation to assert his unbroken faith that God will triumph, even though Samson himself is now cast out from grace:

> This only hope relieves me, that the strife
> With me hath end; all the contest is now
> 'Twixt God and *Dagon; Dagon* hath presum'd,
> Me overthrown, to enter lists with God,
> His Deity comparing and preferring
> Before the God of *Abraham.* He, be sure,
> Will not connive, or linger, thus provok'd,
> But will arise and his great name assert:
> *Dagon* must stoop, and shall e're long receive
> Such a discomfit, as shall quite despoil him
> Of all these boasted Trophies won on me,
> And with confusion blank his Worshippers.   [460–71]

Manoa agrees, in a perfunctory tone, and then goes on to show that his mind is not at all on such matters, but is fixed upon his hope to ransom his son and take him home: "But for thee what shall be done?" Manoa here represents the terms of household common sense, the encouragement to believe that God somehow will perhaps relent, that things simply cannot go on being as unhappy as they are. Samson rejects all these easy consolations in one of the simplest and noblest speeches of the entire play, when Manoa suggests that he might even possibly regain his sight, if only he has patience:[5]

> All otherwise to me my thoughts portend,
> That these dark orbs no more shall treat with light,
> Nor th' other light of life continue long,
> But yield to double darkness nigh at hand:
> So much I feel my genial spirits droop,
> My hopes all flat, nature within me seems
> In all her functions weary of herself;
> My race of glory run, and race of shame,
> And I shall shortly be with them that rest.   [590–98]

The effect of his father's "consolations" has been to make Samson
realize to the full his "sense of Heav'ns desertion," as he cries out
in the great lyrical utterance that follows, a passage expressed,
again, not in blank verse, but in undulating long and short lines
which begin with a few scarcely noticed rhymes, and then utterly
give up all rhymes, as the ode reaches its climax:

> I was his nursling once and choice delight,
> His destin'd from the womb,
> Promisd by Heavenly message twice descending.
> Under his special eie
> Abstemious I grew up and thriv'd amain;
> He led me on to mightiest deeds
> Above the nerve of mortal arm
> Against the uncircumcis'd, our enemies.
> But now hath cast me off as never known,
> And to those cruel enemies,
> Whom I by his appointment had provok't,
> Left me all helpless with th' irreparable loss
> Of sight, reserv'd alive to be repeated
> The subject of thir cruelty, or scorn.
> Nor am I in the list of them that hope;
> Hopeless are all my evils, all remediless;
> This one prayer yet remains, might I be heard,
> No long petition, speedy death,
> The close of all my miseries, and the balm.   [633–51]

That prayer will soon be answered; through the dark night of this
despair, his thoughts are moving in the right way.

Immediately, the contrast between Samson's grandeur of despair and the commonplace musing of the chorus is enforced by
some of the flattest lines and weakest rhymes that Milton ever
wrote:[6]

> God of our Fathers, what is man!
> That thou towards him with hand so *various,*
> Or might I say *contrarious,*
> Temperst thy providence through his short course,
> Not evenly, as thou rul'st
> The Angelic orders and inferiour creatures *mute,*
> Irrational and *brute.*
> Nor do I name of men the common *rout,*
> That wandring loose *about*
> Grow up and perish, as the summer flie.   [667–76]

The chorus is confused and bewildered; but the chosen man is greater than the chorus can here realize, as we are soon to see.

Now, as Samson faces utterly his agonized sense of loss, the external cause of that loss sails into sight with all her streamers waving, perfumed, beautiful, seductive, weeping, penitent (she says), declaring her "conjugal affection," begging forgiveness, asking if she may take him home to her bed and board. Samson's fierceness toward Dalila is a measure of the seductive power that she still holds for him:

> My Wife, my Traytress, let her not come near me.   [725]

> Out, out *Hyæna*; these are thy wonted arts.   [748]

And artful she certainly is. Our opinion of Samson's character is improved here, since we see from the subtlety of her arguments and the appeal of her excuses why and how Samson fell before her earlier persuasions, as he has eloquently described her blandishments in the scene with Manoa. She uses, at first, three arguments, which may be summed up thus: (1) You say I'm weak; well, you're weak too; so let's be weak together. Forgive my weaknesses so that men may forgive your weaknesses. (2) It was love that caused it. I did it to keep you with me:

> I knew that liberty
> Would draw thee forth to perilous enterprises,
> While I at home sate full of cares and fears
> Wailing thy absence in my widow'd bed;
> Here I should still enjoy thee day and night
> Mine and Loves prisoner, not the *Philistines*,
> Whole to my self, unhazarded abroad,
> Fearless at home of partners in my love.
> These reasons in Loves law have past for good,
> Though fond and reasonless to some perhaps:
> And Love hath oft, well meaning, wrought much wo,
> Yet always pity or pardon hath obtain'd.   [803–14]

(3) I did it for my country:

> thou know'st the Magistrates
> And Princes of my countrey came in person,
> Sollicited, commanded, threatn'd, urg'd,
> Adjur'd by all the bonds of civil Duty
> And of Religion, press'd how just it was,

> How honourable, how glorious to entrap
> A common enemy, who had destroy'd
> Such numbers of our Nation.   [850–57]

Samson answers her throughout with careful, steady reasoning;
he is fully in command of his mental powers, as Dalila at last
realizes, when she tries to win him with a hurt and humble manner:

> In argument with men a woman ever
> Goes by the worse, whatever be her cause.   [903–04]

But he answers with strong and bitter wit:

> For want of words no doubt, or lack of breath,
> Witness when I was worried with thy peals.   [905–06]

Seeing him so resolved, she tries the last appeal: whatever is past is
past; let me take care of you; let me make it up to you. We notice
the insidious nature of the temptation she here offers to the blind
man:

>   though sight be lost,
> Life yet hath many solaces, enjoy'd
> Where other senses want not their delights
> At home in leisure and domestic ease,
> Exempt from many a care and chance to which
> Eye-sight exposes daily men abroad.
> I to the Lords will intercede, not doubting
> Thir favourable ear, that I may fetch thee
> From forth this loathsom prison-house, to abide
> With me, where my redoubl'd love and care
> With nursing diligence, to me glad office,
> May ever tend about thee to old age
> With all things grateful chear'd, and so suppli'd,
> That what by me thou hast lost thou least shalt miss.   [914–27]

Samson himself seems almost to believe her here, for at first he
responds more gently:

> No, no, of my condition take no care;
> It fits not; thou and I long since are twain.   [928–29]

But he soon moves on into the tone of more rigorous rejection:

> Nor think me so unwary or accurst
> To bring my feet again into the snare

> Where once I have been caught; I know thy trains
> Though dearly to my cost, thy ginns, and toyls;
> Thy fair enchanted cup, and warbling charms
> No more on me have power, their force is null'd,
> So much of Adders wisdom I have learn't
> To fence my ear against thy sorceries.   [930–37]

Nevertheless, the relative mildness of Samson's manner here seems to make her bolder and to urge her into one final plea: "Let me approach at least, and touch thy hand." Samson's fierce revulsion is a sign of the powerful attraction which she still holds:

> Not for thy life, lest fierce remembrance wake
> My sudden rage to tear thee joint by joint.   [952–53]

And he concludes with a tense and guarded manner, maintaining his firm self-control through bitter and fierce irony:

> At distance I forgive thee, go with that;
> Bewail thy falshood, and the pious works
> It hath brought forth to make thee memorable
> Among illustrious women, faithful wives;
> Cherish thy hast'n'd widowhood with the gold
> Of Matrimonial treason: so farewel.   [954–59]

What shall we make of Dalila here? To what extent does she mean what she says? Is it true, as Samson says, "That malice not repentance brought thee hither"? Is she, as the chorus says, "a manifest Serpent by her sting / Discover'd in the end"? Dalila remains an enigma that neither Samson, nor the chorus, nor the audience, can resolve.[7] Her speeches suggest a complex tissue of motives and impulses: curiosity, a challenge to see if she can draw him back, regret that it turned out worse than she thought it would, physical desire to have Samson back with her again, a desire to defend herself, to prove to herself perhaps that she is not as bad as it may seem. And then at the end we have the natural anger of a woman scorned, which does not necessarily prove her to be a hypocrite throughout, though Samson is surely right in thinking that she would betray him again if he went back. Whatever her nature, whatever her motives, the power of her appeal has certainly accomplished a remarkable change in Samson; she has stirred him out of his sense of loss, stung him into more positive responses.

Samson looks even stronger here if we compare this scene with the scene in Euripides' *The Trojan Women* which it evokes: that scene where Menelaus at last confronts his wife Helen. Menelaus enters cursing Helen, saying that he will kill her now, or take her home and have her killed there. His manner, however, is that of indecisive bluster and torment; and every Greek who watched the play knew perfectly well that Menelaus would never kill her, because in Homer's *Odyssey*, they knew, Telemachus had visited Menelaus and Helen, and had seen them living together again, not at all happily, after the Trojan War. So Menelaus looks weak here in the Greek play, and Helen's cool arguments and unrepentant ways, we know, will overcome his threats. Dalila is far more impressive than the Helen of Euripides, whose brazen reliance on her beauty shows in all her lines; and for this reason too Samson here seems to have much greater strength of mind than Menelaus.

Samson, we see, has now arisen beyond all temptations—and also far beyond the denunciation of the evils of women which we now hear presented in the chorus's inadequate commentary on this complex and moving scene. The chorus presents its conventional anti-feminist satire in what might fairly be called the weakest rhyming of the entire play:

> It is not vertue, wisdom, valour, *wit*,
> Strength, comliness of shape, or amplest *merit*
> That womans love can win or long *inherit*;
> But what it is, hard is to *say*,
> Harder to *hit*,
> (Which way soever men refer *it*)
> Much like thy riddle, *Samson*, in one *day*
> Or seven, though one should musing *sit*.   [1010–17]

The loss of dignity in the poetry is clear; Milton, it seems, is here drastically lowering the tone and manner of the poetry for some particular effect.[8]

> Is it for that such outward *ornament*
> Was lavish't on thir Sex, that inward *gifts*
> Were left for hast unfinish't, judgment *scant*,
> Capacity not rais'd to appr*ehend*
> Or value what is *best*

In choice, but oftest to affect the *wrong?*
Or was too much of self-love *mixt,*
Of constancy no root *infixt,*
That either they love nothing, or not *long?*
. . . .
  Therefore Gods universal *Law*
Gave to the man despotic *power*
Over his female in due *awe,*
Nor from that right to part an *hour,*
Smile she or *lowre:*
So shall he least confusion *draw*
On his whole life, not *sway'd*
By female usurpation, nor *dismay'd.*   [1025–60]

 The jarring impact of the endings here should help to indicate that this is hardly John Milton's final word of wisdom about women. We are warned against this by the weakness of the verse, by the one-sided quality of the view, and by the exaggeration of man's proper power over women. Authority man has—or should have—according to Milton, but never quite a power of this grim variety. Why, then, has Milton brought in such a choric utterance here, weak in itself, and out of tone with the central tendency of Samson's own self-denunciation? True, Samson blames Dalila furiously, for showing the "arts of every woman false like thee," but that is far from saying that nearly every woman is false. The chorus has picked up one aspect of the previous scene and has driven it to the point of caricature. The effect is to relieve the violent tension of the previous scene by a touch of satirical humor, and thus to prepare the way for the next scene, which develops a robustly comic tone, as Samson deflates the bragging and fastidious giant Harapha. Here is the one portion of the play in which we have a glimpse of the old folk-hero: taunting, audacious, primitive in his total confidence in his physical strength:

I only with an Oak'n staff will meet thee,
And raise such out-cries on thy clatter'd Iron,
Which long shall not with-hold mee from thy head,
That in a little time while breath remains thee,
Thou oft shalt wish thy self at *Gath* to boast
Again in safety what thou wouldst have done
To *Samson,* but shalt never see *Gath* more.   [1123–29]

But the glimpse of the primitive hero is brief; Milton very soon transmutes Samson into the dignified champion of God, as Samson declares (with a significant use of the word "Nativity"):

> My trust is in the living God who gave me
> At my Nativity this strength, diffus'd
> No less through all my sinews, joints and bones,
> Then thine, while I preserv'd these locks unshorn,
> The pledge of my unviolated vow.   [1140–44]

And soon Samson declares his willingness to resume the role of God's champion against Dagon, as he proceeds to accept the hope that he had earlier refused to allow:

> All these indignities, for such they are
> From thine, these evils I deserve and more,
> Acknowledge them from God inflicted on me
> Justly, yet despair not of his final pardon
> Whose ear is ever open; and his eye
> Gracious to re-admit the suppliant;
> In confidence whereof I once again
> Defie thee to the trial of mortal fight,
> By combat to decide whose god is God,
> Thine or whom I with *Israel's* Sons adore.   [1168–77]

The hero is fully restored; his great potential has now been revealed; and the play can continue rapidly towards the fulfillment of its triumphant catastrophe. But even in this ending, where the chorus is given many lines of much greater power than in the middle scenes, Milton creates the impression that these men, along with Manoa, have difficulty in grasping the true greatness of Samson's achievement. Their spirits are lifted by the scene with Harapha—to the point where their fine ode, "Oh how comely it is and how reviving," proceeds for thirty fervent lines without a single rhyme—but during the scene with Samson and the Officer, and in the scene with Manoa following Samson's departure, the chorus shows itself bewildered: "How thou wilt here come off surmounts my reach," they say in one deflating line (1380), and they agree completely with Manoa in his hopes for ransoming his son:

> Thy hopes are not ill founded nor seem vain
> Of his delivery, and thy joy thereon

> Conceiv'd, agreeable to a Fathers love,
> In both which we, as next participate.   [1504–07]

The Messenger then describes the center of Samson's great achievement in these words:

> with head a while enclin'd,
> And eyes fast fixt he stood, as one who pray'd,
> Or some great matter in his mind revolv'd.
> At last with head erect thus cryed aloud,
> Hitherto, Lords, what your commands impos'd
> I have perform'd, as reason was, obeying,
> Not without wonder or delight beheld.
> Now of my own accord such other tryal
> I mean to shew you of my strength, yet greater;
> As with amaze shall strike all who behold.   [1636–45]

We note the emphasis on mental action, on reason, and on choice: "Now of my own accord." Samson's greatness lies in his rational choice of a God-given opportunity. But here is what the chorus, in its immediate response, makes of this rational act:

> O dearly-bought revenge, yet glorious!
> Living or dying thou hast fulfill'd
> The work for which thou wast foretold
> To *Israel,* and now ly'st victorious
> Among thy slain self-kill'd
> Not willingly,[9] but tangl'd in the fold
> Of dire necessity, whose law in death conjoin'd
> Thee with thy slaughter'd foes in number more
> Then all thy life had slain before.   [1660–68]

Does the heavy rhyme, once again, help to suggest that this view is not to be taken as the whole truth? The "law" of "dire necessity" plays no part in Milton's universe:[10] by saying that Samson has died "self-kill'd / Not willingly," the chorus shows its initial failure to grasp the deeper meaning of Samson's triumph. Yet, as the chorus proceeds here, the realization of some inward act of "vertue," "illuminated" by God, breaks through:[11]

> But he though blind of sight,
> Despis'd and thought extinguish't quite,
> With inward eyes illuminated
> His fierie vertue rouz'd
> From under ashes into sudden flame . . .   [1687–91]

The latent contradiction between "necessity" and "inward eyes" is
not to be reconciled—nor need it be; it is enough to know that the
chorus at the close has glimpsed something of the essential truth.
As for Manoa, one wonders: his final thoughts are all external[12]—
on washing the "enemies blood" off Samson's body, on having a
proper funeral, on building a proper monument, where

> The Virgins also shall on feastful days
> Visit his Tomb with flowers, only bewailing
> His lot unfortunate in nuptial choice,
> From whence captivity and loss of eyes.   [1741–44]

Still harping on those foreign wives, Manoa can see no relation
between Samson's "nuptial choice" and the opportunity to
achieve, by another choice, his final victory. As Samson knows, it
was not his nuptial choice that led to his "captivity and loss of
eyes"; it was his weakness in dealing with the blandishments of his
chosen mate.

Can we, amid these circumstances, wholly believe Manoa when
he says the words that for some readers have seemed to explain
why the play is not a true tragedy?

> Nothing is here for tears, nothing to wail
> Or knock the breast, no weakness, no contempt,
> Dispraise, or blame, nothing but well and fair,
> And what may quiet us in a death so noble.   [1721–24]

Like everything else that Manoa has said in the play, this is at best
a half-truth, a partial understanding. There is much that is here
for tears, much that is not well and fair. Samson, like all tragic
heroes, has gained his victory within the self, but at terrible cost. It
is the cost of his final understanding that we must ponder, as the
chorus brings the tragedy to a quiet and conventional close. In
these final lines the chorus speaks with an effective firmness, while
the conventionality is marked by its expression in fourteen lines,
rhymed in sonnet-style:

> All is best, though we oft doubt,
> What th' unsearchable dispose
> Of highest wisdom brings about,
> And ever best found in the close.
> Oft he seems to hide his face,

But unexpectedly returns
And to his faithful Champion hath in place
Bore witness gloriously; whence *Gaza* mourns
And all that band them to resist
His uncontroulable intent,
His servants he with new acquist
Of true experience from this great event
With peace and consolation hath dismist,
And calm of mind all passion spent.

Certainly the chorus and Manoa have been uplifted by Samson's achievement; they have received "new acquist / Of true experience" that reaffirms their faith and opens the way toward their salvation. And yet even at the close they seem not quite to grasp the complex meaning of Samson's victory.[13] They stress the "uncontroulable intent" of God, while neglecting the free intent of Samson. They stress the way in which God has borne "witness" to his "faithful Champion," rather than the way in which this faithful man has borne witness to God. The distance between the "Elect" and the "rest" has been maintained. The chorus and Manoa have missed the deep self-discovery of the hero: that he is, by his own willing choice, a chosen son of God.

Nothing could show more clearly the range and reach of Milton's poetical career than a comparison between his volumes of 1645 and 1671. The earlier book derives from a pastoral joy in the physical creation, a sense of relationship between man and nature, though shadowed in places by a growing awareness of mortality and of moral and political evil at work in the world of man. In the later book that joy in the physical creation has been rigorously restrained, and that restraint is conveyed by the rigorous control over sensuous imagery, pagan allusion, and the burgeoning language of Milton's grand style. *Paradise Regain'd*, with its desert setting, is an anti-pastoral, played in the gray country of the mind, without recourse to the fruits of earth. Or perhaps it is better called a pastoral of a kind peculiar to the Bible,[14] a retreat from the city to the wilderness and the sparse pasturing hills of Judaea, such as the Israelites and their prophets made in answer to "the voice of him that crieth in the wilderness, Prepare ye the way of the Lord, make straight in the desert a highway for our God"

PARADISE
REGAIN'D,
A
POEM.

In IV BOOKS.

To which is added

SAMSON AGONISTES.

The Author

JOHN MILTON.

LONDON,

Printed by *J. M.* for *John Starkey* at the
Mitre in *Fleetstreet*, near *Temple-Bar*.
MDCLXXI.

(Isaiah 40:3). The contest of styles that is won by the Son of God in *Paradise Regain'd* finds its fulfillment in the relatively plain style of *Samson Agonistes*, where the play of sensuous imagery is severely pruned and the mode of reasoned speech prevails.[15] The result is a volume of austere greatness, a grandeur of self-abnegation that demonstrates, in both poems, the discovery of the true inner self of the chosen son.

Thus Milton's three great volumes of 1645, 1667, and 1671 might be seen as a triptych. On one side lies the green, youthful, chiefly joyous work of pastoral creation, and on the other the austere, ascetic, reasoned, rigorous work of age. In between lies the master piece, where a pastoral joy in God's Creation lives at the center of the vision, while the sombre tones of a wise and suffering maturity enfold that vision within scenes that reveal the possibilities of tragic failure and redemptive hope. Each of the three panels has an individual integrity, and can be viewed apart. Yet the measure of Milton's greatness lies in a realization of the full ensemble.

Paradise Regain'd
and the *Georgics*

"Oscillation between the heroic and the mundane is characteristic of the *Georgics*," says John Chalker: "It is easy to forget how much of the poem is epic in scope and manner, and how widely the heroic passages range." And he goes on to describe the *Georgics* as "a *montage* involving sudden shifts of subject and mood so that a pattern of comparisons and contrasts is built up which defies easy explanation."[1] The similarity between this account of the *Georgics* and my own view of the "contest of styles" in *Paradise Regain'd* has encouraged me to return to the suggestion made at the outset of the earlier versions of my essay on that poem: that *Paradise Regain'd* bears some analogy with the *Georgics*. The suggestion has not in general been welcomed,[2] perhaps because it was only a suggestion and was not explored in any detail.

The crux of the issue seems to lie in the meaning of the term "middle style," for which the *Georgics* has been taken as the model, at least since the time of Servius: "tres enim sunt characteres, humilis, medius, grandiloquus: quos omnes in hoc invenimus poeta. nam in Aeneide grandiloquum habet, in georgicis medium, in bucolicis humilem pro qualitate negotiorum et personarum."[3] Thus Addison speaks of the *Georgics* as a work written "in the middle Stile": Vergil, he says, "delivers the meanest of his Precepts with a kind of Grandeur, he breaks the Clods and tosses the Dung about with an air of gracefulness."[4]

A reading of the *Georgics* will show that the term *medius* cannot be taken to describe a style that pursues the even tenor of its way along a middle line between the *humilis* and the *grandiloquus*. *Medius* describes a style that allows for frequent oscillations upward and downward from a middle way: on the average the style lies in the middle between the humble and the grand, but it flexi-

bly accommodates a great deal of variation in either direction: it is
medius in the sense of being "intermediate"—"of a middle kind,
resembling each in some degree."

A middle range, however, can be found in the style, like a
thread that holds the poem under control: it is the dignified,
carefully moulded, but unpretentious style found in the poem's
opening lines:

> Quid faciat laetas segetes, quo sidere terram
> vertere, Maecenas, ulmisque adiungere vitis
> conveniat, quae cura boum, qui cultus habendo
> sit pecori, apibus quanta experientia parcis,
> hinc canere incipiam.

Dryden catches the manner to perfection:

> What makes a plenteous Harvest, when to turn
> The fruitful Soil, and when to sowe the Corn;
> The Care of Sheep, of Oxen, and of Kine;
> And how to raise on Elms the teeming Vine:
> The Birth and Genius of the frugal Bee,
> I sing, *Mecaenas,* and I sing to thee.

But then at once the style begins to modulate toward a higher
vein, moving through a series of apostrophes to various gods, and
ending with an appeal to Augustus in something close to an epic
manner:

> vos, o clarissima mundi
> lumina, labentem caelo quae ducitis annum,
> Liber et alma Ceres, vestro si munere tellus
> Chaoniam pingui glandem mutavit arista,
> poculaque inventis Acheloia miscuit uvis,
> et vos, agrestum praesentia numina, Fauni,
> (ferte simul Faunique pedem Dryadesque puellae)—
> munera vestra cano. [1.5–12]

> Ye Deities!, who Fields and Plains protect,
> Who rule the Seasons, and the Year direct;
> *Bacchus* and fost'ring *Ceres,* Pow'rs Divine,
> Who gave us Corn for Mast, for Water Wine;
> Ye Fawns, propitious to the Rural Swains,
> Ye Nymphs that haunt the Mountains and the Plains,
> Join in my Work, and to my Numbers bring
> Your needful Succor, for your Gifts I sing. [trans. Dryden, 7–14]

tuque adeo, quem mox quae sint habitura deorum
concilia incertum est, urbesne invisere, Caesar.
terrarumque velis curam, et te maximus orbis
auctorem frugum tempestatumque potentem
accipiat cingens materna tempora myrto,
an deus immensi venias maris ac tua nautae
numina sola colant, tibi serviat ultima Thule,
teque sibi generum Tethys emat omnibus undis,
anne novum tardis sidus te mensibus addas,
qua locus Erigonen inter Chelasque sequentis
panditur (ipse tibi iam bracchia contrahit ardens
Scorpius et caeli iusta plus parte reliquit)—
quidquid eris (nam te nec sperant Tartara regem,
nec tibi regnandi veniat tam dira cupido,
quamvis Elysios miretur Graecia campos,
nec repetita sequi curet Proserpina matrem)
da facilem cursum, atque audacibus adnue coeptis,
ignarosque viae mecum miseratus agrestis
ingredere et votis iam nunc adsuesce vocari.   [1.24–42]

Dryden, caught up with the grandeur of the passage, expands
Vergil's nineteen lines to thirty-four, of which I quote part, to
illustrate the high tone:

And chiefly thou, whose undetermin'd State
Is yet the Business of the Gods Debate:
Whether in after Times to be declar'd
The Patron of the World, and *Rome's* peculiar Guard,
Or o're the Fruits and Seasons to preside,
And the round Circuit of the Year to guide.
Pow'rful of Blessings, which thou strew'st around,
And with thy Goddess Mother's Myrtle crown'd.
Or wilt thou, *Caesar,* chuse the watry Reign,
To smooth the Surges, and correct the Main?
Then Mariners, in Storms, to thee shall pray,
Ev'n utmost *Thule* shall thy Pow'r obey,
And *Neptune* shall resign the Fasces of the Sea. . . .
But thou, propitious *Caesar,* guide my Course,
And to my bold Endeavours add thy Force.
Pity the Poet's and the Ploughman's Cares,
Int'rest thy Greatness in our mean Affairs,
And use thy self betimes to hear our Pray'rs.   [30–42, 59–63]

When, immediately after this, the poem turns to deal with "mean

Affairs," the style abruptly and appropriately drops down to the middle range:

> Vere novo, gelidus canis cum montibus umor
> liquitur et Zephyro putris se glaeba resolvit,
> depresso incipiat iam tum mihi taurus aratro
> ingemere, et sulco attritus splendescere vomer.
> illa seges demum votis respondet avari
> agricolae, bis quae solem, bis frigora sensit;
> illius immensae ruperunt horrea messes.   [1.43–49]

Dryden's version of this passage seems to elevate the style a bit above the Latin, which here seems to be more direct and perhaps closer to the colloquial, as the translation by Day Lewis may indicate:

> Early spring, when a cold moisture sweats from the hoarhead
> Hills and the brittle clods are loosening under a west wind,
> Is the time for the bull to grunt as he pulls the plough deep-
>   driven
> And the ploughshare to take a shine, scoured clean in the furrow.
> That crop, which twice has felt the sun's heat and the frost twice,
> Will answer at last the prayers of the never-satisfied
> Farmer, and burst his barns with an overflowing harvest.

But shortly after this we find a shift upwards toward the high style, marked by the lists of names characteristic of epic: this is then followed by an equally abrupt shift downward marked by the words "ergo age"—"now let's get to work." The translation by Day Lewis seems quite faithful to the variations upward and downward exhibited by this characteristic passage:

> First you must learn the winds and changeable ways of its
>   weather,
> The land's peculiar cultivation and character,
> The different crops that different parts of it yield or yield not.
> A corn-crop here, grapes there will come to the happier issue:
> On another soil it is fruit trees, and grass of its own sweet will
> Grows green. Look you, how Tmolus gives us the saffron per-
>   fume,
> India its ivory, the unmanly Sabaeans their incense,
> The naked Chalybes iron, Pontus the rank castor,
> And Elis prize-winning mares.
> Nature imposed these laws, a covenant everlasting,
> On different parts of the earth right from the earliest days when

Deucalion cast over a tenantless world the stones
From which arose mankind, that dour race. Now, to business:
As soon as the first months of the year begin, your strong bulls
Should turn the fertile loam and leave the clods lying
For the full suns of summer to bake into a fine dust . . .
See, too, that your arable lies fallow in due rotation,
And leave the idle field alone to recoup its strength:
Or else, changing the seasons, put down to yellow spelt
A field where before you raised the bean with its rattling pods
Or the small-seeded vetch
Or the brittle stalk and rustling haulm of the bitter lupin.
For a crop of flax burns up a field, and so does an oat-crop,
And poppies drenched in oblivion burn up its energy.
Still, by rotation of crops you lighten your labour, only
Scruple not to enrich the dried-up soil with dung
And scatter filthy ashes on fields that are exhausted.[5]

[1.51–66, 71–81]

With the last few lines here we have descended very close to the
humilis, in keeping with the lowly subject:

Alternis idem tonsas cessare novalis
et segnem patiere situ durescere campum;
aut ibi flava seres mutato sidere farra,
unde prius laetum siliqua quassante legumen
aut tenuis fetus viciae tristisque lupini
sustuleris fragilis calamos silvamque sonantem.
urit enim lini campum seges, urit avenae,
urunt Lethaeo perfusa papavera sommo:
sed tamen alternis facilis labor, arida tantum
ne saturare fimo pingui pudeat sola neve
effetos cinerem immundum iactare per agros.   [1.71–81]

   This technique of rising and then cutting back sharply goes on
throughout the poem, as Wilkinson and Otis have both remarked.[6] The effect is particularly notable after the famous passage of the second book devoted to praise of Italy in the higher
style: the translation by Bovie makes the shift clear:

Italian soil has bred a race of heroes,
Marsians, Sabines, toughened generations
From the Western Coast, and tribes of Volscians
Handy with the spear. Great Family names,
Camillus, Decius, Marius, Scipio,
And chief of all, Octavianus Caesar,

Who triumphs now on Asia's farthest shore,
And defends the hills of Rome from the timid foe.
All hail, Saturnian Land, our honored Mother!
For thee I broach these themes of ancient art
And dare disclose the sacred springs of verse,
Singing Hesiod's song through Roman towns.
    Now for the innate qualities of soils:
The color, strength, productive powers of each.
Ground that is hard to deal with, awkward hills,
Thin fields of marl, stone-cluttered undergrowths,
Welcome a grove of Pallas' long-lived olives.
Wild olives, cropping out on every side,
And fields strewn thick with berries, mark the place.
But moist and lush terrain, and fertile flatlands
Thick with grass (the sort we see below
In mountain vales where brooks slip down the rocks
And wash in fertile mud), and southern heights
That favor ferns, the bane of curving ploughs,
Will yield you hardy vineyards full of wine:
This soil is good for grapes . . .   [2.166–91][7]

And the same is true of the passage in book 3 that tells of the epic
battle of the bulls, a passage of twenty-three lines which Dryden
expands to thirty-six, bringing out the mock-heroic elements latent in Vergil and stressing at the end the abrupt shift to a lower
style after the heroic simile:

Not with more Madness, rolling from afar,
The spumy Waves proclaim the watry War.
And mounting upwards, with a mighty Roar,
March onwards, and insult the rocky shoar.
They mate the middle Region with their height;
And fall no less, than with a Mountain's weight;
The Waters boil, and belching from below
Black Sands, as from a forceful Engine throw.
    Thus every Creature, and of every Kind,
The secret Joys of sweet Coition find . . .   [3.367–76]

Equally clear is the contrast set up at the outset of book 3, as
Vergil expresses his hope of ultimately dealing with epic
themes—but at present, he says, such themes are not his occupa-
tion. Then he turns to tell, in a lower style, of the problems of
breeding horses and cattle.
    Meanwhile, as Dryden noted, the entire movement of the *Geor-*

gics shows, within these oscillations, a steady rise in the "Subject": "Virgil has taken care to raise the Subject of each Georgic: In the First, he has only dead Matter on which to work. In the second he just steps on the World of Life, and describes that degree of it which is to be found in Vegetables. In the third, he advances to Animals. And in the last, singles out the Bee, which may be reckon'd the most sagacious of 'em, for his Subject."[8] And the rise in subject is accompanied by an appropriate rise in the level of the characteristic style of each book. The first book, as in *Paradise Regain'd,* is on the whole cast in a lower style than the remaining books, while, as Chalker says, "The most extended epic passages are found in the fourth Book" (p. 26). There the life of the bees is treated in a gently mock-heroic style—gently, because the bees are held up as models for (in Dryden's words) "their prudent and politick Administration of Affairs."[9] Addison well describes the use of the epic techniques here when he says that Vergil

> Ennobles the Actions of so trivial a Creature, with Metaphors drawn from the most important Concerns of Mankind. His Verses are not in a greater noise and hurry in the Battels of *Aeneas* and *Turnus,* than in the Engagement of two Swarms. And as in his *Aeneis* he compares the Labours of his *Trojans* to those of Bees and Pismires, here he compares the Labours of the Bees to those of the *Cyclops.* In short, the last *Georgic* was a good Prelude to the *Aeneis;* and very well shew'd what the Poet could do in the description of what was really great, by his describing the Mock-grandeur of an Insect with so good a grace.[10]

Then at line 280, almost exactly in the middle of the fourth book, Vergil changes his mode of narration to present the "epyllion" of Aristaeus, a story which enfolds the story of Orpheus and Eurydice in a manner that may have influenced Ovid. The parts pertaining to Aristaeus are told in an epic, Homeric manner, as Otis says: "The diction, periodization, metre are almost clamorously epical."[11] Thus we have allusions to such "higher" matters as the shower of Parthian arrows, invocations of the Muse, lists of proper names, and vast geographical excursions, along with the descent of Orpheus to the underworld—all this to relate an aetiological myth of dying and rebirth, telling how a bee swarm is born from the belly of an ox.

One hesitates to press the analogies here, but they seem to press themselves upon us. The fourth book of *Paradise Regain'd* is also told in two different modes of narration. The first part of the last book is given over to the visions of the glories of Rome and Greece, thus completing the long sequence of temptations that began in book 2; the sequence ends at line 364, a little more than half-way through this final book of 639 lines. After a brief transition in which Satan warns the hero that

> Sorrows, and labours, opposition, hate,
> Attends thee, scorns, reproaches, injuries,
> Violence and stripes, and lastly cruel death . . .   [4.386–88]

Milton shifts his mode of narration to tell of three symbolic actions: the storm that seems to adumbrate the Passion, the victory of the Son of God on the pinnacle of the temple, and the banquet and hymn presented to the Son of God by the angels.

Otis points out, in his fine analysis of Vergil's closing epyllion, that the story of Orpheus and Eurydice is enclosed within the story of Aristaeus in such a way as to create a tripartite structure. The Orpheus "panel" is narrated in a sympathetic way, with a concentrated dramatic impact, quite different from the more "diffuse" and objective narration found in the parts dealing directly with Aristaeus. The Orpheus panel tells "with marvellous compression" a story that deals with "the tragedy of human passion." Orpheus "cannot conquer his own impulses which destroy him in the very moment of triumph"—that is, his *furor* ruins his attempt to regain his lost Eurydice. But the Aristaeus myth, on either side of the Orpheus panel, tells a story of miraculous rebirth. Otis presses the point hard:

> What stands out and is meant to stand out is the central Orpheus panel, where the elliptical, concentrated, emotional style and above all, for once, a penetrating vignette of human feeling, come at exactly the point where we are led to expect revelation. The human meaning, the human price of passion, atonement and resurrection emerge in a blaze of light at the decisive, last instant.[12]

It may be valid to feel in this peculiar structure a distant parallel with the way in which the "panel" of Jesus' victory on the pinnacle of the temple stands out, with concentrated power, between the more diffuse narration of the storm (with its famous relaxed sentence: "Mee worse then wet thou find'st not") and the description of the pastoral banquet provided by the angels, followed by their hymn. Perhaps we have been prepared to receive this sort of parallel by the fact that the third books of both poems also display an explicit division into two approximate halves, unlike the first two books of both poems.

The chief difficulty in accepting such analogies with the *Georgics* seems to lie in a tendency to underestimate the wide-ranging implications of that poem. "It used to be thought," says Wilkinson, "that the *Georgics* consisted simply of didactic matter treated as 'poetically' as possible and relieved by set-pieces, mythological examples, similes and so forth."[13] But he points out that classical scholars, for almost fifty years before his book of 1969, had been moving toward a view that sees a high degree of unity and a deeper meaning in the poem.[14] Jackson Knight, for example, has seen the function of what used to be regarded as "digressions"—the heightened passages:

> . . . everything is coloured by contrasts, for it is all framed by a world of imagination; and accordingly nothing is entirely actual. The sheep of the farm are themselves changed, when Vergil, appealing to Pales, goddess of pastures, says that now for such a majestic subject he "must speak in deep-toned harmonics"—*magno nunc ore sonandum.* [*Georgics* 3.294][15]

"It is a serious critical error," says Charles Segal, "to read that great poem as simply a didactic treatise on farming. What it does is to present nature as a vast symbolical framework against which the eternal human themes of love, war, death, work, suffering, and loss are writ large."[16] Jacques Perret, along with Otis, has carried the possible implications of the poem even further:

> . . . through this evocation of rural life an entire philosophy is proposed to us. Virgil's laborer becomes a symbol of all human life, with the result that the poet's exhortations and vehemence produce an immediate emotional response in us . . . I myself may have no feeling for the work of the farmer; yet the images of the poet move me nonetheless: a countryside to recreate, a land to make fruitful, order to establish, a national ideal to animate, a Golden Age to give birth to . . .

It is only quite recently that it has again become possible for us to interpret the *Georgics* in this way, as a poem of human effort, of the building of a country and of the world, as a poem of God's presence in and response to human labor . . . The literary success of the *Georgics* . . . is linked much more closely than is at first apparent to a certain quality of the soul.[17]

Whether or not we agree with these interpretations (as I do), the main point of citing them is to show that Milton, if he is imitating the style and form of the *Georgics* in the renaissance manner, has chosen no unworthy model. We must remember too, that for Dryden and Addison, the *Georgics* was nothing less than Vergil's masterpiece. In the Dedication of his translation to Lord Chesterfield, Dryden speaks of the *Georgics* as "the best Poem of the best Poet," and goes on to say: "*Virgil* wrote his *Georgics* in the full strength and vigour of his Age, when his Judgment was at the height, and before his Fancy was declining." And Addison, in his essay prefaced to Dryden's translations of Vergil, declares that the poem is "the most Compleat, Elaborate, and finisht Piece of all Antiquity."

> The *Aeneis* indeed is of a Nobler kind, but the *Georgic* is more perfect in its kind. The *Aeneid* has a greater variety of Beauties in it, but those of the *Georgic* are more exquisite. In short, the *Georgic* has all the perfection that can be expected in a Poem written by the greatest Poet in the Flower of his Age, when his Invention was ready, his Imagination warm, his Judgement settled, and all his Faculties in their full Vigour and Maturity.

We have no external evidence that Milton shared this remarkably high view of the poem's greatness. As with the question of the middle style, the only strong evidence lies in *Paradise Regain'd* itself. Addison's complaint that the poem has been neglected may suggest that his view was not widely held in the seventeenth century. Yet Dryden was already forty years old when *Paradise Regain'd* was published, and one might think that his views of the *Georgics* had already been established by that time.

However this may be, the evidence of analogy between these two poems is worth pursuing. It can be found by a careful comparison of the two poems, along with the studies of Wilkinson and Otis. Such a comparison may be encouraged by remembering what

Tillyard said long ago, when he remarked that *Paradise Regain'd*
and the *Georgics* were poems of similar length, a little more than
two thousand lines, and that they both were divided into four
books.[18] Some kind of Vergilian analogy, he thought, must reside
in the fact that Milton's opening line, "I who e're while the happy
Garden sung," clearly echoes the lines that used to open the *Aeneid*
in renaissance editions—lines, now widely regarded as authentic,
which allude to Vergil's earlier work in the pastoral and georgic
kinds:

> Ille ego, qui quondam gracili modulatus avena
> carmen, et egressus silvis vicina coegi
> ut quamvis avido parerent arva colono,
> gratum opus agricolis, at nunc horrentia Martis . . .

> I am that poet who in times past made the light melody of pastoral
> poetry. In my next poem I left the woods for the adjacent farm-
> lands, teaching them to obey even the most exacting tillers of the
> soil; and the farmers liked my work. But now I turn to the terrible
> strife of Mars. [trans. Knight][19]

Is Milton suggesting that his career as poet, despite his beginning
with the shepherd's trade, represents a reversal of the Vergilian
pattern, as Milton moves now from a subject not less but *more*
heroic than that of the *Aeneid* into a poem that deals with a subject
above heroic?

Perhaps the best and most tactful solution to the problem is that
implied by Charles Dunster when, in his edition of *Paradise Regain'd* (London, 1795), he described the "species" of the poem as
"the *brief,* or *didactic,* epic" (p. 2). Edward Weismiller, citing this
passage in the recent volume of the *Variorum,* comments wryly on
this "intertwining," this fusion, or confusion of genres:

> That the brief epic is of its nature didactic is perhaps no more
> self-evident than that Hesiod's *Works and Days* (for example) is
> in a true sense epic. And what led a particular critic, no longer
> living, to the intertwining of definitions ordinarily kept separate
> may not be discoverable. Dunster's assignment of *PR* to the
> 'species' he denominates so crisply may on the other hand be in
> part explained by a comment in his concluding note to the
> poem: 'Though it may be said' of *PR,* 'as Longinus has said of
> the *Odyssey,* that it is the *epilogue* of the preceding poem, still the

design and conduct of it is as different, as that of the *Georgics*
from the *Aeneid*.'[20]

Dunster's intertwining of genres may give us a clue to an acceptable solution. What has happened, perhaps, is this: the presence of epic elements in Vergil's *Georgics* allowed Milton to fulfill
his early plan for a brief epic modelled on the book of Job by
merging it with the form and style of the *Georgics*. The presence of
strong epic elements in the style of *Paradise Regain'd* does not in
itself make the poem an epic, unless we are willing to say that for
these reasons the *Georgics* too is a brief epic—with the figure of the
farmer as hero. The "old Corycian swain" in Vergil's fourth book,
says Chalker, "is in a sense the true heroic figure of the *Georgics*"
(p. 26).

In the end it does not matter whether we call *Paradise Regain'd* a
brief epic, or a georgic, as long as we recognize its analogies to the
form and style of Vergil's *Georgics*. If such analogies can be accepted, then Milton's poem of renunciation does not in fact renounce the classics after all. *Samson Agonistes* is "added" to the
volume of 1671, a poem of comparable length and at least equal
power, as though to stress the poet's unbroken allegiance to the
literary modes of Greece and Rome.

Amor and *Furor:*
Anti-heroic Themes
and the Unity of
Ovid's *Metamorphoses*

Ovid's theme of *amor* is introduced in the first tale that occurs after the world has been renewed through the piety of Deucalion and Pyrrha: the story of Phoebus and Daphne opens with the thematic word: "Primus amor Phoebi Daphne Peneia, quem non / fors ignara dedit, sed saeva Cupidinis ira" ("The first love of Phoebus was Daphne, daughter of Peneus, which was not brought about by blind chance, but by the fierce anger of Cupid": 1.452–53). For Apollo, "still exultant" over his heroic conquest of Python, had caught a glimpse of Cupid bending his bow and had said to him in scorn: "What have you to do with a warrior's arms? Weapons such as these are suited to my shoulders" (1.456–57; trans. Innes). Then, after the striking of Cupid's arrow, Apollo's cry to Daphne sets the essential motif: "amor est mihi causa sequendi!" (1.507). In the next book the power of love is pointed up by Ovid's sly remark as Jove is about to undertake the seduction of Europa: "non bene conveniunt nec in una sede morantur / maiestas et amor" ("Majesty and love do not go well together, nor tarry long in the same dwelling-place": 2.846–47; trans. Miller). So too, in book 5, the king of the underworld must submit to the power of Venus, as she sees him inspecting the volcanic region of Sicily. Embracing Cupid, she cries: "O son, both arms and hands to me, and source of all my power, take now those shafts, Cupid, with which you conquer all, and shoot your swift arrows into the heart of that god to whom the final lot of the triple kingdom fell"

(5.365–68; trans. Miller). And so occurs the rape of Proserpine in the field of Enna. Such is the "heroic" warfare of love's empire.

The whole contrast between *maiestas* and *amor* is then summed up in the weaving contest between Pallas and Arachne at the beginning of book 6. The tapestry of Pallas deals majestically with the ancient contest of the gods over the naming of Athens; but Arachne fills her tapestry with scenes depicting the *caelestia crimina* committed by the gods in their erotic escapades. So, from the opening book, on through the story of Pomona in book 14, the power of *amor* transforms the majesty of gods into animals and other earthly semblances, demonstrating an irresistible force summed up in the cry of Galatea: "pro! quanta potentia regni / est, Venus alma, tui!" ("O bountiful Venus, how powerful is your sway!": 13.758–59).

Meanwhile, in book 3, a new god is born, worshipped with new rites: Bacchus, son of Semele. As Pentheus sees and hears these wild rites, he denounces them as a threat to the old heroic code by which he lives: "Quis furor, anguigenae, proles Mavortia, vestras / attonuit mentes?" ("What madness, ye sons of the serpent's teeth, ye seed of Mars, has dulled your reason?") "Can clashing cymbals, can the pipe of crooked horn, can shallow tricks of magic, wo- men's shrill cries, wine-heated madness, vulgar throngs and empty drums—can all these vanquish men, for whom real war, with its drawn swords, the blare of trumpets, and lines of glitter- ing spears, had no terrors?" (3.531–37; trans. Miller). The killing of Pentheus by the Bacchantes at the end of book 3 may thus be taken to indicate the death of the old heroic order. Book 4 then opens with a sustained celebration of the new god, as the women of Thebes—all but the daughters of Minyas—gather for the festi- val of Bacchus, worshipping him under the many names that show his varied and widespread powers.

From here on the powers of Bacchus and Venus are in- tertwined, as the daughters of Minyas, scorning the rites of Bac- chus, tell their many tales of love and passion, beginning with the pitiful love of Pyramus and Thisbe, and ending with the furious passion of Salmacis. This intermingling of the themes of *amor* and *furor* continues throughout the poem, reaching its climax in book 10 and the opening portion of book 11, the section of 805 lines in which the story of Orpheus himself encloses the tales of strange, violent, or perverse passion that he sings to the assembled trees, animals, and birds: Jupiter and Ganymede, Apollo and Hyacinthus, Pygmalion and the statue, the terrible passion of Myrrha for her father, Venus and Adonis, Atalanta and Hippomenes. After all these demonstrations of passion's rage, Orpheus himself is torn to pieces by the mad Ciconian women, who cry: "See, see the man who scorns us!" (11.7). Not even the bard of the rites of Bacchus (11.68, 92–93) can escape the effects of stifled love turned to *furor.* Like Pentheus, he is destroyed by frenzied women associated with the rites of the Bacchantes. By such devices of repetition and ironical reminiscence, by such persistent mingling of *amor* and *furor*—as opposed to the old heroic mode—Ovid's poem weaves itself together into a new kind of epic unity.

Notes

Reference to scholarship on Milton's minor poems and *Paradise Regain'd* is now simplified by the admirable volumes of *A Variorum Commentary on the Poems of John Milton*, vol. 1, *The Latin and Greek Poems*, ed. Douglas Bush, and *The Italian Poems*, ed. J. E. Shaw and A. Bartlett Giamatti (New York: Columbia University Press, 1970); vol. 2, parts 1, 2, and 3, *The Minor English Poems*, ed. A. S. P. Woodhouse and Douglas Bush, *With a review of Studies of Verse Form* by Edward R. Weismiller in part 3 (New York: Columbia University Press, 1972); and vol. 4 [on *Paradise Regain'd*: see below, headnote to chapter 15]; hereafter referred to as *Variorum Commentary*.

Further guidance to scholarship on all of Milton's poetry is given in the excellent introductions and annotations provided by John Carey and Alastair Fowler in their edition (really a small *variorum*) *The Poems of John Milton* (London: Longmans, 1968); hereafter referred to as "Carey and Fowler."

All quotations from Milton's poetry are taken from the text, based upon the first editions, edited by H. C. Beeching, *The Poetical Works of John Milton* (London: Oxford University Press, 1904); I have used the reprint of 1938 (normalizing line-numbers for book 11 of *Paradise Lost*).

Quotations from the Latin text of Vergil are taken from the *Opera*, edited by Frederick A. Hirtzel (Oxford: Clarendon Press, 1900); I have used the reprint of 1950.

Quotations from the Latin text of Ovid's *Metamorphoses* are taken from the volume in the Loeb Classical Library edited with a translation by Frank Justus Miller, 2nd edition, 2 vols. (London: Heinemann, 1921); I have used the reprint of 1966–68.

Quotations from Milton's prose are normally taken from *Complete Prose Works of John Milton*, Don M. Wolfe, general ed., 8 vols. (New Haven: Yale University Press, 1953–); I am especially indebted to the edition of *Christian Doctrine* in vol. 6, translated by John Carey and edited by Maurice Kelley (1973).

Throughout this work, my references to previous scholarship are of necessity highly selective: the *Variorum Commentary* and "Carey and Fowler" must be relied upon to make, by implication, many desirable acknowledgments. I have tried to single out certain books and articles for particular mention whenever they constitute a special debt or provide a parallel or divergent interpretation of some important point of discussion.

I wish to add here a general acknowledgment of the valuable articles and bibliographical aids provided by *Milton Studies, Milton Quarterly,* and *Seventeenth*

Century News. Finally, I wish to express my gratitude for the several volumes of Milton's poetry edited by Merritt Hughes, which I have used in teaching: the two editions of *Paradise Lost* (New York: Odyssey Press, 1935 and 1962); *Paradise Regained, the Minor Poems and Samson Agonistes* (Garden City: Doubleday, 1937); and *Complete Poems and Major Prose* (New York: Odyssey Press, 1957).

CHAPTER 1: The Pastoral Music: *A Maske Presented at Ludlow Castle*

The second part of this chapter is based upon materials presented in my essay "The Music of *Comus*" in *Illustrious Evidence: Approaches to English Literature of the Early Seventeenth Century,* ed. Earl Miner (Berkeley: University of California Press, 1975); "Published under the auspices of the William Andrews Clark Memorial Library." I wish to thank Louise Brown Kennedy for assistance in the preparation of the original essay for the press.

1 See Ovid's account of Chiron's teaching music to Achilles (*Fasti,* 5.379–86) and of Polyphemus' pastoral song to Galatea (*Metamorphoses,* 13.782–869). For the incident in Pholus' cave see the passage in Apollodorus' *Library,* 2.5.4 where at the banquet for Heracles the centaur Pholus opens the wine given by Dionysus to all the centaurs, and thus provokes war with the other centaurs. Anna Rist, in her illuminating commentary on Theocritus' Idyll 7, points out the undercurrent of violence and death in these allusions: "Latent seems to be a suggestion that the human cultivation which is crowned by poetry is purchased at a price." But perhaps the civilizing power of poetry is here implied. See *The Poems of Theocritus,* trans. Anna Rist (Chapel Hill: University of North Carolina Press, 1978), p. 88.

2 *Greek Pastoral Poetry,* trans. Anthony Holden (Harmondsworth: Penguin Books, 1974).

3 An extensive and illuminating study of the theme of music in Milton's early poetry is given in the opening chapter of Jon S. Lawry's *The Shadow of Heaven* (Ithaca: Cornell University Press, 1968). For surveys of musical theory see Leo Spitzer, *Classical and Christian Ideas of World Harmony* (Baltimore: Johns Hopkins Press, 1963); James Hutton, "Some English Poems in Praise of Music," *English Miscellany,* 2 (1951): 1–63; and D. P. Walker, "Orpheus the Theologian and the Renaissance Platonists," *Journal of the Warburg and Courtauld Institutes,* 16 (1953): 100–20. For the relation of Orpheus to Pythagoras see Iamblichus: "a perspicuous paradigm of the Pythagoric theology according to numbers, is in a certain respect to be found in the writings of Orpheus. Nor is it to be doubted, that Pythagoras receiving auxiliaries from Orpheus, composed his treatise Concerning the Gods." *Life of Pythagoras,* trans. Thomas Taylor (London, 1818), p. 105. For the analogy with Orpheus, see especially Angus Fletcher, *The Transcendental Masque* (Ithaca: Cornell University Press, 1971), who also treats the descriptions in lines 86–88 as indicating the "Orphic powers" of the Attendant Spirit (p. 168). See his mention of the Lady's powers as an "Orphic voice" on pp. 170

and 173 and his discussion of the Orphic voice of the poem on pp. 186–91. For the entire topic see S. K. Heninger, *Touches of Sweet Harmony: Pythagorean Cosmology and Renaissance Poetics* (San Marino: Huntington Library, 1974).

4 At the close of his speech in couplets the Genius says he cannot match the music of the spheres, "yet as we go" toward the seat of state, he adds, he will do his best to create music of praise with his "inferior hand or voice." Then in the second song he adds, "Follow me as I sing, / And touch the warbled string," as he leads the group across the lawn to where the Countess is sitting. The final song, perhaps presented as the group arrives at the seat of state, is also presumably sung by the Genius.

5 Ovid, *Metamorphoses,* trans. Mary M. Innes (Harmondsworth: Penguin Books, 1955).

6 See above, headnote, for the translation by Frank Justus Miller.

7 My appreciation of this aspect of Milton's *Maske* was greatly enriched by watching the performance of the work produced by Ars Nova (directed by John Buckingham) in London at St. John's Smith Square, September 1977. The performance was skillfully designed to approximate the original production of 1634.

8 Cf. Fletcher, *The Transcendental Masque,* p. 202.

9 See S. E. Sprott's edition, *A Maske, the Earlier Versions* (Toronto: University of Toronto Press, 1973), p. 196; also *A Maske at Ludlow,* ed. John S. Diekhoff (Cleveland: Press of Case Western Reserve University, 1968), p. [246]. This is the original reading of the Trinity MS, which is revised in accord with the printed version; both versions of the line are therefore Milton's own work.

10 See Vergil's *Eclogues:* 1.2; 6.8.

11 For a detailed discussion of this scene see Hutton, pp. 4–6, 34–38 (note 3 above). The quotations from *The Merchant of Venice* are taken from *The Riverside Shakespeare,* ed. G. Blakemore Evans (Boston: Houghton Mifflin, 1974).

12 For the analogies cf. *Romeo and Juliet,* III.ii.5, *Maske,* 553; *Macbeth,* II.i.51, *Maske,* 553; *Antony and Cleopatra,* II.ii.212–18, *Maske,* 554–59. These analogies are noted by Carey and Fowler. Cf. also *2 Henry VI,* IV.i.3–5 for analogy to *Maske,* 552–53 as noted in the *Variorum Commentary,* II, iii, 924.

13 See John Demaray, *Milton and the Masque Tradition* (Cambridge, Mass.: Harvard University Press, 1968), p. 132, on the uses of listening in *Comus*; also Raymond G. Schoen, "The Hierarchy of Senses in *A Mask,*" *Milton Quarterly,* 7 (1973): 32–37.

14 From Ficino's commentary on the *Timaeus* (*Opera Omnia,* Basel, 1561, p. 1453), as translated by D. P. Walker in *Spiritual and Demonic Magic from Ficino to Campanella* (London: Warburg Institute, 1958), p. 9.

15 "Milton's Haemony," *English Literary Renaissance,* 5 (1975): 81–95. For all quotations in this paragraph see Otten, pp. 84–88.

16 See *OED,* "rash," v^3 (with perhaps overtones of v^1).

17 John Aubrey, *Miscellanies* (London, 1696), p. 111; quoted by Otten, p. 90.

18   For a summary of the many interpretations of Haemony see the *Variorum Commentary*, II, iii, 932–38; also Otten, p. 81n; and Sacvan Bercovitch, "Milton's 'Haemony': Knowledge and Belief," *Huntington Library Quarterly*, 33 (1970): 351–59.

19   Carey and Fowler, p. 266.

20   Euripides, *Alcestis*, trans. Richard Aldington (London: Chatto, 1930), p. 39.

21   On the problem of Chiron's cave see notes in Carey and Fowler, pp. 263–64, and *The Latin Poems of John Milton*, ed. Walter MacKellar (New Haven: Yale University Press, 1930), p. 327; also *Variorum Commentary*, I, 276.

22   See also Angus Fletcher's account of the "triumph of song" in *The Transcendental Masque*, pp. 166–75.

23   See Lewis and Short, *Latin Dictionary*, "carmen."

24   Henry Lawes's autograph manuscript of the songs is on deposit in the British Library (see Coburn Gum, "Lawes Folio," *Milton Newsletter*, 3 [March, 1969], 4–5.) A second manuscript in the British Library is thought to be an eighteenth-century transcript of the autograph: see Andrew J. Sabol, *Songs and Dances for the Stuart Masque* (Providence: Brown University Press, 1959), p. 167; Sabol bases his transcription on this manuscript, which is reproduced in the Fletcher *Facsimile*, I, 340–44 (see next note). Other printed versions of Lawes's music follow the collation of the two musical manuscripts done by Hubert J. Foss for *The Mask of Comus*, ed. E. H. Visiak (Bloomsbury: The Nonesuch Press, 1937), as in Diekhoff, pp. 241–250. See *Variorum Commentary*, II, iii, 739.

25   A facsimile of the Bridgewater MS with transcription is available in *John Milton's Complete Poetical Works Reproduced in Facsimile*, ed. Harris F. Fletcher, 4 vols. (Urbana: University of Illinois Press, 1943–1948), I, 300–39. Fletcher's transcription is reprinted, with useful textual notes, in the collection edited by Diekhoff, pp. 207–40 (see note 9 above). My citations of Bridgewater are taken from Diekhoff. Sprott's *A Maske: The Earlier Versions* includes the versions of Bridgewater, Trinity, and 1637 in parallel columns.

26   This passage is taken from the Foss transcription of Lawes's songs as reprinted in Diekhoff, p. 243. Lineation and initial capitalization have been regularized and slight changes have been made in punctuation. The song version omits six lines of the longer version found at the opening of the Bridgewater MS: see Sprott, pp. 43–45; Diekhoff, p. 210.

27   Milton uses the phrase "The attendant Spirit" in the opening of the published version to refer to the figure called "A Guardian spirit or Daemon" in the Trinity and Bridgewater MSS. As the *Variorum Commentary* points out (II, iii, 853), "In English *daemon* had as one of its meanings . . . 'An attendant, ministering, or indwelling spirit' (*OED:* demon 1b)," but the word also contains specifically platonic overtones. John Arthos (*On A Mask Presented at Ludlow-Castle* [Ann Arbor: University of Michigan Press, 1954], pp. 36–41, 62–66) discusses the platonic doctrine of the demonic as being the realm of the spirit which is both intermediate and intermediary between the divine and the mortal. Sears Jayne ("The Subject of Milton's Ludlow Mask," in

Diekhoff, pp. 184–185) cites Ficino's idea of the platonic Daemon as the agent through which God governs and protects the lower world. For the intricacies of neoplatonic demonology see Frances Yates, *Giordano Bruno and the Hermetic Tradition* (London: Routledge, 1964) and Walker, *Spiritual and Demonic Magic*.

28 By "printed version" I refer to the 1645 printing as the norm: the variants in 1637 and 1673 are very few, though not negligible. The most important variants occur at lines 213, 471, 604, 607, 608, 780. See the *Variorum Commentary* and C. S. Lewis, "A Note on 'Comus,'" *Review of English Studies,* 8(1932): 170–76, reprinted in *Studies in Medieval and Renaissance Literature* (Cambridge: Cambridge University Press, 1966).

29 1645: line 890; the direction occurs in all versions, with minor variations in Trinity: see the helpful table of stage directions appended to the article by John T. Shawcross, "Certain Relationships of the Manuscripts of *Comus*," *Papers of the Bibliographical Society of America,* 54 (1960): 38–56.

30 Eugene Haun, "An Inquiry into the Genre of *Comus*," *Essays in Honor of Walter Clyde Curry* (Nashville: Vanderbilt University Press, 1954), p. 235.

31 But Trinity MS has the direction, "to be said" (*Facsimile,* ed. Harris Fletcher, I, 426, line 9).

32 Haun, "An Inquiry into the Genre of *Comus*," p. 236. There has been a rather extensive and often highly technical debate about the extent to which Milton's *Maske* does, or does not, fit the conventions of the two genres, masque and opera. Gretchen Finney (*Musical Backgrounds for English Literature: 1580–1650* [New Brunswick: Rutgers University Press, 1962], pp 175–94), argues for the relation of the *Maske* to the Italian *dramma per musica,* productions in a mixed form which combined recitative and serious plot with aspects of spectacle or masque. John Hollander (*The Untuning of the Sky: Ideas of Music in English Poetry, 1500–1700* [Princeton: Princeton University Press, 1961], p. 192), and Demaray (*Milton and the Masque Tradition*), disagree with Finney and are opposed to any attempt to relate Milton's *Maske* to the development of early opera. Wilfrid Mellers (*Harmonious Meeting: A Study of the Relationship between English Music, Poetry and Theater, c. 1600–1900* [London: Dobson, 1965], pp. 166–67) argues that the *Maske* is only superficially operatic and that many of the problems of the work are attributable to the fact that it falls between the conventions of poetry and opera. Angus Fletcher (*The Transcendental Masque,* pp. 175–86) provides a summary of the technical debate. He also mentions the possibilities of English blank verse for spoken recitative and asserts that Milton is "a poet whose belief in his own verse was so strong that he could, if he wanted, write an opera without music, *opera senza musica*" (p. 184).

33 See Sprott's edition, pp. 64–65.

34 For the effect of varieties of verse form in Milton's *Maske,* see the essay by Edward Weismiller in the *Variorum Commentary,* II, iii, 1038–52, especially pp. 1049–50.

35 See Carey and Fowler, p. 188; Hollander, *The Untuning of the Sky,* p. 321;

and the *Variorum Commentary,* II, iii, 891. Another interpretation of the Lady's song is given by C. L. Barber ("*A Mask Presented at Ludlow Castle: The Masque as a Masque,*" in Diekhoff, p. 200). While saying that there is no echo except in the hearing and varied responses of Comus and Thyrsis, he argues that the Lady's strength lies in her presumption that "she is in a world inhabited by 'courteous Presences.'" For an extensive discussion of various verbal echoes and musical echo-effects in the poem see Angus Fletcher, pp. 198–209. Agreeing that no echo answers the Lady, Fletcher contends that this failed response becomes, in fact, a positive sign, freeing the Lady from a narcissistic "echo chamber" to await "the true and final echo" which is heavenly.

36 *Romeo and Juliet,* III.ii.18–19.

37 See note 32 above.

38 Samuel Johnson, *Lives of the English Poets,* ed. G. B. Hill, 3 vols. (Oxford: Clarendon Press, 1905), I, 119–120.

39 For the passage from Thomas Randolph's *The Muses Looking-Glasse* frequently cited as an analogue to Comus's temptation speech, see the *Variorum Commentary,* II, iii,773–75.

40 See the essay by Philip Brockbank, "The Measure of 'Comus,'" *Essays and Studies,* 21 (1968): 46–61, for a fine discussion of three kinds of "verbal music" in Milton's masque: the "sensual music" of Comus, the "moral music" of the Elder Brother, and a third kind represented in the Lady's song: "a Miltonic song quite distinct from the sensual music and the moral music, and yet related to both: a transfigured and sublimated sensuality." For this, Brockbank finds the apt term, "Hesperian music" (pp. 55–58).

41 For an excellent treatment of the work from this standpoint, see Gale H. Carrithers, Jr., "Milton's Ludlow *Mask:* from Chaos to Community," *ELH,* 33 (1966): 23–42.

42 See the group of possible sources and analogues for Milton's *Maske* assembled by Watson Kirkconnell in *Awake the Courteous Echo: The Themes and Prosody of Comus, Lycidas, and Paradise Regained in World Literature with Translations of the Major Analogues* (Toronto: University of Toronto Press, 1973), pp. 3–75.

43 For extensive discussion of the relationship of Milton's poem to the masque tradition, and to *Tempe Restored* in particular, see Demaray, *Milton and the Masque Tradition,* pp. 59–96.

44 The terms here reflect my reading of Roy Daniell's important book, *Milton, Mannerism and Baroque* (Toronto: University of Toronto Press, 1963).

CHAPTER 2: The Rising Poet

The present chapter represents an extensive revision and expansion of materials that originally appeared in my essay, "The Rising Poet, 1645," in *The Lyric and Dramatic Milton,* ed. Joseph Summers, Selected Papers from the English Institute (New York: Columbia University Press, 1965), pp. 3–33.

1   See "Chronological Survey," *Variorum Commentary,* II, i, 11–33; and William
    Riley Parker, "Some Problems in the Chronology of Milton's Early Poems,"
    Review of English Studies, 11 (1935): 276–83; "Notes on the Chronology of
    Milton's Latin Poems," in *A Tribute to George Coffin Taylor,* ed. Arnold
    Williams (Chapel Hill: University of North Carolina Press, 1952), pp. 113–
    31.
2   *Latin Poems of John Milton,* ed. Walter MacKellar, p. 358.
3   The translation adapts the versions of Hughes and McCrea: see *John Milton:
    Complete Poems and Major Prose,* ed. Merritt Y. Hughes (New York: Odyssey
    Press, 1957), p. 146; and the translations of the Latin poems by Nelson G.
    McCrea in *The Student's Milton,* ed. Frank Allen Patterson (New York:
    Crofts, 1930), p. 109.
4   See the amusing account in David Masson's *Life of Milton,* 7 vols. (London,
    1859–94), III, 456–59; Masson sees in a passage of *Tetrachordon* a pun on
    Marshall's name. The translation of the Greek verses below is that of Mas-
    son, III, 459. On the other hand, one of my students, Nancy Pollak, has
    suggested that the engraving is meant to show Milton as he appeared in
    1645 at the age of thirty-seven: that is, the portrait represents the older poet
    looking back upon the pleasures of his youth. Perhaps Marshall (unable to
    read Latin?) misunderstood his directions and thought he was supposed to
    portray the poet of 1645. Whatever the case may be, the engraving certainly
    enforces the theme of an older man looking back upon his youth.
5   Brooks and Hardy find in this sonnet the quality "of wry humor, of an ironic
    little joke in which the poet contemplates, a little ruefully but still with a fine
    inner confidence, the place of the poet in a jostling world of men at arms
    and forays and sallies." See *Poems of Mr. John Milton: The 1645 Edition,* ed.
    Cleanth Brooks and John Edward Hardy (New York: Harcourt, 1951), p.
    157; this contains the English poems, accompanied by an important series of
    "Essays in Analysis."
6   *crescentem:* this is the preferred reading of the Oxford text; some MSS and
    editions read *nascentem.*
7   *Virgil: The Pastoral Poems,* trans. E. V. Rieu (Harmondsworth: Penguin
    Books, 1949).
8   Vergil, Eclogue 7, 12–13, trans. Rieu; cf. *Lycidas,* 86.
9   The verbal echoes are explicit, not only from the *Eclogues,* but also from the
    Georgics and the *Aeneid:* see MacKellar's admirable notes to this poem. Ralph
    Condee has now brought together his essays on Milton's Latin poetry (along
    with other essays on Milton) in *Structure in Milton's Poetry* (University Park:
    Pennsylvania State University Press, 1974); his essays on *Ad Patrem, Mansus,*
    and *Epitaphium Damonis* are particularly notable.
10 See *Latin Poems,* ed. MacKellar, p. 347.
11 For the controversy over the dating of *Elegia septima,* see *Variorum Commen-
    tary,* I, 127–29.
12 See *The Reason of Church-government,* prologue to book 2, in *Complete Prose
    Works of John Milton,* ed. Don M. Wolfe (New Haven: Yale University Press,
    1953–), I, 809.

13   See William Riley Parker, *Milton: A Biography*, 2 vols. (Oxford: Clarendon Press, 1968), I, 177; II, 828 n.45.

14   *Prose Works*, ed. Wolfe, I, 321–22. The letter is dated December 4, 1634, and Milton says he made the Greek version of the psalm "before daybreak a week ago"—that is, on or about November 27. Despite some controversy on this point, there can be no reasonable doubt that this is the poem described in the letter: see *Variorum Commentary*, I, 257.

15   For the controversy over the dating of *Ad Patrem*, see *Variorum Commentary*, I, 232–40; and Parker, *Milton*, II, 788–89.

16   See the headnote to the paraphrase of Psalm 114 in the 1645 *Poems*.

17   See *Variorum Commentary*, I, 318–19.

18   Milton's attention to chronology is emphasized in the enlarged edition of his *Poems* in 1673, where the groupings and symmetries of 1645 are blurred by the addition of early and late poems placed in positions dictated by date of composition, not by kind. It seems that Milton's concern to publish, in his last years, a complete, or nearly complete, collection of his shorter poems took precedence over his earlier concern for a well-proportioned volume. Thus *On the Death of a fair Infant*, described as written "Anno aetatis 17," is placed between the psalms written "at fifteen years old" and *The Passion*, composed at age twenty-one. According to the errata sheet of 1673 the poem on the "fair Infant" should have been followed by the lines *At a Vacation Exercise*, dated "Anno Aetatis 19." This was somehow misplaced as the second of three miscellaneous poems (the version of the fifth ode of Horace, the *Vacation Exercise*, and *On the new forcers of Conscience*) added after the expanded group of nineteen sonnets and just before *Arcades* (the sonnets usually numbered 15, 16, 17, and 22 were omitted, undoubtedly because of their risky political content). The *Mask* follows directly after *Lycidas*, without the half title of 1645, and then the English part of the 1673 volume concludes with the two late groups of versified psalms, first the set of 1653 and next the set of 1648—chronology here being discarded in favor of the biblical order.

Among the Latin poems, *Apologus de Rustico & Hero*, a fable of uncertain date in elegiac meter, is added at the very end of the elegiac section; but it is headed with a heavy decorative bar suggesting that it is really *sui generis*. The ode to Rouse (1646) is placed as the final poem of the book, after the *Epitaphium Damonis*. The only other addition is the printing of Milton's satirical Greek verses on his portrait (part of the frontispiece in 1645) after the two Greek poems of 1645, thus observing chronological order. See the important article on chronology in the 1673 volume by John Shawcross, *Studies in English Literature*, 3 (1963): 77–84.

19   *Canzone*, 15; trans. Hughes.

20   "Ridonsi donne e giovani amorosi." Translation from Sonnet 6 by Carey; translation from the *Canzone* by Hughes.

21   For various interpretations of lines 13–14 of Sonnet 7 see *Variorum Commentary*, II, ii, 372–73.

22   See the analysis of the suspended syntax of Sonnet 10 by Alan Rudrum, *A Critical Commentary on Milton's 'Comus' and Shorter Poems* (London: Macmillan, 1967), pp. 87–88. For recent interpretations of all the sonnets (including those not published in 1645) as an integrated sequence revealing the growth toward maturity and old age, see William McCarthy, "The Continuity of Milton's Sonnets," *PMLA*, 92 (1977): 96–109; and Mary Ann Radzinowicz, *Toward Samson Agonistes* (Princeton: Princeton University Press, 1978), pp. 128–44.

23   See the essay on these poems by Don Cameron Allen, *The Harmonious Vision* (Baltimore: Johns Hopkins Press, 1954), pp. 3–23.

24   See the important brief essay by Kester Svendsen in *Explicator*, 8 (May, 1950): Item 49; here Svendsen deals with "the dynamics of the twin poem," showing "the progressive emphasis in both parts on images of sound and music." He notes how, in the finale of *Il Penseroso*, "the many references to sound and in particular to music build toward this conclusion, so that structurally it is the end of a progressive development within both poems."

25   S. Ernest Sprott, *Milton's Art of Prosody* (Oxford: Blackwell, 1953), pp. 17–18.

26   See "Studies of Verse Form in the Minor English Poems" by Edward R. Weismiller in the *Variorum Commentary*, II, iii, 1026–36. Weismiller does not stress the difference in the metric of the companion poems, but he recognizes the difference by citing Sprott's statistics and especially by quoting Carpenter's contrast between the "brisk rocking motion" of *L'Allegro* and "the smoother verse lines" of *Il Penseroso*. See Nan Cooke Carpenter, "The Place of Music in *L'Allegro* and *Il Penseroso*," *University of Toronto Quarterly*, 22 (1952–53): 354–67.

27   See *Variorum Commentary*, II, i, 281–84; and the witty, acute discussion of this controversy by Stanley E. Fish, "What it's like to read *L'Allegro* and *Il Penseroso*," in *Milton Studies*, 7 (1975): 77–99. My own interpretation, though proceeding on different critical principles, is in basic agreement with Fish's view of the differences between the two poems—that the first is delightfully relaxed in its manner and movement, while in the second "our attention is not diffused but concentrated," with an effect of "sustained mental effort" (Fish, pp. 90,94).

28   See J. B. Leishman, *Milton's Minor Poems* (London: Hutchinson, 1969), chapter 6, "*L'Allegro* and *Il Penseroso* in their relation to seventeenth-century poetry."

29   *The Republic of Plato*, trans. Francis MacDonald Cornford (New York: Oxford University Press, 1945), pp. 86–87.

30   *umbrosa Academica:* from the palinode at the end of Milton's *Elegia septima*.

31   The date is omitted in the edition of 1673.

32   See F. T. Prince, *The Italian Element in Milton's Verse* (Oxford: Clarendon Press, 1954), pp. 61–63.

33   A. S. P. Woodhouse, "Notes on Milton's Early Development," *University of Toronto Quarterly*, 13 (1943): 66–101; see p. 75; included in Woodhouse's

The Heavenly Muse: A Preface to Milton, ed. Hugh MacCallum (Toronto: University of Toronto Press, 1972), chapter 2. For others who hold similar views see *Variorum Commentary,* I, 112–15. Parker strongly dissents from this view: see the account of *Elegia sexta* in his *Milton,* I, 67–70.

34   From the translation by Charles Knapp in the Columbia edition of *The Works of John Milton* (New York: Columbia University Press, 1931–38), I, 207.

35   E. K. Rand, "Milton in Rustication," *Studies in Philology,* 19 (1922): 109–35; see pages 110, 124.

36   See *Variorum Commentary,* I, 125–26.

37   *English Madrigal Verse, 1588–1632,* ed. E. H. Fellowes, 3rd edn., revised by Frederick W. Sternfeld and David Greer (Oxford: Clarendon Press, 1967), pp. 156–57. For other analogies see Weismiller's commentary on the stanza-form of the Hymn, *Variorum Commentary,* II, iii, 1019–22.

38   *The Early English Carols,* ed. Richard Leighton Greene, 2nd edn. (Oxford: Clarendon Press, 1977), pp. 48–49. I have omitted the editor's brackets and italics.

39   For a study of the poem in the context of the genre of the literary hymn, with its *topos* of humility, see Philip Rollinson, "Milton's Nativity Poem and the Decorum of Genre," *Milton Studies,* 7 (1975): 165–88. As Rollinson points out, the *topos* of humility is discussed by Ernst Robert Curtius, *European Literature and the Latin Middle Ages,* trans. Willard R. Trask (New York: Pantheon, 1953), pp. 83–85, 407–13; the latter section, Excursus II, "Devotional Formula and Humility," is especially significant for Milton's "humble ode."

40   Lowry Nelson, Jr., *Baroque Lyric Poetry* (New Haven: Yale University Press, 1961), pp. 41–52.

CHAPTER 3: *Lycidas*: Building the Lofty Rhyme

This chapter is a revision of the essay "Who is Lycidas?" that appeared in the issue of *Yale French Studies* devoted to "Image and Symbol in the Renaissance," No. 47 (1972): 170–88. In addition to the *Variorum Commentary,* I wish to acknowledge the help of two collections: *Lycidas: the Tradition and the Poem,* ed. C. A. Patrides (New York: Holt, Rinehart and Winston, 1961); and *Milton's "Lycidas" Edited to Serve as an Introduction to Criticism,* by Scott Elledge (New York: Harper and Row, 1966).

 1   See the classic analysis of the tripartite movement of these poems by Arthur Barker, "The Pattern of Milton's *Nativity Ode," University of Toronto Quarterly,* 10 (1940–41): 167–81.

 2   For the many analogues see the important new study by Ellen Zetzel Lambert, *Placing Sorrow: A Study of the Pastoral Elegy Convention from Theocritus to Milton* (Chapel Hill: University of North Carolina Press, 1976); along with the anthology of precedents for and analogues with *Lycidas* collected by Watson Kirkconnell in *Awake the Courteous Echo,* pp. 79–245.

3   Idyll 7, 13–19: from *The Greek Bucolic Poets,* trans. A. S. F. Gow (Cambridge: Cambridge University Press, 1953). This translation is a revised version of that in Gow's standard edition of *Theocritus,* 2 vols. (Cambridge: Cambridge University Press, 1950), from which I have taken the line numbers.

4   Gilbert Lawall, *Theocritus' Coan Pastorals* (Washington, D.C.: Center for Hellenic Studies, 1967), pp. 80–85, 102–08.

5   The figure Lycidas appears as a gifted singer in a fragment attributed to Bion, which begins with Myrson asking, "Wilt thou sing me some sweet Sicilian song, Lycidas?" (*Greek Bucolic Poets,* trans. Gow, p. 148).

6   Cf. the study of the ninth eclogue by Michael C. J. Putnam, *Virgil's Pastoral Art* (Princeton: Princeton University Press, 1970), pp. 293–341. Putnam perhaps makes the eclogue excessively bleak, yet his view of the poem's presentation of the conflict between the world of song and the world of political power seems basically right, and his contrast with the seventh idyll of Theocritus is excellent: "*Idyl* 7 is a poem about joy in song, about the beauty and variety of poetry, set in the context of a journey to a haven of particular beauty. The ninth eclogue is opposite in tone and meaning. Virgil's road leads not toward the glorious retreat of a harvest festival but out of the country in the direction of the city, through a landscape wherein song is impossible" (p. 338).

7   See James Holly Hanford, "The Pastoral Elegy and Milton's *Lycidas,*" in *John Milton, Poet and Humanist* (Cleveland: Press of Western Reserve University, 1966), pp. 149–51. Hanford assumes that Sannazaro's Phyllis met her death by drowning, but the poem gives no evidence of this. There is no doubt, however, that the latter half of the lament by Sannazaro's Lycidas contains striking analogies to the latter part of Milton's poem, especially in the lines (97–98) where Sannazaro's Lycidas calls to his Phyllis in the heavens or the "Elysian shades," saying, "Look down on us and gently come to us; you shall be ever the godhead (*numen*) of the waters, ever a happy sign to fishermen" (trans. Nash: see next note).

8   Jacopo Sannazaro, *Arcadia and Piscatorial Eclogues,* trans. Ralph Nash (Detroit: Wayne State University Press, 1966), pp. 156–65.

9   The resemblance of these lines to "a broken sonnet" echoing the Petrarchan pattern has been pointed out by Keith Rinehart, *Notes & Queries,* 198 (1953): 103. The rhymes run as follows: xabbaacdacdaxa. For detailed accounts of the rhyme and metrics of the poem see Prince, *The Italian Element in Milton's Verse,* pp. 71–88; Ants Oras, "Milton's Early Rhyme Schemes and the Structure of *Lycidas,*" *Modern Philology,* 52 (1954): 12–22; Joseph Anthony Wittreich, Jr., "Milton's 'Destin'd Urn': the Art of *Lycidas,*" *PMLA,* 84 (1969): 60–70; and Weismiller, *Variorum Commentary,* II, iii, 1057–74.

10 See David Berkeley, *Notes & Queries,* 206 (1961): 178; also *Inwrought with Figures Dim* (The Hague: Mouton, 1974), pp. 33–34.

11 *The Jerusalem Bible,* ed. Alexander Jones (Garden City: Doubleday, 1966).

12 *Webster's New International Dictionary,* 2nd edn. (Springfield, Mass.: Merriam, 1951), "welter," *v.* 2.

13 See Leishman, *Milton's Minor Poems*, pp. 324–26.

14 Barker, "The Pattern of Milton's *Nativity Ode*," pp. 171–72.

15 See the notes on "Amaryllis" and "Neaera" in *Variorum Commentary*, II, ii, 660–61.

16 See Ralph Hone, "The Pilot of the *Galilean* Lake," *Studies in Philology*, 56 (1959): 55–61. We do not need to follow Hone in seeing only the presence of Christ here; Peter is present as well.

17 For the vast and apparently endless controversy over lines 130–31 see *Variorum Commentary*, II, ii, 686–706. Perhaps the most convincing essay on this problem is that by Leon Howard, *Huntington Library Quarterly*, 15 (1952): 173–84.

18 On the consoling, soothing effect of the catalogue see Lambert, *Placing Sorrow*, pp. 172–74.

19 William Madsen (*Studies in English Literature*, 3 [1963]: 1–7) makes the interesting suggestion that Michael is himself speaking here in lines 165–81 ("Weep no more . . . And wipe the tears for ever from his eyes"). I would not go so far, but the lines do seem to be a result of the speaker's appeal, "Look homeward Angel."

20 See especially Revelation 7:17; 14:1–4; 19:6–9; 21:4; 22:1–2; *Variorum Commentary*, II, ii, 728–30.

21 See the fine interpretation of these closing lines by Isabel MacCaffrey, "*Lycidas*: the Poet in a Landscape," in *The Lyric and Dramatic Milton*, ed. Summers, pp. 89–92: "The pastoral scene is re-created; and now it is informed by the presence of the poets who first made these details into poetry, and by the redeemed imagination that has come gradually to understand their meaning."

22 See A. S. P. Woodhouse, "Milton's Pastoral Monodies," in *Studies in Honour of Gilbert Norwood*, ed. Mary E. White (Toronto: University of Toronto Press, 1952), p. 273; included in Woodhouse's *The Heavenly Muse*, chapter 3. Also Isabel MacCaffrey in the essay just cited, p. 67.

PART II: *Paradise Lost:* Poem of Exile

The *Variorum Commentary* on *Paradise Lost* is still in progress, but reference to scholarship on the epic is greatly assisted by the detailed introduction and ample annotations to *Paradise Lost* provided by Fowler in *The Poems of John Milton*, ed. John Carey and Alastair Fowler (London: Longmans, 1968); I am deeply indebted to this edition throughout parts II and III of this book.

CHAPTER 4: Princes of Exile

This chapter is based upon materials presented in the first of a series of three William Lyon Phelps Lectures delivered at Yale University in February 1967 under the general title: "*Paradise Lost:* Poem of Exile." A version of this lecture

was published in *ELH,* 36 (1969): 232–49. The present chapter represents a
further revision.

1   *The Works of John Milton* (New York: Columbia University Press, 1931–38),
    XII, 114–15; I have altered three words in the Masson translation.
2   See the important study by Robert M. Durling, *The Figure of the Poet in
    Renaissance Epic* (Cambridge: Harvard University Press, 1965).
3   St.-John Perse, *Exile and Other Poems,* Bilingual edition, trans. Denis Devlin,
    2nd edn. (New York: Pantheon, 1949), pp. 11–15. Copyright 1940 by the
    Bollingen Foundation, New York.
4   See the perceptive interpretation of the prologue to book 3 by Anne David-
    son Ferry, *Milton's Epic Voice* (Cambridge: Harvard University Press, 1963),
    pp. 25–37.
5   See Augustine, *De Trinitate,* Book 9, where he analyzes the triad: *Mens,
    Notitia, Amor;* see also the analysis of Augustine's trinitarian view of the
    Image of God by Etienne Gilson, *The Christian Philosophy of Saint Augustine*
    (New York: Random House, 1960), pp. 217–24.
6   *OED,* "drug," *sb.* 1.
7   See the sensitive analysis of this simile by Geoffrey Hartman, "Milton's
    Counterplot," *ELH,* 25 (1958): 1–12: "The ripe grain sways in the wind, so
    does the mind which has tended it" (p. 12). See also the quite different view
    in Carey and Fowler (p. 669) where, partly accepting Empson's view, Fowler
    says "the ploughman has to be in some sense 'like' God." Cf. William
    Empson, *Some Versions of Pastoral* (London: Chatto, 1935), p. 172.
8   Ovid, *Metamorphoses,* trans. Rolfe Humphries (Bloomington: Indiana Uni-
    versity Press, 1955).
9   See T. S. Eliot's essay on Marlowe; *Selected Essays, 1917–1932* (New York:
    Harcourt, 1932), p. 100. The controversy over Milton's style is effectively
    resolved in Milton's favor by Christopher Ricks in *Milton's Grand Style* (Ox-
    ford: Clarendon Press, 1963); and by A. Bartlett Giamatti in *The Earthly
    Paradise and the Renaissance Epic* (Princeton: Princeton University Press,
    1966), chapter 6.
10 See *Exile,* p. 35.

CHAPTER 5: The Realms of Light

This chapter stands, with minor revisions, as it appeared in *English Literary Renaissance,* 1 (1971): 71–88. That essay represented an extensive revision and expansion of the second in the series of William Lyon Phelps Lectures delivered at Yale
in 1967; it incorporated passages and thoughts derived from another lecture on
Milton delivered at the University of Western Ontario in February 1970.

1   Cf. Isabel G. MacCaffrey, "The Theme of *Paradise Lost,* Book III," in *New
    Essays on Paradise Lost,* ed. Thomas Kranidas (Berkeley: University of
    California Press, 1969), pp. 58–85.

2 But see the essay by Irene Samuel in *PMLA*, 72 (1957): 601–11, which argues that Milton's God here speaks in the "toneless voice of the moral law" (p. 603). See also the argument by Stanley Eugene Fish, *Surprised by Sin: The Reader in Paradise Lost* (London: Macmillan, 1967), pp. 57–91, where Fish turns the tables on the reader: "In the poem, God's speech represents the essence of Truth, and the reader's response is a judgment on him (a reflection of his 'crookednesse'), not on the dispassionate voice of the Logos" (p. 83). Fish's attractive and influential argument is valid to the extent that Milton is using a device to arouse problems in the reader's mind. The trouble is that the device is awkward and creates more problems than it should. For an extreme version of these problems see William Empson, *Milton's God*, rev. edn. (London: Chatto, 1965), chapter 3.

3 See C. A. Patrides, *Milton and the Christian Tradition* (Oxford: Clarendon Press, 1966), pp. 200–14; and Ernest Sirluck, *Paradise Lost: A Deliberate Epic*, Churchill College Overseas Fellowship Lecture No. 1 (Cambridge: Heffer, 1967), esp. pp. 19–21.

4 Cf. J. B. Broadbent, *Some Graver Subject* (London: Chatto, 1960), p. 157.

5 Cf. Ferry, *Milton's Epic Voice*, chapter 2.

6 For the use of the term "panels" by Brooks Otis in relation to Ovid's *Metamorphoses* see below, chapter 12.

7 Kenneth Burke, *Counter-Statement*, 2nd edn. (Chicago: University of Chicago Press, 1957), pp. 127–28. On Milton's assimilation of comic, satiric, pastoral, and tragic modes to the conventions of heroic poetry, see John M. Steadman, *Epic and Tragic Structure in Paradise Lost* (Chicago: University of Chicago Press, 1976), chapter 2.

8 See Steadman, *Epic and Tragic Structure*, chapters 3–5, for Aristotelian elements. In addition one might see an affinity with the Euripidean prologue of the supernatural agent in Satan's long soliloquy before the action (9.99–178). The voice of the narrator in book 9 seems in places to undertake a choric role, interpreting the series of episodes that constitute the tragedy. One can distinguish eight episodes, each carefully separated by the voice of the narrator: (1) the parting of Adam and Eve: 205–384; (2) Satan's soliloquy at sight of Eve: 473–93; (3) Satan and Eve: preliminary encounter: 532–631; (4) Satan and Eve before the Tree: Eve's Fall: 647–833; (5) Eve's return to Adam: Adam's Fall: 856–989; (6) Adam's invitation to lust: 1017–33; (7) Adam's discovery of shame: 1067–98; (8) the quarrel of Adam and Eve: 1134–86.

9 *OED*, "frail," *a*. 1,2,3.

10 For Milton's openness to highly unorthodox views see the new book by Christopher Hill, *Milton and the English Revolution* (New York: Viking, 1978).

11 Cf. Ferry, *Milton's Epic Voice*, pp. 51–56.

12 Stressed by Frank Kermode in his fine essay "Adam Unparadised," in *The Living Milton*, ed. Frank Kermode (New York: Macmillan, 1961), p. 103. The words *paradisum voluptatis* or *paradiso voluptatis* occur five times in the opening chapters of Genesis (2:8,10,15;3:23,24).

13 Cf. Ferry, *Milton's Epic Voice*, p. 52.
14 For a detailed study of this topic see John Halkett, *Milton and the Idea of Matrimony* (New Haven: Yale University Press, 1970), esp. chapter 4. Also the important essay by Peter Lindenbaum, "Lovemaking in Milton's Paradise," *Milton Studies*, 6 (1974): 277–306; and the lively, acute study by Edward LeComte, *Milton and Sex* (New York: Columbia University Press, 1978).
15 C. S. Lewis, *A Preface to Paradise Lost* (London: Oxford University Press, 1942), chapter 17.
16 The validity of this analogy has now been demonstrated in the new study by Roland Mushat Frye, *Milton's Imagery and the Visual Arts* (Princeton: Princeton University Press, 1978), pp. 227–34. See also Marjorie B. Garber, "Fallen Landscape: The Art of Milton and Poussin," *English Literary Renaissance*, 5 (1975): 96–124.

CHAPTER 6: The Diffusion of Good

About three pages in the latter part of this chapter have appeared previously, in somewhat different form, in portions of my essay in *Ventures*: see headnote to next chapter.

1 For a summary of the numerological interpretations of the poem's structure see Carey and Fowler, pp. 440–43. For the poem's numerological center see Gunnar Qvarnström, *The Enchanted Palace: Some Structural Aspects of Paradise Lost* (Stockholm: Almqvist, 1967), chapter 2; and John T. Shawcross, "The Balanced Structure of *Paradise Lost*," *Studies in Philology*, 62 (1965): 696–718. I should note that I am highly skeptical of the more detailed aspects of the numerological approach; but in discerning the larger aspects of structure the approach is helpful, as one may see in the recent study by Galbraith Miller Crump, *The Mystical Design of Paradise Lost* (Lewisburg: Bucknell University Press, 1975).
2 Cf. Carey and Fowler, note on 7.1, "Descend": "Because from this point onward the course of the poem is steadily downwards." See also Isabel Gamble MacCaffrey, *Paradise Lost as "Myth"* (Cambridge: Harvard University Press, 1959), pp. 57–59.
3 John Peter is right in his estimation of the size of Michael's army: see *A Critique of Paradise Lost* (London: Longmans, 1960), pp. 80–81; but Peter finds God "underhand and deceitful" in thus restricting the number. Empson, surprisingly, does not accept this view of the "equal" armies—apparently because it somewhat detracts from Satan's glory (see *Milton's God*, p. 41); see too the note (on 6.49) in Carey and Fowler, p. 732, where Fowler agrees with Empson in rejecting "Peter's unnecessary speculation that God only allows half of the good angels to fight."
4 For Milton's treatment of Creation see W. B. C. Watkins, *An Anatomy of Milton's Verse* (Baton Rouge: Louisiana State University Press, 1955), pp.

42–86; M. M. Mahood, *Poetry and Humanism* (New Haven: Yale University Press, 1950), chapter 6; and the impressive study by Michael Lieb, *The Dialectics of Creation: Patterns of Birth and Regeneration in Paradise Lost* (Amherst: University of Massachusetts Press, 1970), chapters 1 and 2.

5   Cf. Ricks, *Milton's Grand Style*, pp. 109–17; and Giamatti, *Earthly Paradise*, pp. 302–306.

6   E. M. W. Tillyard, *Studies in Milton* (New York: Macmillan, 1951), pp. 10–13.

7   J. M. Evans, *Paradise Lost and the Genesis Tradition* (Oxford: Clarendon Press, 1968), p. 269; see his entire chapter 10 for Milton's complex presentation of "Nature's Innocence." Barbara Lewalski has independently explored a similar point of view in her important essay "Innocence and Experience in Milton's Eden," in *New Essays on Paradise Lost,* ed. Kranidas, pp. 86–117: "primal man's nature is shown to be complex and constantly developing, not simple and stable" (p. 99). See also the summary of this "newer view of Milton's Paradise" by Lindenbaum in "Lovemaking in Milton's Paradise," pp. 298–302: "The whole emphasis on a difficult Eden and the insistence on the importance of prelapsarian sexual love . . . tend to undermine any hard and fast distinction . . . between pre- and postlapsarian life" (p. 300).

CHAPTER 7: The Power of Choice

The last two-thirds of this chapter, except for a few sentences, was published in *Ventures: Magazine of the Yale Graduate School,* 10 (1970): 37–47; this essay represented the major portion of the last lecture in the series of William Lyon Phelps Lectures delivered at Yale in 1967.

1   Milton's theme of "choice" is the basis for the illuminating explorations by Leslie Brisman in *Milton's Poetry of Choice and Its Romantic Heirs* (Ithaca: Cornell University Press, 1973). For the importance of "choice" in the poem see the careful study by Jon Lawry in *The Shadow of Heaven,* chapter 4: "'Most Reason is that Reason Overcome': Choice in *Paradise Lost.*"

2   See the similar interpretation by Arnold Stein in *The Art of Presence: The Poet and Paradise Lost* (Berkeley: University of California Press, 1977), pp. 99–101: for his subtle interpretation of the following argument between Adam and Eve see pp. 112–21.

3   See the studies by Evans and Lewalski noted above (chapter 6, n. 7). For the idea that Eve is "not sincere" in her suggestion, see Tillyard, *Studies in Milton,* p. 17.

4   A. J. A. Waldock, *Paradise Lost and Its Critics* (Cambridge: Cambridge University Press, 1947), pp. 56–57.

5   See the studies of Evans and Lewalski noted above (chapter 6, n. 7).

CHAPTER 8: The Winding up of the Action

The germ of this chapter lies in a small portion of *The Paradise Within* (New Haven: Yale University Press, 1964), pp. 135–40.

1   *The Spectator,* ed. Donald F. Bond, 5 vols. (Oxford: Clarendon Press, 1965), III, 329–30 (No. 357).

2   See Fowler's discussion in his introduction (pp. 432–33) and in many of his annotations to *Paradise Lost* in Carey and Fowler.

3   See Philippians 2:7: "and took upon him the form of a servant"; Genesis 3:21: "Unto Adam also and to his wife did the Lord God make coats of skins, and clothed them"; John 13:14–16: "If I then, your Lord and Master, have washed your feet; ye also ought to wash one another's feet . . . . The servant is not greater than his lord"; Luke 6:27–29: "Love your enemies, do good to them which hate you. . . . and him that taketh away thy cloke forbid not to take thy coat also." The curious usage of "repaid" (in the sense of "given in return"—the beasts, perhaps, were not slain, but were given new skins, "as the snake") may echo Proverbs 13:21: "to the righteous good shall be repayed."

4   In his classic essay, "The Crisis of *Paradise Lost,*" to which this chapter is deeply indebted: see his *Studies in Milton,* pp. 8–52, especially pp. 31–32.

5   See the note on 10.289–93 in Carey and Fowler, p. 940.

6   It might be noted that both in Vergil and in Ovid the phrase occurs in a less than heroic context. Cf. the similar phrase in Vergil's first eclogue (23), and the significant variation of the phrase in *Paradise Regain'd* (4.563–64): "to compare / Small things with greatest."

7   Fowler notes that "the simile gains most force from a silent allusion to the well-known story that Xerxes wept while reviewing his army, at the thought that within a century such multitudes would all be dead" (Carey and Fowler, p. 942). The simile thus forms a tacit link with Satan's tears at reviewing his army (1.620).

8   *Metamorphoses,* 4.576–603. The allusion thus links with Milton's reference to "Hermione and Cadmus" (9.503–06) cited above in chapter 4.

9   *Metamorphoses,* 4.614–20; 1.438–47.

10 I am thinking of the soliloquies of Medea (*Metamorphoses,* 7.11–72), Scylla, daughter of Nisus (8.44–80), Althaea (8.481–511), Byblis (9.474–516), and Myrrha (10.320–55). A relation to Adam's soliloquy (and also to Satan's earlier soliloquies) may be suggested by William Anderson's comment on these Ovidian passages: "The many soliloquies in the central part of the *Metamorphoses* all, to a certain extent, analyze the meaning of critical moral terms. Each speaker, aware of the moral responsibilities implicit in the word or words under discussion, tries to evade these formal obligations; and, when reason fails to justify such evasion or change, he or she then lets emotions overcome reason and morality. Knowingly, they undertake *nefas* or *scelus,* and usually they experience the consequences soon after in their moral depths" ("Multiple Change in the *Metamorphoses,*" *Transactions of the American Philological Association,* 94 (1963): 1–27: see pp. 20–21. Adam of course comes to a different conclusion, after the manner of a renaissance imitation.

11 Tillyard, *Studies in Milton,* pp. 39–42; Joseph H. Summers, *The Muse's Method: An Introduction to Paradise Lost* (London: Chatto, 1962), pp. 176–85.

12 Milton's technique here seems to be an elaborate expansion of a favorite Ovidian device: "date munera templis / nec timida gaudete fide! dant munera templis, / addunt et titulum: titulus breve carmen habebat" (*Metamorphoses*, 9.791–93); "Dignane, cui grates ageret, cui turis honorem / ferret, Adoni, fui? nec grates inmemor egit, / nec mihi tura dedit." (*Met.* 10.681–83). See also *Heroides*, 3.5–6; 4.143–44; *Amores*, 3.5.7–8; and Milton's playful use of such devices in his Ovidian *Elegia quinta*, 6–7, 33, 122, 129–30. For further examples of this rhetorical technique, see below, chapter 13.

CHAPTER 9: "A Poem Written in Ten Books"

This chapter represents a greatly revised version of my essay "Camoens and Milton" in *Ocidente: Revista Portuguesa de Cultura,* 35 (1972): 45–58; part of a large special number celebrating the 400th anniversary of the publication of *Os Lusíadas,* and including papers presented at the University of Connecticut (Storrs) as part of a symposium honoring this anniversary.

1 F. T. Prince, "On the Last Two Books of *Paradise Lost,*" *Essays and Studies,* n.s. 11 (1958): 38–52: see pp. 49–51. The difficulty, I suppose, is that the experience of readers and habits of reading differ too widely to make this a basis for critical judgment.

2 A summation of the issues concerning books 11 and 12, with wise suggestions for their resolution, is given by Balachandra Rajan in *The Lofty Rhyme* (London: Routledge, 1970), chapter 6; on pp. 168–69 Rajan provides a full bibliography of writings on the topic, up to 1966. To this one should add: Stanley Fish, *Surprised by Sin* (1967), chapter 7; Dennis Burden, *The Logical Epic* (1967), chapter 9; Mary Ann Radzinowicz, "'Man as a Probationer of Immortality,'" in *Approaches to Paradise Lost,* ed. C. A. Patrides (London: Arnold, 1968), pp. 31–51; Jon S. Lawry, *The Shadow of Heaven,* pp. 267–88; Jason Rosenblatt, "Adam's Pisgah Vision," *ELH,* 39 (1972): 66–86; and Joseph Anthony Wittreich, Jr., "'A Poet amongst Poets': Milton and the Tradition of Prophecy," in *Milton and the Line of Vision,* ed. Wittreich (Madison: University of Wisconsin Press, 1975), pp. 97–142; see esp. pp. 129–42.

3 See *Essays of John Dryden,* ed. W. P. Ker, 2 vols. (Oxford: Clarendon Press, 1926), I, 268; II, 29; and *Spectator,* No. 369: ed. Bond, III, 386.

4 See *Facsimile,* ed. Harris Fletcher, II, 20–23.

5 *Mansus,* 80–81, trans. MacKellar.

6 *Epitaphium Damonis,* 168–71; trans. Hughes.

7 See *Prose Works,* ed. Wolfe, I, 812–14.

8 Cf. James H. Sims, "Echoes of Camoens' *Lusiads* in Milton's *Paradise Lost* (I-IV)," *Revista Camoniana,* 3 (1971): 135–44; "'Delicious Paradise' in *Os Lusíadas* and in *Paradise Lost,*" *Ocidente,* 35 (1972): 163–72; and "Christened Classicism in *Paradise Lost* and *The Lusiads,*" *Comparative Literature,* 24 (1972); 338–56.

9 See Arthur Barker, "Structural Pattern in *Paradise Lost,*" *Philological Quar-*

terly, 28 (1949): 17–30; esp. pp. 21–23. For other views see J. R. Watson, "Divine Providence and the Structure of *Paradise Lost,*" *Essays in Criticism,* 14 (1964), 148–55; and Wittreich's theory about the number 12, in *Milton and the Line of Vision,* ed. Wittreich, pp. 131–34. Also Crump, *The Mystical Design of Paradise Lost.*

10 [This number for the note was unplanned!] For the Pythagorean (and Augustinian) significance of the number 10 in relation to the edition of 1667 see Qvarnström, *The Enchanted Palace,* chapter 4. One may disagree with details, but there is force in the argument that Pythagorean theory is involved in Milton's grouping of his ten books into sets of 4:3:2:1, or, counting by the occurrence of the four prologues, 2:4:1:3; for the groupings bear an uncanny parallel with the "divine tetractys" of Pythagoras, in which the sum of the numbers 1234 equals 10. See the pioneer study among the numerological interpreters: James Whaler, *Counterpoint and Symbol, Anglistica,* vol. 6 (Copenhagen, 1956); and Carey and Fowler, pp. 440–43, 851–52. Also Shawcross, "The Balanced Structure of *Paradise Lost,*" pp. 708–10.

11 C. M. Bowra, *From Virgil to Milton* (London: Macmillan, 1945) pp. 238–39.

12 For an explanation of the function of this vision and a fine interpretation of the *Lusiad* see Giamatti, *The Earthly Paradise,* pp. 210–26; esp. pp. 221–23.

13 *Prose Works,* ed. Wolfe, II, 551–53.

14 This and the following prose translations are taken from *The Lusiads,* trans. William C. Atkinson (Harmondsworth: Penguin Books, 1952). Fanshawe's translation is available (with the heavy use of capital letters in 1655 reduced) in the edition by J. D. M. Ford (Cambridge, Mass.: Harvard University Press, 1940).

15 For judicious correction of the usual modern view of romantic criticism see the introduction by Joseph Anthony Wittreich, Jr., to his collection *The Romantics on Milton* (Cleveland: Press of Case Western Reserve University, 1970).

16 The role of "the voice of the bard" has been explored by Ferry, *Milton's Epic Voice* (1963); by myself, in *The Paradise Within* (1964); by William G. Riggs, *The Christian Poet in Paradise Lost* (Berkeley: University of California Press, 1972); and by Arnold Stein, *The Art of Presence* (1978), a climactic study of remarkable subtlety and depth.

CHAPTER 10: Trials of Faith

This chapter represents a drastic revision and re-thinking of the last three sections of my essay on *Paradise Lost* in *The Paradise Within* (pp. 141–67). I have been greatly helped in my revision by two friendly, but judiciously critical review-articles: Arnold Stein, "The Paradise Within and the Paradise Without," *Modern Language Quarterly,* 26 (1965): 586–600; and Isabel G. MacCaffrey, "The Meditative Paradigm," *ELH,* 32 (1965): 388–407. In Mrs. MacCaffrey's recent death the scholarly world has lost a great teacher, a deep, original mind, and a generous spirit.

1 *The Works of John Dryden,* ed. E. N. Hooker and H. T. Swedenberg, Jr., 18
   vols. (Berkeley: University of California Press, 1956–), II, 109.
2 Two essays dealing with the theological design have been most helpful in my
   revision: one by Mary Ann Radzinowicz (see above, chapter 9, note 2), and
   the other by Barbara Lewalski, "Structure and the Symbolism of Vision in
   Michael's Prophecy," *Philological Quarterly,* 42 (1963): 25–35. The notes to
   books 11 and 12 in Carey and Fowler have also been particularly instructive
   here.
3 Cf. Carey and Fowler, note on 11.355, p. 998.
4 Cf. L. D. Lerner, "The Miltonic Simile," *Essays in Criticism,* 4 (1954): 297–
   308; esp. p. 307.
5 See "faith" and "faithful" in 12. 113, 128, 152, 154, 295, 306, 409, 427, 449,
   462, 481, 488, 527, 529, 536, 571, 582, 599, 603.
6 Summers, *The Muse's Method,* p. 206.
7 The "Arguments" were first published in the re-issue of *Paradise Lost* in
   1668, when they were printed together before the poem; in 1674 they were
   distributed to stand at the head of each book, the arguments for the original
   books 7 and 10 being broken up to head the newly divided books. The
   above quotation is from 1674; in 1668 the equivalent to this part of the
   argument is less precise in its opening portion: "thence from the Flood
   relates, and by degrees explains, who that Seed of the Woman shall be; his
   Incarnation, Death [etc.]." See *Facsimile,* ed. Harris Fletcher, II, 177–89.
8 William G. Madsen, "The Idea of Nature in Milton's Poetry," in *Three Studies
   in the Renaissance* (New Haven: Yale University Press, 1958), pp. 258–59.
9 Cf. Broadbent, *Some Graver Subject,* pp. 88–90.
10 This formulation is indebted to my reading of Stanley Fish's *Surprised by Sin:*
   see esp. his account of the last books, chapter 7.
11 My thinking here is strongly influenced by the stimulating study by Herbert
   N. Schneidau, *Sacred Discontent: The Bible and Western Tradition* (Berkeley:
   University of California Press, 1976), esp. chapters 2 and 3.
12 Cf. Addison's remark on book 12: "If *Milton's* Poem flags anywhere, it is in
   this Narration, where in some places the Author has been so attentive to his
   Divinity, that he has neglected his Poetry" (*Spectator,* No. 369: ed. Bond, III,
   386).

CHAPTER 11: The Solitary Way

This chapter represents an extensive revision of the essay under this title which
appeared in *The Author in His Work: Essays on a Problem in Criticism* [in honor of
Maynard Mack], ed. Louis L. Martz and Aubrey Williams, with an introduction
by Patricia Meyer Spacks (New Haven: Yale University Press, 1978), pp. 71–84;
this essay was originally composed as a lecture, "*Paradise Lost* and the Idea of
Pilgrimage," delivered at the Vermont Renaissance Symposium in April 1975.
The present version incorporates the equivalent of a half-dozen pages from
various portions of *The Paradise Within.*

1   The illustration is derived from Raphael: see Marcia R. Pointon, *Milton and English Art* (Manchester: Manchester University Press, 1970), p. 15; and Helen Gardner, "Milton's First Illustrator," *Essays and Studies,* n.s. 9 (1956): 27–38; see pp. 34–35. See also Merritt Y. Hughes, "Some Illustrators of Milton: The Expulsion from Paradise," *Journal of English and Germanic Philology,* 60 (1961): 670–79; Kester Svendsen, *Milton and Science* (Cambridge, Mass.: Harvard University Press, 1956), pp. 107–13; and Dick Taylor, Jr., "Milton's Treatment of the Judgment and the Expulsion in *Paradise Lost,*" *Texas Studies in English,* 10 (1960): 51–82. Pictorial representations of the Expulsion in the Middle Ages and the Renaissance have now been thoroughly explored by Roland Mushat Frye in his monumental study *Milton's Imagery and the Visual Arts* (1978), pp. 308–15, with this conclusion: "I know of nothing like [Milton's presentation] in pictorial art: when Michael takes the hands of Adam and Eve in his hands and leads them through the gate, we have a radically new version of an old and familiar scene" (pp. 312–13). The only flaw in Frye's otherwise excellent interpretation is his misreading of 12.632–34, where Frye takes "before them" (which refers to the cherubim descending from "the other Hill") to refer to Adam and Eve, and thus mistakes Milton's use of the traditional motif: "In pictorial art," Frye says, "that 'brandisht' sword always *followed* Adam and Eve, driving them before it with greater or lesser implications of immediate physical harm, whereas Milton reverses its position, and explicitly places it 'before them,' where it was 'high in front advanced'. . . . So used, the sword becomes processional, leading them forth in dignity and grace rather than driving them in terror" (p. 311). But the sword is behind them, as the Argument to book 12 says.
2   Peter Sterry, *A Discourse of the Freedom of the Will* (London: 1675), p. 99.
3   See the notes to these lines in Carey and Fowler, pp. 485–86.
4   See Ricks, *Milton's Grand Style,* chapter 4, and Christopher Grose, *Milton's Epic Process* (New Haven: Yale University Press, 1973), chapter 6, for summation and perceptive extension of critical views on the similes. For an acute study of all aspects of Milton's imagery see MacCaffrey, *Paradise Lost as "Myth",* chapter 5. Also Ferry, *Milton's Epic Voice,* chapter 3; and Hartman, "Milton's Counterplot."
5   Cf. MacCaffrey, *Paradise Lost as "Myth",* pp. 181–84; and the detailed study of Milton's Hell by Broadbent, *Some Graver Subject,* pp. 80–124.
6   See above, note 2. Milton shared in some measure this view that the Image of God in man has not been utterly destroyed, but retains some vestiges of its original creative power: see *De Doctrina,* 1.12: "it cannot be denied that some traces of the divine image still remain in us, which are not wholly extinguished by this spiritual death. . . . These traces remain in our intellect" (trans. Carey: *Prose Works,* ed. Wolfe, VI, 396). This view is the implicit basis of his treatise *Of Education* and derives from his close affiliation with Platonic thought: see Irene Samuel, *Milton and Plato* (Ithaca: Cornell University Press, 1947).
7   Cf. MacCaffrey, *Paradise Lost as "Myth",* chapter 6: "Satan's Voyage."

 8 *OED,* "pilgrimage," *sb.* 1.
 9 Augustine, *De Trinitate,* 14.20; *Later Works,* trans. John Burnaby, Library of Christian Classics, vol. 8 (London: SCM Press, 1955), pp. 118–19.
10 An excellent account of Milton's Paradise is given by John R. Knott, Jr., in *Milton's Pastoral Vision: An Approach to Paradise Lost* (Chicago: University of Chicago Press, 1971); Knott's footnotes provide a running bibliography of writings on the subject. See especially Broadbent, *Some Graver Subject,* chapter 6; Giamatti, *The Earthly Paradise,* chapter 6; Arnold Stein, *Answerable Style* (Minneapolis: University of Minnesota Press, 1953), pp. 52–74; Northrop Frye, *The Return of Eden* (Toronto: University of Toronto Press, 1965); and Joseph E. Duncan, *Milton's Earthly Paradise: A Historical Study of Eden* (Minneapolis: University of Minnesota Press, 1972).
11 Cf. Ferry, *Milton's Epic Voice,* pp. 55–56.
12 Cf. C. S. Lewis, *A Preface to Paradise Lost,* pp. 47–50.
13 For a fine analysis of the hymn see Summers, *The Muse's Method,* chapter 3.

Coda Many of the studies cited for particular points in the foregoing chapters have had, over the years, a more pervasive part in the development of the ideas presented in this account of *Paradise Lost.* I should like to include within this general acknowledgment my gratitude to a few more studies for which no particular mention has arisen, especially to the first on this list, which formed my introduction to Miltonic studies:

E. M. W. Tillyard, *Milton* (London: Chatto, 1930).

Maurice Kelley, *This Great Argument* (Princeton: Princeton University Press, 1941).

Arthur E. Barker, *Milton and the Puritan Dilemma* (Toronto: University of Toronto Press, 1942).

Douglas Bush, *Paradise Lost in Our Time* (Ithaca: Cornell University Press, 1945).

Thomas Greene, *The Descent from Heaven* (New Haven: Yale University Press, 1963); especially chapter 12.

Michael Fixler, *Milton and the Kingdoms of God* (Evanston: Northwestern University Press, 1964).

Merritt Y. Hughes, *Ten Perspectives on Milton* (New Haven: Yale University Press, 1965).

Helen Gardner, *A Reading of Paradise Lost* (Oxford: Clarendon Press, 1965).

Thomas Kranidas, *The Fierce Equation: A Study of Milton's Decorum* (The Hague: Mouton, 1965).

Irene Samuel, *Dante and Milton* (Ithaca: Cornell University Press, 1966).

John M. Steadman, *Milton and the Renaissance Hero* (Oxford: Clarendon Press, 1967), and *Milton's Epic Characters* (Chapel Hill: University of North Carolina Press, 1968).

William Madsen, *From Shadowy Types to Truth* (New Haven: Yale University Press, 1968).

CHAPTER 12: The Anti-heroic Epic

1   *The Life Records of John Milton,* ed. J. Milton French, 5 vols. (New Brunswick: Rutgers University Press, 1949–58), V, 110, 327.

2   Or perhaps, as one of my students, Paul Leopold, has suggested, Milton knew his Vergil by heart and had no need for a reader!

3   See Douglas Bush's indispensable chapter on Milton in *Mythology and the Renaissance Tradition in English Poetry* (Minneapolis: University of Minnesota Press, 1932), pp. 248–68. Also Jonathan H. Collett, "Milton's Use of Classical Mythology in *Paradise Lost,*" *PMLA,* 85 (1970): 88–96.

4   Quintilian, *Institutio Oratorio,* 10.1.88, trans. H. E. Butler, 4 vols., Loeb Classical Library (London: Heinemann, 1920–22), IV, 50–51.

5   Brooks Otis, *Ovid as an Epic Poet* (Cambridge: Cambridge University Press, 1966); 2nd edn., revised, 1970. The second edition is important because in it Otis has drastically changed his view of Ovid's flaws in writing heroic passages; he now sees these passages as parody; see the wholly re-written "Conclusion" to the 1970 edition. Robert Coleman, "Structure and Intention in the *Metamorphoses,*" *Classical Quarterly,* 21 (1971): 461–77.

6   Charles Paul Segal, *Landscape in Ovid's Metamorphoses, Hermes: Einzelschriften,* 23 (Wiesbaden, 1969). For the *topos* of the *locus amoenus* see Curtius, *European Literature and the Latin Middle Ages,* chapter 10.

7   G. Karl Galinsky, *Ovid's Metamorphoses* (Berkeley: University of California Press, 1975); see esp. pp. 19–25, 99. Also Otis (1970), pp. 335–38. Such views have been encouraged by the analytic catalogue of Ovid's "interventions" by Michael v. Albrecht, *Die Parenthese in Ovids Metamorphosen und ihre dichterische Funktion* (Hildesheim: Georg Olms, 1964).

8   Cf. Galinsky, pp. 24, 44–45; and Charles Segal, "Myth and Philosophy in the *Metamorphoses,*" *American Journal of Philology,* 90 (1969): 257–92; see esp. pp. 289–92.

9   In a highly illuminating article William S. Anderson finds a unifying factor in the theme of transformation by *love*—metamorphosis which consists not only in physical change, but primarily in psychological and moral changes that occur when *forma* (shape) is affected by *forma* (beauty): see "Multiple Change in the *Metamorphoses,*" *Transactions of the American Philological Association,* 94 (1963): 1–27. Otis is right, then, in saying that love "is the power that lifts the *Metamorphoses* to epic scope and unity" (1966: p. 334), while at the same time the power of love is used to deflate "divine majesty" and heroic dignity (p. 104). See Appendix 2 for a summary view of the anti-heroic action of *amor* and *furor.*

10 See Otis, *Ovid as an Epic Poet,* pp. 84–87 (pagination up to p. 306 is the same in both editions); the charts here are taken from Otis.

11 Notably Otis, in the revised "Conclusion" to his book: see his acknowledgment of the scholars who have motivated his change of mind. See also Coleman, "Structure and Intention in the *Metamorphoses,*" pp. 474–77; and

William S. Anderson's introduction to his edition of the *Metamorphoses, Books 6–10* (Norman: University of Oklahoma Press, 1972).

12 Cf. Otis (1970), pp. 346–47.

13 See Otis (1966), p. 323: "when he tried to treat heroic themes in a serious or a Virgilian way, he met an absolute check, and fell into the worst sort of bathos. His misfortune was that his epic plan and purpose could not be made to fit his peculiar abilities and deficiencies."

14 See Galinsky, *Ovid's Metamorphoses,* pp. 129–40. Coleman ("Structure and Intention," pp. 474–75) effectively takes issue with this view; in the Lapith-Centaur episode he says Ovid "is in reality pouring scorn upon the whole epic tradition of the aggrandizement of war. The epic tone here is therefore parodic" (p. 474). "What Ovid has done in fact is to deflate the whole heroic ideal, as set forth in the Homeric tradition and recently re-stated by Virgil in close and complex symbolic relation with the Augustan myth" (p. 475).

15 See Arnold Stein, *Answerable Style,* pp. 17–37; Broadbent, *Some Graver Subject,* pp. 218–28; Lieb, *Dialectics of Creation,* chapter 4; and the definitive article by Stella Revard, "Milton's Critique of Heroic Warfare in *Paradise Lost* V and VI," *Studies in English Literature,* 7 (1967): 119–39.

16 Hesiod, *Theogony,* 664–721.

17 Davis P. Harding, *Milton and the Renaissance Ovid* (Urbana: University of Illinois Press, 1946), pp. 67–79.

18 *Oechalia* is the reading of 1674; 1667 reads *Oealia,* evidently a misprint.

19 Repetition in Ovid is most frequent in small patterns, such as Anderson points to when he analyses the repetitions in "*deseruere sui nymphae* vineta Timoli, / *deseruere suas nymphae* Pactolides undas" (6.15–16), or in the "type of repetition" that he calls "peculiarly Ovidian"—the technique where "in a first clause he will use a finite verb, and the second clause will begin with the active or past participle of that verb"—as in "'a! piget, a! non est' *clamabat* 'tibia tanti.' / *clamanti* cutis est summos direpta per artus" (6.386–87); see *Metamorphoses, Books 6–10,* ed. Anderson, pp. 21–23. Nims points out a famous, longer example in the tale of Cephalus and Procris, where the word "aura" ("breeze") is skillfully repeated: "repetebam frigus et umbras / et quae de gelidis exibat vallibus *aura:* / *aura* petebatur medio mihi lenis in aestu, / *auram* exspectabam, requies erat illa labori. / '*aura*' (recordor enim), 'venias' cantare solebam. . . ." (7.809–13). Then a few lines later the repetition is compounded by a play on *aurem* ("ear"), followed by a striking repetition of words in the next line: "vocibus ambiguis deceptam praebuit *aurem* / nescio quis nomenque *aurae* tam saepe vocatum / esse putat *nymphae: nympham* mihi credit amari" (7.821–23). See the introduction by John Frederick Nims to his edition of Golding's translation of the *Metamorphoses* (New York: Macmillan, 1965), pp. xxx–xxxi.

20 Orpheus in the *Metamorphoses* pleads before Dis and Persephone in words that remind one of Milton's Hell and Chaos: "per ego haec loca plena

timoris, / per Chaos hoc ingens vastique silentia regni, / Eurydices, oro, properata retexite fata." ("I beg you, by these awful regions, by this boundless chaos, and by the silence of your vast realms, weave again Eurydice's destiny, brought too swiftly to a close." (10.29–31; trans. Innes). The music of Orpheus was successful, but his mission failed through his failure to obey divine command. Milton's bard, taught by a higher Muse, has returned "safe" to the realms of light.

CHAPTER 13: Pastoral Love: Versions and Subversions

1 Beyond the general resemblances, Thomas Newton noted that Milton "has expresly imitated some passages" from Ovid here; he calls attention to the close rhetorical imitation of *Metamorphoses*, 3.434–36,457–60: see Newton's edition of *Paradise Lost*, 2nd edn., 2 vols. (London, 1750), I, 294–95.
2 See Burden, *The Logical Epic*, pp. 83–85.
3 See above, chapter 8, n.12; chapter 12, n.19.
4 Gordon Williams, in his lecture on Vergil's fourth eclogue, has noted: "Patterned phrases, with symmetrical elements of repetition, are a characteristic feature of Theocritus' poetry." For examples he refers to the excellent summary of this Theocritean technique in *Theocritus: Select Poems*, ed. K. J. Dover (London: Macmillan, 1971), pp. xlv–xlviii. See Colloquy 7 (1973) in the series issued by The Center for Hermeneutical Studies in Hellenistic and Modern Culture, p. 16.
5 *Minor Latin Poets*, trans. J. Wight Duff and Arnold M. Duff, Loeb Classical Library, rev. edn. (London: Heinemann, 1935).
6 I have altered the opening phrases of the Loeb translation in order to stress the exact imitation of Calpurnius.
7 *Metamorphoses, Books 6–10*, ed. Anderson, p. 483 (note to 10.99).
8 See Harding, *Milton and the Renaissance Ovid*, p. 31; and Donald Lemen Clark, *John Milton at St. Paul's School* (New York: Columbia University Press, 1948), chapters 7 and 8.
9 See *Metamorphoses*, 4.256–70 (Clytie), 283 (Crocus), 10.162–219 (Hyacinthus). But, as so often in Milton, the Ovidian reminiscence here is mingled with another classical allusion: regarding the violet, crocus, and hyacinth, Newton pointed out, "Our author has taken this from Homer, who makes the same sort of flowers to spring up under Jupiter and Juno as they lay in conjugal embraces upon mount Ida, Iliad. XIV. 347." (*Paradise Lost*, ed. Newton, 2nd. edn., I, 314.) My point here, as elsewhere in this chapter, is not to argue that Ovid is the sole reminiscence, but that, when all the allusions are taken together, the presence of Ovid is dominant.
10 Segal, *Landscape in Ovid's Metamorphoses*, esp. section IV. See also Hugh Parry, "Ovid's *Metamorphoses*: Violence in a Pastoral Landscape," *Transactions of the American Philological Association*, 95 (1964): 268–82.

CHAPTER 14: The Ultimate Design

1 See above, chapter 9, n. 16.
2 See Brooks Otis, *Virgil: A Study in Civilized Poetry* (Oxford: Clarendon Press, 1964), chapter 3, "The Subjective Style"; and *Ovid as an Epic Poet* (1970), pp. 335–38.
3 Cf. Durling, *The Figure of the Poet in Renaissance Epic;* Durling deals with the narrator in Horace's *Satires* and Ovid's *Ars amatoria* and *Remedia amoris,* not with the *Metamorphoses.* But the techniques of the narrator in these elegiac poems point the way toward the voice of the narrator in Ovid's epic (see pp. 26–43). Durling goes on to deal with Chaucer, Petrarch, Boiardo, Ariosto, Tasso, and Spenser. But in this connection one should not overlook the extensive interventions of the poet found in Lucan and Statius: see Gordon Williams, *Change and Decline: Roman Literature in the Early Empire* (Berkeley: University of California Press, 1978), pp. 232–38.
4 Cf. T. F. Brunner, "The Function of the Simile in Ovid's *Metamorphoses,*" *Classical Journal,* 61 (1966): 354–63; and S. G. Owen, "Ovid's Use of the Simile," *Classical Review,* 45 (1931): 97–106.
5 See Hermann Fränkel, *Ovid, A Poet between Two Worlds* (Berkeley: University of California Press, 1945), pp. 101–11; and Otis, pp. 280, 291, 304–05, where he says "the history is not really assimilated to the myth," and speaks of "the barely disguised perfunctoriness of much of his historical liaison." Also Douglas Little, "The Speech of Pythagoras in Metamorphoses 15 and the Structure of the Metamorphoses," *Hermes,* 98 (1970): 340–60; and L. P. Wilkinson, *Ovid Recalled* (Cambridge: Cambridge University Press, 1955), pp. 221–26.
6 See Coleman, "Structure and Intention," p. 472; and Charles Segal, "Myth and Philosophy in the *Metamorphoses:* Ovid's Augustanism and the Augustan Conclusion of Book XV," *American Journal of Philology,* 90 (1969): 257–92. Also the acute older article by Frank J. Miller, "Ovid's *Aeneid* and Vergil's: A Contrast in Motivation," *Classical Journal,* 23 (1927): 33–43.
7 See Galinsky, p. 195; and Wilkinson, pp. 235–36, where he speaks of Ovid's catalogues as done "in the Hesiodic manner revived by the Alexandrians." Gordon Williams regards Ovid as virtually the "inventor" of this particular technique, which, he notes, "became a distinct stylistic feature of later epic," especially in Statius (*Change and Decline,* p. 215). The catalogue from Ovid's *Fasti* cited below is taken from the edition in the Loeb Classical Library, trans. Sir James George Frazer (London: Heinemann, 1931).
8 T. S. Eliot, "Milton" (1936), in *On Poetry and Poets* (London: Faber, 1957), p. 144.
9 Coleman, "Structure and Intention," p. 472.
10 This and all subsequent translations from Ovid's book 15 are by F. J. Miller.
11 See Segal, "Myth and Philosophy in the *Metamorphoses*," pp. 287–88; and Kenneth J. Pratt, "Rome as Eternal," *Journal of the History of Ideas,* 26 (1965): 25–44; see esp. pp. 25–28.

CHAPTER 15: *Paradise Regain'd:* The Interior Teacher

This chapter stands substantially as it appeared in *The Paradise Within,* chapter 4, with a new conclusion and the omission of the first four pages. That chapter was itself a revision of the essay *"Paradise Regain'd:* The Meditative Combat" which appeared in *ELH,* 27 (1960): 223–47. The earlier versions of this essay opened with a suggestion that *Paradise Regain'd* bears some analogy with Vergil's *Georgics;* I have removed discussion of this possibility to an appendix, in order to explore the whole matter in some detail. Reference to scholarship on *Paradise Regain'd* is now fortunately made easy by the publication of the volume dealing with this poem in *A Variorum Commentary on the Poems of John Milton,* vol. 4, ed. Walter MacKellar, *With a Review of Studies of Style and Verse Form* by Edward R. Weismiller (New York: Columbia Univeristy Press, 1975). The problem of the poem's genre has been carefully studied by Barbara Lewalski in *Milton's Brief Epic* (Providence: Brown University Press, 1966), with two important results: we can now understand the tradition that led Milton to say that the Book of Job provided a "brief model" for an epic; and we can now see the great variety of short biblical poems before *Paradise Regain'd* that might be called "brief epics." Few of them, however, display an action that bears a significant resemblance to *Paradise Regain'd.* Consequently, her investigation seems rather to confirm the view of Northrop Frye that the structure of the poem is "a technical experiment that is practically *sui generis."* "None of the ordinary literary categories apply to it," says Frye, "its poetic predecessors are nothing like it and it has left no descendants." He goes on to suggest that "its closest affinities are with the debate and with the dialectical colloquy of Plato and Boethius, to which most of the Book of Job also belongs." He notes, however, that "these forms usually either incorporate one argument into another dialectically or build up two different cases rhetorically; Milton's feat of constructing a double argument on the same words, each highly plausible and yet as different as light from darkness, is, so far as I know, unique in English literature" (*The Return of Eden* [Toronto: University of Toronto Press, 1965], pp. 135–36). MacKellar, after citing this passage, goes on to say: "Nor is it unique only in English literature. Among numerous Italian and French Biblical poems of the 16th and 17th centuries, I have found none which even remotely resembles *Paradise Regained.* Milton, in short, displays a singular independence of traditional literary forms" (*Variorum Commentary,* IV, 10).

The poem, paradoxically, becomes *sui generis* by reason of what Stuart Baker calls an "interplay of genres," in his persuasive essay "Sannazaro and Milton's Brief Epic," *Comparative Literature,* 20 (1968): 116–32. Baker sees Milton's poem, like Sannazaro's *De partu virginis,* as mingling epic motifs with elements drawn from "meditation, prophecy, debate, and the pastoral landscape" (p. 131)— and to these I would add elements drawn from the "didactic" genre, as described by Addison: "No rules therefore that relate to *Pastoral,* can any way affect the *Georgics,* since they fall under that class of Poetry, which consists in giving plain and direct instructions to the reader; whether they be Moral duties, as those of *Theognis* and *Pythagoras;* or Philosophical speculations, as those of *Aratus* and *Lucretius;* or Rules of practice, as those of *Hesiod* and *Virgil"* (Addison, *Miscel-*

laneous Works, ed. A. C. Guthkelch, 2 vols. [London: Bell, 1914], II, 4). Edward Weismiller *(Variorum Commentary,* IV, 297–317) has given a shrewd and fair-minded account of the various critical views that contribute to this support for finding the key to the poem in the "interplay of genres" and the "complex intermingling of styles." Stanley Fish has provided new insight into the interiority of the poem in his essay "Inaction and Silence: The Reader in *Paradise Regained,*" in the important collection: *Calm of Mind: Tercentenary Essays on Paradise Regained and Samson Agonistes in Honor of John S. Diekhoff,* ed. Joseph A. Wittreich, Jr. (Cleveland: Press of Case Western Reserve University, 1971), pp. 25–47.

1   Both this quotation and the epigraph to Part IV are taken from Augustine's *De Magistro,* 11.38; 12.40: *Augustine: Earlier Writings,* trans. John H. S. Burleigh, Library of Christian Classics, vol. 6 (London: SCM Press, 1953), pp. 95–96.

2   Milton, *De Doctrina,* 1.15: *Prose Works,* ed. Wolfe, VI, 432.

3   Cf. Tillyard, *Milton,* pp. 313–14: "the normal style of the poem is deliberately chastened or dimmed."

4   For the wide range of interpretations possible here see the study of the third temptation given by Elizabeth Marie Pope in *Paradise Regained: The Tradition and the Poem* (Baltimore: Johns Hopkins Press, 1947), chapter 7. Also the article by A. S. P. Woodhouse, "Theme and Pattern in *Paradise Regained,*" *University of Toronto Quarterly,* 25 (1955–56): 167–82, esp. p. 181; included in Woodhouse's *The Heavenly Muse,* chapter 10.

5   See, for example, Don Cameron Allen, *The Harmonious Vision* (Baltimore: Johns Hopkins Press, 1954), pp. 110–15; and Tillyard, *Milton,* p. 307.

6   I believe that this functional view of the basic style of *Paradise Regain'd* was suggested to me by certain remarks of W. Menzies in his essay, "Milton: the Last Poems," *Essays and Studies,* 24 (1938): 80–112; see esp. pp. 109–11. A similar view is developed by Jacques Blondel in the introduction (really a sizable monograph) prefaced to his bilingual edition of *Paradise Regain'd* (Paris: Aubier, 1955); see esp. pp. 92–110 *passim.*

7   F. M. Cornford, *Before and After Socrates* (Cambridge: Cambridge University Press, 1950), chapter 2, esp. pp. 50–51.

8   Milton's *Prose Works,* ed. Wolfe, VI, 735. See MacKellar's account of the Christian reconciliation of magnanimity with humility in the *Variorum Commentary,* IV, 41–43; and Steadman's important chapter 6, "The Critique of Magnanimity," in *Milton and the Renaissance Hero.* For the essential and pervasive influence of John on Milton's poem see the significant article by Ira Clark, "*Paradise Regained* and the Gospel according to John," *Modern Philology,* 71 (1973): 1–15.

9   Arnold Stein, *Heroic Knowledge* (Minneapolis: University of Minnesota Press, 1957), p. 89. For a discussion of the ways in which Milton "intrudes" throughout the poem, see the adverse criticism by W. B. C. Watkins, *Anatomy of Milton's Verse,* pp. 113–25. For a favorable view of the narrator's role see Roger H. Sundell, "The Narrator as Interpreter in *Paradise Regained,*" *Milton Studies,* 2 (1970): 83–101.

10   Cf. Stein, *Heroic Knowledge,* pp. 50–51, where he speaks of "the charming development of Satan rising as advocate to defend the elevated virtue of his opponent" and treating us to "a delightful piece of mythological debunking by a puritanical Satan."

11   See the excellent analysis of the sequence of the temptations according to Plato's *Republic* by Irene Samuel, *Plato and Milton,* pp. 69–129.

12   See Allan H. Gilbert, "The Temptation in *Paradise Regain'd,*" *Journal of English and Germanic Philology,* 15 (1916): 599–611, esp. pp. 606–07. Also Pope, *Paradise Regained: the Tradition and the Poem,* p. 67.

13   For helpful discussion of the problems here see Irene Samuel, "Milton on Learning and Wisdom," *PMLA,* 64 (1949): 708–23; Lewalski, *Milton's Brief Epic,* chapter 11; and Rajan, *The Lofty Rhyme,* chapter 8.

14   *The Ferrar Papers,* ed. B. Blackstone (Cambridge: Cambridge University Press, 1938), pp. 60–63; I have expanded abbreviations and altered the punctuation slightly.

15   Milton, *Prose Works,* ed. Wolfe, VI, 194.

16   See the searching and wholly convincing study of the "companionable" nature of the two poems by Arthur Barker in "Calm Regained through Passion Spent," in *The Prison and the Pinnacle,* ed. Balachandra Rajan (Toronto: University of Toronto Press, 1973), pp. 3–48, esp. p. 35: "As the young Christ isolates himself in the wilderness of this world to engage in wholly interiorized and self-closeted meditation, so Samson, however unintelligent and uncontemplative, is forced by the wrath of his just God and the pains of enslaved defeat to withdraw into himself. As Christ meets a series of temptations by a series of cold repudiations, so Samson meets the series of his renewed temptations by a series of repudiations through which his despair is transformed into a cold anger which is the expression of the contempt for the world proper to his new spirituality . . ."

17   See headnote to next chapter.

18   Tertullian, *De Praescriptionibus Haereticorum,* chapter 7; see the translation by Peter Holmes in the *Ante-Nicene Christian Library,* ed. Alexander Roberts and James Donaldson (Edinburgh: Clark, 1870), XV, 9–10. The apostles taught in the "porch of Solomon" (Acts 3:11); the quotation about "simplicity of heart" comes from Wisdom of Solomon 1:1.

19   Clement of Alexandria, *Stromateis,* 1.5; see *Ante-Nicene Christian Library,* ed. Roberts and Donaldson, IV, 366. I have quoted the superior translation of this passage by Henry Bettenson in *Documents of the Christian Church* (London: Oxford University Press, 1947), p. 10.

20   Milton, *De Doctrina,* 1.12; trans. Carey; *Prose Works,* ed. Wolfe, VI, 396.

CHAPTER 16: *Samson Agonistes:* The Breath of Heaven

The present chapter stands substantially as it appeared in *Milton Studies,* 1 (1969): 115–34, under the title "Chorus and Character in *Samson Agonistes,*" an essay which was in turn based upon a lecture, "Tragic Transformation in *Samson Agonistes,*" delivered at the University of Pittsburgh in January 1968 as part of a series celebrating the tercentenary of *Paradise Lost.* I have here omitted the opening paragraphs and have written a new conclusion.

The volume of the *Variorum Commentary* devoted to *Samson Agonistes* has not yet appeared, but a worthy surrogate is now available in the recent book by Mary Ann Radzinowicz, *Toward Samson Agonistes: The Growth of Milton's Mind* (Princeton: Princeton University Press, 1978); along with its own illuminating commentary, this provides a thorough bibliography, detailed footnotes on points of controversy, and ample consideration of all major studies of the poem. Her view of the chorus and of Manoa is quite divergent from my own, but the strength of her objections has convinced me that my original essay tended to over-state the case, and I have therefore moderated my views in places.

1 See the analysis of this prologue by Arnold Stein, *Heroic Knowledge,* pp. 138–43.

2 Cf. Stein, pp. 145–46.

3 The question has been ably treated by John Huntley in "A Revaluation of the Chorus's Role in Milton's *Samson Agonistes,*" *Modern Philology,* 64 (1966–67): 132–45; Huntley throughout presents an excellent argument for his view that the members of the chorus "are neither vicious nor saintly, but represent the vast ambivalent mass of mankind which neither knows what it feels nor feels what it knows" (p. 139). For the controversy on this point see Radzinowicz, *Toward Samson Agonistes,* pp. 62–64, 98–99; and Anthony Low, *The Blaze of Noon* (New York: Columbia University Press, 1974), pp. 118–26. Lynn Sadler suggests that the rhyming platitudes demonstrate the chorus's effort to apply legalistic Old Testament wisdom to Samson; see "Coping with Hebraic Legalism: The Chorus in *Samson Agonistes,*" *Harvard Theological Review,* 66 (1973): 353–68. The problem is related to the effect of "rhythmic strangeness" in *Samson,* which Edward Weismiller has defended in his fine essay on the metrics of the play: "Again we must assume that the strangeness is intended; but we do well to recognize it as a strangeness produced in the first place by a kind of controlled metrical-rhythmical disorientation, and persisting as a strangeness of proportioning—a complex effect for which the reading of stanzaic verse, even Milton's own stanzaic verse, has hardly prepared us" (see "The 'Dry' and 'Rugged' Verse," in *The Lyric and Dramatic Milton,* ed. Summers, pp. 115–52; esp. pp. 135–36).

4 A suggestion close to this was made long ago by A. J. Wyatt: see his edition of *Samson Agonistes* in the "University Tutorial Series" (London, 1892), pp. 9–10, where he asserts that "Milton's use of rhyme here is so far in accord with his previous renunciation of it, that he intends in the rhymed passages to produce a curious effect of contempt or aversion." After listing most of the "chief passages" of rhyme, Wyatt adds that these passages were "doubtless introduced in almost every case with a purpose, probably to indicate scorn or some kindred feeling." Wyatt's suggestion is cited by W. R. Parker in his article, "The Date of *Samson Agonistes,*" but rejected on the grounds that "a sympathetic application of Wyatt's theory accounts for not half of the riming passages; and Wyatt himself, in a list of 'the chief passages,' omits the

superb final chorus, the intricate rime pattern of which is reminiscent of a sonnet" (see *Philological Quarterly,* 28 (1949): 148–49). Wyatt's view is extravagant, but has some truth in it. Roberts W. French describes the choric rhymes as "superfluous decoration" which emphasizes the chorus's confidence in false convictions: see "Rhyme and the Chorus of *Samson Agonistes,*" *Laurel Review,* 10 (1970): 60–67.

5 For a contrasting view of Manoa's character, see Low, *The Blaze of Noon,* pp. 123–32; and Radzinowicz, *Toward Samson Agonistes,* pp. 337–38.

6 For strong disagreement with this point, see Low, pp. 210–14.

7 For varied opinions of Dalila see Don Cameron Allen, *The Harmonious Vision,* pp. 88–90; Thomas Kranidas, *Studies in English Literature,* 6 (1966): 125–37; and the commentaries of Low (pp. 144–58) and Radzinowicz (pp. 36–50, 99–101, 212–17).

8 Cf. *Heroic Knowledge,* p. 177, where Stein speaks of the "comic tone" and the "light verse" of this chorus. In this passage Low sees rather an expression of "near-incoherent exasperation" (p. 214).

9 Radzinowicz (p. 263), in dealing with these lines, breaks off the quotation after "Not willingly"—but the rest of the passage is essential to the meaning. Earlier (p. 107) she describes the effect of the catastrophe on the chorus in a way that seems to reveal the contradiction between the Greek view of "necessity" and the Christian view of "illumination": "As a group they accept the tragic, they do not push it away. Samson *was* 'tangl'd in the fold of dire necessity.' His enemies were 'fond'; 'insensate . . . or to sense reprobate,' they invited their own ruin. Samson's triumph lies not in their defeat but in himself: 'with inward eyes illuminated' he revived, and his virtue reflourished though his body died."

10 See Milton's *De Doctrina,* 1.3: "neither God's decree nor his foreknowledge can shackle free causes with any kind of necessity" (trans. Carey: *Prose Works,* VI, 166).

11 I now agree with Huntley's view on this point: see "Revaluation of the Chorus's Role," p. 144.

12 Franklin R. Baruch makes a similar point about the funeral rites in "Time, Body, and Spirit at the Close of *Samson Agonistes,*" *ELH,* 36 (1969), pp. 324–25. See Low's objection to this point of view, pp. 128–32.

13 Baruch seems to support this argument when he says that "the image that the Chorus offers of themselves is not the justifiable one of a group inspired to a moral choice and action by a noble example, but rather a contented, peaceful lot, well out of the active process that Milton always envisioned at the unalterable center of true Christian being" (p. 338).

14 Cf. Schneidau, *Sacred Discontent,* chapter 3.

15 Cf. Radzinowicz, pp. 22–23, 351.

APPENDIX 1: *Paradise Regain'd* and the *Georgics*

1 John Chalker, *The English Georgic* (London: Routledge, 1969), pp. 24, 209; see his whole opening chapter.

2 But see Douglas Bush, *English Literature in the Earlier Seventeenth Century*, 2nd edn., revised (Oxford: Clarendon Press, 1962), pp. 414–15; and, more recently, the corroborative essay, written from a thematic point of view, by Andrew V. Ettin, "Milton, T. S. Eliot, and the Virgilian Vision: Some Versions of Georgic," *Genre*, 10 (1977): 233–58.

3 *Servii Grammatici Qui Feruntur in Vergilii Carmina Commentarii*, ed. G. Thilo and H. Hagen, 4 vols. (Leipzig, 1881–1902), III, fasc. 1, pp. 1–2.

4 See Addison's "Essay on the *Georgics*" prefixed to John Dryden's translation, *The Works of Vergil* (London, 1697): Addison, *Miscellaneous Works*, ed. Guthkelch, II, 9.

5 *The Eclogues and Georgics of Virgil*, trans. C. Day Lewis (Garden City: Doubleday-Anchor, 1964); the translation of the *Georgics* was originally published in 1940; copyright 1940 by Oxford University Press.

6 See Brooks Otis, *Virgil: A Study in Civilized Poetry*, pp. 164–65, 167, 186; L. P. Wilkinson, *The Georgics of Vergil* (Cambridge: Cambridge University Press, 1969), pp. 71–107; esp. pp 88–89.

7 *Georgics*, trans. Smith Palmer Bovie (Chicago: University of Chicago Press, 1956).

8 See "The Argument" at the head of Dryden's translation of the fourth book of the *Georgics*.

9 *Ibid.*

10 Essay prefixed to Dryden's translation; Addison, *Miscellaneous Works*, pp. 10–11.

11 Otis, *Virgil*, p. 194.

12 Otis, *Virgil*, pp. 190–214; see esp. pp. 201, 208, 211–214.

13 Wilkinson, *The Georgics of Vergil*, p. 71.

14 Wilkinson, pp. 71–75. See also pp. 314–15 for a bibliography of studies on the structure of the *Georgics* since 1924.

15 W. F. Jackson Knight, *Roman Vergil* (London: Faber, 1944), p. 152.

16 Segal, *Landscape in Ovid's Metamorphoses*, p. 2.

17 Jacques Perret, "The *Georgics*," trans. M. Brooks, in *Virgil*, ed. Steele Commager (Englewood Cliffs: Prentice-Hall, 1966), pp. 37–38, 40; from Perret's *Virgile* (Paris: Editions du Seuil, 1959).

18 Tillyard, *Milton*, p. 322.

19 *The Aeneid*, trans. W. F. Jackson Knight, rev. edn. (Harmondsworth: Penguin Books, 1958).

20 *Variorum Commentary*, IV, 298. For Dunster's final remark here see his edition, p. 267. Dunster follows this with stress upon the poem's relation to the genre of the *Georgics*: "The *Paradise Regained* has something of the *didactic* character; it teaches not merely by the general moral, and by the character and conduct of its hero, but has also many positive precepts every where interspersed. It is written for the most part in a style admirably condensed, and with a studied reserve of ornament: it is nevertheless illuminated with beauties of the most captivating kind."

List of Illustrations

The above identifications have been aided by information in
Marcia Pointon's *Milton and English Art* (Manchester: Manchester
University Press, 1970), and in Suzanne Boorsch's study, "The
1688 *Paradise Lost* and Dr. Aldrich," *Metropolitan Museum Journal,*
6(1972): 133–50. Boorsch provides convincing evidence for attributing the unsigned designs for book 2 (partly after Mantegna)
and book 12 (after Raphael) to Henry Aldrich, rather than to
Medina; but the evidence for the unsigned design for book 1 is
indeterminate.

Index

The index has been designed to serve also as a bibliographical guide; for each book or article cited, the first page-entry for the notes will provide a full reference. Modern translations are normally indexed only for the full reference. The following abbreviations have been used: *PL: Paradise Lost; PR: Paradise Regain'd; SA: Samson Agonistes.*